Rethinking Global History

Despite three decades of rapid expansion and public success, global history's theoretical and methodological foundations remain under-conceptualised, even to those using them. In this collection, leading historians provide a reassessment of global history's most common analytical instruments, metaphors and conceptual foundations. *Rethinking Global History* prompts historians to pause and think about the methodology and premises underpinning their work. The volume reflects on the structure and direction of history, its relation to our present and the ways in which historians should best explain, contextualise and represent events and circumstances in the past. In chapters on fundamental concepts such as scale, comparison, temporality and teleology, this collection will guide readers to assess the extant literature critically and write theoretically informed global histories. Taken together, these chapters provide a unique and much-needed assessment of the implications of history going global. This title is also available as open access on Cambridge Core.

STEFANIE GÄNGER is Professor of Modern History at Heidelberg University. She is the author of *A Singular Remedy. Cinchona Across the Atlantic World, 1751–1820* (Cambridge University Press, 2020) and *Relics of the Past. The Collecting and Study of pre-Columbian Antiquities in Peru and Chile, 1837–1911* (Oxford University Press, 2014).

JÜRGEN OSTERHAMMEL is Professor Emeritus of Modern and Contemporary History at the University of Konstanz. His books in English include *The Transformation of the World: A Global History of the Nineteenth Century* (Princeton University Press, 2014). With Akira Iriye, he is the general editor of *A History of the World* (6 vols., Harvard University Press, 2012–24).

T0371551

Rethinking Global History

Edited by

Stefanie Gänger

Heidelberg University

Jürgen Osterhammel

University of Konstanz

Shaftesbury Road, Cambridge CB2 8EA, United Kingdom

One Liberty Plaza, 20th Floor, New York, NY 10006, USA

477 Williamstown Road, Port Melbourne, VIC 3207, Australia

314–321, 3rd Floor, Plot 3, Splendor Forum, Jasola District Centre,
New Delhi – 110025, India

103 Penang Road, #05–06/07, Visioncrest Commercial, Singapore 238467

Cambridge University Press is part of Cambridge University Press & Assessment,
a department of the University of Cambridge.

We share the University's mission to contribute to society through the pursuit of
education, learning and research at the highest international levels of excellence.

www.cambridge.org
Information on this title: www.cambridge.org/9781009444040

DOI: 10.1017/9781009444002

© Cambridge University Press & Assessment 2024

This publication is in copyright. Subject to statutory exception and to the provisions of
relevant collective licensing agreements, with the exception of the Creative Commons
version the link for which is provided below, no reproduction of any part may take
place without the written permission of Cambridge University Press & Assessment.

An online version of this work is published at doi.org/10.1017/9781009444002
under a Creative Commons open access license CC-BY- NC 4.0 which permits re-
use, distribution and reproduction in any medium for non-commercial purposes
providing appropriate credit to the original work is given and any changes made
are indicated. To view a copy of this license visit https://creativecommons.org/
licenses/by-nc/4.0.

When citing this work, please include a reference to the DOI 10.1017/
9781009444002

First published 2024

A catalogue record for this publication is available from the British Library.

*A Cataloging-in-Publication data record for this book is available from the
Library of Congress.*

ISBN 978-1-009-44404-0 Hardback
ISBN 978-1-009-44402-6 Paperback

Cambridge University Press & Assessment has no responsibility for the persistence or
accuracy of URLs for external or third-party internet websites referred to in this
publication and does not guarantee that any content on such websites is, or will remain,
accurate or appropriate.

Contents

Part III   Configurations and *Telos*

Figures

Contributors

JEREMY ADELMAN is the Henry Charles Lea Professor Emeritus of History at Princeton University and the Director of the Global History Lab at the University of Cambridge.

CHRISTINA BRAUNER is Assistant Professor of Global History of the Late Middle Ages and the Early Modern Period at the University of Tübingen.

STEFANIE GÄNGER is Professor of Modern History at Heidelberg University.

VALESKA HUBER is Professor of Contemporary History at the University of Vienna.

JAN C. JANSEN is Professor of Modern History at the University of Tübingen.

DÁNIEL MARGÓCSY is Professor in the History of Science, Technology and Medicine at the University of Cambridge.

JÜRGEN OSTERHAMMEL is Professor Emeritus of Modern and Contemporary History at the University of Konstanz.

DOMINIC SACHSENMAIER is Professor of 'Modern China with a Special Emphasis on Global Historical Perspectives' at the University of Göttingen.

SUJIT SIVASUNDARAM is Professor of World History at the University of Cambridge.

ALESSANDRO STANZIANI is Professor of Economic and Social History at the *École des Hautes Études en Sciences Sociales* in Paris.

PIM DE ZWART is Associate Professor in Economic and Environmental History at Wageningen University.

Acknowledgements

It was about five years ago – in the summer of 2019 – that we began sketching a first outline of this volume, and we have incurred many debts in the intervening period.

The book would not have been possible without the Balzan Prize, awarded to Jürgen Osterhammel for his contribution to the field of global history in 2018 by the Fondazione Internazionale Premio Balzan in Milan. Balzan projects are commonly directed jointly by the prizewinner and a more junior co-director; Stefanie Gänger happily accepted the invitation to co-direct the project early in 2019. We would like to thank the members of the Balzan General Prize Committee, chaired by Luciano Maiani, for their interest in the project. The foundation's general secretary, Suzanne Werder, and her staff in Milan have generously provided all sorts of helpful support. We are also very grateful to the former rector of the University of Freiburg, Hans-Joachim Schiewer, and to the Freiburg Institute for Advanced Studies (FRIAS), especially its then director Bernd Kortmann and his successor, Ralf von den Hoff, for agreeing to host the Balzan Project in Global History.

Somewhat unusually, the volume came into its own via an orchestrated, directed process: instead of starting with an open call for papers, we chose an international group of scholars, both senior and at post-doctoral stages in their careers, according to their expertise. We suggested subjects to them, which over the course of long conversations gradually morphed into chapter headings: centrism, direction, teleology, among others. We discussed the authors' draft papers in two consecutive workshops held in January and September 2021 – online, since the volume came into its own during the years of the pandemic. We are grateful to Jan C. Jansen for first proposing the idea of that procedure, to Peer Vries for his advice in our quest for potential contributors and, of course, to our indefatigable authors, for taking up the challenge. We would like to gratefully acknowledge their encouraging, constructive and stimulating suggestions and feedback, both to one other and on our concept, framework and introduction.

We are also grateful to the fellows and visiting members of the Balzan–FRIAS research group at Freiburg University who have taken the time to discuss project outlines, read parts of the manuscript and suggest changes: Debjani Bhattacharyya, Jesús Bohorquez, Jennifer Eaglin, Benjamin W. Goossen, Enrique Martino, Anna Olenenko and Lianming Wang. At various stages along the publication process, Sven Beckert, Javier Francisco, Chen Hao, Susann Liebich and Martin Rempe joined our conversations about various aspects of the project and contributed valuable suggestions and comments. Tom Theis, Albert Loran and Christian Stenz kindly agreed to listen in and take notes during our workshops, as a basis for later revisions. We presented initial outlines of the project and the introduction for the volume at other venues and seminars too. We are particularly grateful to Jan C. Jansen and Jakob Vogel for the invitation to present drafts of the introduction in Duisburg-Essen in May 2021 and at the Centre Marc Bloch in Berlin in November 2020, and for the comments and feedback we received on these occasions.

We also owe a great debt to Cambridge University Press: to the two anonymous referees for helpful and supportive comments, and to Lucy Rhymer and her team for their interest, kind guidance and valuable suggestions. Our proofreader and adviser on matters of language, Robert Savage, meticulously worked his way through our prose, adjusting our word choice, fixing our grammar and flagging questionable assertions. We are also very grateful to Lea-Marie Trigilia and Tom Theis for providing the perfect back-of-the-book index. The open access publication of this book has been made possible through generous funding by the universities of Konstanz and Heidelberg, and the European Research Council (ERC) under the European Union's Horizon 2020 research and innovation programme (grant agreement no. 849189).

The book stands at the intersection of global history and historical theory. For Stefanie Gänger, it is part of an ongoing engagement with both the language of global history and with historical epistemology; she owes much to conversations held over the years, first in the Cambridge World History Seminar, then the Konstanz-based Leibniz Prize Group 'Global Processes' and more recently, the Heidelberg 'Cultures of Validation (Geltungskulturen)' network. For Jürgen Osterhammel, it is the culmination of a long involvement with questions of historical methodology inspired by teachers and colleagues of whom only a few can be mentioned by name: Gangolf Hübinger, Jürgen Kocka, Hartmut Kaelble, Lutz Raphael, Jörn Rüsen, Chris Lorenz and the late Ernst Schulin.

Introduction
Rethinking History, Globally

Stefanie Gänger and Jürgen Osterhammel

Historians, whatever their area, period or subfield, are well advised to occasionally rethink the premises of their research, writing and 'craft' – that is, to think again or further about them, and to reconsider them with a view to amendment. Like any conscientious scholar, they ought to sometimes take a step back from their routine and habitual ways, to reassess their basic discourses and stances, their position and practice, and recall the explicit and the tacit, perhaps even unconscious, assumptions and conventions underlying their research. The present volume is premised on the conviction that it is not advisable to leave these kinds of reflections entirely to specialised philosophers or theorists of history, who often have little first-hand research experience. Rather, it is of fundamental importance that ordinary historians, too, reflect on 'their daily task', as Marc Bloch put it – on their methods, craftsmanship and conceptual basis.[1]

This volume is an attempt to do just that with regard to global history. A rethinking of global history, the editors and contributors assembled in the volume hold, is both necessary and timely. Despite three decades of rapid expansion and considerable public success, global history – or whatever is presented under that label – is still in need of studies that spell out the implications and consequences, the possibilities and risks of history going global. This is even more pressing because the ground on which global historians stand is moving fast. Much of the field's self-image, conceptual basis and success rests on what is ultimately a tautology: that global history is the history

---

[1] Marc Bloch, *The Historian's Craft* (New York: Knopf, 1953; reprinted Manchester: Manchester University Press, 2015), 16. Other prominent examples of this kind of self-reflection by eminent practitioners include Johann Gustav Droysen, *Grundriß der Historik* (Leipzig: Veit 1868). For a recent edition, Johann Gustav Droysen, *Historik*, 3 vols., ed. Peter Leyh and Horst Walter Blanke (Stuttgart–Bad Canstatt: Frommann–Holzboog, 1977–2020); Edward Hallett Carr, *What Is History?* (London: Macmillan, 1961); Paul Veyne, *Writing History: Essays on Epistemology* (Middletown: Wesleyan University Press, 1984); John Lewis Gaddis, *The Landscape of History: How Historians Map the Past* (Oxford: Oxford University Press, 2002). Related genres are scholarly autobiographies, such as John H. Elliott, *History in the Making* (New Haven: Yale University Press, 2012), or interviews, for instance those collected in Carolien Stolte and Alicia Schrikker (eds.), *World History–A Genealogy: Private Conversations with World Historians, 1996–2016* (Leiden: Leiden University Press, 2017).

befitting a global age, connected histories suitable for a connected world.[2] That is unlikely to suffice in the long run. By the third decade of the twenty-first century, with globalisation in crisis and universal values under threat, our era remains irrefutably global – with our present predicaments, from warfare to climate change, meaningful only on a global scale – but no longer consistently or affirmatively, let alone enthusiastically so. Historians are unlikely to be startled by this turn of events; as scholars of the past, they are familiar with processes of contraction, disillusionment and fragmentation. If global history is to remain a fitting, fruitful approach for our present and the future, however, our 'guild' must rethink its craft accordingly and forge a more robust, enduring and timely form of global history, both attuned and impervious to the winds of change that are sweeping through the world today.

Theory, Methodology and Epistemology of Global History

While around 1980, and even 1990, global history was a promise, today it is a library. Alongside a vast range of research monographs, there are by now several volumes that introduce the subject of global history to students, professional historians and a general public[3] that reflect on the practice and overall situation of world and global history in various societies, past and present,[4] and that canvass the field's politics, both analytically and programmatically.[5]

---

[2] Diego Olstein, *Thinking History Globally* (Basingstoke: Palgrave Macmillan, 2015), x–xi, 2; Sebastian Conrad, *What Is Global History?* (Princeton: Princeton University Press, 2016), 2.

[3] Patrick Manning, *Navigating World History: Historians Create a Global Past* (New York: Palgrave Macmillan, 2003); Pamela K. Crossley, *What Is Global History?* (Cambridge: Polity Press, 2008); Pierre-Yves Saunier, *Transnational History* (Basingstoke: Palgrave Macmillan, 2013); James Belich et al. (eds.), *The Prospect of Global History* (Oxford: Oxford University Press, 2016); Roland Wenzlhuemer, *Doing Global History: An Introduction in Six Concepts* (London: Bloomsbury, 2020); Rolf-Ulrich Kunze, *Global History und Weltgeschichte: Quellen, Zusammenhänge, Perspektiven* (Stuttgart: Kohlhammer, 2017); Laurent Testot (ed.), *L'histoire globale: Un autre regard sur le monde* (Auxerre: Sciences Humaines Éditions, 2008); Laura Di Fiore and Marco Meriggi, *World History: Le nuove rotte della storia* (Rome: Laterza, 2011); Eric Vanhaute, *World History: An Introduction* (London: Routledge, 2013); Masashi Haneda, *Toward Creation of a New World History* (Tokyo: Japan Publishing Industry Foundation for Culture, 2018); Conrad, *What Is Global History?*; Olstein, *Thinking History Globally.*

[4] Sven Beckert and Dominic Sachsenmaier (eds.), *Global History, Globally: Research and Practice Around the World* (London: Bloomsbury, 2018); Hervé Inglebert, *Le monde, l'histoire: Essai sur les histoires universelles* (Paris: Presses Universitaires Françaises, 2014); Hervé Inglebert, *Histoire universelle ou Histoire globale? Les temps du monde* (Paris: Presses Universitaires Françaises, 2018); Dominic Sachsenmaier, *Global Perspectives on Global History: Theories and Approaches in a Connected World* (Cambridge: Cambridge University Press, 2011); Matthias Middell and Lluís Roura (eds.), *Transnational Challenges to National History Writing* (Basingstoke: Palgrave Macmillan, 2013).

[5] Alessandro Stanziani, *Eurocentrism and the Politics of Global History* (London: Palgrave Macmillan, 2018); Alessandro Stanziani, *Les entrelacements du monde: Histoire globale, pensée globale, XVIᵉ-XXᵉ siècles* (Paris: CNRS Éditions, 2018); C. A. Bayly, 'History and

A number of books and articles assess global history's future prospects[6] or situate it in the tradition of a cosmopolitan, world, or 'general' historiography[7]. However, despite that impressive output and incessant debates about what global history 'really' is, the field remains to some extent oblivious to the rules and formalities that guide its forms of inquiry and argumentation and to the tacit assumptions underlying much of its practice. Only a handful of authors – notably, Sebastian Conrad, Michael Lang and, in the early days of the debate, Raymond Grew – have hitherto sought a dialogue between the new global history and the established concerns of historical theory.[8] One might argue that the constellation of practice surging ahead and theoretical reflection trailing behind is an expected and common one. After all, Minerva's owl spreads its wings only with the falling of dusk. The opposite is possible, however. Some of the most important historiographical innovations, from the rise of the *Annales* school in the 1920s and 1930s to the reinvention of social history in the 1960s and 1970s, were concerted programmes of empirical research and theoretical, self-conscious reflection.[9]

The present volume is devoted to a reassessment of global history's most common metaphors, analytical instruments and cognitive practices. The project is theoretical and methodological neither in the sense of wilful pedantry nor in that of conceit; its expectation is not that of outwitting the practising historian. Rather, it is methodological in the sense of being (self-) reflective. It (re-)considers what it means for a historian to think 'globally' and examines the mental grids, cognitive instruments and linguistic devices

World History', in Ulinka Rublack (ed.), *A Concise Companion to History* (Oxford: Oxford University Press, 2011), 3–25.

6 James Belich et al., 'Introduction: The Prospect of Global History', in Belich et al., *The Prospect of Global History*, 3–22; Jeremy Adelman, 'What Is Global History Now?', *Aeon*, 2 March 2017, https://aeon.co/essays/is-global-history-still-possible-or-has-it-had-its-moment.

7 See Sanjay Subrahmanyam, *On the Origins of Global History: Inaugural Lecture Delivered on Thursday 28 November 2013* (Paris: Collège de France, 2013); Stefan Berger, *History and Identity: How Historical Theory Shapes Historical Practice* (Cambridge: Cambridge University Press, 2022), 261–83.

8 See, for instance, Conrad, *What Is Global History?*; Michael Lang, 'Globalization and Its History', *Journal of Modern History* 78, 4 (2006), 899–931; Michael Lang, 'Histories of Globalization(s)', in Prasenjit Duara et al. (eds.), *A Companion to Global Historical Thought* (Malden: Wiley-Blackwell, 2014), 399–411; Raymond Grew, 'On the Prospect of Global History', in Bruce Mazlish and Ralph Buultjens (eds.), *Conceptualizing Global History* (Boulder, CO: Westview Press, 1993), 227–49; Raymond Grew, 'Expanding Worlds of World History', *Journal of Modern History* 78, 4 (2006), 878–98.

9 Peter Burke, *The French Historical Revolution: The Annales School, 1929–2014*, rev. and updated 2nd ed. (Cambridge: Polity Press, 2015); Jürgen Kocka, *Sozialgeschichte: Begriff, Entwicklung, Probleme* (Göttingen: Vandenhoeck & Ruprecht, 1986), 23–6; Heinz-Gerhard Haupt and Jürgen Kocka (eds.), *Comparative and Transnational History: Central European Approaches and New Perspectives* (New York: Berghahn, 2009); Geoff Eley, *A Crooked Line: From Cultural History to the History of Society* (Ann Arbor: University of Michigan Press, 2005).

that are helpful (or, indeed, detrimental) in organising that sort of thinking. The volume shares concerns generally associated with the philosophy or theory of history, in that it reflects on the structure and direction of history, its relation to our present, and the ways in which historians can best explain, contextualise and represent events and circumstances in the past.[10] The project is also an epistemological endeavour since it examines the validity and scope of global historical knowledge and considers the field's particular epistemic values and standards.[11] It is an exercise in epistemology, too, in the sense that it engages in reflections on the emergence of global historical objects of knowledge[12] – how 'the global', 'circulation' or 'connection' became thinkable: that is, how they coalesced and amalgamated into coherent categories, paradigms and domains of inquiry that continue to shape scholarly practice.[13]

Global history is usually not defined by way of method but either through its objects – global moments,[14] worldwide connections[15] or phenomena that occur globally – or as a political attitude, 'way of seeing' and perspective that transcends the nation-state and the we-group: non-parochial, inclusive, anti-Eurocentric and cosmopolitan.[16] Indeed, its practitioners rarely think of global history as a set of distinctive methods, let alone as an approach that may require cognitive instruments different from those common to historical studies in general – as a site of methodological innovation, progress and inventiveness.

---

[10] On the theory of history, see the general surveys in Aviezer Tucker (ed.), *A Companion to the Philosophy of History and Historiography* (Oxford: Blackwell, 2009); Chiel van den Akker (ed.), *The Routledge Companion to Historical Theory* (London: Routledge, 2022); Daniel Little, 'Philosophy of History', *The Stanford Encyclopedia of Philosophy*, First published 18 February 2007; substantive revision 13 October 2016, https://plato.stanford.edu/archives/sum2017/entries/history/.

[11] An excellent survey of the evolution of 'epistemology', mainly in the French tradition that emphasises the social production of knowledge, is Hans-Jörg Rheinberger, *Historische Epistemologie zur Einführung* (Hamburg: Junius, 2007); see also Hans-Jörg Rheinberger, *On Historicizing Epistemology: An Essay* (Stanford: Stanford University Press, 2010). In English-language philosophy 'epistemology' is more akin to German *Erkenntnistheorie* and focuses on the justification of (scientific) knowledge.

[12] Uljana Feest and Thomas Sturm, 'What (Good) Is Historical Epistemology? Editors' Introduction', *Erkenntnis* 75, 3 (2011), 285–302, here 292.

[13] Lorraine Daston, 'Introduction: The Coming into Being of Scientific Objects', in Lorraine Daston (ed.), *Biographies of Scientific Objects* (Chicago: University of Chicago Press, 2000), 1–14, here 6, 9.

[14] Sebastian Conrad and Dominic Sachsenmaier, 'Introduction: Competing Visions of World Order. Global Moments and Movements, 1880s–1930s', in Sebastian Conrad and Dominic Sachsenmaier (eds.), *Competing Visions of World Order: Global Moments and Movements, 1880s–1930s* (New York: Palgrave Macmillan, 2007), 1–25.

[15] See, for instance, Olstein, *Thinking History Globally*, 14. A helpful sociological systematisation is John Urry, 'Mobilities and Social Theory', in Bryan S. Turner (ed.), *The New Blackwell Companion to Social Theory* (Malden: Wiley-Blackwell, 2009), 477–95.

[16] See, for instance, Conrad, *What Is Global History*, 3–5. Sven Beckert once referred to global history as a 'way of seeing': see C. A. Bayly et al., 'AHR Conversation: On Transnational history''', *American Historical Review* 111, 5 (2006), 1441–61, here 1454.

The most widely used 'method' that global historians routinely refer to is comparison; some of the few theoretically sophisticated concepts in the field are those of entanglement, connected history and *l'histoire croisée*.[17] Instead, global historians rely on the semantics of 'mobility', 'connectivity' and 'networks' – usually with no reference to network theory, or at best a passing nod – as a kind of surrogate theory.[18] Most of these terms are metaphorical and figurative, however: 'circulation', connectivity, 'flow' or, indeed, 'the global'[19] are metaphors rather than concepts and, as such, prior to them, as Hugo Fazio has argued. They conjure up feelings and – in a tradition going back to Aristotle – help make similarities visible,[20] but they are less useful in establishing differences and in specifying the exact meaning of a historical event or process.[21] This, however, is what concepts are supposed to do. While they may be used flexibly in view of the world's semantic diversity, they should be defined as sharply as possible – Max Weber's legacy in the humanities. One ought not to abandon conceptual clarity for the sake of literary description and narration.[22]

Observers of the field have noted that when global historians are challenged, respond to criticism of their field, or seek to defend the solidity of their craftsmanship, they tend to avoid addressing the issue of method, let alone that of methodological innovation. Rather, they fall back on the historian's

---

[17] See, for instance, Sanjay Subrahmanyam, 'One Asia, or Many? Reflections from Connected History', *Modern Asian Studies* 50, 1 (2016), 5–43; Michael Werner and Bénédicte Zimmermann, 'Beyond Comparison: Histoire Croisée and the Challenge of Reflexivity', *History and Theory* 45, 1 (2006), 30–50.

[18] For additional observations, see Jürgen Osterhammel, 'Global History 2020: Fragility in Stability', *Balzan Papers* 3 (2020), 11–30; Jürgen Osterhammel, 'Global History', in Peter Burke and Marek Tamm (eds.), *Debating New Approaches to History* (London: Bloomsbury, 2018), 21–48.

[19] See, for instance, Stefanie Gänger, 'Circulation: Reflections on Circularity, Entity and Liquidity in the Language of Global History', *Journal of Global History* 12, 3 (2017), 303–18; Stuart A. Rockefeller, 'Flow', *Current Anthropology* 52, 4 (2011), 557–78; Jürgen Osterhammel, 'Globalifizierung. Denkfiguren der neuen Welt', *Zeitschrift für Ideengeschichte* 9, 1 (2015), 5–16.

[20] See Andreas Hetzel, 'Metapher, Metaphorizität, Figurativität', in Andrea Allerkamp and Sarah Schmidt (eds.), *Handbuch Literatur und Philosophie* (Berlin: De Gruyter, 2021), 125–36, here 128. It is impossible here to survey the long history of theories of metaphor. About twenty-five such theories are discussed in Luzia Goldmann, *Phänomen und Begriff der Metapher. Vorschlag zur Systematisierung der Theoriegeschichte* (Berlin: De Gruyter, 2019). We are not aware of a similar work in English.

[21] For this observation, see Hugo Fazio, 'La historia global: ¿encrucijada de la contemporaneidad?', *Revista de Estudios Sociales* 23 (2006), 59–72, here 59, 61.

[22] On the adjustment of precision in the use of ideal-types by Max Weber and his followers, see the case study Mikhail Ilyin, 'Patrimonialism. What Is Behind the Term: Ideal Type, Category, Concept or Just a Buzz Word?', *Redescriptions* 18, 1 (2015), 26–51. Still essential for the categorisation of categories is David Collier and James E. Mahon Jr., 'Conceptual "Stretching" Revisited: Adapting Categories in Comparative Analysis', *American Political Science Review* 87, 4 (1993), 845–55.

most conventional skills and research methods, stressing their reliance on primary sources, historical depth and context.[23] This is not to say that global historians should not be judged by similar standards as historical scholarship in general, that its practitioners should not treat their sources with the same circumspection or forgo the established rules of source criticism. It is to say, however, that one would expect 'a new prospect to have methodological implications', as Peer Vries put it; it cannot suffice for its practitioners to visit more archives and master more languages than other historians.[24] Indeed, in regarding global history as a prospect *with methodological implications*, to appropriate Vries's phrase, we are emphasising both its specificity and its openness. In our view, global history, though it may often be a distinct *field* within historical studies in institutional terms, is invariably also an approach with methodological implications applicable – albeit with varying success – to many different historical subdisciplines and neighbouring fields within the humanities: think of global histories of art, medicine or music, to name but a few examples. It is not, nor should it be, thought of as fundamentally different from, let alone superior to, the many other methodological and theoretical approaches historians embrace whenever their subject requires it.

Global history and other relational approaches to history may be said to need conceptual and theoretical awareness even more urgently than other fields of history. Only in exceptional cases have historians with a global purview ventured into explicit theory-building; Martin Mulsow's 'reference theory of globalised ideas' is one of those daring deeds: an attempt to suggest a general framework for global intellectual history.[25] Their overall hesitancy is all the more paradoxical since global histories are a theoretical enterprise by definition. Their practitioners cannot treat their parameters as though they were a given; the very choice of a timeframe, a spatial arena or a suitable unit of analysis requires reflection. None of them are sanctioned by tacit – that is, in many cases, national – conventions.[26] Even the use of categories of analysis or comparison – seemingly neutral, but ultimately European concepts such as class, dynasty, revolution or bourgeoisie – requires a measure of theoretical consideration.[27] Historians going global are also in need of conceptual

---

[23] Peer Vries, 'The Prospects of Global History: Personal Reflections of an Old Believer', *International Review of Social History* 64, 1 (2019), 111–21, here 119.

[24] Vries, 'The Prospects of Global History', 119.

[25] Martin Mulsow, 'A Reference Theory of Globalized Ideas', *Global Intellectual History* 2, 1 (2017), 67–87. See also the comprehensive application of this theory in Martin Mulsow, *Überreichweiten. Perspektiven einer globalen Ideengeschichte* (Berlin: Suhrkamp, 2022).

[26] Jürgen Osterhammel, 'Global History and Historical Sociology', in Belich et al., *The Prospect of Global History*, 23–43, here 25.

[27] See, for instance, Christof Dejung et al. (eds.), *The Global Bourgeoisie: The Rise of the Middle Classes in the Age of Empire* (Princeton: Princeton University Press, 2019); Jeroen Duindam, 'A Plea for Global Comparison: Redefining Dynasty', *Past & Present* 242, Supplement 14 (2019), 318–47. For a collection of basic essays in (global) conceptual history, see

reflections since many of the classic analytical instruments commonly employed by historians require some reduction of complexity – to explain, to periodise or to compare. These tasks are naturally more difficult, and in need of theoretical reflection and guidance, in endeavours that deal with an unusual convolution and abundance of evidence and factors. Global historians might likewise want to engage in theoretical reflections on the matter of perspective and authorial vantage point in history writing: after all, global history's initial battle cry was a revisionist impulse, an assault on Eurocentrism, now widely considered a fundamental shortcoming of the modern social sciences and humanities at large.[28] But how to actually write a history without a centre or, indeed, one with a diversity of voices and vantage points, given that any narrative requires a minimum of coherence?

Historians adopting global perspectives would also be well advised to engage in critical epistemological introspection because of the tacit political assumptions underlying and informing their scholarly practice. Global history 'rests on the notion of global integration as a defining feature', as Sebastian Conrad put it;[29] its understanding of history is inseparable from the telos of continuously increasing global integration, one that leads to a state where 'everyone lives inside a global web, a unitary maelstrom of cooperation and competition'.[30] Any self-respecting historian, global or not, will firmly reject the association with teleology – by common understanding, one of the worst of historiographical sins – but it is hard to refute the reproach that a certain *telos* and sense of direction is implicit in every global historian's very research interest: in the spread of ideas, the making of connections and the formation of networks; in the shrinking of distance, 'entanglement' and 'transcultural-ity'. Global history has recently come under critique – both from within and outside the field – for its sense of proportion, or, rather, its lack thereof: for overstating the significance of 'influences', both inward and outward, over internal causes.[31] These points are well taken; indeed, a penchant for overstating the weight of connections is a logical defect in a field devised to look for

Margrit Pernau and Dominic Sachsenmaier (eds.), *Global Conceptual History* (London: Bloomsbury, 2016).

[28] This is linked to extensive debates on the role of colonialism and racism in the history of the humanities. See Andrew Valls (ed.), *Race and Racism in Modern Philosophy* (Ithaca: Cornell University Press, 2005); Oliver Eberl, *Naturzustand und Barbarei: Begründung und Kritik staatlicher Ordnung im Zeichen des Kolonialismus* (Hamburg: Hamburger Edition, 2021); and numerous studies on individual thinkers, such as Katrin Flikschuh and Lea Ypi (eds.), *Kant and Colonialism: Historical and Critical Perspectives* (Oxford: Oxford University Press, 2014).

[29] Conrad, *What Is Global History*, 101; or, as Conrad puts it elsewhere more subtly, 'it takes structured integration as a context, even when it is not the main topic'. 90, also 129.

[30] John R. McNeill and William H. McNeill, *The Human Web: A Bird's-eye View of World History* (New York: Norton, 2003), 5.

[31] David A. Bell, 'Questioning the Global Turn: The Case of the French Revolution', *French Historical Studies* 37, 1 (2014), 1–24, here 23.

evidence of these. Again, this is where method is bound to be useful, to rein in the imagination. Global historians using quantitative methods, for instance – formalising, at least in some basic sense, their arguments – would invariably weigh the relative importance of 'influences' more carefully, and endeavour to comprehend the reach and meaning of 'the global' in the past with greater precision. A quantitative approach might also help them define thresholds for 'globality', take the measure of mobility, and establish sounder criteria for speaking of 'integration', 'connectivity' and interrelatedness. At any rate, a certain hesitancy about methodology and theory, which may materialise from time to time as a backlash against excessive theorising, is detrimental to any field. To an approach like global history, with its particular need of conceptual, methodological and theoretical guidance, it is self-defeating.[32]

The present volume addresses global historians in particular for the obvious reason that many of the concepts and metaphors that are their daily bread – think of scale or distance – do not have the same relevance in other fields of history. And yet, much of what is said in the following pages should be of interest to historians more broadly. Of course, every historian ought to occasionally pause and reflect on the conceptual basis of their work: on the place of explanation – and its relation to narration – in it; on how to tackle the issue of *telos*, perspective and directionality in history writing or to establish robust, consensual criteria; on when they should speak of 'more', 'fewer' or 'better'. Indeed, in its particular need of theorisation, global history can also serve to challenge and add to theories of historiography more broadly. Narrativist theory, for instance, as discussed in the chapter on explanation by Jürgen Osterhammel in this volume, usually refers to very simple set-ups of more or less linear narratives within a limited spatial arena. The kinds of discontinuous stories connecting disparate venues that global historians contend with challenge and add complexity to conventional conceptions of narratives.[33] Reflections on periodisation, likewise discussed in this volume in the chapter by Christina Brauner, similarly benefit from global historical debates, given that the chronopolitics involved in our conceptions of time, temporality and temporal regimes are nowhere so evident as in colonial and imperial legacies. Or take the issue of teleology. Global history is not the only example of an approach that, after renouncing one form of teleology – in its case, that of Eurocentrism and nationalism[34] – has unwittingly adopted a new sense of direction: that of global integration. Indeed, since the late 1700s historians have again and again renounced one *telos* and replaced it with another, from

---

[32] For a sensible defence of theory, see Gary Wilder, 'From Optic to Topic: The Foreclosure Effects of Historiographic Turns', *American Historical Review* 117, 3 (2012), 723–45.

[33] See Gabriele Lingelbach (ed.). *Narrative und Darstellungsweisen der Globalgeschichte* (Berlin: De Gruyter Oldenbourg, 2022).

[34] Conrad, *What Is Global History*, 3–4.

eschatology to progress to nationalism. More recently, teleology has made another (re-)appearance in the form of an apocalyptic Anthropocene discourse and environmental histories premised upon the *telos* of continuous natural degradation.[35] This is not a call to foolishly deny climate change or environmental destruction and degradation, of course. It is to say, however, that other areas of historiography are also infused with a sense of direction and would be as well advised as global historians to critically reflect on whether this might not be to the detriment of their understanding of historical complexity and contingency.

The global perspective, in short, is not just a minor adjustment of focal length. Global history shares the basic logic and cognitive infrastructure of historical studies in general. It adds complications and theoretical challenges, however, that are of interest even to those who are unconcerned with or indifferent to global historians' empirical results. Microanalyses, studies that limit their purview to one village, town or country, and other 'discrete' forms of history have long injected fresh perspectives into historical theory, questioned the validity of paradigms, and challenged simplifications in their attention and sensitivity to agency, idiosyncrasy and detail. So, too, global and other relational forms of history can be a touchstone for historical theory.[36] Together, they allow us to test the premises and value of historical theory, its soundness and its scope.

Shifting Ground: Global History in the 2020s

A systematic rethinking of the global historian's craft is all the more important because the world is changing fast. Global history, though standing in an ancient tradition of world or 'general' history, is conceptually and theoretically a creature of the 1990s, the formative decade of theorisation and euphoria about globalisation.[37] At the time, the conclusion to half a century of political decolonisation, an ebb of international tensions, a bright economic outlook

---

[35] Such a 'declinist' perspective is not limited to prognostic books (e.g. David Wallace-Wells, *The Uninhabitable Earth: Life After Warming* [New York: Tim Duggan, 2019]), but also informs substantial historical accounts such as Daniel R. Headrick, *Humans Versus Nature: A Global Environmental History* (Oxford: Oxford University Press, 2020), and Laurent Testot, *Cataclysms: An Environmental History of Humanity* (Chicago: University of Chicago Press, 2020). Historians have challenged environmental catastrophism for some time now from the perspective of Indigenous societies, who suffered its consequences long prior to western societies and were not equally culpable of it. For a critique of 'the Anthropocene as a teleological fact', see Zoe Todd, 'Indigenizing the Anthropocene', in Heather Davis and Etienne Turpin (eds.), *Art in the Anthropocene: Encounters Among Aesthetics, Politics, Environment and Epistemology* (London: Open Humanities Press, 2015), 241–54, here 251.

[36] See, for instance, Francesca Trivellato, 'Is There a Future for Italian Microhistory in the Age of Global History?', *California Italian Studies* 2, 1 (2011), http://dx.doi.org/10.5070/C321009025.

[37] A key text summarising the thinking of that decade is David Held et al., *Global Transformations: Politics, Economics and Culture* (Cambridge: Polity, 1999).

and the rise of information technology seemed to open up the prospect of a borderless world, of irreversible, peaceful integration, and – with few voices dissenting[38] – of an end to ideological and religious cleavages. As a scholarly project of growing prestige and respectability, global history took shape in the context of that decade's sanguine outlook and in the spirit of 'one-worldism', palpable to this day in global historians' 'enthusiasm for movement, mobility, and circulation',[39] their basic vocabulary of effortless flows and their tacit belief in a perpetually increasing 'connectivity'.[40]

That kind of muted confidence can no longer inspire and support global history. There is no need to rehearse at length the long series of setbacks for cosmopolitan hopes in the twenty-first century: the rise of nationalist 'my-country-first'-ism and isolationism, the inability of 'global governance' to tame the selfishness of great powers, the use of information technology for digitised surveillance and cyber warfare rather than liberation or, indeed, the disintegrating effects of the Covid-19 pandemic and the attendant containment measures. This is not to say that globalisation has lost its relevance; in fact, on some levels, the world has become more integrated than ever, with political and economic shocks reverberating globally, or with a nuclear threat and climate catastrophe endangering all of humanity in a finite, closed world.[41] After all, the greatest possible globality is attained when there is nowhere to hide from disaster. What globalisation has lost is its innocence and any appearance of inherent goodness on the one hand, and all semblance of consistency, uniformity and dependability on the other. Rather, today's world reveals the dialectics of entanglement: not in terms of a simple see-saw between integration and disintegration, globalisation and deglobalisation, but in terms of multiple levels of integration standing in a possibly contradictory relation to one another and drifting apart. The pandemic, for instance, brought worldwide physical mobility to a standstill, unravelled global supply chains and revealed a dire lack of global solidarity in the distribution of vaccines, while at the same time enhancing digital communication on a global scale, not to mention showing us how the virus would leave no corner of the world unscathed. The war against

---

[38] From different political perspectives: Samuel Huntington, *The Clash of Civilizations and the Remaking of World Order* (New York: Simon & Schuster, 1996); Paul Hirst and Grahame Thompson, *Globalization in Question: The International Economy and the Possibilities of Governance* (Cambridge: Polity Press, 1996).
[39] Conrad, *What Is Global History*, 210.
[40] Gänger, 'Circulation'; Rockefeller, 'Flow'; Osterhammel, 'Globalifizierung'.
[41] See Sabine Höhler, *Spaceship Earth in the Environmental Age* (London: Routledge, 2017); for the background in intellectual and media history, see David Kuchenbuch, *Welt-Bildner: Arno Peters, Richard Buckminster Fuller und die Medien des Globalismus, 1940–2000* (Vienna: Böhlau, 2021). The future is no longer seen as 'open' and malleable but as a source of danger and doom, as recent discussions of historical time have argued. See, for instance, Zoltán Boldizsár Simon, *History in Times of Unprecedented Change: A Theory for the 21st Century* (London: Bloomsbury Academic, 2019).

Ukraine that started on 24 February 2022 caused the disruption of international grain markets and led to an unprecedented isolation of a major country, while simultaneously triggering a large refugee movement, an exceptionally unanimous global public opinion (at least in the arena of the United Nations),[42] and a global energy crisis. Pipelines transmogrified into weapons of economic strangulation, while interdependence lost its 'inter'-prefix and turned from seemingly reciprocal to hierarchically constraining.

If global history is the history for our time, what happens when the times are a-changing, as Christina Brauner puts it in this volume? The 1990s created the specific historical conditions for the invention of epistemic categories such as 'the global', 'connectivity', 'flow' and 'circulation'. By the 2020s, the historical conditions that brought about this sort of 'global talk'[43] have changed and, in some measure, vanished. Recent developments are invalidating several of the assumptions and images that continue to inform global historical discourse and require us to rethink it. It is imperative, for one thing, to reflect on the value judgements implicit in our writing and terminology: our idea of globalisation as a benign process, our obsession with movement, so palpable especially in the pioneering years of global history, or the ultimately positive connotations long attached to terms such as 'connectivity', 'flow' and 'circulation'.[44] Recent experiences such as refugee crises, the pandemic, climate catastrophe and nuclear threat remind us not only of the unpleasant, toxic and lethal side of global 'connectivity', but also drive home the fact that 'connectivity' is not necessarily about free choice, inclusion and unrestricted agency. It can befall us, haunt and torment us against our will. Global historians will no longer speak of connectivity, circulation and mobility with quite the same ease and innocence; different, perhaps less anthropocentric semantics – 'contagion', even the much-maligned 'diffusion'[45] – might well have to be added to their vocabulary to express global experiences in the past and the present.

The association of the modern era with unchecked and unprecedented mobility, long held to be an iron law in global historical scholarship, is also

---

[42] On the concept of a global public, see Valeska Huber and Jürgen Osterhammel, 'Introduction: Global Publics', in Valeska Huber and Jürgen Osterhammel (eds.), *Global Publics: Their Power and Their Limits, 1870–1990* (Oxford: Oxford University Press, 2020), 1–60.

[43] Paul A. Kramer, 'How Did the World Become Global? Transnational History, Beyond Connection', *Reviews in American History* 49, 1 (2021), 119–41, here 133.

[44] For a critique of what has been called 'happy transculturalism', see, for instance, Monica Juneja and Christian Kravagna, 'Understanding Transculturalism: Monica Juneja and Christian Kravagna in Conversation', in Fahim Amir et al. (ed.), *Transcultural Modernisms* (Berlin: Sternberg, 2013), 23–33, here 31–2.

[45] Damon Centola, *How Behavior Spreads: The Science of Complex Contagion* (Princeton: Princeton University Press, 2018); Adam Kucharski, *The Rules of Contagion: Why Things Spread – and Why They Stop* (London: Profile Books, 2020). The concept of 'diffusion' has been successfully employed in the study of technological globalisation; see, for example, James W. Cortada, *The Digital Flood: The Diffusion of Information Technology Across the US,*

shaken. This is not to deny an increase in the level of migration after 1850 on account of advances in transportation technology;[46] if mobility can be banned or made next to impossible from one day to the next by governmental strategies for disease containment, however, 'acceleration' is a changing variable rather than a force of nature. The premise of growing integration, likewise, is not only bordering on the trivial: global population growth and improved technical means of transport and communication will inevitably lead to a proliferation of contacts; our present experience makes that basic belief untenable. Indeed, one might consider replacing the concept of 'globalisation' or 'global integration' with approaches that take into account the various levels of integration and their possibly contradictory relation to one another – to move to a level beneath that undifferentiated macro-process and 'framing device', as Jan C. Jansen puts it in this volume, by thinking in terms of 'heterodox' global processes with varying directionalities, velocities and reaches; even cyclical, contingent and chaotic processes that encompass expansion and contraction, termination and reversal.[47] Not only must global historians pay more heed to 'global imaginaries' expressive not of cosmopolitan yearnings but of fear and endangerment from the world; they also ought to consider more seriously the possibility of past worlds that were 'devoid of connectivity' – idiosyncratic, asynchronous and insular.[48] At any rate, when the 'facts change',[49] conventions of thought and language must be re-examined.

Global history cannot be a history out of sync with the present, to be sure; in some measure, however, it must dissociate and distance itself, not just from the 1990s, but also from its presentism, broadly speaking.[50] This is not to deny history's necessary relation to the present nor the fact of its invariably changing

---

Europe, and Asia (Oxford: Oxford University Press, 2012), and this path-breaking study: Vernon W. Ruttan, *Technology, Growth and Development: An Induced Innovation Perspective* (Oxford: Oxford University Press, 2001).

[46] Jan Lucassen and Leo Lucassen, 'The Mobility Transition Revisited, 1500–1900: What the Case of Europe Can Offer to Global History', *Journal of Global History* 4, 3 (2009), 347–77.

[47] Peter Laslett, 'Social Structural Time: An Attempt at Classifying Types of Social Change by Their Characteristic Paces', in Tom Schuller and Michael Young (eds.), *The Rhythms of Society* (London: Routledge, 1988), 17–36; Wolfgang Knöbl, 'After Modernization: Der Globalisierungsbegriff als Platzhalter und Rettungsanker der Sozialwissenschaften', *Vierteljahreshefte für Zeitgeschichte* 68, 2 (2020), 279–318, here 313; Wolfgang Knöbl, *Die Soziologie vor der Geschichte: Zur Kritik der Sozialtheorie* (Berlin: Suhrkamp, 2022); Andreas Wimmer and Reinhart Kössler (eds.), *Understanding Change: Models, Methodologies, and Metaphors* (Basingstoke: Palgrave Macmillan, 2005).

[48] Giorgio Riello, 'The World in a Book: The Creation of the Global in Sixteenth-Century European Costume Books', *Past & Present* 242, Supplement 14 (2019), 281–317, here 286, 295, 302, 316. On early modern global imaginaries, see also C. A. Bayly, '"Archaic" and "Modern" Globalization in the Eurasian and African Arena, c. 1750–1850', in A. G. Hopkins (ed.), *Globalization in World History* (London: Pimlico, 2002), 47–73, here 52–54.

[49] Tony Judt, *When the Facts Change: Essays 1995–2010* (New York: Penguin, 2015).

[50] François Hartog, *Regimes of Historicity: Presentism and the Experience of Time* (New York: Columbia University Press, 2015).

with the times. But a global history less reliant on concepts with evident expiry dates, more aware of the historicity of its own premises, more careful and conscious in its use of categories, would promise to be more impervious to the winds of change. It is likely to be less of a 'trend' and more of an approach or, indeed, a set of methods, in history that is here to stay. The present volume does not presume to foretell what global history will look like many years from now; we are no astrologers. Rather, it is about what it *might* look like. Many historians shy away from the prescriptive or normative, and for good reason. In an academic world of proliferating 'turns' and competing trends, blowing one's own trumpet too loudly tastes of the vulgar. At the same time, assessing the present state of a scholarly field will never be an entirely neutral or unbiased activity. Inasmuch as ours is a critical exercise, it is bound, and indeed designed, to uncover failings and weaknesses, reveal room for improvement and avenues for further exploration. Some amount of gate-keeping is indispensable for any line of scholarship. Again, our critique is no swansong farewell to a failed promise – quite the contrary. We simply believe that academic fields improve through the intellectual exercise of destabilising and stabilising, of disassembling and reconstructing, their premises, terms and concepts. To us, global history is a methodological approach that is teeming with possibilities, with stories to be told. We criticise it not because we think it has 'had its moment'[51] – incidentally, the very Jeremy Adelman, to whom that assertion is attributed, never thought it had[52] – but because in dissociating it from the moment it is bound to live longer, to evolve and to thrive. Any survey of the present by necessity points to the future. The present volume takes such a path of cautious normativity.

Rethinking the Premises

In an ideal world, one would assemble a group of specialists and charge them with compiling a multi-volume dictionary of 'key terms in global history', an endeavour along the lines of Reinhart Koselleck and his co-editors' encyclopedic, eight-volume project of *Geschichtliche Grundbegriffe* (Basic Concepts in History), an indispensable tool for any German-speaking historian.[53] The present book, inevitably, falls short of such comprehensive ambition. Rather, it

---

[51] Adelman, 'What Is Global History Now'.
[52] See the response by Jeremy Adelman to Richard Drayton and David Motadel, 'Discussion: The Futures of Global History', *Journal of Global History* 13, 1 (2018), 1–21, here 18.
[53] Otto Brunner et al. (eds.), *Geschichtliche Grundbegriffe: Historisches Lexikon zur politisch-sozialen Sprache in Deutschland*, 7 vols. (Stuttgart: Klett-Cotta, 1972–97); see also the extensively revised English translation of a French work: Barbara Cassin (ed.), *Dictionary of Untranslatables: A Philosophical Lexicon* (Princeton: Princeton University Press, 2014).

offers a selection of concepts and themes that, we hope, strikes a balance between coherence and diversity.

The instruments at the disposal of the historian can be arranged on a scale between precision and vagueness, between 'hard' methods and 'soft' visions. Some of the topics in this volume are located at the 'hard' end of the spectrum: comparison, explanation, periodisation and quantification are well-established set-pieces in the methodology of history and the social sciences. They are canvassed in Part I, which is devoted to methodological forms of inquiry and argumentation in global history. Jürgen Osterhammel's chapter discusses the particular difficulties that explanation, or the asking of why-questions – invariably reliant on a certain reduction of complexity – poses for a historiography dealing with an unusual plurality and abundance of evidence. Explanation seems to have somewhat gone out of fashion; many global historians prefer storytelling and colourful narratives to explanation and analysis. No narrative goes without deliberation, however; even the most compelling story contains an explanation, albeit an implicit one that does not reveal its premises, selection and contingency. Closely related to the challenges attendant on explanation are those related to comparison on a global scale, a topic discussed by Alessandro Stanziani. Stanziani dwells on the difficulties of choosing 'neutral' parameters for comparison, on the discourse of singularity and other implicit comparisons, and on forgoing or finding 'other' models when fundamentally different entities are being brought together for the purpose of noting similarities and differences. Every comparison requires a meta-language, an exercise in commensurability, that will commonly be more intricate on a global scale, and thus in particular need of conceptual reflection and guidance.

Questions of time and temporality, too, addressed in Christina Brauner's chapter, pose a challenge for global history. Brauner discusses the difficulties of periodising on a global scale and with a claim to universal validity, given the diversity of temporalities, temporal regimes and cultures of time in the world of the past. Take the much-debated concept of the 'global Middle Ages', for instance. Is it a way of ensuring contemporaneousness and inclusiveness – a place within history for all – or a mere continuation of Eurocentric pretentiousness? This part concludes with a chapter by Pim de Zwart on quantitative approaches in global history – in other words, on arguing with numbers: a topic properly within the remit of economic historians but with much wider repercussions. The rise of the digital humanities is bound to bring numbers to the fore; we might as well dispel whatever qualms we have about them and learn to employ them with a view to crafting a more robust form of global history.

Other topics in the volume are nearer the 'soft' end of the spectrum in that they are devoted to metaphors and even verbal images (*Sprachbilder*) rather than sharply defined concepts and categories. First in line is, of course, 'the global' – a notion invoked time and again in academic as well as popular global history writing but which rarely receives the careful consideration it urgently requires.[54] As Peer Vries has pointed out, the terms 'global' and 'globalisation' may well be appealing to some practitioners in their very fuzziness, suggestiveness and vagueness. Their alluring imprecision, however, precludes a vigilant assessment of their potential, on the one hand, and of the analytical limitations and constraints of a global perspective, on the other.[55] In his chapter, Sujit Sivasundaram gauges the meaning of 'the global', by all accounts global history's most basic concept, stressing its constructedness and contingency: how the globe is not a given but a historic artifice – the only given is the earth, incidentally an oblate spheroid rather than globular – and how the meaning of and associations with globality have changed over time, in relation to our historical actors' cosmos and its geographical, social and communicational limits.[56] Sivasundaram's chapter adds to and is complementary to debates in other fields that have sought to come to terms with 'the global', such as sociological systems-theory[57] and international relations discourses.[58]

Closely related to 'the global' is another image: that of the 'sphere', with its implied ability to regulate access through both inclusion and exclusion. Global historians tend to reject a 'container' type view of the past which is often seen as emblematic of old-fashioned methodological nationalism.[59] Still, some kind of structuration is indispensable, with spheres as an interesting candidate, as Valeska Huber shows in her chapter. It is one of many examples global historians might consider taking up in order to diversify their vocabulary. The last chapter in Part II concerns another fundamental, much-used concept in global historical discourse: that of 'scale'. Dániel Margócsy's chapter questions both the self-evidence of the concept – the very idea of 'levels of analysis' – as well as the all-too-entrenched dichotomies of micro–macro or global–local it has entailed; it points, at the same time, to the concept's

---

[54] For a similar critique, see Duncan Bell, 'Making and Taking Worlds', in Samuel Moyn and Andrew Sartori (eds.), *Global Intellectual History* (New York: Columbia University Press, 2013), 254–79, here 256.

[55] Vries, 'The Prospects of Global History', 116; Cooper's comments on 'globalisation' remain indispensable: Frederick Cooper, *Colonialism in Question: Theory, Knowledge, History* (Berkeley: University of California Press, 2005), 91–112.

[56] See Christoph Markschies (ed.), *Atlas der Weltbilder* (Berlin: Akademie-Verlag, 2011). On the politics of 'global speak', see Olaf Bach, *Die Erfindung der Globalisierung. Entstehung und Wandel eines zeitgeschichtlichen Grundbegriffs* (Frankfurt a.M.: Campus, 2013); Sabine Selchow, *Negotiations of the 'New World': The Omnipresence of 'Global' as a Political Phenomenon* (Bielefeld: Transcript, 2017).

[57] Rudolf Stichweh, 'World Society', in Ludger Kühnhardt and Tilman Mayer (eds.), *The Bonn Handbook of Globality* (Cham: Springer, 2019), vol. 1, 515–26.

[58] Jens Bartelson, *Visions of World Community* (Cambridge: Cambridge University Press, 2009); Jens Bartelson, 'The Social Construction of Globality', *International Political Sociology* 4, 3 (2010), 219–235.

[59] See, for instance, Conrad, *What Is Global History*, 4.

usefulness if handled carefully, premised partly on recent theoretical reflections in geography. Like Sivasundaram's or Stanziani's contributions, Margócsy's study retraces the semantic evolution of the concept in question. Historians, after all, even when they engage in methodological reflections, are unable to abandon their habitual interest and expertise in change, to good effect.

Contributions in Part III expose unquestioned 'configurations',[60] biases and assumptions that guide global historians' work and put them up for careful inspection. Jan C. Jansen's chapter reflects critically on global histories' tacit directionality, especially the implicit assumption of a continuously growing global integration. Rather than passing judgement on a historiographical sin or seeking to refute the reproach that a certain *telos* and sense of direction is implicit in global historians' thinking and writing, the chapter turns the debate about teleology into one about the theoretical foundations of history – especially, but not exclusively, global history – at large. It uses teleology as a stimulus to think creatively and provocatively about direction, coherence and processes in the writing of history more broadly. As does Jeremy Adelman, whose chapter is concerned with another form of *telos* in the global history literature: the alleged demise of distance in the modern era. Global history is often defined as the historical study of objects that are separated by, but that cover and overcome sizeable distance, both geographical and cultural; yet its practitioners rarely reflect on distance as a subject and as a narrative. Adelman's chapter not only exposes how the collapse and surmounting of physical distance in the modern era has entailed other forms of (social, legal, racial) distance, but also canvasses ideas about strangeness and familiarity, the 'arc of history' and distance as both variable, and effect more broadly.

Stefanie Gänger's chapter, in turn, is concerned with the implicit, unspoken assumptions that guide and inform global histories that consider aspects of the material world. Its particular interest is in the grounds on which historians associate matter and material culture with a specific scale, context or level of observation: with world-making, the global scale and 'connectivity', but also with the concrete, the particular and the intimate, the latter presumably a substrate of their own societies' socioreligious texture. The last chapter in the volume, written by Dominic Sachsenmaier, examines yet another unquestioned assumption – that of global history's downright renunciation of 'centrism'. Surveying Eurocentrism, Sinocentrism and other forms of centrism, the chapter unmasks the illusion of a non-centred vantage point of uncontaminated authorial oversight. It employs the concept of centrism as a lens to reflect on perspective, viewpoint and the possibility and desirability of writing histories without a centre more broadly. The piece ultimately relates to a political question: if any history requires a narrative gradient

---

[60] On the concept of (con)figuration, see Norbert Elias, *What Is Sociology?* (New York: Columbia University Press, 1978), 128–33.

or centre, is global history unavoidably related to hegemonies inside and outside of global academia – European, US-American and more recently Chinese?

Many more concepts and images would merit the kind of reflection that this volume attempts to offer. One of its main purposes is to inspire and encourage further research and reflection along the lines suggested in it. We could have included contributions on the concepts of 'network', 'periphery', 'chain' – as in commodity chain, for instance – or 'diffusion', the latter one of many naturalistic metaphors in global history. Much remains to be said about the idea of 'context' – particularly the deceptive self-evidence of a 'global context', as the context of all contexts, in which events or processes tend to be 'embedded'[61] – and the idea of 'order', or, indeed, orders. The idea of connections and connectivity would certainly have been worth a chapter, too; but then, that topic is so ubiquitous and obvious that it is taken up at many places across the volume.[62] A few more classical issues, models and ideal-types in global and other relational forms of history surely deserve a closer look, such as 'agency', 'structure' or the complex field of 'translation', which is both a designation for a precise linguistic operation and a general metaphor for intercultural conversion and metamorphosis.

Further contributions in our project's spirit will hopefully transcend the linguistic, geographical and historiographical limitations of our volume, which, except for Sachsenmaier's chapter, centres on material written in Western European languages. Some future collection of essays might broaden the purview to a worldwide perspective, inquiring, for instance, into East African views of 'the global', Polynesian concepts of time or Japanese constructions of maritime space.[63] Its authors and editors, who might not be Europeans as we mostly are, will hopefully be reflective of their own sociocultural premises, too, and not give in to a very European and modern longing for originality, 'unchanging certainty' and 'endangered authenticities',[64] nor, after renouncing the telos inherent in Eurocentrism and global integration, succumb to a new sense of direction, hoping to find radically different ontologies and fundamental alterity out there. Indeed, a thoroughgoing 'decolonisation' of the historiographical vocabulary is difficult, if not impossible, for the modern era. Students of history

---

[61] This topic has attracted the attention of the *doyen* of intellectual history: J. G. A. Pocock, 'On the Unglobality of Contexts: Cambridge Methods and the History of Political Thought', *Global Intellectual History* 4, 1 (2019), 1–14.

[62] For interesting suggestions on various forms, functions and effects of connectivity in other fields, see Anna Lowenhaupt Tsing, *Friction: An Ethnography of Global Connection* (Princeton: Princeton University Press, 2005).

[63] See Richard Reid, 'Time and Distance: Reflections on Local and Global History from East Africa', *Transactions of the Royal Historical Society* 29 (2019), 253–72; Warwick Anderson et al. (eds), *Pacific Futures: Past and Present* (Honolulu, HI: University of Hawai'i Press, 2018); Takashi Shiraishi, *Empire of the Seas: Thinking about Asia* (Tokyo: Japan Publishing Industry Foundation for Culture, 2021).

[64] Rey Chow, *Writing Diaspora: Tactics of Intervention in Contemporary Cultural Studies* (Bloomington: Indiana University Press, 1993), 36, 51–3, 118.

outside Europe, North America and Australia – the archetypal 'West' – nowadays discuss the same authors, regardless of their geographical location and cultural background, notwithstanding an asymmetry in the business of academic translations that leads to a very uneven reception. What is more, not every concept forged in Western historiography is hopelessly tainted and untransferable. Questions of closeness and distance or the dichotomy between materiality and spirituality are common to many cultural contexts.[65] So too is an understanding of the temporal form of historical change; indeed, the study of temporalities is a particularly fruitful field in this regard.[66] Explanation, comparison and counting, though they can be implemented in varying ways, are cognitive procedures of unbounded generality.[67] The *logic* of using sources, constructing historical arguments and making bias transparent, too, is not culturally specific. This is not to say that future historians should not historicise, 'provincialise' and contextualise their concepts and assumptions; rather, that they should do so without succumbing to the illusion that there is radical alterity, purity and authenticity to be found out there.

Global history has come under attack from several angles. The more fundamental criticism has come not so much from within their own global community of scholars, but from two external factions: from historians who object to decentring, relating and comparing their national histories for fear of diminishing the stature of the nation-state on the one hand,[68] and, on the other, from postcolonial and decolonial scholarship increasingly reluctant about putting the former victims of imperial violence and exploitation within the same analytical framework as the perpetrators.[69] Both lines of attack deny the universality of

---

[65] On the premise that materiality is that which ought to be transcended, the merely apparent 'behind which lies that which is real', see Daniel Miller, 'Materiality: An Introduction', in Daniel Miller (ed.), *Materiality* (Durham: Duke University Press, 2005), 1–50, here 1.

[66] See, as a model study, Wayan Jarrah Sastrawan, 'Temporalities in Southeast Asian Historiography', *History and Theory* 59, 2 (2020), 210–26.

[67] See Angelika Epple and Walter Erhart, 'Practices of Comparing. A New Research Agenda between Typological and Historical Approaches', in Angelika Epple et al. (eds.), *Practices of Comparing: Towards a New Understanding of a Fundamental Human Practice* (Bielefeld: Transcript, 2020), 11–38. Though not ambitiously 'global', a seminal collection is Willibald Steinmetz (ed.), *The Force of Comparison: A New Perspective on Modern European History and the Contemporary World* (New York: Berghahn, 2019). A hotbed of methodological advances in comparison is now ethnology/anthropology: see Michael Schnegg and Edward D. Lowe (eds.), *Comparing Cultures: Innovations in Comparative Ethnography* (Cambridge: Cambridge University Press, 2020).

[68] See, for instance, the criticism brought forth against Patrick Boucheron (ed.), *Histoire mondiale de la France* (Paris: Seuil, 2017); the wider debate is aptly summarised in Damiano Matasci, 'L'histoire mondiale: Un modèle historiographique en question', *Revue Suisse d'Histoire* 71, 2 (2021), 333–46, here 335–6.

[69] The relationship between global history and postcolonial studies would have been an additional topic of great complexity given the numerous positions subsumed under those general labels. For a good juxtaposition of postcolonialism and globalisation studies, see Nicolas Bancel, *Le postcolonialisme* (Paris: Que sais-je?, 2019), 110–16.

the human experience and the existence of a common ground that makes it basically possible to converse, relate and compare anything to anything else. Though methodologically and conceptually a creature of the 1990s, global history has deep roots in older forms of world or general historical writing that comprehend the world in its widest conceivable extent as it was known, or knowable, at a given place and time. General history – as in the Arabic tradition, for instance – is a history that transcends the historian's 'we-group'; a history of Us *and* Them.[70] Unlike world history, which starts out from the division of humanity into units – civilisations, religious ecumenes, empires or world regions – global history stands in that 'general' tradition in its deliberate de-emphasising of units or, where they cannot be ignored, in regarding them as 'produced' or constructed rather than as given.[71] If the field takes that legacy and approach seriously, there is no fundamental obstacle to a global conversation about concepts, images and methods. Indeed, global historians ought to stand their ground on this. Not only is their approach one that allows us to decide which metaphors, forms of inquiry and ideas to dismiss on the grounds of their utter idiosyncrasy and which to retain, or take up, because they are sufficiently general or ample; their relational approach also allows for a global conversation that we desperately need today. Some will object that a proper dialogue is impossible when reception and influence between Western and other countries remain asymmetrical.[72] And, to be sure, the distribution of resources – from journal licences to visiting fellowships – is deeply unequal, as is that of academic freedom from political, ideological and religious pressure, vital for a kind of history that, from the point of view of rulers and guardians of orthodoxy, refuses to be 'useful' in any obvious way. While there can be no doubt that imbalance remains an obstacle to relations and exchange, however, it is also the best reason to nurture them; relations can, at best, help redress imbalance. To resort, once more, to cautious normativity: global history is, and ought to be, a 'general' kind of history; it can and should be a history for all of humanity, an approach through which people relate to each other.

---

[70] Subrahmanyam, *On the Origins of Global History.*
[71] See, for instance, Olstein, *Thinking History Globally*, 51.
[72] Margrit Pernau and Dominic Sachsenmaier, 'Introduction: Global History, Translation and Semantic Changes', in Pernau and Sachsenmaier, *Global Conceptual History*, 1–28, here 17.

Part I

Forms of Inquiry and Argumentation

1   Explanation
The Limits of Narrativism in Global History

Jürgen Osterhammel

Next to overcoming Eurocentrism – and perhaps any other form of value-laden centrism – the other big promise made by global history is to widen horizons, multiply the forms of human experience considered by the historian and increase the number of voices that are recovered from the past. Yet richness is not an end in itself. If the temptation of empirical overabundance is not resisted, world history turns into an ocean of the picturesque and the world historian into an old-fashioned polymath.

The obvious remedy is to employ concepts, patterns and strategies of emplotment with the purpose of giving shape to historical representation. In other words, sheer description tends to exhaust itself. In one of the most underrated contributions to historical theory, Siegfried Kracauer put it like this: 'One might also say that the historian follows two tendencies – the realistic tendency which prompts him to get hold of all data of interest, and the formative tendency which requires him to explain the material in hand.'[1] It seemed to be a matter of course for Kracauer, writing in the 1960s, to equate the 'formative tendency' with 'explanation'. As his subsequent discussion shows, Kracauer uses the term quite broadly – similar to how another great theorist, the Hungarian philosopher Ágnes Heller, was later to employ it when she wrote that 'explanation' was identical to 'making something understood'.[2] In other words, to explain means 'to make sense' of what historians find in their sources. It also means to translate the past into the present and make it comprehensible while, ideally, not obliterating its strangeness.

Explanation builds upon description. It is the attempt to impart meaning to the evidence by distinguishing outcomes from causes and then tracing specific causes *behind* specific outcomes. Ágnes Heller adds an anthropological afterthought, which she does not really follow up: '"Why" is *the* elementary question, the first real question of a child. "How" is more sophisticated; it is a diffident "why".'[3] Explanation responds to a very basic human need; it is

---

[1] Siegfried Kracauer, *History: The Last Things Before the Last* (New York: Oxford University Press, 1969), 47.
[2] Ágnes Heller, *A Theory of History* (London: Routledge & Kegan Paul, 1982), 159.
[3] Heller, *A Theory of History*, 170.

a naive expression of pristine amazement. Description – Kracauer's 'realistic tendency' – already belongs to the answer. It requires care, even precision, a certain distance of the describing observer from the object under examination. It is by no means easy to give a good description, of historical events or of anything else. In a third step, to pick up Heller's train of thought, explanation re-enters, fortified with method. Sense-making becomes systematic, follows certain conventional rules of logic and argumentation and sometimes aims at higher orders of abstraction.[4]

It should, therefore, be taken with a pinch of salt if historians deny any intention to explain, as was fashionable at the peak of the cultural turn. The more historians turned away from politics and economics, and the closer they drew to literary studies and certain tendencies in cultural anthropology, the lower fell the regard in which explanation was held. This was all the more true for the related concept of 'causation'. In the 1980s, as R. Bin Wong aptly points out, 'causation was no longer as central a concern of historians as it once was'.[5] Neither was explanation.

Though it is impossible to speak about explanation without mentioning 'causes', I shall avoid the concept of 'causation'. In analytical epistemology, 'explanation' and 'causation' or 'causality' are different if related topics.[6] Among philosophers, causality presently seems to be the more exciting of the two. There is now consensus that (a) causation unfolds in processes, and (b) that it can be probabilistic. Other aspects of the topic are more controversial.[7] The present chapter focuses on explanation, leaving aside causality.

I shall argue, *empirically*, that not all kinds of global history aim at explanation, but a lot do – sometimes explicitly, often in subcutaneous, implicit and hidden ways that should be brought to light. While I agree with Siegfried Kracauer that not everything in the social and political past is (rationally) explicable and that we must reckon with the existence of 'irreducible entities',[8] I want to show that explanation ought to matter for the field of history, but even more so for that of global history, which is confronted with

---

[4] A radical position was taken by Collingwood with reference to human action: 'When he [the historian] knows what happened, he already knows why it happened.' R. G. Collingwood, *The Idea of History*, rev. ed., ed. Jan van der Dussen (Oxford: Clarendon Press, 1993), 214.

[5] R. Bin Wong, 'Causation', in Ulinka Rublack (ed.), *A Concise Companion to History* (Oxford: Oxford University Press, 2011), 27–54, here 28.

[6] James Woodward, 'Scientific Explanation', *Stanford Encyclopedia of Philosophy*, 24 September 2014, https://plato.stanford.edu/archives/win2019/entries/scientific-explanation/, sect. 7.1 ('somewhat independent'); also Aviezer Tucker, 'Causation in Historiography', in Aviezer Tucker (ed.), *A Companion to the Philosophy of History and Historiography* (Oxford: Blackwell, 2009), 98–108, here 99.

[7] For a summary of the main theories see Bert Leuridan and Thomas Lodewyckx, 'Causality and Time: An Introductory Typology', in Samantha Kleinberg (ed.), *Time and Causality Across the Sciences* (Cambridge: Cambridge University Press, 2019), 14–36, here 17–29.

[8] Kracauer, *History*, 29.

unusually rich and diverse evidence. Explanation is an important tool for reducing complexity in a 'formative' (Kracauer) way.

To be sure, there is a wide variety of explanatory approaches, none of them particular to global history. In actual practice, explanations are of differing quality, on a scale from brilliant to utterly unconvincing.[9] It is an important task of scholarly critique to assess that quality in individual cases. The only *general* rule is a formal one that holds true for history as it does, more or less, for all scholarship: the imperative to avoid monocausality. Yet, under special circumstances, explanations have to be monocausal. Ancient Pompeii was destroyed in AD 79 by a volcanic eruption and by nothing else. Still, historians usually steer clear of monocausality and unilinear determinism. The decline and fall of the Western Roman Empire require a much more complex explanatory design than the end of Pompeii. At the same time, explanations should be elegant and parsimonious, stopping short of overcomplexity. Such overcomplexity may degenerate into long lists of factors that are suspected to be operative in a vaguely specified manner. In their practical work, historians are likely to look for graspable, intuitively plausible explanations; they prefer – or should prefer – controlled simplification to comprehensive fuzziness. Not everything is related to everything else – as a vulgar notion of globality tends to imply. The business of explanation consists, to a large extent, of taking decisions about what is relevant and what is less so in making sense of a particular historical constellation.

Since explanation has rarely been discussed in the theoretical literature on global history, this chapter begins with a brief overview of what historical theory and the methodology of the social sciences may have to offer global historians.

General Theories of Explanation

The word 'explanation' basically refers to two different things. Firstly, it can mean to give reasons – often moral justifications – for one's own actions or those of other humans. As Charles Tilly has put it, human beings are 'reason-giving animals'.[10] For historians, this is an object of study. We look in the sources for attempts by historical actors to provide reasons and motives for their actions, and we do not expect such explanations to be 'logical' or 'rational'. Secondly, to explain something can mean to account for states of affairs by identifying connections between 'causes' and 'effects' – in other

---

[9] For a brilliant discussion of depth, completeness, purpose and other parameters of historical explanations (and of the role of such parameters in theoretical accounts of explanation) see Veli Virmajoki, 'What Should We Require from an Account of Explanation in Historiography?' *Journal of the Philosophy of History* 16, 11 (2022), 22–53.

[10] Charles Tilly, *Why?* (Princeton: Princeton University Press, 2006), 8.

words, by providing *causal* analysis. In this case, reasons and causes are established by the analyst, sidelining the self-expressions of the actors or taking a distancing view of them. The second meaning of 'explanation' transcends subjective intentionality and encompasses 'structural' considerations that often require hindsight and transgress the awareness of the historical actors. The question of 'why people do what they do' is not answered best by those people themselves.[11]

The philosophical theory of explanation derives from Aristotle and, in modern times, from John Stuart Mill's *System of Logic* (1843).[12] Its application to history basically begins with Carl Gustav Hempel's 1942 theory of explanation that went through various modifications up to its final version developed in the 1960s – still a benchmark approach.[13] Ever since the later Hempel, the theory rests on two assumptions: (a) it is nominalist or constructivist and does not require the assumption that causes 'exist in reality'; (b) it presupposes that a specific effect and its specific cause, or causes, are connected by something more general: not necessarily an invariable and time–space-insensitive 'natural law' or 'iron law of history', but perhaps a more limited regularity.[14] That regularity should be empirically rich as well as theoretically plausible, for instance when historians cite a well-established sociological theorem or an evidence-based insight from demography to help them account for a specific phenomenon in social history or the history of population.

General theories of explanation are nowadays worded much less rigorously than they used to be in the days of Carl G. Hempel.[15] They often allow for

---

[11] Murray G. Murphey, *Philosophical Foundations of Historical Knowledge* (New York: State University of New York Press, 1994), 283.

[12] Martin Carrier, *Wissenschaftstheorie zur Einführung*, 4th ed. (Hamburg: Junius, 2017), 28–35.

[13] Carl Gustav Hempel, 'The Function of General Laws in History', *Journal of Philosophy* 9, 2 (1942), 35–48; Carl Gustav Hempel, *Aspects of Scientific Explanation and Other Essays in the Philosophy of Science* (New York: Free Press, 1965); James H. Fetzer (ed.), *The Philosophy of Carl G. Hempel: Studies in Science, Explanation and Rationality* (Oxford: Oxford University Press, 2001). Hempel's original intention was to defend the methodological unity of science and the humanities rather than provide a fully articulated theory of historical explanation. See Fons Dewulf, 'Revisiting Hempel's 1942 Contribution to the Philosophy of History', *Journal of the History of Ideas* 79, 3 (2018), 385–406, here 388–92. A major pre-Hempelian attempt, undertaken in the footsteps of Max Weber, to integrate formal and logical elements into a comprehensive theory of historical and sociological knowledge was Raymond Aron, Introduction à la philosophie critique de l'histoire: Essai sur les limites de l'objectivité historique, new ed. and rev. and annotated by Sylvie Mesure (Paris: Gallimard, 1986). See also Iain Stewart, *Raymond Aron and Liberal Thought in the Twentieth Century* (Cambridge: Cambridge University Press, 2020), 61–6.

[14] Bert Leuridan and Antony Froeyman, 'On Lawfulness in History and Historiography', *History and Theory* 51, 2 (2012), 173–92, here 182–3.

[15] Overviews are: Wesley C. Salmon, *Four Decades of Scientific Explanation* (Minneapolis: University of Minnesota Press, 1989); Oswald Schwemmer, 'Erklärung', in Jürgen Mittelstrass (ed.), *Enzyklopädie Philosophie und Wissenschaftstheorie*, 2nd ed. (Stuttgart: Metzler, 2005), vol. 2, 381–7.

'contexts' of various kinds. Such 'pragmatic' theories[16] have become acceptable, and even influential, as a result of the historicising and relativising turn in
the philosophy and sociology of science inaugurated by Thomas S. Kuhn and
others in the 1960s. Wesley C. Salmon, perhaps the most influential philosophical theorist of explanation in the generation after Hempel, has allowed for
'causal networks' and 'etiological explanations'.[17] In the last phase of his
work, Hempel himself used 'soft' formulations such as asking what 'made
a difference' or how 'relevant' causal factors were. He also envisaged 'fine-
grained mechanical explanations'[18] that generate knowledge about 'how things
work'.[19] Today's major authority on explanation, James Woodward, even
permits counterfactuals (i.e. sentences of the type 'What if things had been
different …?').[20] In sum, the general theory of explanation is nowadays
perhaps less parsimonious and elegant than in Carl Gustav Hempel's foundational design of 1942, but much closer to the actual practice of scientists and
less prescriptive than it used to be. Even so, philosophers still look for *general*
criteria to assess the quality of particular explanations and to detect logical
flaws in them.

Historians are busy people and unlikely to spend much time on the intrica-
cies of the general theory of explanation. Still, denying its relevance would be
an anachronistic relapse into crude dichotomies of science versus humanities,
'nomothetic' (law-based) versus 'idiographic' (case-based) disciplines or
quantitative versus qualitative approaches. It would be a denial of the basic
methodological unity of all the sciences.[21] The boundaries between the famous
'two cultures' have become porous, not least through the rise of digital awareness in the humanities, including global history, where sometimes datasets of
enormous volume and variety have to be processed.

In Defence of (Historical) Explanation

The heyday of debates on *historical* explanation was in the 1960s and 1970s.
For our time, Paul A. Roth, one of the few remaining exponents of an 'analytical' theory of history in a loosely conceived Hempelian tradition, diagnoses

[16] Woodward, 'Scientific Explanation', sect. 6.
[17] Wesley C. Salmon, *Scientific Explanation and the Causal Structure of the World* (Princeton: Princeton University Press, 1984), 269–70.
[18] Quoted in Wesley C. Salmon, *Causality and Explanation* (New York: Oxford University Press, 1998), 365.
[19] Salmon, *Causality and Explanation*, 77.
[20] James Woodward, *Making Things Happen: A Theory of Causal Explanation* (Oxford: Oxford University Press, 2003).
[21] Wolfgang Spohn, 'Normativity Is the Key to the Difference Between the Human and the Natural Sciences', in Dennis Dieks (ed.), *Explanation, Prediction, and Confirmation* (Berlin: Springer, 2011), 241–51, here 242; see also Edward O. Wilson, *Consilience: The Unity of Knowledge* (New York: Knopf, 1998).

'an almost total neglect of historical explanation within philosophy of science'.[22] This is generally true for the 'formal' theory of history (in German: *Historik*), which has to be distinguished, following Ernst Troeltsch, from the 'material' philosophy of history that grapples with the big sweep of 'real' history.[23]

The formal theory of history and the numerous programmatic self-reflections of historians tend to be almost silent on explanation. When historians ponder what they are actually doing, they rarely come to the conclusion that they elaborate explanations. The latest careful discussion of historical explanation, using numerous examples from the historiographical literature, dates from the previous century.[24] Achim Landwehr, a prolific German theorist, sees the historian's task in the description of complexity and declines any further ambition; he does not even mention the issue of explanation.[25] Jörn Rüsen has downgraded the relative position of explanation within his comprehensive system of historical knowledge from version to version.[26] Reinhart Koselleck, who is enlightening on almost any question within the theory of history, was largely reticent on matters of explanation. Global historians, too, are diffident on the issue of explanation. Sebastian Conrad, today's foremost theorist of global history, does not show much interest in it. Where he touches upon the matter, he apologises to the reader that his brief remarks might appear 'rather technical and inconsequential'.[27] Diego Olstein has interesting things to say about contextualisation, comparison and connections, but next to nothing on explanation.[28]

Why this white spot on the map of historical theory? There are at least three possible answers:

(a) Historians believe that explanation is something to be left to cliometricians, with their social-scientific minds, and to schematic historical sociologists, as it is no primary concern of the mainstream. They are reluctant to admit that, whether they are aware of it or not, they answer 'why'

---

[22] Paul A. Roth, 'Philosophy of History', in Lee McIntyre and Alex Rosenberg (eds.), *The Routledge Companion to Philosophy of Social Science* (London: Routledge, 2017), 397–407, here 397.

[23] Ernst Troeltsch, *Der Historismus und seine Probleme: Erstes Buch: Das logische Problem der Geschichtsphilosophie* (Tübingen: Mohr Siebeck, 1922), 67–8. This distinction has recently been revived by Johannes Rohbeck, *Integrative Geschichtsphilosophie in Zeiten der Globalisierung* (Berlin: de Gruyter, 2020).

[24] Chris Lorenz, *Konstruktion der Vergangenheit. Eine Einführung in die Geschichtstheorie* (Cologne: Böhlau, 1997). The Dutch original of this book was published in 1987; it was never translated into English.

[25] Achim Landwehr, *Die anwesende Abwesenheit der Vergangenheit: Essay zur Geschichtstheorie* (Frankfurt: S. Fischer, 2016), 209–31.

[26] The latest one is Jörn Rüsen, *Historik: Theorie der Geschichtswissenschaft* (Cologne: Böhlau, 2013), 162–5.

[27] Sebastian Conrad, *What Is Global History?* (Princeton: Princeton University Press, 2016), 214.

[28] Diego Olstein, *Thinking History Globally* (Basingstoke: Palgrave Macmillan, 2015).

questions all the time. Few historians are likely to endorse the unequivocal assertion made by the Canadian philosopher Mario Bunge: 'All the historical sciences have the same aim, namely, to discover what happened and why it happened: they seek truth and explanation, not just yarn.'[29] And not everyone would agree with Paul Veyne when he says that 'to explain more is to narrate better'.[30]

(b) A second explanation of non-explanation would be that this is not what the public expects from science in general, and from historical studies in particular. The public is said to be keen on 'yarn'. This, too, is dubious. The pandemic year 2020 was a time when science – from virology to empirical social research – faced an unprecedented demand for discovering the causes of our multiple predicaments. Explanations were indispensable for finding remedies and practical solutions and for predicting the future. Historians were quite successful in explaining how we got to where we are – and, more specifically, how and *why* similar causes led to diverging outcomes.[31] After Russia started its full-scale invasion of Ukraine in February 2022, historians of Eastern Europe were in great demand to give reasons for the Russian leadership's motives, goals and conduct against the backdrop of the long-term history of the region.

(c) The third possible reason for the occlusion of explanation in historical theory comes closer to the mark: a powerful 'narrativist turn' since the 1970s, set in motion and sustained by cultural theorists and literary critics, gained intellectual hegemony at the expense of the analytical theory of history. It seemed to be closer to the activity of *writing* history than the abstract deliberations of the logicians in the Hempel tradition. Narrativist theorists believe that history is about constructing plots whose rootedness in evidential research, or the lack of it, is of subordinate importance to theory. While few working historians were (and are) persuaded that this approach offers an adequate description of what they are actually doing, narrativism conquered Anglo-American theory and came to lead a life of its own. The much more nuanced narrativism of the French philosopher Paul Ricœur was not as influential internationally as it should have been. Nor was Michel Foucault's non-analytical concept of 'genealogy'.[32]

[29] Mario Bunge, *Social Science under Debate: A Philosophical Perspective* (Toronto: University of Toronto Press, 1998), 257.
[30] Paul Veyne, *Writing History: Essays on Epistemology* (Middletown: Wesleyan University Press, 1984), 93.
[31] Peter Baldwin, *Fighting the First Wave: Why the Coronavirus Was Tackled So Differently across the Globe* (Cambridge: Cambridge University Press, 2021); Adam Tooze, *Shutdown: How Covid Shook the World's Economy* (New York: Viking, 2021).
[32] Gerry Gutting, 'Foucault's Genealogical Method', *Midwest Studies in Philosophy* 15, 1 (1990), 145–56; Joseph Vogl, 'Genealogie', in Clemens Kammler et al. (eds.), *Foucault-Handbuch* (Stuttgart: Metzler, 2008), 255–8.

Despite Foucault's worldwide celebrity, few global historians have so far worked in such a genealogical mode.

In sum, explanation is a permanent concern and standard procedure of all historical sciences, including archaeology, palaeontology, historical demography and so on. Its current neglect in the formal theory of history does not mirror its real significance.

Analytical and Narrativist Theories

The analytical theory of history applies thought patterns from the logic of scientific research to the humanities and is primarily concerned with methodology. Reaching its high point in the influential works of Arthur C. Danto (1965) and Louis O. Mink (1987),[33] and represented today by Paul A. Roth and, with certain limitations, Aviezer Tucker,[34] it addresses the central theme of how historians establish the truth, or other forms of epistemic authority, of their verbal propositions. Analytical theorists have never shown much interest in analysing texts written by ordinary historians. They usually deal with brief and simple speech acts. Though this can hardly be otherwise for the sake of philosophical clarity, it limits the impact of analytical theory outside its own circles. Most historical explanations are complex argumentative constructions that cannot be reduced to atomistic events and isolated propositional sentences. Correspondingly, analytical theorists tend to have a reductive and old-fashioned understanding of real-life historiography, which they prefer to see as a linear chronicle of political events.

Paradoxically, the same is true for the arch opponent of the analytical school: narrativist theory. It is simply much easier to tell – and to analyse using the tools of narratology – a tale in the style of *l'historie événementielle* than to express multivariable causal arguments in narrative form.[35] Thus, both schools of theory suffer from an inbuilt bias against all kinds of structural history and also against cultural history of a more sophisticated bent.

Narrativist theory, to this day labouring under the shadow of Hayden White's celebrated *Metahistory: The Historical Imagination in Nineteenth-Century Europe* (1973),[36] must not be taken too seriously in its far-reaching agnostic

---

[33] Arthur C. Danto, *Analytical Philosophy of History* (Cambridge: Cambridge University Press, 1965); Louis O. Mink, *Historical Understanding* (Ithaca: Cornell University Press, 1987).

[34] Roth, 'Philosophy of History'; Paul A. Roth, *The Philosophical Structure of Historical Explanation* (Evanston: Northwestern University Press, 2020); Aviezer Tucker, *Our Knowledge of the Past: A Philosophy of Historiography* (Cambridge: Cambridge University Press, 2004).

[35] Tim Burke, 'Complexity and Causation', *Soundings: An Interdisciplinary Journal* 90, 1–2 (2007), 33–47, here 37.

[36] Hayden White, *Metahistory: The Historical Imagination in Nineteenth-Century Europe* (Baltimore: Johns Hopkins University Press, 1973).

claims: that historians are unable to establish anything like the 'truth' about the past, that their utterances lack an extralingual referent and so on.[37] White himself has impressively analysed a handful of nineteenth-century historiographical classics that were written in co-evolution with the historical novel. His approach, and the more mundane and technical methods of the narratology of literary historians,[38] however, fail to do justice to research-based historical scholarship and its textual strategies, which are not primarily governed by literary techniques of spinning a tale. Moreover, form and rhetoric, though important for historical studies, are not essential for them. Whether the Gordian Knot can be cut by postulating something like 'narrative explanation' – in Jörn Rüsen's view a 'discursive practice' that synthesises all aspects of historical writing[39] – remains controversial. A recent survey of the literature concludes 'that it is hard to say what a narrative explanation precisely consists of'.[40] A new and promising approach to the connection between narration and argumentation suggested by a team of authors around the Spanish philosopher Paula Olmos has yet to reach the historiographical debate.[41] So far, narrativism has difficulty offering criteria for assessing the quality of a specific explanation. To put it bluntly, any explanation seems to be acceptable as long as it is disguised as a good read.

A recent work by the Finnish theorist Jouni-Matti Kuukkanen fails to inspire more confidence than earlier narrativist theory. His *Postnarrativist Philosophy of Historiography* (2015) is the epitome of ultra-narrativism. The author, proud to represent 'the dominant school',[42] is interested 'not so much in the generation of historical knowledge and explanation as in the forms in which it is presented',[43] and he dismisses Carl G. Hempel's covering law theory, and with it analytical theory as a whole, as '(in)famous',[44] unworthy of philosophical attention. Kuukkanen wants to liberate – in an age of interdisciplinarity – the humanities from 'disciplinary externalism', a term that appears to refer to the purported straitjacket of the natural sciences.[45] He sees no way of assessing

[37] For a critique, see C. Behan McCullagh, *The Truth of History* (London: Routledge, 1998).
[38] Peter Hühn (ed.), *Handbook of Narratology*, 2nd ed. (Berlin: de Gruyter, 2014).
[39] Jörn Rüsen, *Rekonstruktion der Vergangenheit. Grundzüge einer Historik*, vol. 2: *Die Prinzipien der historischen Forschung* (Göttingen: Vandenhoeck & Ruprecht, 1986), 37–47; Rüsen, *Historik*, 65–6.
[40] Gunnar Schumann, 'Explanation', in Chiel van den Akker (ed.), *The Routledge Companion to Historical Theory* (London: Routledge, 2022), 269–84, here 273. A leading theorist, Paul A. Roth, has recently reopened the debate (*Philosophical Structure of Historical Explanation*, chapters 2 and 5); whether practising historians will feel provoked to respond remains to be seen.
[41] Paula Olmos (ed.), *Narration as Argument* (Cham: Springer, 2017).
[42] Jouni-Matti Kuukkanen, *Postnarrativist Philosophy of Historiography* (Basingstoke: Palgrave Macmillan, 2015), 14.
[43] Kuukkanen, *Postnarrativist Philosophy of Historiography*, 15.
[44] Kuukkanen, *Postnarrativist Philosophy of Historiography*, 15.
[45] Kuukkanen, *Postnarrativist Philosophy of Historiography*, 20.

the intrinsic worth of works of history. Rather, he subscribes to something like textual Darwinism: 'The plausibility of a historical thesis depends on its impact within the argumentative field.'[46] The winner takes all.

More nuanced theoretical suggestions went down on the battlefield between the two tendencies, but deserve a new look. This applies to the philosopher Maurice Mandelbaum, with his urbane and learned attempt to bridge the chasm between the analytical and the narrativist schools.[47] Mandelbaum argues realistically that rather than spin linear plots, historians construct multilayered 'sequences' into which they incorporate explanatory elements.[48] The task of the historian is not so much to string together the pieces of a story as to clarify the relations between the various elements in a two-dimensional tissue. Mandelbaum also makes the important point that in analysing change historians should never forget 'external' factors.[49] It is always a promising working hypothesis, says Mandelbaum, that there is an 'outside' to one's particular field of investigation – in other words, an external arena from where forces may impinge on what at first sight looks like a closed system: for instance, a nation-state. Though Mandelbaum is never quoted by global historians, his insights are much more pertinent for global history's concerns than anything offered by current narrativism or analytical theory.

Another author worth (re)discovering is the Austrian sociologist, philosopher and historian of ideas Karl Acham, who began his career with an excellent summary and critique of the analytical school.[50] He has since reflected deeply on what Hempel already allowed for as 'explanation sketches': less rigorous than strictly universalist 'nomological' explanations and able to accommodate the plurality of factors and scales characteristic of the humanities.[51] After many decades of struggling against the eviction of 'meaning' (*Sinn*) by a methodology of history subservient to the natural sciences, another veteran, the aforementioned Jörn Rüsen, has finally arrived at a sceptical verdict on narrativism to which he had always shown a close affinity. In Rüsen's view, the triumph of that school has led to the consequence that 'the problem of rationality was suppressed [*verdrängt*] rather than solved', and, along with it, the question of the scientific nature (*Wissenschaftlichkeit*) of the work performed

[46] Kuukkanen, *Postnarrativist Philosophy of Historiography*, 165.
[47] Maurice Mandelbaum, *The Anatomy of Historical Knowledge* (Baltimore: Johns Hopkins University Press, 1977); Maurice Mandelbaum, *Philosophy, History, and the Sciences: Selected Critical Essays* (Baltimore: Johns Hopkins University Press, 1984); and see Louis O. Mink, 'Review Essay on Maurice Mandelbaum, "The Anatomy of Historical Knowledge"', *History and Theory* 17, 2 (1978), 211–23.
[48] Mandelbaum, *Anatomy of Historical Knowledge*, 25–8.
[49] Mandelbaum, *Anatomy of Historical Knowledge*, 113.
[50] Karl Acham, *Analytische Geschichtsphilosophie: Eine kritische Einführung* (Freiburg: Alber, 1974).
[51] Karl Acham, *Vom Wahrheitsanspruch der Kulturwissenschaften: Studien zur Wissenschaftsphilosophie und Weltanschauungsanalyse* (Vienna: Böhlau, 2016), 245–79.

by historians.[52] Following up on this, a slightly different answer to narrativism might be: the principal aim of historical studies is not to tell stories but to ask questions and provide the strongest possible rational justification for the answers given to those questions on the basis of the best available evidence.[53]

In sum, both major schools within the formal philosophy of history - the disciples of Carl G. Hempel and the followers of Hayden White – offer only limited access to what Marc Bloch called *le métier de l'historien*, especially to the questions of how historians explain in actual practice and how their explanations might be improved. The analytical tendency, however, has a sense for the interplay between the general and the particular in historical reasoning and maintains the idea of an intersubjectively valid logic in the service of truth, whereas the narrativists lack respect for historical research and assimilate historical writing to the construction of fictional tales.

Sequences and Mechanisms: Explanation in the Social Sciences

The social sciences are close neighbours of historical studies. Both deal with individual and collective human behaviour; both study change over time; both differ from the natural sciences in that it is impossible (history) or difficult (social sciences) for them to observe reality directly or under laboratory conditions. A few remarks shall be offered about sociology, a discipline that since the days of Émile Durkheim and Max Weber has occupied a middle ground between *Verstehen* (hermeneutical understanding) and *Erklären* (explanation).[54]

Unlike philosophers of history, sociologists are not interested in telling historians what to do. Thus, we have to reverse the perspective. Is there anything historians can learn from sociologists when it comes to explanation? Three points may be worth exploring further.

(a) *Historical* sociology has always been a decidedly explicatory discourse, comparison being its preferred method.[55] One of its favoured approaches is a dynamic comparison between developmental paths and trajectories.

[52] Rüsen, *Historik*, 162.
[53] This is not a novel approach. See Marc Bloch, *Apologie pour l'histoire, ou Métier d'historien*, ed. Étienne Bloch (Paris: Armand Colin, 1993), 99–106.
[54] Of enduring relevance on relations between sociology and history is Peter Burke, *History and Social Theory* (Cambridge: Polity Press, 1992); see also Jeroen Bouterse, 'Explaining *Verstehen*: Max Weber's Views on Explanation in the Humanities', in Rens Bod et al. (eds.), *The Making of the Humanities*, vol. 3: *The Modern Humanities* (Amsterdam: Amsterdam University Press, 2014), 569–82; Thomas Haussmann, *Erklären und Verstehen: Zur Theorie und Pragmatik der Geschichtswissenschaft* (Frankfurt am Main: Suhrkamp, 1991).
[55] Jürgen Osterhammel, 'Global History and Historical Sociology', in James Belich et al. (eds.), *The Prospect of Global History* (Oxford: Oxford University Press, 2016), 23–43; A. A. van den Braembussche, 'Historical Explanation and Comparative Method: Toward a Theory of the History of Society', *History and Theory* 28, 1 (1989), 1–24.

Historians tend to complain about the remoteness of historical sociologists from primary sources and of a certain formalism or schematism in their comparative thought experiments. Yet, in the best case, the chosen explanatory set-ups are complex as well as transparent, involving neatly defined factors and plausible hypotheses about the interplay between those factors over time.[56] The entire Great Divergence debate – to many observers quintessential global history – owes a lot to the social science methodology of comparison.[57]

(b) A relatively new concept, explicitly conceived of as a way to facilitate causal explanations, is that of the mechanism.[58] Such an approach would either look at psychological mechanisms that make individual and collective behaviour more or less predictable,[59] or postulate medium-range and small-scale regularities between certain causes and certain effects in 'processes involving large populations and interacting networks of organisations'.[60] Mechanisms as regularities of limited scope partly fulfil the requirements for 'covering laws' which are essential in Hempel's nomological model of explanation. They also show a family resemblance with Reinhart Koselleck's 'patterns of repetition', a fascinating though under-elaborated element of Koselleck's mature, and rather sketchy, theory of history.[61]

---

[56] A good example is Jack A. Goldstone, *Revolution and Rebellion in the Early Modern World* (Berkeley: University of California Press, 1991).

[57] Craig Calhoun, 'Explanation in Historical Sociology: Narrative, General Theory, and Historically Specific Theory', *American Journal of Sociology* 104, 3 (1998), 846–71; James Mahoney and Dietrich Rueschemeyer (eds.), *Comparative Historical Analysis in the Social Sciences* (Cambridge: Cambridge University Press, 2003); James Mahoney, 'Comparative-Historical Methodology', *Annual Review of Sociology* 30, 1 (2004), 81–101; James Mahoney and Kathleen Thelen (eds.), *Advances in Comparative-Historical Analysis* (Cambridge: Cambridge University Press, 2015); Nicolas Delalande et al. (eds.), *Dictionnaire historique de la comparaison: Mélanges en l'honneur de Christophe Charle* (Paris: Éditions de la Sorbonne, 2020).

[58] A concise survey is Nancy Cartwright, 'Causal Inference', in Nancy Cartwright and Eleonora Montuschi (eds.), *Philosophy of Social Science: A New Introduction* (Oxford: Oxford University Press, 2014), 308–26, here 319–21.

[59] Jon Elster, *Explaining Social Behavior: More Nuts and Bolts for the Social Sciences* (Cambridge: Cambridge University Press, 2007).

[60] Renate Mayntz, 'Causal Mechanism and Explanation in Social Science' (MPIfG Discussion Paper 20/7) (Cologne: Max-Planck-Institut für Gesellschaftsforschung, 2020), 5; Renate Mayntz, 'Mechanisms in the Analysis of Macro-social Phenomena', *Philosophy of the Social Sciences* 34, 2 (2004), 237–59; Renate Mayntz, *Sozialwissenschaftliches Erklären: Probleme der Theoriebildung und Methodologie* (Frankfurt am Main: Campus, 2009). From a different theoretical angle, see Peter Hedström and Richard Swedberg (eds.), *Social Mechanisms: An Analytical Approach to Social Theory* (Cambridge: Cambridge University Press, 1998).

[61] Reinhart Koselleck, 'Wiederholungsstrukturen in Sprache und Geschichte', *Saeculum: Jahrbuch für Universalgeschichte* 57, 1 (2006), 1–16; English translation in Reinhart Koselleck, *Sediments of Time: On Possible Histories*, transl. and ed. Sean Franzel and Stefan-Ludwig Hoffmann (Stanford: Stanford University Press, 2018), 158–74.

(c) A recent innovation in theoretical sociology is the use of temporal sequences and 'syntaxes' for purposes of explanation.[62] That concept involves the close study of temporal shifts and conjunctures and may help to better describe the concatenation of causal factors that historians like to employ in a less systematic fashion than sociologists. Sequencing works best when it is seen as preparing explanation rather than replacing it. Similarly, within the vast field of theories of time, sociological contributions stand out in their resolve to overcome the antagonism of experienced or subjective time against measured or objective time. They are particularly good at dissecting complex processes into their constituent elements and at postulating causal connections between those elements.

What these three sociological approaches have in common is that they reveal the bare bones of their explicatory arrangements in a way that can alert historians to their own strategies of reasoning. The explicatory or 'configurational' models[63] used by (historical) sociologists tend to be much more intricate, and therefore better attuned to the practice of historians, than the often reductive and simplistic ideas about nomological, intentional or narrative explanation cherished by analytical and narrativist philosophers of history alike.[64]

How Do (Global) Historians Explain?

In the study of historiographical texts, explanation has received much less attention than rhetoric and narrative emplotment. There are surprisingly few in-depth analyses of how historians actually practice explanation, even with regard to the great classics of the historiographical canon. Tim Rood's *Thucydides: Narrative and Explanation* and Jonas Grethlein's wide-ranging work on ancient historiography can serve as models for what is deplorably lacking for other authors and epochs.[65] Even less is known about the crafting of the routine research output in today's discipline. How do normal historians handle explanation? Since actual practice remains obscure, firm foundations are lacking for normative assessments: what is a good explanation?

---

[62] Andrew Abbott, *Processual Sociology* (Chicago: University of Chicago Press, 2016); Aljets Enno and Thomas Hoebel, 'Prozessuales Erklären. Grundzüge einer primär temporalen Methodologie empirischer Sozialforschung', *Zeitschrift für Soziologie* 46, 1 (2017), 4–21.

[63] John R. Hall, *Culture of Inquiry: From Epistemology to Discourse in Sociohistorical Research* (Cambridge: Cambridge University Press, 1999), 216–30.

[64] Rüsen, *Rekonstruktion der Vergangenheit*, 24–47.

[65] Tim Rood, *Narrative and Explanation* (Oxford: Clarendon Press, 1998); Jonas Grethlein, *Experience and Teleology in Ancient Historiography: 'Futures Past' from Herodotus to Augustine* (Cambridge: Cambridge University Press, 2013); referring to modern history: Arnd Hoffmann, *Zufall und Kontingenz in der Geschichtstheorie* (Frankfurt am Main: Klostermann, 2005).

Nobody should expect a straightforward and universally valid answer. *How* we explain depends to a large extent on *what* we want to explain. Explanations in intellectual history are different from those in economic history. It is one thing to discover the reasons behind an individual political decision, quite another to account for a macro-process such as the outbreak of a multi-state war, the collapse of an empire, or a trajectory of economic development or implosion. A plausible guess is that what is difficult to analyse in most fields of historical study is even more difficult for *global* history. Though this should not be misunderstood as a claim to superiority, global history has to handle more factors and variables and a greater number of diverse actors and social configurations than is the case for most other fields of history. The ritualised assurance that global history is, or should be, multi-archival and multi-lingual is just a consequence of the fact that it is a rather complicated, disparate and sometimes messy affair. Since explanation is a way to reduce complexity, the burden that lies on explanation in global history is a particularly heavy one. It has to tame – to use a buzzword – 'vibrant' plurality.

Under these circumstances, critical interventions that probe the soundness (Woodward) of argumentation and explanation are highly welcome. I single out three of them.

Firstly, several distinguished historians, not known as sworn enemies of global history, have applied the emergency brake to a merry-go-round of high-sales publishing and launched a vehement attack against 'fake global history'.[66] 'Global history', the critics declare, 'has become an excuse for authors to make outlandish claims, based on the belief that they will not be subject to the usual scholarly scrutiny.'[67] Such 'outlandish claims' include sloppy explanations. The general justification of this charge derives from two related observations. On the one hand, there is a certain pressure in the 'trade' section of the book market even for respectable historians to exaggerate the colourfulness of their materials and the drama of their interpretations. On the other, wide-ranging works that cut across academic compartmentalisation are difficult to assess in terms of specialised scholarship. They easily slip through the net of responsible scrutiny and are applauded by overwhelmed reviewers for superficial virtues such as daring assertions, unparalleled comprehensiveness or the alleged uncovering of secrets.

Secondly, and closer to the issue of explanation, Princeton historian David A. Bell has undertaken an interesting thought experiment.[68] Bell, an expert on

[66] Cornell Fleischer et al., 'How to Write Fake Global History', in *Cromohs – Cyber Review of Modern Historiography*, 9 September 2020, https://doi.org/10.13128/cromohs-12032.
[67] My own example is a book on European empires: Jürgen Osterhammel, Review of Jason C. Sharman, 'Empires of the Weak', *Neue Politische Literatur* 65, 2 (2020), 302–304.
[68] David A. Bell, 'Questioning the Global Turn: The Case of the French Revolution', *French Historical Studies* 37, 1 (2014), 1–24. A few of Bell's book reviews have a similar thrust: David

Europe around 1800, raises a helpful question: 'What is gained from placing it [the French Revolution] in a global perspective, and what is lost?'[69] For 'French Revolution' one can easily substitute any major historical phenomenon or mega-event that has conventionally been considered within a non-global context and is now seen through the unaccustomed spectacles of global history. Bell supports his major question with a long lists of complaints about the over-ambitiousness of historiographical globalisers. While one does not have to follow him through all the twists and turns of his philippic, his focus on the French Revolution ensures that explanation occupies centre stage in his inter-vention. Very few episodes in history have been linked to more *why*-questions than the French Revolution. Why did a major upheaval occur in France and not elsewhere? Why in 1789? Why did the Ancien Régime succumb? Why did the Revolution go through a process of radicalisation? And so on. These questions have usually been raised and answered within a French or a European frame-work. A global approach, still under debate, suggests longer concatenations covering the entire North Atlantic space or even regarding French domestic developments as part of a general world crisis.[70] Bell offers a useful distinction of general applicability when he insists that 'inward influences' – the causal impact of external actors and events – and 'outward influences' – effects, often long-term and unspecific, reaching out into the world – follow different logics.[71] This is generally true. Some local events have global ramifications, most others do not. (Not every assassination of the member of a royal house leads, as did the shots of 28 June 1914 at Sarajevo, to global war.) In reverse, the fact that an event acquired universal significance does not always mean that its origins were 'global'; most 'world religions' have distinctly local roots.

From the vantage point of the historiographical practitioner, David Bell confirms a lesson also to be learned from the methodology of explanation: if additional – in this case, 'global' – factors are being added to an explanatory model, hypotheses are needed that specify precisely the possible causal con-nections between the new factors and the other elements of the model. Invoking an atmospheric 'globality' does not explain anything. Nor are fuzzy 'waves' that 'sweep' around the globe proper candidates for independent variables and fundamental causes. It is from theorists such as Maurice Mandelbaum and from the sociological analysis of temporal sequences that one should take away the

A. Bell, 'Did Britain Win the American Revolution?', *New York Review of Books* 67, 7 (23 April 2020), 46–7; David A. Bell, 'I Wanted to Rule the World', *London Review of Books* 42, 23 (3 December 2020), 25–6.
[69] Bell, 'Questioning the Global Turn', 4.
[70] Alan Forrest and Matthias Middell (eds.), *The Routledge Companion to the French Revolution in World History* (London: Routledge, 2016).
[71] Bell, 'Questioning the Global Turn', 4–6.

imperative to disaggregate complex processes into their constituent parts and look for *specific* connections rather than for general connectivity.

Thirdly, Peer Vries, whose early work in the formal theory of history sharpened his later acuity as a global economic historian,[72] sums up his experience as a pioneer of the field in a stern admonition: 'More energy should be devoted to determining the exact extent and impact of the various kinds of "contacts" and "exchanges" of which global historians are so fond.'[73] Calling for 'more methodological awareness', Vries goes on to note that the seemingly avant garde label of global history camouflages a lot of scholarly practices that are 'strikingly traditional'.[74] A new kind of history – as long as that ambition is kept alive – requires methodological adjustments and innovations. A global perspective, this is Vries's persuasive argument, is always worth a try even though it cannot claim a priori superiority over conventional approaches.

Varieties of Explanation in Global History

Even if Peter Perdue, a distinguished historian of China, exaggerates when he says that the term 'global history' nowadays 'can refer to almost anything',[75] it remains true that many different kinds of history have comfortably settled under the umbrella of global history. That umbrella becomes even wider if one includes the more popularising trends within the global history discourse – in other words, those books that shape public impressions of what global history is about and why it is important. The discrepancy, for instance, between global microhistory and those macro-approaches that border on historical sociology and consider the 'very long run' is so enormous that a shared strategy of explanation is almost ruled out. Thus, there is no manner of explanation that is a distinctive feature of global history.

Still, a few basic ways of handling explanation can be discerned:

(1)   Non-Explanation

A great deal of what goes under the label of global history was never meant to explain anything. I suggest calling this the 'panoramic' approach, to be distinguished from 'analytical' global history. Entirely legitimate, panoramic global history appears in the shape of various globalising genres. One such genre are

---

[72] Peer Vries, *Vertellers op drift: Een verhandeling over de nieuwe verhalende geschiedenis* (Hilversum: Verloren, 1990).
[73] Peer Vries, 'The Prospects of Global History: Personal Reflections of an Old Believer', *International Review of Social History* 64, 1 (2019), 111–21, here 118.
[74] Vries, 'The Prospects of Global History', 119.
[75] Peter C. Perdue, 'From the Outside Looking In: The Annales School, the Non-Western World, and Social Science History', *Social Science History* 40, 4 (2016), 565–74, here 569.

the fashionable globalised histories of particular nation-states, patterned on *L'histoire mondiale de la France.*[76] They do not count as explanatory history simply because they pursue only modest analytical aims. These voluminous tomes have to be seen as synthetic statements intended for national education.

A second non-explicatory genre are general histories of the world. Nowadays they are wary of big questions and the corresponding big answers. William H. McNeill, writing in the halcyon days of the Pax Americana, put a major puzzle into the title of his work: *The Rise of the West.*[77] Yet his treatment remained safely in the descriptive mode and deserves to be remembered mainly for its imaginative periodisation and a few crisp chapter headings ('Moslem Catalepsy, 1700–1840 AD', etc.). McNeill told a story. He did not distinguish systematically between causes and effects and therefore did not offer an explanatory model, let alone a theory.

McNeill's master of sorts, Arnold J. Toynbee, had been of a different cast of mind. Especially in his best decade, the 1930s, Toynbee was a dedicated explainer and anything but a spinner of epic tales. While Toynbee's lack of interest in sociology and ethnology makes even his best works – the first six volumes of *A Study of History*[78] – look old-fashioned, his approach to explanation was rational and unpretentious. He did not believe in perennial 'laws of history' and, in a sense, anticipated the middle-range 'causal mechanisms' (Renate Mayntz) and 'patterns of repetition' (Reinhart Koselleck) mentioned earlier.[79]

Today, the better one-volume world histories are playful philosophical reflections decked out with illustrative pluckings from the past.[80] When the burden of writing a history of the entire world is shouldered in scholarly earnestness, all sorts of rump explanations are attempted with hardly ever a sense of satisfaction. With everything remaining half-said, unintended monocausality can hardly be avoided.[81] In a nutshell, much of published global history is never meant to serve as a stepping stone towards explanation. It is merely exhibitive: materials from all over the world are assembled and displayed, enriching people's knowledge and strengthening their sense of diversity and their cosmopolitan outlook.

---

[76] Patrick Boucheron (ed.), *Histoire mondiale de la France* (Paris: Seuil, 2017).
[77] William H. McNeill, *The Rise of the West: A History of the Human Community* (Chicago: University of Chicago Press, 1963).
[78] Arnold J. Toynbee, *A Study of History*, vols. I–VI (London: Oxford University Press, 1934–9).
[79] Jürgen Osterhammel, 'Arnold J. Toynbee and the Problems of Today', *Bulletin of the German Historical Institute Washington* 60 (2017), 69–87.
[80] Michael Cook, *A Brief History of the Human Race* (New York: Norton, 2003); Yuval Noah Harari, *Sapiens: A Brief History of Humankind* (London: Vintage, 2014).
[81] Merry Wiesner-Hanks, *A Concise History of the World* (Cambridge: Cambridge University Press, 2015).

(2)   Pan-Explanation and Explanation Through Comparison

The other end of the spectrum of explanatory intensity is marked by works where comparison is used to identify those variables that make a causal difference. These works are global – in a non-methodical way – if they straddle commonly respected cultural boundaries. 'Non-methodical' means that the logical strategies used in a comparison between Britain and France and in a comparison between France and Japan are basically the same. The only two differences, certainly requiring careful attention, are (a) a greater obtrusiveness of the 'cultural' dimension that cannot be disregarded or bracketed in a ceteris paribus way; and (b) a greater relevance of 'emic' (as distinct from 'etic') nomenclatures – in other words, 'local' or 'indigenous' terminologies. To illustrate the second point with examples from comparative social history: *samurai* in a Japanese, *shenshi* (scholar-officials) in a Chinese, *gentry* in an English and *noblesse de robe* in a French context are local categories that are almost impossible to translate and difficult to subsume under generic terms of higher abstraction and universality.

The apotheosis of comparativism in global history was attained in the Great Divergence Debate.[82] Here *everything* revolves around explanations in response to one of the biggest *why*-questions ever asked: Why did 'the West' (or Europe, North-Western Europe, etc., respectively) achieve worldwide superiority in the modern era? What accounts for the increasing economic disparities between different parts of the world? The debate started almost a century before the publication of Kenneth Pomeranz's famous book[83] with Max Weber's titanic effort, undertaken at a time when the social and economic study of Asian societies had barely begun, to account for the emergence of rational capitalism in the Occident by contrasting it with supposedly dead-end trajectories in China, India and elsewhere. In the early twenty-first century, the debate has been the most important laboratory for macro-historical explanation through comparison. Regardless of innumerable disagreements among a vast array of authors, the participants share a few commonalities.

Though history books would be unreadable without narrative, no participant in the debate relies on narrative alone to produce explanations in the sense of the theorists' 'narrative explanation'. Mirroring developments in the real world, general attention in these explanations has shifted from probing the 'rise' of Europe to finding reasons for the delayed 'rise' of China. Thus, the

---

[82] This sprawling debate has yet to find its detached critic and historian. Almost all comments are from participants. This applies also to the otherwise excellent overview: Prasannan Parthasarathi and Kenneth Pomeranz, 'The Great Divergence Debate', in Thirthankar Roy and Giorgio Riello (eds.), *Global Economic History* (London: Bloomsbury Academic, 2019), 19–37.

[83] Kenneth Pomeranz, *The Great Divergence: China, Europe, and the Making of the Modern World Economy* (Princeton: Princeton University Press, 2000).

explanandum remained more or less the same across more than a century – why did the 'normal' disparities in wealth, power and cultural creativity between major parts of the world result in *one* dramatic bifurcation, a great divergence among so many small divergences?[84] – whereas the candidates for the losing and winning positions changed several times. Concurrently, the basic parameters – or variables, in the language of quantification – of explanation have kept shifting, which complicates the debate considerably. What was it that diverged in the first place? Economic growth, capitalism, scientific ingenuity, power/imperialism or modernity at large? All those aspects are related but by no means identical.

In this teeming mass of sophisticated reasoning, monocausal explanations singling out culture, the environment or institution-building as the causal factor of last resort have not entirely disappeared. Yet there seems to be general consensus in favour of more complex models of explanation that meet the criteria of a multi-factorial design combined with parsimonious elegance. Pomeranz's model shares these virtues with earlier contributions such as E. L. Jones' pioneering contribution of 1981.[85] Subtle disagreements continue in regard to claims of explanatory 'power'. Solutions to the big riddle of original bifurcation have moved from strong determination (i.e. a broad and powerful 'Western tradition' rooted in the Middle Ages or even Greek Antiquity[86]) to weak determination through small differentials that engendered huge effects. This shift from necessity to contingency reflects a general transformation of – mainly Western – thinking from structuralism to postmodernism or poststructuralism, and also an evolution in theories of explanation as they incorporated probabilistic elements. Such a general intellectual stance, however, will not remain uncontested since those who see themselves as victors in historical struggles do not like to be told that they prevailed by mere chance. The current Chinese leadership and the scholars who happen to agree with it, for instance, insist on a deeply rooted ('5,000 years') path-dependency and thus on the unassailable necessity and legitimacy of the country's ever-growing strength. The politics of explanation includes the question of how much explanatory weight one is projecting onto the past.

Much more remains to be said about the Great Divergence Debate. Addressing a major problem of world *history*, it is nevertheless conducted with intellectual tools pioneered by comparative sociologists from Max Weber to Charles Tilly, Theda Skocpol and Jack Goldstone. It is a truly

---

[84] On bifurcation, see Gottfried Schramm, *Fünf Wegscheiden der Weltgeschichte* (Göttingen: Vandenhoeck & Ruprecht, 2004).

[85] E. L. Jones, *The European Miracle: Environments, Economies and Geopolitics in the History of Europe and Asia* (Cambridge: Cambridge University Press, 1981).

[86] Michael Mitterauer, *Why Europe? The Medieval Origins of Its Special Path* (Chicago: University of Chicago Press, 2010).

transdisciplinary exercise. But is there anything specifically *global* about it? Surely the geographic scope of the cases considered is worldwide even if holistic 'civilisations' have been replaced by economic macro-regions as the preferred units of analysis. At the same time, the logical set-ups of explanation and the comparative procedures do not differ very much from those at closer range. Once 'culture' no longer counts as the major explicative variable,[87] the Great Divergence ceases to be a 'transcultural' issue. Thus, there is no longer a fundamental methodological gap between an intra-European comparison and one targeting different regions in China, India or Europe.

The Great Divergence Debate confirms the point that systematic comparison remains one of the most fruitful explanatory tools in the social sciences. Attempts to discredit comparison by playing it off against 'relational' history have failed as far as methodology is concerned. The basic compatibility of comparison and the analysis of transfer was already established two decades ago.[88] Remarkably, comparison has recently been rediscovered in the 'soft' humanities – for instance, in literary studies – even among those of a basically post-modernist persuasion.[89] However, outside of economic history, fields characterised by a preponderance of *why*-questions are relatively rare. Usually, explanation is set in wider descriptive frames. For example, it is an interesting problem of global *cultural* history why certain religions and some languages expand – and may even become 'world religions' and 'world languages' – while others stay local and do not 'travel'.[90] Admittedly, these are not the *central* concerns of religious history and the history of languages, but they are very important issues for a history of cultural interaction that adopts a global perspective.

(3)   Mixed Explanations

Between the extremes of non-explanation and pan-explanation, a wide middle ground opens up where the search for causes is mixed up with a host of other considerations. These cases are 'global' to the extent – one should remember David Bell's discussion of explanations of the French Revolution – that

---

[87] As it did in David S. Landes, *The Wealth and Poverty of Nations: Why Some Are so Rich and Some so Poor* (New York: Norton, 1998).

[88] Hartmut Kaelble and Jürgen Schriewer (eds.), *Vergleich und Transfer: Komparatistik in den Sozial-, Geschichts- und Kulturwissenschaften* (Frankfurt am Main: Campus, 2003); see also Michel Espagne, 'Comparison and Transfer: A Question of Method', in Matthias Middell and Lluís Roura (eds.), *Transnational Challenges to National History Writing* (Basingstoke: Palgrave Macmillan, 2013), 36–53.

[89] For instance: Rita Felski and Susan Stanford Friedman (eds.), *Comparison: Theories, Approaches, Uses* (Baltimore: Johns Hopkins University Press, 2013).

[90] For an overview, see Marek Tamm, 'Introduction: Cultural History Goes Global', *Cultural History* 9, 2 (2020), 135–55.

external and 'long-distance' vectors are accorded special prominence in relation to internal ones. This also means that causal chains and sequences – what has been called 'the transitivity of causation'[91] – are usually longer than in internalist explanations. The factors impinging from the outside are often difficult to identify and trace to their origins. Characteristic, therefore, are forms of comparison that are incomplete, rudimentary or implicit and subcutaneous in a plurality of cases not strictly conforming to methodological requirements and standards. One could speak of 'wild' explanations, depending on the individual case, of quasi-explanations, crypto-explanations or proto-explanations, sometimes even of pseudo-explanations that qualify impolitely as 'fake global history'. Since in the humanities the line between academic and popular forms of expression is much more difficult to draw than in the natural sciences, the rigour of explanation, comparison and other logic-bound methodical procedures can be softened in many grades and shades. James Woodward, the great philosophical authority on causal explanation, suggests some kind of 'continuity' between causal explanation in science and 'causal knowledge of a more mundane, everyday sort'.[92] In extreme cases, conspiracy 'theorists' concoct their own explanations of historical phenomena that can be perfectly consistent and formally rational, but based on substantially mistaken and irrational premises. Systems of delusion and closed worldviews derive their attractiveness to their true believers from a claim to be able to make sense of anything.

(4)   Explanations as Counterfactual Thought Experiments

While philosophy takes counterfactuals very seriously,[93] manuals of historical method are likely to admonish us that they should be avoided, and no less an authority than Richard J. Evans has expressed well-considered reservations against the abuse of thought experiments for fanciful speculation about alternative pasts.[94] The genre of fictitious 'alternate histories' is an old one and is well-developed in contemporary popular culture. Laurent Binet's novel *Civilisations* (2019),[95] in which Columbus fails and the Incas invade Europe, even won a prize from the Académie Française. Serious historians have peppered their books with speculations about China winning the Opium War

[91] John Dupré, *The Disorder of Things: Metaphysical Foundations of the Disunity of Science* (Cambridge, MA: Harvard University Press, 1993), 197.
[92] Woodward, *Making Things Happen*, 19.
[93] David K. Lewis, *Counterfactuals* (Cambridge, MA: Harvard University Press, 1973).
[94] Richard J. Evans, *Altered Pasts: Counterfactuals in History* (Waltham, MA: Brandeis University Press, 2013).
[95] Laurent Binet, *Civilizations* (Paris: Grasset, 2019) [English translation: *Civilisations*, trans. Sam Taylor (London: Vintage, 2021)].

and sending a punitive Armada to Britain.[96] Even so, few global historians are likely to risk their reputation with similar literary experiments. Still, one might pause and ponder whether we do not perform counterfactual thought experiments all the time. When we prepare a multi-factorial explanation of a complex phenomenon, is it not a normal, if pre-methodical, mental procedure to remove a factor – or to neutralise it to ceteris paribus status – and imagine the consequences of its deletion or disregard? Or to *add* another factor and see what happens? Perhaps it is worth considering Cass Sunstein's advice to 'dismiss counterfactual history when it is based on false historical claims' and when it crosses the boundary between the plausible and the fantastic,[97] without rejecting it for experimental purposes: 'any causal claim is an exercise of counterfactual history'.[98] Shouldn't one simply add counterfactual speculation to the toolkit of historical heuristics?

(5)   Explanation and Context

Almost anything can be placed within 'a global context' – in other words, a context of all contexts that encompasses the various national and regional contexts commonly handled in historiography. Global history could even be defined as an exercise in context maximisation. Bookshops are full of volumes on 'X in global [world] history'. However, context as such is no virtue and no end in itself. It may be interesting to learn what happened elsewhere at the same time, or to draw parallels across the world, or to discover sources created by travellers and other eye-witnesses from afar whose existence had so far been overlooked by historians. Yet descriptive context as such does not explain anything. In each individual case, context has to be reduced to specific and traceable connections. To put it in more technical language: how does one select causally *relevant* contexts from among a huge repository of *virtual* contexts? How does one translate context into particular variables that correspond with classes of information found in the sources – in other words, variables that can be 'tested' empirically? How does one make claims about quantities – how much is 'much'? – and proportions, about the relative power of impacts and the strength, stability and persistence of effects?

---

[96] Ian Morris, *Why the West Rules – for Now: The Patterns of History, and What They Reveal about the Future* (New York: Farrar, Straus and Giroux, 2013), 3–11. A wide-ranging survey of the literature of counterfactual history and the various logics and purposes attached to it is Quentin Deluermoz and Pierre Singaravélou, *A Past of Possibilities: A History of What Could Have Been* (New Haven: Yale University Press, 2021).

[97] Cass R. Sunstein, 'Historical Explanations Always Involve Counterfactual History', *Journal of the Philosophy of History* 10, 3 (2016), 433–40, here 437.

[98] Sunstein, 'Historical Explanations', 434.

(6)   Explaining Dynamics

While it may be correct to say that global historians tend to privilege the synchronic over the diachronic dimension – in other words, space over time – they are still keenly interested in dynamics. Global history is by no means a static discourse. The very centrality of mobility as a research topic speaks against such a suspicion. Dynamics enter the picture in two rather different shapes. On the one hand, the motive of long-term 'change' is being projected on the planet as a whole. Climate change and the shrinking of biodiversity are anthropogenic processes of worldwide scope. Does global history possess the intellectual tools necessary for making a significant contribution to explaining these processes? Probably, these kinds of macro-dynamics require micro-scaled and detailed analyses of their origins and consequences. On the other hand, global history is likely to be better equipped for understanding 'diachronic' dynamics – that is, processes that can best be observed as they move 'horizontally' from place to place. The frequently noted obsession of global studies with mobility and flows points in this direction. Processes of relocation and diffusion, of expansion and contraction, of the formation and metamorphosis of networks are rewarding objects of description. 'Contagion' has become a key term for global histories of disease and financial panics. But how to go beyond description? How to come up with accounts for motion that are neither unilinear and mechanical (A leads to B, B to C, etc.) nor tautological (mobility increases because the world is accelerating, and so on)? Would that not be a good opportunity to incorporate into explanatory models certain middle-range mechanisms and regularities of spreading and infectious connectivity drawn from epidemiology or financial market research?

That final question leads us back to the elementary options in the formal theory of history. Unfortunately, the squaring of the circle has not been accomplished: A concept of 'analytical narratives' was never elaborated adequately,[99] although it is intuitively obvious what such narratives might look like.[100] Global history – a wide umbrella covering very different approaches – cannot be content with producing narratives and, if explaining is intended at all, relying on the miracles wrought by a phantom called 'narrative explanation'. Rather, explanation has to be made explicit as a logical procedure, with a little help from analytical theories of history, constrained as they largely have been by a fixation on a conventional history of political events. More promising are social science methodologies,

---

[99]   Robert H. Bates et al., *Analytic Narratives* (Princeton: Princeton University Press, 1998) is not really helpful.
[100] A model of its kind is C. A. Bayly, *The Birth of the Modern World 1780–1914: Global Connections and Comparisons* (Oxford: Blackwell, 2004).

especially middle-range theories, mechanisms and patterns of repetition. Such analytical devices can be incorporated into complex, though not overloaded explanatory sketches. In the event of success, global history is not just an exercise in diversity but makes a deprovincialised past speak to the future.

2 Comparison
Its Use and Misuse in Social and Economic History

Alessandro Stanziani

A few years ago, Gareth Austin, a well-known economic historian specialising in Africa, took up Kenneth Pomeranz and R. Bing Wong's proposal to develop a form of 'reciprocal comparison' in which Africa (Austin's case) and China (Pomeranz and Wong's) would not be compared exclusively to the Western model as the exemplary scenario and exclusive yardstick.[1] The fundamental aim of these proposals was to break free from the 'Eurocentrism' underlying most economic history analysis. As Austin asserted, the point was not to reject any general model of economic development but rather to widen the definitions of city, market and private property to include practices found in non-European worlds.

Unfortunately, in practice, this claim turned into its reverse: Pomeranz and Austin ended up assigning to non-European countries features usually associated with more or less idealised Western countries. Thus, the Yangzi had real competitive markets and private property rules, while Ghana and other African countries might have had the same if corruption had not intervened. While at first sight it seems politically correct not to call Africans 'underdeveloped' or 'naturally hostile' to capitalism, ascribing them a proto-market economy was not empirically true and expressed a vision of comparison modelled on faith in the one capitalist world after the collapse of 'actually existing socialism'. Unlike the economic anthropology of the 1960s and the 1970s, which scoured the world for 'alternative' economic rationalities, this new approach sought to show that capitalist values had been globally widespread for centuries. Yet after the enthusiasm for globalisation and global history, after the long financial crisis and the return of nationalisms in response precisely to globalisation, we need something other than mere enthusiasm for capitalist values. It makes no

---

[1] Gareth Austin, 'Reciprocal Comparison and African History: Tackling Conceptual Eurocentrism in the Study of Africa's Economic Past', *African Studies Review* 50, 3 (2007), 1–28; Kenneth Pomeranz, *The Great Divergence: China, Europe, and the Making of the Modern World Economy* (Princeton: Princeton University Press, 2000), 8; R. Bin Wong, *China Transformed: Historical Change and the Limits of European Experience* (Ithaca: Cornell University Press, 1997).

sense to compare the Chinese, the African or the Indian 'case' exclusively to an ideal model of the West.

A first solution would be to take a closer look at non-Western values and categories of thought, such as Buddhism, Hinduism and Islam. Anthropologists, along with specialists in area studies and the second generation of subaltern studies (the first being mostly concerned with the social history of the peasantry), advanced this solution when making explicit or implicit comparisons. Thus, Dipesh Chakrabarty's approach has the virtue of questioning the categories we use when we think about our world in comparison to others, and insisting on the need to take the values of other cultures into consideration.[2] It is perfectly legitimate to wonder if there are equivalents in other cultures to Western notions such as human rights, civil society, cosmopolitanism[3] or even religion and secularism.[4] This attention to 'alternative' values is necessary and welcome, but it also carries a risk. The insistence on 'genuine' Hindu, Chinese or Muslim values is a feature of nationalist political projects, but it also influenced several attempts made by Western specialists in so-called area studies to oppose the European perspective to a world history seen from a Chinese, Islamic or African perspective.[5]

This is a dangerous path: by emphasising more or less monolithic entities called 'cultures' or 'civilisations' or 'area studies', historians tend to overlook the cross-pollination and reciprocal influences that occur between 'cultures', which are never monolithic entities. This is one of the chief criticisms that 'connected history' has levelled against subaltern studies. Sanjay Subrahmanyam, and supporters of entangled or connected history in general, has persistently stressed how European values and practices have been profoundly affected by inter-actions and exchanges with non-European worlds.[6] Connected history has sought to overcome this wall of opposing civilisations and, while initially strongly critical of comparisons, Subrahmanyam recently acknowledged the possibility of using them.[7]

---

[2] Dipesh Chakrabarty, *Provincializing Europe. Postcolonial Thought and Historical Difference* (Princeton: Princeton University Press, 2000).

[3] Karen O'Brien, *Narratives of Enlightenment: Cosmopolitan History from Voltaire to Gibbon* (Cambridge: Cambridge University Press, 1997); Corinne Lefèvre et al. (eds.), *Cosmopolitismes en Asie du Sud: Sources, itinéraires, langues, XVIe-XVIIIe siècles* (Paris: EHESS, 2015).

[4] Nilufer Göle, 'La laïcité républicaine et l'islam public', *Pouvoirs* 115, 4 (2005), 73–86.

[5] One recent example of this attitude: James Belich et al. (eds.), *The Prospect of Global History* (Oxford: Oxford University Press, 2016).

[6] Sanjay Subrahmanyam, *Is Indian Civilization a Myth?* (Delhi: Permanent Black, 2013); Serge Gruzinski, *Les quatre parties du monde: Histoire d'une mondialisation* (Paris: Seuil, 2004).

[7] Sanjay Subrahmanyam, 'Between Eastern Africa and Western India, 1500–1650: Slavery, Commerce, and Elite Formation', *Comparative Studies in Society and History* 61, 4 (2019), 805–34.

At the same time, the opposition between comparison, presumed to be subject-ive, and connection, viewed as objective and obvious, weakens entangled history and connected history in general.[8] It seems senseless to oppose *l'histoire croisée* and connected history to comparative history.[9] This is all the more relevant since comparisons actually connect entities, and create relationships between them, precisely by looking for analogies and differences. They also connect objects by comparing them according to a list of criteria. The connections found in archives are no less subjective than the comparisons made by the historian. Archives and documents are never ready-made; they are the product of the efforts made by the administrations, companies and actors at their source, and later by archivists and their classifications, and ultimately by historians who select a given document and present it in an equally particular way. In fact, each comparison requires a meta-language and, if not a proper translation, at least an exercise of commensurability between terms and within a given methodological framework.[10]

Therefore, this chapter will not question the terms of comparison and analogy in abstract methodological models; instead, it will place actors and debates in their appropriate historical context in order to understand why they were interested in comparison and why, in a given context, they practised it in one particular way and not in another. Moreover, each context will be resolutely transregional and comparison will be identified as a cross-cultural practice. I will therefore take my distance from current arguments relating comparison only to European colonial expansion.[11] This is certainly true in some periods and for some authors, but not for all. Infra-European tensions and competition were no less important in justifying comparisons than encounters with non-European worlds. The history of comparative investigations reveals precisely that the identification of 'us' and the 'others', of Europe, or the West, and the 'rest' was an extremely variegated exercise in both its approach and its conclusions, and it contributed to the mutual identification, and not just oppos-ition, of all these terms. The interesting point to identify is how these multiple levels of comparison, geopolitical tensions and cultural transfers intervened in specific contexts. Even if comparison has been practised since Antiquity (both in Western and Asian historiographies),[12] or, even more radically, as some

---

[8] Michael Werner and Bénédicte Zimmermann (eds.), *De la comparaison à l'histoire croisée* (Paris: Seuil, 2004).

[9] Heinz-Gerhard Haupt and Jürgen Kocka (eds.), *Comparative and Transnational History: Central European Approaches and New Perspectives* (New York: Berghahn, 2009).

[10] Willibald Steinmetz (ed.), *The Force of Comparison. A New Perspective on Modern European History and the Contemporary World* (New York: Berghahn, 2019), in particular 'Introduction', 1–33.

[11] Clifford Geertz, *The Interpretation of Cultures* (New York: Basic Books, 1973); Ann Laura Stoler, *Along the Archival Grain* (Princeton: Princeton University Press, 2009).

[12] Marcel Detienne, 'Rentrer au village: Un tropisme de l'hellénisme?', *L'Homme* 157, 1 (2001), 137–49; G. E. R. Lloyd, *The Ambitions of Curiosity: Understanding the World in Ancient Greece and China* (Cambridge: Cambridge University Press, 2000).

anthropologists and biologists argue, since the Palaeolithic, and even if it became more widely used in the Middle Ages in its analogic forms, I will mostly focus on the period from the eighteenth century to the present day. This is not to follow Michel Foucault who, in *Les mots et les choses* (1966), argued that comparison presented a major break in the seventeenth century, when the episteme moved from analogy to classification and distinction.[13] The problem is that there is little empirical evidence of such a shift. Instead, as we will see, the two forms of comparison coexisted over the long run. Thus, my focus on the last three centuries responds to the epistemological evidence: comparison, as a form of translation, and analytical reflection are coessential to the relationships between the so-called human sciences, social sciences and natural sciences. The very possibility of identifying and separating these fields became relevant only from the eighteenth century onwards. I will begin with the eighteenth-century Enlightenment and its comparative philosophical anthropology; I will then move to the nineteenth century (Karl Marx, Max Weber) and the twentieth, examining the use and misuse of Weber (and Marx) during the decolonisation process and the Cold War, before arriving at global history nowadays. I will also evoke the Durkheimian approach to the comparative history of societies and its historical translation in the French *Annales* school, not to forget the comparative approaches in social and economic anthropology. I will conclude by suggesting some possible ways to practise comparisons in a global perspective.

Eurocentric Comparison: A Stain on the Enlightenment?

The Enlightenment raised two major relevant questions in comparison: on the one hand, the Eurocentrism of comparatism; on the other, the epistemological tension between historical sources and broader philosophical categories and thought. On the first point, subaltern, orientalist, post-modernist and finally global studies strongly criticise the Enlightenment as the source of Eurocentrism. In their view, most eighteenth-century authors explicitly or implicitly compared a more or less idealised European civilisation to 'other' backward areas and civilisations.[14] Along a similar line, nowadays supporters of 'multiple modernities' erroneously mix up present-day approaches and those of the Enlightenment.[15] In fact, most of today's critical judgements reflect less

---

[13] Michel Foucault, *Les mots et les choses: Une archéologie des sciences humaines* (Paris: Gallimard, 1966), ch, 2, in particular 68–72.

[14] On these critics, Sebastian Conrad, *What Is Global History?* (Princeton: Princeton University Press, 2016); Alessandro Stanziani, *Eurocentrism and the Politics of Global History* (New York: Palgrave, 2018).

[15] *Multiple Modernities*, special issue of Daedalus 129, 1 (2000); Dominic Sachsenmaier et al. (eds.), *Reflections on Multiple Modernities: European, Chinese and Other Interpretations* (Leiden: Brill 2002).

the original aim of eighteenth-century authors than their influential interpretations over the following centuries. In the eighteenth century, comparison was made not on the basis of economic or sociological models – these fields did not yet exist – but starting from philosophy and physiology. Most authors compared the attitudes individuals had to 'developing' their body and personality; the category of 'backwardness' (retardation) was first applied to individuals (their bodily or psychological backwardness). But then, differences between individual capacities were turned into differences in social status in order to criticise the 'old regime'. This passage from the individual to society finally led to different societies being compared in time and space.[16] However, authors never compared different modernities and civilisations for the very simple reason that they constantly employed the term 'civilisation' in the singular: there was not a European or an Indian or Arab civilisation, but one single civilisation of humankind. The question instead was whether different values contributed equally to progress and civilisation, or whether some values, institutions and people were more advanced than others. The first approach imagined multiple scales of time and values and therefore compared countries in order to understand their possible mutual influence.[17] The latter attitude, by contrast, imagined that some countries were more advanced than others on the scale of time and that their values would ultimately prevail over the rest. Jean-Jacques Rousseau and Pietro Giannone were in the first group, together with the later versions of the Abbé Raynal's *Histoire des deux Indes*. Diderot and Montesquieu, as well as many 'economists' – the French physiocrats – tended to express the second attitude.

However, Europeans did not just reflect on the 'others'. For much of the eighteenth century, for example, the French and the British constantly compared themselves to each other in terms of economic and social progress, warfare, science, population, techniques and so forth. This was because of the fierce competition between the two powers in Europe and on a global scale as they went about consolidating their respective empires. These two stakes – the nation and the empire – went together. Moreover, this was not just a European attitude, but one that was widespread in China, the Ottoman Empire and Russia, among others, where local elites compared themselves with the European powers.[18] In all these cases, comparisons expressed not only the influence of contradictory attitudes that Western European thinkers exerted outside of their country, but also the emergence of new paradigms of

---

[16] Michael Eggers, *Vergleichendes Erkennen: Zur Wissenschaftsgeschichte und Epistemologie des Vergleichs und zur Genealogie des Komparatistik* (Heidelberg: Winter, 2016).
[17] Jürgen Osterhammel, *Unfabling the East: The Enlightenment's Encounter with Asia* (Princeton: Princeton University Press, 2018).
[18] Alessandro Stanziani, *Les entrelacements du monde* (Paris: CNRS Éditions, 2018).

comparison in non-European countries.[19] Several authors reflected on comparison and expressed similar methodologies, some looking for 'universal values' and others associating the very notion of 'specificity' with longue durée persistent features in culture, institutions and the like. Reciprocal influence between thinkers in these areas was the rule. For example, Diderot believed in the reforming potential of Catherine the Great and the French monarchy.[20] Based on this belief, he distinguished between nations that had already achieved their highest level of civilisation and were starting to degenerate and those that remained closer to nature and could strive for a higher level of order and morality while avoiding the evils of civilisation. He placed America and Russia among the latter.[21]

After the 1770s, major political and social events pushed several philosophers to redefine their notion of progress, and therefore the object and content of their comparisons. The Pugachev uprising in Russia (1773–75) and the protests by masters and apprentices against the abolition of the guilds in France rapidly led to a revision of the enlightened monarchs' projects in both countries. From the 1780s on, Diderot and Condillac associated their scepticism about enlightened despotism with a more general criticism of European civilisation.[22] In other words, the encounter with Russia not only led French authors to reflect on France and Europe, but also to eventually reverse the tension between 'advanced' and 'backward' countries. In turn, this was not a one-way cultural exchange between a presumed 'centre' and a 'periphery' of Europe (Russia); beyond the impact of the Russian experience on French reflections on modernity, this two-way avenue of reflection produced original thinking in Russia itself. Here, besides followers of French revolutionary thinkers such as Alexander Nikolayevich Radishchev,[23] others adopted a more moderate attitude. Mikhailo Mikhailevich Shcherbatov claimed to be inspired by the French *philosophes* when he suggested keeping Peter the

---

[19] Sheldon Pollock, *The Language of the Gods in the World of Men: Sanskrit, Culture, and Power in Premodern India* (Berkeley: University of California Press, 2006); José Rabasa and Daniel Woolf (eds.), *The Oxford History of Historical Writing*, vol. 3: *1400–1800* (Oxford: Oxford University Press, 2012).

[20] Denis Diderot, 'Questions de Diderot et réponses de Catherine II sur la situation économique de l'Empire russe', in Maurice Tourneux, *Diderot et Catherine II* (Paris: Calmann Lévy, 1899), 532–57.

[21] Denis Diderot, 'Observations sur le Nakaz de Catherine II', in Denis Diderot, *Oeuvres politiques* (Paris: Garnier, 1963), 329–458, here 365.

[22] Michèle Duchet, *Anthropologie et histoire au siècle des Lumières: Buffon, Voltaire, Rousseau, Helvétius, Diderot* (Paris: Maspero, 1971), 134–5.

[23] Vladimir I. Moriakov, *Iz istorii evoliutsii obshchestvenno-politicheskikh vzgliadov prosvetitelei kontsa XVIII veka: Reinal' i Radishchev* [On the History of the Evolution of the Socio-political Orientations of Institutors During the Eighteenth Century: Raynal and Radishchev] (Moscow: Izdatel'stvo Moskovskogo Universiteta, 1981).

Great's Table of Ranks.[24] These reinterpretations of the French Enlightenment
in Russia did not express the 'distortions' of Russian authors but instead
reflected the ambivalences of the Enlightenment itself and the cross-
pollination across the Urals. They were anything but a monolithic 'centre
versus periphery' phenomenon, as critics of European cultural imperialism
often state.

In short, comparison in the Enlightenment expressed a philosophical attitude
which sought to identify an epistemological framework to reflect on human
civilisation as a whole. Within this overall attitude, one tendency consisted in
measuring 'backward' areas in the light of the most advanced ones, while,
conversely, another approach considered that the 'corruption' of Europe could
be solved by learning from the 'savage' areas. How did the nineteenth century
modify this exchange? To answer this question, we need to consider three
major trends in comparative approaches during the nineteenth century, linked
with the names of Marx, Durkheim and Weber.

Marx: Champion of Comparative Eurocentrism?

Nineteenth-century comparisons owed much to the emergence of positivism
and the influence the natural sciences had on the social sciences. The former
further developed reflections and practices on classifications which, once
adopted by the social sciences, encouraged normative attitudes: comparison,
based on the classification of societies, was a tool not just to understand but also
to orient social change and public policies. In this context, Marxist forms of
comparison raised two major concerns: on the one hand, again, the
Eurocentrism of this approach; on the other, the tension between a general
model and 'local' exceptions. As a great admirer of Charles Darwin, and also
with the aim of criticising 'vulgar socialism', Marx sought to fill the gap
between these fields. This is one of the reasons why Dipesh Chakrabarty
considers Marx's approach poorly suited to explaining contexts such as India.
But this is not the only point; the relevant question is why and how did Marx
himself imagine 'Europe', 'India' and 'Asia' and compare them? During
the second half of the nineteenth century, the question arose in the main
countries of Europe as to whether the 'historical laws of development' were
the same everywhere. At that time, several countries in Southern and Eastern
Europe, and also outside Europe (Japan, Latin America), stopped closing
themselves off to European influence and instead sought to steer their own
path to industrialisation and 'modernisation'.

---

[24] See 'Razmotrenie o voprose: Mogut li dvoriane zapisyvat'sia v kuptsy [Notes on the Question:
Can Nobles Register as Merchants?]', in Mikhail M. Shcherbatov, *Neizdannye sochineniia*
[Unpublished Works] (Moscow: Sotsekgiz, 1935), 139–58.

In this context, in the first volume of *Capital*, as earlier in the *Critique of Political Economy* and *The Communist Manifesto*, Marx accused classical political economy of putting forward abstract theories and laws that failed to take into account the historically situated nature of capitalism. He opposed the abstraction of economics to concrete, empirical analyses of societies and their history. In reality, he was less critical of models in general than of those who dehistoricised capitalism, such as the authors of the classical school. Indeed, his own approach led him to identify simultaneously the historical singularity of capitalism and its 'general laws'. Marx adopted comparatism, but only to insert it into the wider laws of history. As a Hegelian, Marx was not against general theories and historical laws, only certain interpretations of this process. Marx did not criticise political economy for abstraction as such, but rather the particular form that naturalised capitalism. Instead, he proposed a schema meant to be both historical and general, with claims to universality. The passage from feudalism to capitalism is valid everywhere, along with the main characteristics of capitalist dynamics: alienation and commodification of labour, the monetisation of trade and commodity fetishism that inevitably accompany the trend towards a lower profit rate, alternating periods of crisis and expansion and the existence of the famous 'reserve army' of proletarians. Historical determinism and the philosophy of history come together in a positivist approach in which history serves less to question than to validate a general scheme.

Yet, as was the case for the Enlightenment, Marx also sometimes produced new attitudes when he moved beyond Germany or Britain. It is important to understand, even beyond an author's initial intention, the role cross-cultural influences played (and play) in comparative historical investigation. Thus, the opposition between Slavophiles and Westernisers in nineteenth-century Russia stemmed precisely from the issue that concerns us here: comparison in its epistemological and historical dimensions. Starting in the 1840s, first Slavophiles and then Westernisers such as Alexander Herzen saw the Russian peasant commune as a historical singularity that could allow the country to move directly into modernity without going through a capitalist phase of development. The debate over the commune was inseparable from the comparison between Russia and Western Europe. This debate was at once ideological (the role of the peasantry in the revolution), empirical (how to prove the arguments used) and methodological (how to make comparisons). That is why this debate inevitably ended up being combined with the debate over method in the science of society. Marx did it, and Russian intellectuals did it as well. 'Those who invoke private property', noted Nikolay Gavrilovich Chernyshevsky, 'think that progress in sociology and economics, as in natural science, consists in moving from simple to more complex forms'. From this point of view, by limiting specialisation, the commune did not contribute to backwardness but rather anticipated the future evolution of the developed countries.[25]

But how were these conclusions to be reconciled with the Marxist thought with which these authors associated themselves? In other words, if historical laws existed, how could historical varieties be explained? One single path for each country, or multiple paths? The answer to these questions had an impact on the theory and practice of comparison itself: it offered a choice between normative comparison and historical determinism, on the one hand, and heuristic comparison and historical bifurcations, on the other. How so?

In a letter addressed to Nikolay Konstantinovich Mikhailovsky in 1877, Marx said he thought Russia could take a different route from the one in the West. Four years later, in a letter to Vera Zasulich, he wrote that the peasant commune was the basis for the social regeneration of Russia.[26] By turning his focus towards Russia and empirically casting doubt on his theory, Marx ended up unlocking it. Yet Marx was uncertain in this turn, and after him Engels pushed to standardise Marxism into a kind of orthodoxy which ignored the 'alternative paths' in history. This type of normative comparison has never disappeared from Marxist thought in all its variants; even worse, 'late Marx' seems even to have been forgotten again, after the parenthesis of 'development studies' during the Cold War. Would Max Weber and his followers provide an alternative?

The Use and Misuse of Max Weber

Towards the end of the nineteenth century, reflections on comparison took some new turns. First, the general social and political context focused attention on countries that were 'catching up' (such as Germany and the United States), inspiring new reflections on the putative 'decadence' of former leading countries, such as China or even, paradoxically, Britain. Meanwhile, the emergence of Japan encouraged comparative reflections on non-European areas and their presumed 'backwardness'. Modernisation and the role of the state therefore acquired a major relevance in comparative investigations in history. Beyond this field, anthropology found new life in global investigations of 'local' people. In this context, physical and biological anthropology made use of natural sciences to classify and hierarchise peoples, while ethnography and

---

[25] Nikolai G. Chernyshevskii, 'Ob Obshchinnom vladenii' [On Community Ownership] 1858, reproduced in Sochineniia [Works], vol. 2 (Geneva: Elpidine, 1879). Regarding these debates: Alessandro Stanziani, L'économie en revolution: le cas russe. 1870–1930 (Paris: Albin Michel, 1998).

[26] Stanziani, L'économie en révolution. For the letters between Marx and the Russians: Teodor Shanin (ed.), Late Marx and the Russian Road: Marx and the 'Peripheries of Capitalism' (New York: Monthly Review Press, 1983).

cultural anthropology sought to compare by putting the accent on 'cultural specificities', and, eventually, comparative linguistics.[27] I will return to anthropology in the final part of this chapter.

Among the authors who contributed most to reflections on comparisons in this period, one reference is at least as important as Marx: Max Weber. He had enormous influence at the time and his ideas keep surfacing today in comparative and global history studies, via Charles Tilly, R. Bin Wong and Kenneth Pomeranz, among others – this despite criticism of Weber by specialists in area studies and anthropologists such as Jack Goody.[28] We should be careful to distinguish Weber's thought from the many approaches more or less inspired by him. Let us take one example among others: religion. Serious proof has never been found to substantiate the favourable connection between Protestantism and capitalism, or the tensions between Catholicism and Confucianism on the one hand, and capitalism on the other. Yet these elements continue to be evoked as if they were established truths – except when they are reversed entirely nowadays and Confucianism is invoked to explain China's economic success.[29]

Weber certainly had a Eurocentric approach, as did Marx before him. At the same time, when he wrote on China or India and compared them to Europe in terms of rationality, state, the economy, accounting and science, he posed a far greater challenge to his period and was much more nuanced than his critics usually argued. His main goal was not to oppose civilisation to backwardness and rationality to irrationality but to explain historical trajectories starting from social complexities. To be sure, Weber sought to explain the success of the West; but, at the same time, his explanations were far more complex than those of dozens of authors who claimed to be inspired by Weber. Much recent criticism of Weber applies more to 'Weberian authors' than to Weber himself.[30]

Unlike Karl Marx or Émile Durkheim, Weber gave priority to comparison rather than to 'whole' dynamics (without neglecting them). This style of reasoning had its roots in the German 'historical school' of economics and in the attempt to insert the 'nation' into wider dynamics while preserving it as one possible unit of comparison. However, unlike the first generation of the historical school (Friedrich List, for example), looking for the 'nation' in a still divided Germany, and unlike the second generation (Wilhelm Roscher, among others), reflecting on the tension between casuistic and general historical laws,

[27] Matei Candea, *Comparison in Anthropology: The Impossible Method* (Cambridge: Cambridge University Press, 2019).
[28] Jack Goody, *The East in the West* (Cambridge: Cambridge University Press, 1996); Haupt and Kocka, *Comparative and Transnational History*; Wong, *China Transformed*.
[29] Jan Rehmann, *Max Weber: Modernization as Passive Revolution: A Gramscian Analysis* (Leiden: Brill, 2013); Peter Ghosh, *Max Weber and the Protestant Ethic: Twin Histories* (Oxford: Oxford University Press, 2014).
[30] James M. Blaut, *Eight Eurocentric Historians* (New York: Guilford Publications, 2000).

Weber pioneered a multi-scale and multi-angle comparative method. The crucial element in this process lay in the choice of the fields, on the one hand, and the variables, on the other. First, the fields: society, religion and the economy. All three enter into Weberian architecture to provide a fully integrated analysis of society. Next, within each field, Weber selected what he considered the relevant variables. For example, the comparison between Europe – mainly Britain – and China was made by focusing on private property or the role played by science in technological innovation, power struggles between entrepreneurs, capitalists and wage earners and so on. Capitalism was distinguished by the pursuit of profit and the rational organisation of production factors.[31] Weber's strength lay in conceiving a framework of comparative analysis that remained unchallenged for decades and which often served to legitimise the supremacy of the West, or, rather, of its ideal type.[32] He shared with Marx the idea that profits and wage labour were the main features of capitalism. However, unlike Marx he did not seek to predict the course of history: normativity made way for a heuristic of the 'model' that aimed at opening doors and asking questions rather than identifying the 'laws of history'. The global perspective was equally different: Marx reasoned in terms of extension; he presumed that the historical path of England, more or less idealised, would extend to the rest of the world. Weber did not imagine the future of other countries but instead sought to compare ideal types with empirical realities. He thus did not share Marx's obligation to consider the case of India or Russia and ask if they fitted into his scheme.

What is important to retain here is the relationship Weber maintained between comparison and ideal types.[33] This link was crucial to incorporating historical analysis into a sociological perspective. Comparison requires constant terms; without them, it becomes impossible. According to Weber, this was the price to pay for reconciling logical rigour with empirical analysis. Not all these features would be taken up by Weber's disciples.

Comparative history as it developed after the Second World War would have been impossible without the intellectual diaspora of Russian and Central European authors in the United States, originating from the collapse of the Austro-Hungarian and Russian empires as well as the rise of Nazism. Friedrich A. von Hayek, Ludwig von Mises, Karl Polanyi, Alexander Gerschenkron,

---

[31] Max Weber, *Wirtschaft und Gesellschaft* (Tübingen: Mohr Siebeck, 1922); translated as Max Weber, *Economy and Society: An Outline of Interpretive Sociology*, ed. Guenther Roth and Claus Wittich, 2 vols. (Berkeley: University of California Press, 1978). The *Max-Weber-Gesamtausgabe* (Tübingen: Mohr Siebeck) has re-edited the work in eight volumes: I/22,1 to I/22,5, I/23 to I/25 (1999–2015).

[32] Wolfgang J. Mommsen, *Max Weber and German Politics, 1890–1920* (Chicago: University of Chicago Press, 1984).

[33] Fritz K. Ringer, *Max Weber's Methodology: The Unification of the Cultural and Social Sciences* (Cambridge, MA: Harvard University Press, 1997).

Wassily Leontief, Albert Hirschmann and Simon Kuznets were just some of those who left continental Europe. Their sensibility and approaches owed much to the multiple encounters between the Germanic and Russian cultures, to which they added an always difficult dialogue with the Anglophone worlds (most of them were critical of American consumerism).[34] These experiences encouraged not just comparisons in their approach but, what is more, comparisons in which cross-cultural experiences were crucial.

To these multiple influences another must be added: the global Cold War, in which tensions between the two superpowers were transmuted into investigations (and subsequent policies) about the origins and solutions to 'backwardness'. Alexander Gerschenkron is famous for his *Economic Backwardness in Historical Perspective*. It involved proposing a scale of comparison to account for economic growth as well as for so-called 'obstruction' factors. Like Max Weber and others before him, Gerschenkron began by drawing up a list of Western characteristics on which his comparison would be based. He, too, emphasised cities, the bourgeoisie, markets and private property. Yet unlike Marx and, to some extent, Weber, he thought it was possible to arrive at industrialisation (but not capitalism) without a bourgeoisie. In other words, Gerschenkron gave new value to the late Marx's investigation on the Russian path. He did not use it to explain the general laws of history, but instead to identify historical and future solutions to 'underdevelopment'. 'Backward' countries (to use the jargon of the 1960s and 1970s) such as Prussia and Russia had 'substituting factors', notably the state. This was a clever solution to the problem raised by the need to reconcile particular features and historical specificities with general dynamics. If backwardness and diversity go together, then it is possible to conceive of alternative paths.[35]

One might wonder, however, whether this solution really eliminates the confusion between historical time and logical time. Yet these two terms – the notions of backwardness and historical temporalities – are hardly compatible. In reality, economic backwardness refers to logical time (as identified in an economic model, for instance). Contrary to appearances, Gerschenkron did not compare Russia to England in specific historical contexts. Instead, he opposed an ideal image of the West (and of England in particular) to an equally ideal image of nineteenth-century Russia. English economic development was associated with the early introduction of a parliament, privatisation of the commons and, hence, the formation of a proletariat available for agriculture and industry.

---

[34] See, for example, Nicholas Dawidoff, *The Fly Swatter: Portrait of an Exceptional Character* (New York: Vintage Books, 2002), a biography of Alexander Gerschenkron; Jeremy Adelman, *Worldly Philosopher: The Odyssey of Albert O. Hirschman* (Princeton: Princeton University Press, 2013).

[35] Alexander Gerschenkron, *Economic Backwardness in Historical Perspective* (Cambridge, MA: Harvard University Press 1962).

In contrast, Russia was associated with market towns – and therefore with a bourgeoisie – as well as the presence of an absentee landed gentry living off serf labour. These were ideal types instead of complex historical realities. This approach paid a heavy tribute to the climate of the Cold War.

Normative Comparison: From the Cold War to the Great Divergence

This work was part of a broader debate in the 1950s and 1960s. With decolonisation, economists raised the problem of (under)development and what should be done to remedy it. In the context of the Cold War, this issue was inseparable from the question of which economic and political form the new states would take: capitalism or socialism. The components of this debate were globalised. They not only compared the economic achievements of the USSR to those of the West, but also the trajectories of China, India and the countries in the Americas, Africa and Asia that were gaining their independence at the time. In fact, the debate over modernisation implied a strongly determinist philosophy of history, Eurocentric categories and postulates and, ultimately, circular explanatory arguments.[36] Herein lies the essential connection between Weber, Gerschenkron and development economics: Eurocentrism was the very basis of comparisons using ideal types. These comparisons, often centred on the twin notions of backwardness and progress, reflected issues that were not only intellectual but also political and therefore normative. The comparisons were not so much anachronistic as atemporal.

The normativity of comparison even increased over time, well beyond Gerschenkron's approach. In particular, Walt W. Rostow put forward his theory of stages of growth in open opposition to socialism. He showed that the stages of growth were universal and that it was impossible to follow a path imposed from on high, as in the USSR. History served to validate the Western-style itinerary and the arrow of time moved in only one direction. Paradoxically, Rostow reproduced Marx's argument, according to which the most advanced countries showed backward countries the way ahead.

In a similar vein, when Karl August Wittfogel published *Oriental Despotism*, the Cold War was at its height.[37] Using his Marxist training and Marx's notion of the 'Asiatic mode of production', the author described the USSR under Stalin as 'despotism'. From this viewpoint, he was putting the Soviet Union in the same category as earlier forms of Asian power that were said to have developed highly despotic societies by controlling hydraulic

---

[36] Frederick Cooper et al., *Confronting Historical Paradigms: Peasants, Labor, and the Capitalist World System in Africa and Latin America* (Madison: University of Wisconsin Press, 1993).
[37] Karl A. Wittfogel, *Oriental Despotism. A Comparative Study of Total Power* (New Haven: Yale University Press, 1957).

resources. Wittfogel contrasted this type of organisation with slave-owning societies and feudal societies. Instead of slaves or serfs, oriental despotic societies subjugated the entire population to the will of high-ranking bureaucrats. What was really at stake in Wittfogel's book was this: at the time of the Cold War, the USSR was viewed as a despotic system not only by liberals and conservatives but also by socialists and communists critical of Stalinism and the Soviet Union. For Wittfogel, as for Montesquieu and Marx before him, the analysis of Asia was actually intended as a discussion of political relationships within the 'West'. In other words, we should not make the mistake of considering every opposition between 'us' and the 'others' as lacking tensions within the 'us'.

There is another methodological insight to discuss in this kind of comparison: the relationship between causality and temporality. For example, comparative history and the sociology of state construction (at the very core of Max Weber, Charles Tilly, Theda Skopcol, Barrington Moore and Victor B. Lieberman) have often taught us to think in terms of nation-states. Even if an author such as Charles Tilly declares at the outset that we must avoid projecting recent constructions on the past, he cannot help doing so himself.[38] That is one of the consequences of studying the past in order to find the origins of the present. This reasoning raises two types of questions: it starts from the results and assumes the chronological antecedents were 'causes', even though there is no evidence, for example, that the growth of England was actually linked to the adoption of the Bill of Rights in 1689 or that Venice lost its power because it was unable to produce a state like France. In the absence of empirical materials, the authors added a causality which is impossible to demonstrate. The solution lies very conveniently in *post hoc ergo propter hoc*. Temporal succession becomes synonymous with causality. Is it possible to shatter this kind of tautological reasoning?

A first attempt to solve this problem comes from the so-called debate on 'the Great Divergence', inspired by the title of Kenneth Pomeranz's book. In Pomeranz's approach, the Great Divergence is mainly related to colonial expansion and factor endowments. While Western Europe benefitted from its American colonies, and later from American markets and resources, Russian despotism and power limited Asian (mainly Chinese) expansion. We are apparently at the other end of the spectrum from classical Weberian approaches: instead of trying to fit the data into a model, here the data are used to confirm or disprove earlier studies without any pre-judgement. To be sure, these approaches do not fall into the trap of facile comparison mentioned earlier. They also avoid celebrating the West and, like every other global history

---

[38] Charles Tilly, *Coercion, Capital and European States, AD 990–1991* (Cambridge, MA: Blackwell, 1990).

approach, those used by proponents of the Great Divergence also propose important solutions to the question of how the singularities of the various parts of the world are interlinked and how they are connected to a larger whole (e.g. the comparison between the Lower Yangzi region and Lancashire leads to a reassessment of European and Chinese dynamics as a whole). This was a huge step forward from previous comparisons in terms of backwardness. But what about the model itself?

Pomeranz explains the Chinese dynamic according to the same criteria used for Europe – in particular, demographic growth, the protection of private property and the commercial and proto-industrial dynamic.[39] In other words, like Weber, David S. Landes, Karl Polanyi, Marx and so many others before him, Pomeranz retains the idealised British model made of privatisation of common lands, proletarianisation, industrialisation, bourgeois and individualist mentality, and so forth, and then extends it to China. Thus, Pomeranz overturns Weber but maintains his comparative method – which confirms the strength and polyvalence of the Weberian approach. At the same time, from a political standpoint, the whole debate over the Great Divergence stems from neoliberal Western intellectual orthodoxy after the fall of the Berlin Wall: markets and capitalism dominate the recent centuries of world history; institutions and perhaps factor endowments influence historical outcomes, not 'mentalities' or different economic attitudes (as anthropologists had expressed them). Finally, research work on the Great Divergence is problematic from the standpoint of political philosophy: how long will economic history – whether global or not – have to focus exclusively on growth and on 'who was first'? The history of Russia – as well as the new Asian capitalism of China and India today – show that economic growth and markets are perfectly compatible with a lack of democracy and unequal social rights.

Marc Bloch or How to Reconcile Philology and Comparison

The First World War was experienced everywhere as a fundamental shift that broke up the old order. The United States asserted itself as the leading global power, while France and Great Britain, despite victory, were left to cope with the difficulties of reconstruction. Hostility to global economic, political and social dynamics stoked populist nationalism in Europe, Asia and parts of Africa and the Americas.[40] During the interwar period, historiographical nationalism reached heights never before achieved, even in the nineteenth century.[41] The

---

[39] Pomeranz, *Great Divergence*.
[40] Stefan Berger et al. (eds.), *Narrating the Nation: Representations in History, Media and the Arts* (New York: Berghahn, 2008).
[41] Katherine Verdery and Ivo Banac (eds.), *National Character and National Ideology in Interwar Eastern Europe* (New Haven: Yale Center for International and Area Studies, 1995).

political role of nationalist history found its most extreme embodiment in the
totalitarian states, where Hitler, Mussolini and Stalin made the rewriting of
history the core of their respective political projects. Now nation and ethnicity
became strongly connected and social Darwinism penetrated historical
discourse.[42] In 1920, Lucien Febvre published an article in the *Revue de
synthèse historique* setting forth the political and social role of history in
a 'world in ruins'.[43] Febvre was not looking for a theory, but rather for an
approach to history that would explain, among other things, the World War and
its origins. This is where the global nature of history comes in: a global
perspective is not as important in developing a political project for society
(as was the case for Marx and Oswald Spengler, among many others) as it is in
connecting different levels of history. Global history was *histoire totale*. Febvre
emphasised that 'posing problems correctly – the *how* and *why* –expressed the
end and means of history. When there are no problems, there is no history –
only narratives and compilations.'[44] The other issue pertained to the use of
language in analysing societies distant from the historian in time or space.
Febvre noted that mastering the language used is an absolute prerequisite to
undertaking a historical study.

Marc Bloch also insisted on linguistic proficiency in his *Apologie pour
l'histoire ou Métier d'historien* (1949) and in his famous article on historical
comparison from 1928.[45] It is not by chance that, even nowadays and not only
in France, historians who criticise comparativism and 'socio-history' refer to
Bloch as one of the few acceptable methods for comparison. What essentially
distinguishes Bloch and Febvre from Weber and his followers is mastery of
languages and a rejection of general abstract models of analysis. Febvre
maintained that researchers should not undertake analyses of a region unless
they were proficient in the language; Bloch demanded similar linguistic proficiency. His approach shows the distance that separates him from Max Weber,
Émile Durkheim and Francois Simiand.[46] Bloch thought categories evolved
over time, which accounts for his scepticism with regard to diachronic

---

[42] Anthony D. Smith, *The Ethnic Origins of Nations* (Oxford: Blackwell, 1986).

[43] Lucien Febvre, 'L'histoire dans le monde en ruines', *Revue de synthèse historique* 30, 1 (1920), 1–15.

[44] Lucien Febvre, 'Propos d'initiation: Vivre l'histoire', in Lucien Febvre, *Combats pour l'histoire* (Paris: Colin, 1992), 18–33.

[45] Marc Bloch, *Apologie pour l'histoire, ou Métier d'historien*, ed. Étienne Bloch (Paris: Armand Colin, 1993) [English translation: Bloch, *The Historian's Craft* (New York: Knopf, 1953)]; Marc Bloch, 'Pour une histoire comparée des sociétés européennes', *Revue de synthèse historique* 46, 1 (1928), 15–50; Marc Bloch, 'A Contribution towards a Comparative History of European Societies', in *Land and Work in Mediaeval Europe. Selected Papers*, trans J. E. Anderson (London: Routledge & Kegan Paul, 1966), 44–81.

[46] Etienne Anheim and Benoit Grévin, 'Choc des civilisations ou choc des disciplines? Les sciences sociales et le comparatisme', *Revue d'histoire moderne et contemporaine* 49, 4 (2002), 122–46.

comparisons and his preference for synchronic comparisons. Moreover, in keeping with his insistence on knowing the sources and the language, Bloch restricted himself to comparisons within the 'Western' and Germanic European context and excluded Russia from his investigation. According to him, this was not only because he did not know Russian, but also because Russia did not belong to the same civilisation as France and Germany and therefore comparison would be useless.[47] Bloch's approach invites us to think about relevant scales for comparison: even admitting for the moment that only synchronic comparison is justified, how does one go about choosing the relative spaces?

Bloch took for granted the relevance of comparisons within Europe. Of all his positions, this is perhaps the one that was most influenced by the interwar context; the tensions within European space motivated Bloch's desire to claim its homogeneity despite the First World War and the conflict between France and Germany. These were indeed major challenges, especially when viewed from Strasbourg where Bloch lived. As a result, contrary to his own method, he assumed far more than he demonstrated the homogeneity of Europe and its relevance to making suitable comparisons. Despite the general success of this approach over decades, he was confusing the historian's skills with analytical relevance. No doubt within the community of historians, as it was understood in France and in Europe and which Bloch defended in his work, the knowledge of languages was assumed to be indispensable for studying a region and producing comparisons and/or circulatory analyses. The refusal to make comparisons for reasons of 'language' or 'civilisation' is just as weak as making comparisons based on generalist models. This actually was a first important departure from the Enlightenment priority accorded to the 'model' or general concepts over empirical findings and which was inherited, in different ways, by Marx and Weber. The strength of this approach is to return sources, languages and archives to the core of the comparative investigation. The price paid was a methodological underdetermination of the epistemological status of the origin of archives themselves, the selection of documents by the historians and the role of language across time and space, as we have shown in Bloch's definition of 'Europe'. Anthropology provides a possible solution to this problem.

Anthropology and Comparisons: A Dialogue with Historians and Economists?

To a certain extent, anthropology is always comparative, although not necessarily explicitly so.[48] Some major anthropologists, Evans-Pritchard among them, even argued the impossibility of achieving ultimate comparisons in

[47] Bloch, 'Pour une histoire comparée des sociétés européennes'.
[48] Candea, *Comparison in Anthropology*.

anthropology; in doing so, they developed wonderful analyses on comparison itself.[49] In fact, 'biological' and nowadays 'evolutionary' anthropology insist on comparison as a natural artefact of the human mind, while, at the opposite end, cultural anthropology stresses the limits of comparison and its artificial nature. The former approach made use of the inductive method of the natural sciences when comparing and emphasised the differences, 'all other things being equal'. This branch of anthropology was and still is close to economics, which adopted a similar method. By contrast, the latter approach sustained the so-called concomitant variations when comparing cases – that is, a complex set of multiple variations within and between the compared items. Anthropology offered a further device: it deconstructed the binary of 'us' and the 'other' so widespread in historical studies, in particular in imperial, colonial and postcolonial investigations. This approach overcame the notion of 'specificity' and therefore put an end to the comparison, if not the opposition, between essentialised 'cultures' and 'area studies'.

Instead, circulation and translations became part of the comparison itself. Comparison was no longer a tool to confirm a given model but, on the contrary, an attitude to negotiate in situ the tensions between the 'universal' and the 'particular' while stressing the multiplicity of historical paths.[50] By subjecting the very notion of 'culture' to scrutiny, anthropology pushed historians to redefine their reasoning in terms of well identified 'cultures' or 'civilisations'. No 'culture' is isolated from all others, and its representations and self-representations go well beyond the conventional opposition between 'realities' and 'representations', so dear to economic and some social historians. It is not by chance that anthropologists are usually critical of the very notion of 'area studies', as ahistorical, essentialist stabilisation of cultural identities.[51] However, such a radical relativism and indistinction of the subject and the object, as embraced by Clifford Geertz and his followers, does not find unanimous consensus among anthropologists and historians.[52] Among historians, the interface between post-modernist and post-colonialist deconstructivism and new reflective, critical reconstructions of the past has generated a multitude of approaches, including Carlo Ginzburg's historical

[49] Edward E. Evans-Pritchard, *Social Anthropology* (London: Cohen & West, 1951).

[50] Jane Comaroff and John Comaroff (eds.), *Millennial Capitalism and the Culture of Neoliberalism* (Durham: Duke University Press, 2001); Arturo Escobar, *Encountering Development: The Making and Unmaking of the Third World* (Princeton: Princeton University Press, 1995).

[51] Jane Guyer, 'Anthropology in Area Studies', *Annual Review of Anthropology* 33 (2004), 499–523; Philippe Descola, *Par-delà nature et culture* (Paris: Gallimard, 2005) [English translation: *Beyond Nature and Culture*, trans. Janet Lloyd (Chicago: University of Chicago Press, 2013)]; Geertz, *The Interpretation of Cultures*.

[52] Comaroff and Comaroff, *Millennial Capitalism*; Marshall Sahlins, *Stone Age Economics* (Chicago: Aldine de Gruyter, 1972); George Steinmetz (ed.), *The Politics of Methods in the Human Sciences* (Durham: Duke University Press, 2005).

morphologies, Ann Laura Stoler's ethnography in and of the archives, and Natalie Zemon Davis's and Alf Luedtke's historical anthropology, to name a few.[53]

Meanwhile, from the early twentieth century, economic anthropology sought to articulate a different (from mainstream economics) relationship with history and other social sciences.[54] Hundreds of anthropological historical studies on local communities and their 'economic' behaviour all around the world saw the light of day. Intense debates over 'multiple economic rationalities', and the denial of supposedly economic relationships existing independently from cultural and social features, marked this huge trend during much of the twentieth century.[55] In the second half of the century, these were not just theoretical debates: concrete policies to be adopted in 'developing countries' were a major stake. Did 'Africans' or 'Indians' have to act like Londoners at the stock exchange to escape from poverty? The most interesting concern was that this attitude ultimately raised questions about economic behaviour and the boundaries between economic, social and cultural life in 'advanced' countries themselves. According to many anthropologists, optimising agents, as mainstream economics called them, were a fiction everywhere.[56] In short, the supposedly 'local' was not only connected to other 'local' entities and therefore to the global, but required that theories and interpretations of the 'West' itself be reframed. Historians, above all those who were close to microhistory, seemed extremely sensitive to this argument.[57] It is from this crossroads between history, anthropology and other social sciences that we may reflect on the present state and future orientation of comparative history.

[53] Carlo Ginzburg, *Clues, Myths and the Historical Method* (Baltimore: Johns Hopkins University Press, 1989); Stoler, *Along the Archival Grain*; Natalie Zemon Davis, *Fiction in the Archives* (Stanford: Stanford University Press, 1990); Alf Luedtke, *History of Everyday Life* (Princeton: Princeton University Press, 1995).

[54] Raymond Firth, *Primitive Economics of the New Zealand Maori* (London: Routledge, 1929); Edward E. Evans-Pritchard, *The Nuer: A Description of the Modes of Livelihood and Political Institutions of a Nilotic People* (Oxford: Oxford University Press, 1940); Marcel Mauss, *Essai sur le don* (Paris: Presses Universitaires de France, 2012).

[55] For a synthesis see Chris Hann and Keith Hart, *Economic Anthropology* (Cambridge: Polity Press, 2011).

[56] Arjun Appadurai (ed.), *The Social Life of Things: Commodities in Cultural Perspective* (Cambridge: Cambridge University Press, 1986); Clifford Geertz et al., *Meaning and Order in Moroccan Society* (Cambridge: Cambridge University Press, 1979); David Graeber, *Toward an Anthropological Theory of Value: The False Coin of Our Own Dreams* (New York: Palgrave, 2001); Maurice Godelier, *Rationalité et irrationalité en économie* (Paris: Maspero, 1968); Claude Meillassoux, *L'anthropologie économique des Gouro de Côte d'Ivoire* (Paris: Mouton, 1964).

[57] Giovanni Levi, *Le pouvoir au village: Histoire d'un exorciste dans le Piémont du xviie siècle* (Paris: Gallimard, 1989).

Which Way?

The question this chapter sought to raise is not just how and whether historians should practise comparison but also, and more importantly, why historical comparisons matter in the political arena. In the eighteenth century, comparison was grounded in philosophy and expressed the deep involvement of 'philosophers' in the public sphere. To a certain extent, comparative history was part of political philosophy, which explains the criticisms most 'philosophers' raised vis-à-vis philology as a purely descriptive tool for 'antiquarians'. At the same time, it would be a mistake to associate this comparative philosophical history with Eurocentrism. This was true for some but not all authors, precisely because the Enlightenment expressed contrasting attitudes towards the 'centrality' of Europe, its notions and the idea of progress.

The nineteenth century took a different approach. According to Marx, progress must come from the most advanced countries, above all Britain, and the categories of capital, labour, capitalism, exploitation and accumulation, although derived from a more or less stylised 'European' (actually British–German) perception, were supposed to be universally acceptable. Comparison was absorbed into the general laws of history.

Socio-economic comparative history acquired increasing importance in the public sphere during the twentieth century, precisely in relation to global phenomena such as the transmutation of Europe and increasing nationalist movements in the colonial world during and after decolonisation. Max Weber and his legacy were at the very core of comparative history for many decades. As such, Weber's studies could lead to Eurocentric attitudes (in particular, on China or the role of Protestantism), but also to their opposite (studies on law and authority, parts of his economic history). As for Marc Bloch and the *Annales* school, multiple epistemological options and empirical conclusions were available.

This was not the case after Bloch for multiple reasons: the emergence of totalitarianisms and their use of history produced more rigid and tautological attitudes in liberal history as well. The Cold War and decolonisation exacerbated the problem rather than solving it, as we have seen with the debates around Alexander Gerschenkron, despite his attempts to identify multiple paths of development. Ironically, the end of the Cold War had an unexpected effect on comparative history: at first, renewed enthusiasm for the global gave rise to new ventures in comparative history, as attested by the debate on the Great Divergence. This debate marked the end of economic anthropology and of multiple paths to 'modernity'. Comparison became a politically correct tool to confirm that Africans, Chinese and Indians were equally keen to embrace capitalism if only they had not been invaded by Western powers and later lived with corrupt governments. With the financial crisis, the opposition to globalisation and the new rise of nationalism, comparative approaches met with success among nationalist and civilisationist historians and observers, who stressed the radical opposition between Europe and Islam, the United States and the others, India or China and the West, and the like.

Is there another way to make use of comparison in the era of the global return of nationalisms? The answer is yes, but we need first to overcome some limitations in history teaching and history writing, beginning with the persistent institutional and analytic accent put on the so-called 'singularity' or 'specificity' of area studies.[58] Several authors have reflected on comparison and expressed similar methodologies, some looking for 'universal values', others associating the very notion of 'specificity' with persistent longue durée features, in culture, institutions and the like. 'Specificity', the very core of comparison, was identified in the 'soul' of the country, its traditions, customs and sometimes language and religious beliefs – we would say its structural longue durée components. Specificity is a structuralist notion today and was so in the past. Area studies still mention undefined 'specificities' of an area as synonymous with incommensurability and incomparability.[59]

Sometimes, singularity is translated into uniqueness: a given region is said to be sui generis and therefore incomparable because unlike any other. Any justification of this position would require an explicit comparison, whereas this practice is rejected in the name of the very specificity and uniqueness of one area or another.[60] Together with its opposite – universalism and a single time scale – this was the most important legacy the Enlightenment left to historical comparisons. Such 'singularity' is also associated with the longue durée; persistent features may account for the presumed singularity of an area: its environment, culture, language, religion and state.[61] In defining civilisations and area studies, the longue durée approach turns into a boomerang: what began as a heuristic tool (how to justify Europe instead of the Mediterranean? China instead of the Han culture?) becomes an intellectual prison.[62]

Nor can reciprocal comparison solve the problem, despite Austin's and Pomeranz's assertions to the contrary. The answer is not to claim that all areas are equal, but to critically identify their multiple and variable (in time) singularities. These can only be detected in a connected history of the notions and practices of 'singularities' themselves. It does not suffice to say that France

---

[58] Robert H. Bates, 'Area Studies and the Discipline: A Useful Controversy?' *PS: Political Science & Politics* 30, 2 (1997), 166–70.

[59] David Ludden, 'Area Studies in the Age of Globalization', *FRONTIERS: The Interdisciplinary Journal of Study Abroad* 6, 1 (2000), 1–22.

[60] Werner and Zimmermann, *De la comparaison à l'histoire croisée*.

[61] Marc Raeff, 'Un Empire comme les autres?', *Cahiers du monde russe* 30, 4 (1989), 321–7.

[62] For a critique of these approaches, see Sanjay Subrahmanyam, 'Connected Histories: Notes Towards a Reconfiguration of Early Modern Eurasia', *Modern Asian Studies* 31, 3 (1997), 735–62.

is like or unlike Senegal and Japan; presumed 'specificities' must be examined and not assumed; they have to be put into a dynamic historical global framework in which connections and comparison intervene. Areas are not monolithic entities existing by themselves but mobile configurations which respond to both sources and questions.

At the same time, as the history of comparison shows, a second shift is needed in contemporary historical practices. Schemes underlying historical comparative investigations are, explicitly or not, drawn from social sciences; they need to be historically decentred. What does this mean? To this day, global history reproduces the different paths to comparison inherited from previous centuries: neo-Marxists such as Immanuel Wallerstein or Giovanni Arrighi compare in order to identify a single path to post-capitalism. The world-system is a tautological model which leaves no room for historical bifurcations: the scene was set in the sixteenth century and ever since the periphery has been condemned to be a periphery and the core to be a core. Recent BRIC paths invalidate this theory. Paradoxically, globality is found again in a universal path, or even in a universal, pre-existing form of economic rationality. It is not by chance that some variants of the Great Divergence thesis combine Wallersteinian and neo-Marxist approaches: profit maximisation, exploitation and domination explain the 'divergence'.

The problem is that historical comparison is based on 'schemes', if not rigid 'models', derived from philosophy, political economy, sociology, political sciences and anthropology. Comparisons are therefore often tautological because most of the social sciences are not only Eurocentric but also normative fields: they not only ask questions, they also pretend to give answers which fit the model and, where possible, they aim at predicting the future (economics constantly does so) while providing suggestions to the public sphere. Once the social sciences become normative, their use of history produces tautological schemes. And when normativity is combined with Eurocentric (and, recently, Sinocentric, Indocentric and Afrocentric) values and categories, then we are locked in historical 'centric' determinism and comparison is bound to fail.

However, there is no need to fall into this trap and we can still make comparisons which are neither deterministic nor 'centric'. These two moves are interrelated. On the one hand, schemes may provide a heuristic, helping to pose questions instead of providing ready answers. If the answers do not fit the model, in particular in history, this means that historical research has genuinely contributed to our understanding of the world. This is the first contribution global history can make to the social sciences through comparatism: it can transform the normative into the heuristic.

On the other hand, much more than history, the social sciences are extremely 'centric' (in this case, mostly Eurocentric), even if nowadays attempts are made to decentralise the social sciences by basing them on presumed 'Chinese',

'Islamic', 'African' or 'Indian' categories. Thus, global historians must dare not just to 'historicise' the social sciences (as Marx, Weber and many others already argued), but to historicise them into a global perspective. Despite some recent attempts, a 'global history' of political economy, sociology, anthropology, linguistics, legal studies and so forth, that is not conceived as a series of chapters on, say, economics in India, in Japan, African sociology and the like, has yet to be written. In short, problematising the so-called 'specificity' of an area instead of taking it for granted, while mobilising the decentred social sciences, is the main goal of a heuristic and not normative comparatism in global history.

3   Time
Temporality in Global History

Christina Brauner

Time, it has been argued, is the 'last fetish' of the historians' tribe.[1] If this is true, global history has played, and continues to play, a peculiar role in that cult, at the same time acting as a devout believer and a fervent iconoclast. This ambivalence is connected to the diverse and divergent approaches assembled under the flag of 'global history'. Global historians' struggle with temporality points to problems of historical scholarship more broadly but also opens up possibilities for rethinking the discipline.

The Time of Global History

Time takes a central yet ambiguous role in the discourse of global history, as its definition demonstrates: global history, or so we are told, is the history our global and globalised present requires. It is, above all, required to explain the genesis of this global present, by studying historical globalisation processes or exploring the genealogy of growing connections. But global history's claim to timeliness also operates on methodological levels: here, the reference to the global present serves to call for viewpoints beyond the national restraints of traditional historiography.[2]

As this rhetoric of timeliness shows, global history is situated within the discourse of globalisation.[3] This does not mean that global history can only be written as a history of globalisation; on the contrary, a growing number of

---

[1] Chris Lorenz, 'Der letzte Fetisch des Stamms der Historiker. Zeit, Raum und Periodisierung in der Geschichtswissenschaft', in Fernando Esposito (ed.), *Zeitenwandel. Transformationen geschichtlicher Zeitlichkeit nach dem Boom* (Göttingen: Vandenhoeck & Ruprecht, 2017), 63–91; for an abridged translation see Chris Lorenz, '"The Times They Are a-Changin": On Time, Space and Periodization in History', in Mario Carretero et al. (eds.), *Palgrave Handbook of Research in Historical Culture and Education* (London: Palgrave Macmilan, 2017), 109–31.

[2] Cf. Bruce Mazlish, 'An Introduction to Global History', in Bruce Mazlish and Ralph Buultjen (eds.), *Conceptualizing Global History* (Boulder: Westview Press, 1993), 1–24, here 1–2. For a structurally similar yet far more nuanced argument see Sebastian Conrad, *What Is Global History?* (Princeton: Princeton University Press, 2016), 1–3.

[3] For a critical reflection, cf. Jürgen Osterhammel, 'Von einem hohen Turm? Weltgeschichte und Gegenwartsdiagnose', in Jürgen Osterhammel, *Die Flughöhe der Adler: Historische Essays zur*

global historians have set out to criticise this paradigm of globalisation. Yet the connection to the discourse remains present, even if in the form of critique.[4]

Evoking present-day concerns to frame and legitimise historical studies in general, or certain research agendas in particular, is, of course, not peculiar to global history. Some may call such references 'presentist' and mean this as a reproach. From an epistemological perspective, though, all history is and must be presentist, as the viewpoint historians think and write from is necessarily located in the present.[5] However, when globalisation theorists claim an unprecedented novelty of the global present, a more specific understanding of presentism is at play. It assumes a fundamental rupture between past and present, just as it is central to François Hartog's definition of presentism as the 'regime of historicity' which governs our order of time today.[6] In global history, such presentist reasonings lead to an uneasy co-existence with the discipline's quest for historicisation, seeking to trace and explain the genesis of globalisation processes. With regard to the identity of the field, too, there are tensions between claims to novelty and the quest for venerable ancestors and 'pedigree'.[7] While such discussions concern the beginnings of global history both as subject matter and scholarly field, the contours of the global present itself, too, are far from clear: When does it begin? And what kind of future does a global present have?[8]

globalen Gegenwart (Munich: C.H. Beck, 2017), 203; Jürgen Osterhammel and Stefanie Gänger, 'Denkpause für Globalgeschichte', *Merkur* 855 (2020), 79–86, here 79.

[4] Cf., for example, Frederick Cooper, 'Globalization', in Frederick Cooper (ed.), *Colonialism in Question: Theory, Knowledge, History* (Berkeley: University of California Press, 2005), 91–112, here 93; Geoff Eley, 'Historicizing the Global, Politicizing Capital: Giving the Present a Name', *History Workshop Journal* 63, 1 (2007), 154–88, here 158; Jürgen Osterhammel, 'Globalizations', in Jerry H. Bentley (ed.), *The Oxford Handbook of World History* (Oxford: Oxford University Press, 2011), 89–104, here 92. On globalisation critique, see Olaf Bach, *Die Erfindung der Globalisierung: Entstehung und Wandel eines zeitgeschichtlichen Grundbegriffs* (Frankfurt am Main: Campus, 2013), 191–8.

[5] Ethan Kleinberg, 'Hiding (from the Present) in the Past', *History of the Present* 13, 2 (2023), 265–74; Cf. David Armitage, 'In Defense of Presentism', in Darrin M. McMahon (ed.), *History and Human Flourishing* (Oxford: Oxford University Press, 2023), 59–84; Marcus Colla, 'The Spectre of the Present: Time, Presentism and the Writing of Contemporary History', *Contemporary European History* 30, 1 (2021), 124–35.

[6] François Hartog, *Régimes d'historicité: Présentisme et expériences du temps*, expanded ed. (Paris: Éditions du Seuil, 2012), 13, 16–17. English translation: *Regimes of historicity. Presentism and experiences of time*, transl. by Saskia Brown (New York: Columbia University Press, 2015), 17f.

[7] For an exchange about this, see Richard Drayton and David Motadel, 'Discussion: The Futures of Global History', *Journal of Global History* 13, 1 (2018), 1–21, here 20–1. This resonates with the contradictory temporality of globalisation discourse itself, characterised both by historicist and ahistoricist tendencies; see Olaf Bach, 'Ein Ende der Geschichte? Entstehung, Strukturveränderungen und die Temporalität der Globalisierungssemantik seit dem Zweiten Weltkrieg', *Vierteljahrshefte für Zeitgeschichte* 68, 1 (2020), 128–54, here 151–4.

[8] Kalle Pihlainen, 'Historians and "the Current Situation"', *Rethinking History* 20, 2 (2016), 143–53; Dipesh Chakrabarty, 'Where is the Now?', *Critical Inquiry* 30, 2 (2004), 458–62. See also the editors' introduction to this volume.

Still, the global present has a peculiar temporal identity: it is a present that claims to have become, finally and fully, a time of contemporaries.[9] This claim is, above all, buttressed by allusions to an unprecedented experience of synchronicity – or at least the possibility of such experience – which is very much at the heart of globalisation definitions.[10] Hartmut Rosa, for instance, discusses globalisation as 'time-space compression' and characterises it 'temporally' as the 'dissolution of stable rhythms and sequences following the ubiquitous contemporisation (*Vergleichzeitigung*) of even the noncontemporaneous'.[11]

Indeed, when global historians refer to 'our present', they equally presuppose an all-encompassing yet somewhat fuzzy community of experience. Moreover, synchronising approaches to the past have become a signature practice of global history. They serve not only to transcend traditional divides and seek out connections otherwise invisible but have also been championed as an antidote to lingering 'centrisms' of various kinds. Both on a historical and a historiographical plane, however, the effects of synchronisation remain ambiguous: Does it lead to the emergence of a homogenous time regime, or rather reinforce or even foster a plurality of times?[12] And what is, after all, the 'noncontemporaneous' that is, in Rosa's wording, 'contemporised' in a globalising world?

Obviously, global history has its time. Reflecting on the consequences this entails for the practice of global historians leads to more general questions about temporality and historicity. It prompts us to consider the 'politics of time' or 'chronopolitics' inherent in our own scholarly practices and the institutional settings we inhabit.[13]

This chapter discusses how questions of time and temporality shape and challenge historical studies in general and global history in particular. Firstly, the chapter shows why time can be understood as history's 'last fetish', as Chris

---

[9] Cf. Peter Osborne, 'The Fiction of the Contemporary', in Peter Osborne (ed.), *In Anywhere or Not at All: Philosophy of Contemporary Art* (London: Verso, 2013), 15–36.

[10] For an overview see Paul Huebener et al., 'Exploring the Intersection of Time and Globalization', *Globalizations* 13, 3 (2016), 243–55; Lynn Hunt, 'Globalization and Time', in Berber Bevernage and Chris Lorenz (eds.), *Breaking up Time: Negotiating the Borders between Present, Past, and Future* (Göttingen: Vandenhoeck & Ruprecht, 2013), 199–215, here 201–3; Lynn Hunt, *Measuring Time, Making History* (Budapest: Central European University Press, 2008), 75–80.

[11] Hartmut Rosa, *Social Acceleration. A New Theory of Modernity* (New York: Columbia University Press, 2013, 217, with a list of diverse 'forms of contemporisation' (219–20).

[12] For the plural temporalities emerging from attempts at synchronisation, see Vanessa Ogle, *The Global Transformation of Time, 1870–1950* (Cambridge, MA: Harvard University Press, 2015).

[13] For an often-quoted definition, see Charles S. Maier, 'The Politics of Time. Changing Paradigms of Collective Time and Private Time in the Modern Era', in Charles S. Maier (ed.), *Changing Boundaries of the Political. Essays on the Evolving Balance between the State and Society, Public and Private in Europe* (Cambridge: Cambridge University Press, 1987), 151–78, here 151–3. Recently, it served as a starting point for Christopher Clark's 'time-history' of German regimes: Christopher Clark, *Time and Power. Visions of History in German Politics, from the Thirty Years' War to the Third Reich* (Princeton: Princeton University Press, 2019), 14–15. See also Fernando Esposito and Tobias Becker, 'The Time of Politics, the Politics of Time, and Politicized Time: An Introduction to Chronopolitics', *History and Theory* 62 (2023), 3–23.

Lorenz has phrased it, and how this makes itself known among global historians. The chapter moves on to consider the politics of periodisation as a particular challenge for decentring history, taking up the debate about the 'Global Middle Ages' as an example. Finally, it turns to synchronisation and contemporaneity as important concerns in global history, containing a promise and a problem at the same time.

The 'Fetish' of Time and the Pursuit of Global History

There is no history without time. Still, time has long been something of a 'blind spot' within the field.[14] It takes a double role, featuring as the seemingly empty and transparent *medium* in which 'history unfolds' and as the *product and means* of historical narrative and representation. Recently, in the wake of what has eagerly been hailed as the 'temporal turn', time increasingly appears as a specific *subject* of study.[15] Given this multiplicity of roles, it is important to distinguish between analytical and historical notions of time and temporality or – taking up a distinction from anthropology – the perspective of the scholarly observer (etic) and those of the actors involved in the field observed (emic).

Following Lorenz's diagnosis, historical scholarship even suffers from 'chronocentrism', with temporal units, markers and divisions as its arguably most important denominators. This chronocentrism is perhaps most evident in the guise of periodisation, in terms of both historiographical operation and institutional structure.[16] For global historians, periodisation presents a particular challenge. Thomas Bauer, a scholar of Islamic history and Arabic literature, has nailed this with perfection when he begins his essay *Warum es kein islamisches Mittelalter gab* ('Why there were no Islamic Middle Ages') as follows:

Compare the following two sentences:
    'Charlemagne was an important European ruler of the Tang period.'
    'Hārūn ar-Rašīd was an important Near Eastern ruler of the Middle Ages.'[17]

The two sentences perform periodisation as a standard historiographical procedure, classifying historical phenomena in an apparently meaningful way

---

[14] Lorenz, 'Der letzte Fetisch', 64–5. Famous exceptions are, of course, Reinhart Koselleck and Fernand Braudel.

[15] For an overview, see, for example, Matthew S. Champion, 'The History of Temporalities. An Introduction', *Past & Present* 243, 1 (2019), 247–54.

[16] See Kathleen Davis, *Periodization and Sovereignty. How Ideas of Feudalism and Secularization Govern the Politics of Time* (Philadelphia: University of Pennsylvania Press, 2008).

[17] Thomas Bauer, *Warum es kein islamisches Mittelalter gab: Das Erbe der Antike und der Orient*, 2nd ed. (Munich: C. H. Beck, 2019), 11 (my translation). On periodisation of Islamic history, see also Konrad Hirschler and Sarah Bowen Savant, 'Introduction: What Is in a Period? Arabic Historiography and Periodization', *Der Islam* 91, 1 (2014), 6–19.

by assigning them to certain conventional units of time. The periodisation schemes they allude to – the European tripartite model of Antiquity–Middle Ages–Modernity and the Chinese dynasty–based model – are both part and parcel of specific historiographical traditions.[18] The European model, however, has managed to gain currency well beyond the context from which it originated: even if its specific usage can be shaped by very different concerns (as we shall see), its proliferation is nonetheless tied to a long history of Western hegemony and colonisation. Perhaps it is when both sentences begin to ring similarly strange or familiar that global history has achieved some success.

Striving to evade Eurocentric and other universalising periodisation schemes, some scholars have turned to chronology for an alternative and seemingly 'neutral' order of things.[19] Take, for example, the 'national global histories' that have recently been published in various European countries. In the *Histoire mondiale de la France* (2017), which set the model for the whole genre, chronology is chosen as an antidote against the 'illusory continuities of traditional narrative'. The volume thus abstains from any overarching narrative but presents the reader with a multitude of chapters or 'fragments' all linked to one specific year and arranged in strict chronological order.[20]

Yet such an order is neither neutral nor given. Every chronology presupposes the choice of a particular calendar. It is a choice we rarely think about in everyday life – indeed, such routinised phenomena are the often nearly invisible yet perhaps most pervasive effects of a politics of time. Moreover, chronology can also shape what is perceived as 'history' as such: by privileging 'events' over processes and the longue durée, it presents history as a sequence of distinct temporal units.[21] It is such an equation of 'historical' and 'chronological time' that Lorenz has identified as one of history's chronocentric 'idols'.[22]

A chronological framework, though, can also provide a starting point for more nuanced approaches to historical temporalities. So, even within the strict sequential order of the *Histoire Mondiale de la France*, the practitioner may question the very unity of historical time. Exploring the hoard of Ruscino, historian and archaeologist François-Xavier Fauvelle, for instance, prompts his

---

[18] On the Middle Ages and the European model, see n. 44; on dynastic periodisation in Chinese historiography, see Richard van Glahn, 'Imagining Pre-modern China', in Richard van Glahn and Paul J. Smith (eds.), *The Song-Yuan-Ming Transition in Chinese History* (Cambridge, MA: Harvard University Asia Center, 2003), 35–70.

[19] Patrick Boucheron et al., *France in the World: A New Global History*, trans. Teresa Lavender Fagan et al. (London: Gallic Books, 2021), 7–15, here 9.

[20] Boucheron, 'Ouverture', 14–15, commenting on the potential neglect of the *longue durée*.

[21] Cf. Gavin Lucas, 'Archaeology and Contemporaneity', *Archaeological Dialogues* 22, 1 (2015), 1–15, esp. 3–7; see also William M. Reddy, 'The Eurasian Origins of Empty Time and Space. Modernity as Temporality Reconsidered', *History and Theory* 55, 3 (2016), 325–56.

[22] Lorenz, 'Der letzte Fetisch', 90–1.

readers to think not only about the presence of the past and the limits of our present knowledge, but also about past futures of the early-eighth-century Mediterranean world. Fauvelle sets the scene by directly addressing his reader:

Imagine yourself there. . . . The place you are standing is called Ruscino. . . . You live there amid familiar ruins. As soon as the alert is sounded, you hide your tools . . . Neither historians nor archaeologists know who you are nor what you did there. . . . You're living in the provinces, but in a province that is no longer the province of anything. You are living in the outskirts of Perpignan, but you don't know that because Perpignan does not yet exist.

His essay thus also shows how literary strategies – rather than theoretical reflection – can be used to make visible historical contingencies and different temporalities.[23]

Others have rediscovered chronology itself as a possible way to move *beyond* 'historical time'. Discussing the challenges the Anthropocene poses to concepts of time and history, Helge Jordheim suggests that chronology could serve to integrate timescales beyond those of human and social life. It allowed us to relate historical time to geological temporalities but also to the life cycles of microbes and viruses. To serve such a critical aim, chronology must not be taken as a given temporal order but a knowledge practice in itself – which is, as Jordheim highlights, indeed a return to a pre-modern understanding.[24]

The most pervasive 'blind spot' in historians' relation to time is perhaps the temporalising work they themselves perform, especially in drawing a line between past and present.[25] This line is constitutive for the very field of historiography. It is also part of a specific temporal regime, namely that of modern historicity. Here, with the dissociation of experience and expectations, history has first emerged as the collective singular of a unified past and the present became oriented towards an open and malleable future.

Historicising historicity, this specific constellation of temporal relations, has become a major concern in recent years, with Reinhart Koselleck's work leading the way. With his analysis of historicity as a specific temporal regime emerging in the so-called *Sattelzeit* ('saddle period'), Koselleck has made a decisive and unmatched contribution to denaturalising history itself. His role in inspiring critical reflection on questions of temporality and the regime of historicity – also

---

[23] François-Xavier Fauvelle, '719. L'Afrique frappe à la porte du pays des Francs', in Boucheron et al., *Histoire mondiale de la France*, 124–9; for the English translation: '719. Africa knocks on the Franks' Door' in Boucheron et al., *France in the World*, 87–92, quote at 87f.

[24] Helge Jordheim, 'Return to Chronology', in Marek Tamm and Laurent Olivier (eds.), *Rethinking Historical Time: New Approaches to Presentism* (London: Bloomsbury Academic, 2019), 43–56.

[25] See Berber Bevernage and Chris Lorenz, 'Breaking up Time. Negotiating the Borders between Present, Past, and Future – Introduction', in Bevernage and Lorenz, *Breaking up Time*, 7–35, esp. 22–6.

far beyond the narrow field of historiography – can hardly be overestimated and, indeed, continues to grow.[26] At the same time, Koselleck has also left us with a substantial notion of modernity, maybe even with the last and possibly most refined refuge of such an understanding.[27] As Lynn Hunt has put it: 'If modernity exists – and I still want to admit some doubts on this score – then it is at least in large measure a category having to do with the experience of time.'[28]

Approaching modernity through the lens of temporality and historicity provides a sophisticated and reflexive understanding. Still, as with all attempts at conceptualising modernity, it is inextricably tied to the 'pre-modern', situated before and/or outside of European modernity. This 'pre-modern' remains cast in terms of 'deficit', measured against the yardstick of modern historicity: it has no open future, no sense of the difference of the past as past. Hence, the temporal understanding of modernity, too, can be read as a – even if sophisticated – reproduction of an old binary, contrasting the history of the West with its pre-modern Other.

In response, an interdisciplinary critique has emerged, ranging from postcolonial studies and global history to medieval studies.[29] In terms of historical critique, this has led to explorations of temporalities outside of modern Europe, adding historical depth and differentiation to a debate long centred on the *Sattelzeit* and its aftermath.[30] This helps to make visible conflicting temporal

---

[26] The growing attention is also due to recent translations of his work: see Reinhart Koselleck, *Futures Past: On the Semantics of Historical Time*, transl. Keith Tribe (Columbia University Press: New York, 2004); Reinhart Koselleck, *Sediments of Time. On Possible Histories*, transl. and ed. by Sean Franzel and Stefan-Ludwig Hoffmann (Stanford: Stanford University Press, 2018). Cf. Niklas Olsen, *History in the Plural: An Introduction to the Work of Reinhart Koselleck* (New York: Berghahn Books, 2012), esp. 217–31, and Helge Jordheim, 'Against Periodization. Koselleck's Theory of Multiple Temporalities', *History & Theory* 51, 2 (2012), 151–71.

[27] For an account of the *Sattelzeit* (*c*.1750–1850) as the period of transition to modernity and the need to historicise history, see Reinhart Koselleck, 'On the Need for Theory in the Discipline of History' in Koselleck, *The Practice of Conceptual History: Timing History, Spacing Concepts*, transl. by Todd Samuel Presner et al. (Stanford: Stanford University Press, 2002), 1–20, with a strong emphasis on the heuristic character of the period concept (5).

[28] Hunt, *Measuring Time*, 75; see also Lorenz, 'Der letzte Fetisch', 75–80, 91, and Allegra Fryxell, 'Time and the Modern: Current Trends in The History of Modern Temporalities', *Past & Present* 243, 1 (2019), 285–98.

[29] Cf. Dipesh Chakrabarty, *Provincializing Europe: Postcolonial Thought and Historical Difference* (Princeton: Princeton University Press, 2000), esp. ch. 1; Davis, *Periodization and Sovereignty*, ch. 3, esp. 87–95; Prathama Banerjee, 'Time and the Limits of the Political: Anti-Historical Excursions from South Asia', *2nd Berlin Southern Theory Lecture* (Berlin: FU Berlin / ZMO Berlin, 2020), www.zmo.de/fileadmin/Inhalte/Publikationen/Berlin_Southern_Theory_Lecture/bstl_2_banerjee_2020_1.pdf. See also Theo Jung, 'Das Neue der Neuzeit ist ihre Zeit: Reinhart Kosellecks Theorie der Verzeitlichung und ihre Kritiker', *Moderne. Kulturwissenschaftliches Jahrbuch* 6 (2010/2011), 172–84.

[30] See, for example, Matthew Champion, *The Fullness of Time. Temporalities of the Fifteenth-Century Low Countries* (Chicago: The University of Chicago Press, 2017), esp. 7–12 for taking issue with Koselleck's understanding of medieval temporality. Medievalist critique has, in particular, focused on the problem of futures and futurity: Klaus Oschema and Bernd Schneidmüller eds., *Zukunft im Mittelalter: Zeitkonzepte und Planungsstrategien* (Ostfildern:

orders and, indeed, chronopolitics in what is much too often understood in terms of a given 'culture'.[31] Sometimes, though, this historical critique seems to falls prey to a certain precursorism: tracing the emergence of open futures and 'historical consciousness' ever further back in time, for instance, retains and, in fact, reinforces the basic tenets of 'modernity-as-temporality'.[32] Lately, critics have taken issue with the presumed domination of historicity itself, pointing to alternative and conflicting temporalities within European modernity.[33] Moreover, criticising historicity has also brought forth conceptual reflections on the inherent Eurocentrism of history as a discipline rooted in such an understanding – indeed, the very venture of historicising history presents a paradox in itself.[34] Here, the full power of the 'fetish' plays out: historicising historicity has the paradoxical effect of simultaneously questioning and perpetuating the historically bound understanding of history as a discipline. Global history, perhaps more than many other fields, needs to engage the practical consequences of this paradox.

The Politics of Periodisation and the Case of the 'Global Middle Ages'

Many historians happily leave conceptual debates and reflections about the discipline's epistemological foundations to those specialising in the philosophy and theory of history and the pages of respective journals such as *History & Theory* or *Rethinking History*. The problem of time and temporality, though, is particularly apt to demonstrate how allegedly 'theoretical' questions concern the everyday work of historians. To do so, this section focuses on a practice that is, at the same time, a banal operation and a highly political business: periodisation.[35] For global historians, periodisation presents a particularly

Thorbecke, 2021); Felicitas Schmieder ed., *Mittelalterliche Zukunftsgestaltung im Angesicht des Weltendes/Forming the Future Facing the End of the World in the Middle Ages* (Cologne: Böhlau, 2015).

[31] See, for example, Kathleen Davis and Michael Puett, 'Periodization and the 'Medieval Globe': A Conversation', *The Medieval Globe* 2, 1 (2015), 1–14, esp. 8–12; Davis, *Periodization and Sovereignty*, 16–17, 88–95.

[32] Cooper's thought-provoking critique of 'multiple modernities' comes to mind here; Frederick Cooper, 'Modernity', in Cooper, *Colonialism in Question*, 113–49, here 133. Cf. Dipesh Chakrabarty, 'The Muddle of Modernity', *American Historical Review* 116, 3 (2011), 663–75.

[33] Cf. Fryxell, 'Time and the Modern'.

[34] Cf. Fernando Esposito, 'The Two Ends of History and Historical Temporality as a Threatened Order', in Ewald Frie et al. (eds.), *Dynamics of Social Change and Perceptions of Threat* (Tübingen: Mohr Siebeck, 2018), 221–39, esp. 232–9.

[35] As Chakrabarty has phrased it: 'The periodizing instinct and the political instinct are deeply connected'; Chakrabarty, 'Where Is the Now', 459. See, for example, Jacques Le Goff, *Faut-il vraiment découper l'histoire en tranches?* (Paris: Éditions du Seuil, 2014); Eric Hayot, 'Against Periodization; Or, On Institutional Time', *New Literary History* 42, 4 (2011), 739–56; Jürgen

acute challenge. As one of the most prominent manifestations of universalising Eurocentrism, it is central to all attempts at decentring historical studies. It is not only tied to the interplay of appropriation and critique, but also leads to wide-ranging questions about institutional and conceptual change.[36]

The notion of a 'Global Middle Ages' has enjoyed a remarkably dynamic career since the 2010s: journals and handbooks advocate the study of 'medieval worlds' and 'The Medieval Globe', central conventions of medievalists have prominently debated 'the Global Middle Ages' and first jobs in the field have been advertised.[37] This career has come somewhat unexpectedly. Indeed, the wording 'Global Middle Ages' itself presents – once more – a kind of paradox.[38] As mentioned earlier, the 'Middle Ages' are part and parcel of a traditional European periodisation scheme that has been exported to the world. For this reason, the term has been heavily criticised by postcolonial scholarship and historians of the non-European world. Such critique is exacerbated by the fact that 'medieval' functions not only as a geographically but also as a temporally 'mobile category' around the globe: used as a signifier for 'backwardness', the 'medieval' plays a principal role in the temporalisation of difference.[39] Equally, historians of Europe themselves have long, and strongly, criticised the concept.[40]

So why does the 'Middle Ages' enjoy such a career precisely in the field of global history? While definitions have often remained vague, the 'Global Middle Ages' serves a clearly designated function: it was designed as an

---

Osterhammel, 'Über die Periodisierung der neueren Geschichte', *Berlin-Brandenburgische Akademie der Wissenschaften, Berichte und Abhandlungen* 10 (2006), 45–64.

[36] See, for example, Jerry H. Bentley, 'Cross-Cultural Interaction and Periodization in World History', *American Historical Review* 101, 3 (1996), 749–70; Kenneth Pomeranz, 'Teleology, Discontinuity and World History. Periodization and Some Creation Myths of Modernity', *Asian Review of World Histories* 1, 2 (2013), 189–226; Thomas Maissen et al. (eds.), *Chronologics: Periodisation in a Global Context*, 9 October 2018, https://chronolog.hypotheses.org/.

[37] Cf. Geraldine Heng, *The Global Middle Ages: An Introduction* (Cambridge: Cambridge University Press, 2021); Catherine Holmes and Naomi Standen, 'Defining the Global Middle Ages (AHRC Research Network AH/K001914/1, 2013-15)', *Medieval Worlds* 1 (2015), 106–17. For a recent overview and comment, see Roy Flechner, 'Review Article: How Far is Global?', *Medieval Worlds* 12 (2020), 255–66, and Christina Brauner, 'Das "globale Mittelalter" und die Gegenwart der Geschichtswissenschaft', *traverse* 28, 2 (2022), 41–62.

[38] Uhlig speaks of an 'anachronistic, even oxymoronic character'; Marion Uhlig, 'Quand "Postcolonial" et "Global" riment avec "Médiéval"': Sur quelques approches théoriques anglo-saxonnes', *Perspectives médiévales* 35 (2014), https://doi.org/10.4000/peme.4400, sect. 2. See also Kim M. Phillips, 'Travel, Writing, and the Global Middle Ages', *History Compass* 14, 3 (2016), 81–92, here 87.

[39] See, for example, Davis, *Periodization and Sovereignty*; Carol Symes, 'When We Talk about Modernity', *American Historical Review* 116, 3 (2011), 715–26.

[40] Cf. C. Warren Hollister, 'The Phases of European History and the Nonexistence of the Middle Ages', *Pacific Historical Review* 61, 1 (1992), 1–22; Timothy Reuter, 'Medieval: Another Tyrannous Construct?', *The Medieval History Journal* 1, 1 (1998), 25–45; Bernhard Jussen, 'Richtig denken im falschen Rahmen? Warum das "Mittelalter" nicht in den Lehrplan gehört', *Geschichte in Wissenschaft und Unterricht* 67, 9–10 (2016), 558–76.

instrument of critique – directed against traditional notions of the 'medieval' and its 'Eurocentric straight jacket'.[41]Overall, this aims at a more inclusive understanding of the past.[42] Some of the most prominent champions propose a programmatic understanding of the 'Global Middle Ages' as a venture to decolonise medieval studies.[43]

Roughly and conventionally located between 500 and 1500, the 'Global Middle Ages' provides a heuristic framework that allows scholars to bring together coeval phenomena and processes formerly treated separately, to seek out unusual comparisons and to discover unknown or neglected connections. It resonates with a preference for a seemingly neutral chronological order, as outlined earlier, and points to the important role attributed to synchronicity in global history.

There are, however, also a few attempts to build a period concept with a specific period identity. Naomi Standen and Catherine Holmes, for example, who in 2012 initiated the interdisciplinary network 'Towards a Global Middle Ages', advocate such a 'strong' concept. They define the 'Global Middle Ages' as 'a period of human history with distinctive characteristics; and as a powerful concept to "think with"', set apart from a more amorphous global 'pre-modernity'. So far, Holmes and Standen propose to understand it as a phase of 'dynamic change and experiment when no single part of the world achieved hegemonic status', as a 'time of options and experiments'.[44] While such an understanding would certainly counter traditional narratives of both the Middle Ages and Western domination in globalisation processes, the specificity of the suggested characteristics remains controversial. Indeed, many global historians are sceptical about any kind of 'strong' periodisation schemes operating on a global scale and claiming universal validity.[45]

Whether one subscribes to 'strong periodisation' or not, Holmes and Standen's proposal clearly shows that thinking about the 'Middle Ages' in a global perspective also carries critical potential for global history, its periodisation and the

---

[41] Peter Frankopan, 'Why We Need to Think About the Global Middle Ages', *Journal of Medieval Worlds* 1, 1 (2019), 5–10, here 9.

[42] Bryan C. Keene, 'Introduction: Manuscripts and Their Outlook on the World', in Bryan C. Keene (ed.), *Toward a Global Middle Ages: Encountering the World through Illuminated Manuscripts* (Los Angeles: The J. Paul Getty Museum, 2019), 5–34, here 8; see also Walter Pohl and Andre Gingrich, 'Medieval Worlds: Introduction to the First Issue', *Medieval Worlds* 1 (2015), 2–4, here 2.

[43] Heng, *Global Middle Ages*; Geraldine Heng, 'Early Globalities, and Its Questions, Objectives, and Methods: An Inquiry into the State of Theory and Critique', *Exemplaria* 26, 2–3 (2014), 234–53; Sierra Lomuto, 'Becoming Postmedieval: The Stakes of the Global Middle Ages', *postmedieval: A Journal of Medieval Cultural Studies* 11, 4 (2020), 503–12.

[44] Catherine Holmes and Naomi Standen, 'Introduction', in Catherine Holmes and Naomi Standen (eds.), *The Global Middle Ages* (Oxford: Oxford University Press, 2018), 1–41, here 2–3, 6; cf. Naomi Standen, 'Colouring outside the Lines. Methods for a Global History of Eastern Eurasia, 600-1350', *Transactions of the Royal Historical Society* 29 (2019), 27–63.

[45] Pohl and Gingrich, 'Medieval Worlds', 2; Osterhammel, 'Über die Periodisierung'.

definition of the 'global' itself. Indeed, no matter which terminology is chosen, every discussion of medieval history – or, for that matter, of any other 'pre-modern' period – from such a perspective has to engage with the temporality inherent in global history, just as it needs to engage with the inextricable connection between global history and the discourse of globalisation: Is there such a thing as 'globalisation' in a pre-modern world? Can the 'Middle Ages' actually be global? And, if so, what does 'global' mean in this context?

Such questions concern issues controversial within global history at large, and medievalists have approached them in various ways. Some stress the limited and fragmentary character of medieval connections, as judged against current models of globalisation and global modernity. Against this backdrop, Michael Borgolte, a pioneer of global medieval history in Germany, has argued in favour of an 'Eurafrasian era' in place of the 'Global Middle Ages'.[46] While such an approach clearly sets global history apart from the history of globalisation, it still operates within the framework of globalisation narratives. According to its logic, a truly 'global period' only becomes possible with the beginning of globalisation. Indeed, the emerging periodisation scheme itself visualises the process of spatio-temporal integration.[47] Other scholars have called for a thorough and critical engagement with such a notion, aiming at a historicisation of globality.[48] Such pleas resonate with current critical reflections on 'globalism' from within the social sciences and contemporary history, drawing attention to its inherent teleology and hegemonic bias.[49] Studying 'globalities' in the *longue durée* may help to foster reflection on the remnants of modernisation theory in the discourse of globalisation and, once more, on the embeddedness of global history in this discourse.[50]

[46] Michael Borgolte, 'Sprechen wir doch einfach vom eurafrasischen Zeitalter', *Frankfurter Allgemeine Zeitung*, 29 August 2018, 11. and his opus magnum: *Die Welten des Mittelalters. Globalgeschichte eines Jahrtausends* (München: C.H. Beck, 2022), here 13–31. In his view, medievalists study 'transcultural entanglements' in contrast to 'globalisation' as a twentieth-century phenomenon; see Michael Borgolte, 'Mittelalter in der größeren Welt: Mediävistik als globale Geschichte', in Michael Borgolte, *Mittelalter in der größeren Welt. Essays zur Geschichtsschreibung und Beiträge zur Forschung*, ed. Tillmann Lohse and Benjamin Scheller (Berlin: De Gruyter: 2014), 533–46, esp. 536–38.

[47] Cf. Christian Grataloup, 'Les Périodes sont des régions du Monde', *ATALA Cultures et sciences humaines* 17 (2014) [special issue 'Découper le temps: Actualité de la périodisation en histoire'], 65–1.

[48] For example, Amanda Power and Caroline Dodds Pennock, 'Globalizing Cosmologies', *Past and Present* 238, Supplement 13 (2018), 88–115, esp. 90–4; Alicia Walker, 'Globalism', *Studies in Iconography* 33 (2012) [special issue 'Medieval Art History Today – Critical Terms'], 183–96, esp. 185–7.

[49] See, for example, Tim Ingold, 'Globes and Spheres: The Topology of Environmentalism', in Tim Ingold, *The Perception of the Environment: Essays on Livelihood, Dwelling and Skill* (London: Routledge, 2000), 209–18, here 210–11; Simon Ferdinand et al. (eds.), *Other Globes: Past and Peripheral Imaginations of Globalization* (Cham: Palgrave Macmillan, 2019).

[50] Cf. Wolfgang Knöbl, 'After Modernization: Der Globalisierungsbegriff als Platzhalter und Rettungsanker der Sozialwissenschaften', *Vierteljahrshefte für Zeitgeschichte* 68, 2 (2020), 297–317; Urs Stäheli, 'The Outside of the Global', *The New Centennial Review* 3, 2 (2003), 1–22.

No matter what definition of the global and the medieval they propose, all protagonists of the debate share the belief that global perspectives can serve as a critique of the 'Middle Ages' as we know it. The 'Global Middle Ages' act as a successful formula for this critique, although (or perhaps because) it pinpoints the paradox this venture entails. Indeed, scholars have reflected upon this in different ways: While some stress the provisional and, finally, transitory status of the 'Global Middle Ages' – for want of a better term – others frame the paradox as a strategy of deconstruction. Geraldine Heng, prominent champion of the 'Global Middle Ages' as a decolonising project, seeks to employ the notion of the Global Middle Ages to upturn 'old tyrannies of periodisation in the West' from within. To do so, she draws on the 'asynchrony of global temporalities'. To establish this asynchrony, she relies on modernity as a yardstick, defined, though, as a recurrent 'transhistorical phenomenon', as 'repetition-with-difference'. Heng uses this to identify 'modernities' across the medieval globe *before* their European manifestations. Pointing, for instance, to industrialised mass production and printing technology in China, she integrates Chinese history into the framework of medieval history and establishes its comparative 'advance' over Europe.[51] This certainly helps to unsettle both long-standing narratives about the 'West and the Rest' and institutional divisions within academia. Yet, the 'muddle of modernity' remains: can a 'transhistorical' concept of 'modernity' help us to do away with the dichotomy of the medieval and the modern? For instance, if we search for industrial revolutions *avant la lettre*, doesn't this reinforce European developments as a blueprint and yardstick of global synchronicity? In short: where does 'breaking' a concept 'from within' lead?[52]

Such questions point to more general discussions within postcolonial studies about subversion, appropriation and change.[53] To explore the longer history of these discussions, let us briefly consider how the concept of the 'Middle Ages' has been employed to claim a place *within* history. In Indian and African historiography, for instance, it has been introduced by some to break with periodisation schemes structured around the pre-colonial/colonial divide.[54]

---

[51] Heng, 'Early Globalities', 235–8; see also Heng, *Global Middle Ages*, 20–1.
[52] For a related critique cf. Chakrabarty, 'The Muddle of Modernity'.
[53] For an early discussion see Anne McClintock, 'The Angel of Progress: Pitfalls of the Term Post-Colonialism', *Social Text* 31–2 (1992), 84–98; and the response by Stuart Hall, 'When was "the Post-Colonial"? Thinking at the Limit', in Iain Chambers and Lidia Curti (eds.), *The Postcolonial Question. Common Skies, Divided Horizons* (London: Routledge, 1995), 242–60. Cf. also Russell West-Pavlov, *Temporalities* (London: Routledge, 2013), 165–6; Gabriela De Lima Grecco and Sven Schuster, 'Decolonizing Global History? A Latin American Perspective', *Journal of World History* 31, 2 (2020), 425–46, here 442–3.
[54] See also Brajadulal Chattopadhyaya, *The Making of Early Medieval India* (Delhi: Oxford University Press, 1994), esp. 1–10; Daud Ali, 'The Idea of the Medieval in the Writing of South Asian History. Contexts, Methods and Politics', *Social History* 39, 3 (2014), 382–407, esp. 388–90.

Against such a divide, perpetuating assumptions of a static and ahistorical 'precolonial' age, François-Xaver Fauvelle has positioned the 'African Middle Ages' as a marker of 'historical value'.[55] Locating the period between the eighth and the fifteenth centuries AD, he identifies the advent of Islam and the onset of direct European contact and Atlantic trade as relevant caesura. These dates are tied to external factors, to be sure, yet bear witness to the entanglements that connect African and Eurasian pasts. Fauvelle also singles out the specific documentary regime that characterises the period and continues to shape our knowledge practices. The 'African Middle Ages', he argues, is a move towards a more inclusive and truly globalising view of the 'medieval world', with Europe and Africa both studied as provinces of 'a global world that deserves to be called medieval based only on its distinctive way of being global'.[56] Some reviewers have appreciated Fauvelle's attempt at periodisation 'in terms of global history' and stress the importance of integrating African history into mainstream historiography as well as public discourse.[57] Other commentators, in contrast, are more sceptical and object to what they perceive as a return of Eurocentrism, or even 'exoticism'.[58]

The 'African Middle Ages', however, are no invention of Fauvelle's. Comparable notions had already surfaced in African historiography and debates about intellectual decolonisation in the 1950s and 1960s.[59] They are tied to attempts at synchronising European and African history, frequently to the advantage of the latter and frequently through means of comparisons, with a particular interest in the history of slavery and serfdom.[60] Here, striking parallels to the agenda of the Global Middle Ages today emerge. And, just as

[55] François-Xaver Fauvelle, *The Golden Rhinoceros. Histories of the African Middle Ages* (Princeton: Princeton University Press, 2018), 10.
[56] Fauvelle, *Golden Rhinoceros*, 11; cf. François-Xaver Fauvelle, *Leçons de l'histoire de l'Afrique: Leçon inaugurale prononcée le jeudi 3 octobre 2019* (Paris: Collège de France, 2020), https://doi.org/10.4000/books.cdf.9292, esp. sec. 9–14.
[57] Claire Bosc-Tiessé, 'Penser et écrire l'histoire d'un Moyen Âge en Afrique: Une lecture de François-Xaver Fauvelle-Aymar, *Le rhinocéros d'or. Histoires du Moyen Âge africain*', *Afriques. Débats et lectures*, 27 July 2015, http://journals.openedition.org/afriques/1702; Marie-Laure Derat, 'Moyen Âge africain: Plaidoyers pour des histoires de l'Afrique', *Médiévales: Langue, textes, histoire* 79, 2 (2021), 209–20, esp. 209–11.
[58] Cf. Arno Sonderegger, Review of Fauvelle, 'Das goldene Rhinozeros', *Stichproben: Wiener Zeitschrift für kritische Afrikastudien* 17, 33 (2017), 134–41; Bauer, *Warum es kein islamisches Mittelalter gab*, 151–3.
[59] Sylvie Kandé, 'African Medievalisms. Caste as a Subtext in Ahmadou Kourouma's Suns of Independence and Monnew', in Nadia Altschul and Kathleen Davis (eds.), *Medievalisms in the Postcolonial World: The Idea of 'the Middle Ages' Outside Europe* (Baltimore: Johns Hopkins University Press, 2009), 301–24, here 302–8.
[60] See, for example, Philippe Decraene, 'Le Mali médiéval', *Civilisations* 12, 2 (1962), 250–8; Cheikh A. Diop, *L'Afrique noire pré-coloniale: Étude comparée des systèmes politiques et sociaux de l'Europe et de l'Afrique Noire, de l'antiquité à la formation des états modernes* (Paris: Présence africaine, 1960). For a more extensive discussion, cf. Brauner, 'Das "globale Mittelalter"'.

today, such approaches were by no means uncontroversial: would a celebration of the African Middle Ages, with its grand empires of Ghana and Mali, help to decolonise the history of the continent? Or is it in danger of reproducing European notions of historicity, located in rulers and states?[61]

As Kathleen Davis and Nadia Altschul have observed, 'the medieval occupies a fraught, paradoxical role in postcolonial politics'.[62] When prominent protagonists of postcolonial scholarship – namely, members of the Subaltern Studies Group – engaged with European medievalists' debates on feudalism and the peasant economy, this helped them take a stance with regard to the Indian present and future.[63] Similarly, the contested meanings of the Chinese Renaissance are less connected to scholarly debates about Eurocentrism than to discussions about different visions of Chinese identity and political futures.[64]

The global proliferation of the Middle Ages is a postcolonial phenomenon itself, shaped by local appropriations that are part of specific *local* discussions and politics.[65] Reflecting on these 'multiple Middle Ages' leads us to reconsider the question of critique and change. From an analytical point of view, the transfer and transformation of concepts can be the subject of global conceptual history.[66] But it constitutes a methodological and, indeed, a practical challenge for all historians, as they themselves take part in processes of translation and entanglement. In this sense, the Global Middle Ages can serve as an example of global history's potential to question concepts and institutions, but also for the difficulties and challenges such attempts at transformation face. This, as

---

[61] See Finn Fuglestad, 'The Trevor–Roper Trap or the Imperialism of History: An Essay', *History in Africa* 19 (1992), 309–26.

[62] Nadia Altschul and Kathleen Davis, 'The Idea of "the Middle Ages" Outside Europe', in Altschul and Davis, *Medievalisms in the Postcolonial World*, 1–26, here 12. On ambiguities of postcolonial histories, cf. also Fuglestad, 'Trevor–Roper Trap'; Achille Mbembe, *Critique of Black Reason* (Durham: Duke University Press, 2017), 28–31; V. Y. Mudimbe, *The Invention of Africa. Gnosis, Philosophy, and the Order of Knowledge* (Bloomington: Indiana University Press, 1988), here 35–48.

[63] Bruce W. Holsinger, 'Medieval Studies, Postcolonial Studies, and the Genealogies of Critique', *Speculum* 77, 4 (2002), 1195–227.

[64] Pablo A. Blitstein, 'A Global History of the "Multiple Renaissances"', *Historical Journal* 64, 1 (2021), 162–84. See also Thomas Maissen and Barbara Mittler (eds.), *Why China Did Not Have a Renaissance – and Why That Matters. An Interdisciplinary Dialogue* (Berlin: de Gruyter, 2018).

[65] For selected case studies, see Marwa Elsharky, 'The Invention of the Muslim Golden Age: Universal History, the Arabs, Science, and Islam', in Dan Edelstein et al. (eds.), *Power and Time. Temporalities in Conflict and the Making of History* (Chicago: University of Chicago Press, 2020), 80–102; Sanjay Subrahmanyam, 'Region, Nation, World: Remarks on Scale and the Problem of Periodisation', in Maissen et al., *Chronologics*, 23 April 2018, https://chronolog .hypotheses.org/270; Sebastian Conrad, 'What Time Is Japan? Problems of Comparative (Intercultural) Historiography', *History and Theory* 38, 1 (1999), 67–83.

[66] For recent approaches to global conceptual history see, e.g., Margrit Pernau and Dominic Sachsenmaier (eds.), *Global Conceptual History. A Reader* (London: Bloomsbury Academic, 2016); Margrit Pernau, 'Provincializing Concepts: The Language of Transnational History', *Comparative Studies of South Asia, Africa and the Middle East* 36, 3 (2016), 483–99.

Suzanne Conklin Akbari has reminded us, is not only a language game: Speaking about 'medieval Ethiopia', for instance, also means claiming a place for Ethiopian studies within the medievalist community and access to its resources.[67] Politics of periodisation have their very material effects, too.

At the Same Time: Simultaneity and the Dialectics of Non-Coevalness

Global history is often understood in terms of space and spatial expansion. Yet it is also characterised by specific attention to time. 'The concern with synchronicity, with the contemporaneous even if geographically distant', Sebastian Conrad suggests, 'has become the hallmark of global approaches'.[68] Numerous books and studies have followed such an approach, often choosing one specific year as their observational unit.[69] As we have seen, studying what happens at the same time in different places can contribute to dismantling traditional periodisation schemes. It serves as a powerful tool to counter the 'denial of coevalness' and the confinement to the 'waiting room' of history, in Chakrabarty's felicitous wording. In this sense, synchronicity seems to contain a promise of equality, set to counter exclusions and divisions of traditional historiography. But what concepts of time underwrite synchronisation itself? The issue of synchronisation showcases how global historians approach time as iconoclasts and believers at the same time.

The very formation of Western scholarship is tied to the temporalisation of difference and the allocation of different temporalities. In his influential study *Time and the Other: How Anthropology Makes Its Object* (1983), Johannes Fabian argues that anthropology as a discipline was built on a 'denial of coevalness'. It assigned its subject of study – the allegedly 'primitive' cultures – to a time different from the one inhabited by the scholarly observer, a time before history and historical change. Precisely for this reason, studying 'primitive peoples' was thought to allow for insights into the deep past of 'our own' civilised societies. The 'denial of coevalness', in fact, was a denial of diversity, as all societies were supposed to follow the same scheme of development (if they developed at all).[70]

---

[67] Suzanne C. Akbari, 'Where Is Medieval Ethiopia? Mapping Ethiopic Studies within Medieval Studies', in Keene (ed.), *Toward a Global Middle Ages*, 82–93.

[68] Conrad, *What Is Global History*, 150. See also Adrien Delmas, 'De la Simultanéité en histoire globale', *L'Atelier du Centre de recherches historiques* 20 (5 April 2019), https://doi.org/10.4 000/acrh.9586, sec. 1.

[69] Just to name a few examples: Valerie Hansen, *The Year 1000. When Explorers Connected the World – and Globalization Began* (New York: Scribner, 2020); Christian Caryl, *Strange Rebels: 1979 and the Birth of the 21st Century* (New York: Basic Books, 2013); Serge Gruzinski, *What Time Is It There? America and Islam at the Dawn of Modern Times* (Cambridge: Polity, 2010).

[70] Johannes Fabian, *Time and the Other. How Anthropology Makes Its Object* (New York: Columbia University Press, 1983); see also Johannes Fabian, 'The Other Revisited: Critical

While explicit denials of coevalness are on the retreat, the basic framework survives in the institutionalised division of labour between the disciplines, especially in the divide between history and area studies. Synchronising approaches can help to make visible these persistent divisions and potentially contribute to their undoing. This is also, as we have seen, what the champions of the 'Global Middle Ages' propose. According to Jürgen Osterhammel, a focus on simultaneity characterises global history at large: global history 'highlights the simultaneity of societies in various parts of the world … Few literary devices have been more successful in overcoming Eurocentric habits of seeing.'[71] Pitted against the temporalisation of difference, simultaneity becomes associated with a promise of equality and equivalence.

The issue of 'being at the same time', however, is trickier than it might seem. Some ambiguity already appears when we consider the vocabulary that is usually employed but rarely reflected upon. Compare, for instance, the different terms used in the statements quoted so far – namely, 'simultaneity', 'synchronicity', 'coevalness' and 'contemporaneity'. Although these terms might appear similar or even synonymous at first glance, on closer scrutiny one finds that they contain allusions to different temporalities and, in fact, point to a conflation of emic and etic notions of time. If we want to unpack the different concepts and layers of temporality involved, some analytical distinctions might be helpful. *Simultaneity*, for one thing, can be understood in terms of an analytical framework of calendrical or chronological time: referring to things, events, processes happening at the same time from an external observer's point of view, without any necessary connection between them drawn by internal observers. *Synchronicity*, on the other hand, usually designates the active relating of phenomena and processes that result from the 'work of synchronisation', as Helge Jordheim has called it.[72] Understanding synchronicity as a product of making relations rather than a given helps to uncover the economic and political rationales involved and consider unexpected outcomes. As Vanessa Ogle has astutely demonstrated, attempts at a global standardisation of time in order to synchronise 'the world' have led to a greater variety of times, to hybridisation and the co-existence of different temporalities.[73] Historians are also engaged in the 'work of synchronisation' – for instance, by integrating

Afterthoughts', *Anthropological Theory* 6, 2 (2006), 139–52. Cf. Berber Bevernage, 'Tales of Pastness and Contemporaneity: On the Politics of Time in History and Anthropology', *Rethinking History* 20, 3 (2016), 352–74; John D. Kelly, 'Time and the Global: Against the Homogeneous, Empty Communities in Contemporary Social Theory', *Development and Change* 29, 4 (1998), 839–71, here 860–4.
[71] Osterhammel, 'Globalizations', 94.
[72] Helge Jordheim, 'Multiple Times and the Work of Synchronization', *History and Theory* 53, 4 (2004), 498–518.
[73] Ogle, *The Global Transformation of Time*.

distinct yet simultaneous phenomena in the same narrative and one explanatory framework, regardless of potential connectivity or historical perceptions.

In line with this distinction, studying global history through the lens of simultaneity does not necessarily imply a focus on connectivity and connections. Simultaneity is tied to an observer's (etic) perspective and does not presuppose that the observed actually experience each other as 'being at the same time' or share the same understanding of time and temporality. Such a framework of observation is what champions of the Global Middle Ages as an inclusive approach and 'chronological container' aim at: a framework that opens up space for comparison and historiographical synchronisation.

Coevalness and *contemporaneity* are linked to an actively and consciously shared time.[74] Sometimes, 'intersocietal contemporaneity' is distinguished from 'interpersonal coevalness'. Yet, more often than not, contemporaneity and coevalness are used interchangeably and refer to experiences of time as shared time.[75] Sharing time contains a promise of commonality, maybe even of potential equality. For better or worse, it presupposes that there is one single time 'we all' are living in.[76] As we have seen, a central tenet of globalisation discourse posits the 'global present' as that time in which we all have become, fully and finally, contemporaries.

Tracing such temporal characteristics of globalisation, historians have turned to the study of 'global events' or 'global moments': 'global moments', according to the influential definition proposed by Dominic Sachsenmaier and Sebastian Conrad, are 'events with global repercussions', 'events of a popular significance that appealed to people in discrete and distant locations'. Such moments, Sachsenmaier and Conrad suggest, are characteristic of the 'high time of globalisation since the late nineteenth century', resulting from a preceding emergence of a 'global consciousness throughout much of the world'.[77] Global moments, in their reading, are thus tied to specific historical

---

[74] Cf. Bevernage, 'Tales of Pastness', 367–9; María I. Mudrovcic, 'The Politics of Time, the Politics of History. Who Are My Contemporaries?', *Rethinking History* 23, 4 (2019), 456–73, here 459–62 on the term's history.

[75] I will follow this usage here when discussing the relevant literature; otherwise, the term 'coevalness' is preferred.

[76] An influential distinction between the two terms goes back to Fabian, *Time and the Other*, 24–5, 30–1. Referring to Alfred Schütz, he defines coevalness as 'intersubjective time', connoting 'a common, active "occupation", or sharing, of time' (31) and even defined as a 'condition of communication' that cannot be denied (32). 'Contemporary', in contrast, is understood as 'co-occurrence' in 'typological time' (like a period). For a critical discussion, see Bevernage, 'Tales of Pastness', 360–7; Kevin Birth, 'The Creation of Coevalness and the Danger of Homochronism', *Journal of the Royal Anthropological Institute* 14, 1 (2008), 3–20, here 11–12.

[77] Sebastian Conrad and Dominic Sachsenmaier, 'Introduction: Competing Visions of World Order: Global Moments and Movements, 1880s–1930s', in Sebastian Conrad and Dominic Sachsenmaier (eds.), *Competing Visions of World Order. Global Moments and Movements, 1880s–1930s* (Basingstoke: Palgrave Macmillan, 2007), 1–28, here 12–13, 15–16.

conditions, showcasing how the process of globalisation brings about experiences of a 'shared time' worldwide.

The term itself, however, has been put to more generalised use and expanded to periods well before the late nineteenth century. Indeed, we read, for instance, about Polybius' 'global moment' in the context of shifting Roman discourses about mobility, or find the eruption of the Indonesian volcano Samalas discussed as a 'global moment' in the 1250s.[78] This travelling concept thus brings us back to the relation between simultaneity, synchronicity and contemporaneity: Polybius' 'global moment' is discussed in terms of historical perceptions of shared time and practices of synchronisation. The Samalas eruption as a global event, in contrast, emerges from analytical observation of simultaneous processes and phenomena, as the result of synchronisation of disparate materials and timescales, not least through global comparison. The notion of 'global events' has thus travelled far from its origins, pointing, once more, to the importance of precise terminology. It equally illustrates the fascination of synchronisation that goes beyond a mere observational device – indeed, past simultaneity seems to contain a promise of potential contemporaneity.

Contemporaneity, despite its claim to unity, comes with its own Other. Remember, for instance, how Rosa characterised globalisation 'temporally' as the 'dissolution of stable rhythms and sequences following the ubiquitous contemporisation (*Vergleichzeitigung*) of even the noncontemporaneous'.[79] Evidently, this alludes to the often-quoted figure of the *Gleichzeitigkeit des Ungleichzeitigen* (which roughly translates as 'contemporaneity of the non-contemporaneous'). However, while this figure is often employed to assert an ecumenical vision of pluritemporality, Rosa hints at the final dissolution of such diversity in an encompassing contemporaneity.

But what is the contemporaneous, after all? And how can Rosa distinguish it from the 'non-contemporaneous'? The statement contains a normative understanding of contemporaneity – implying, once more, a distinct unity of times in time.[80] Peter Osborne has described the notion of contemporaneity as an '*operative* fiction: it *regulates the division* between the past and present within the present', bound up with the project of 'global modernity'. Given 'growing

[78] Cf. Elena Isayev, 'Polybius's Global Moment and Human Mobility through Ancient Italy', in Martin Pitts and Miguel J. Versluys (eds.), *Globalisation and the Roman World. World History, Connectivity and Material Culture* (Cambridge: Cambridge University Press, 2015), 123–40; Martin Bauch, 'Chronology and Impact of a Global Moment in the 13th Century: The Samalas Eruption Revisited', in Andrea Kiss and Kathleen Pribyl (eds.), *The Dance of Death in Late Medieval and Renaissance Europe: Environmental Stress, Mortality and Social Response* (Abingdon: Routledge, 2020), 214–32.
[79] Rosa, *Social Acceleration*, 217, with a list of diverse 'forms of contemporisation' (219–20).
[80] Cf. Achim Landwehr, 'Von der "Gleichzeitigkeit des Ungleichzeitigen"', *Historische Zeitschrift* 295, 1 (2012), 1–34, here 3–10. For an example, see Koselleck's usage of the figure, relating to 'our own experience to have contemporaries who live in the Stone Age': Koselleck, 'Need for Theory', 8.

social interconnectedness', 'constructions of the contemporary increasingly appear as inevitable'. In this transition from 'fictional to historical narrative', he locates the role of the 'global histories of the present' that aim at 'an empirically consistent hypothetical unity of the present, beyond pure heteronomy or multiplicity'.[81] When we observe the role of the 'global present' in global history, we observe this operative fiction in action.

While these normative implications of 'being at the same time' are often invisible, they come to the forefront when we compare the topos of the 'contemporaneity of the non-contemporaneous' to the figure of anachronism. While the two figures are structurally related, they come with starkly different value judgements. One of the most thought-provoking analyses of anachronism has been proposed by Jacques Rancière. For Rancière, anachronism is less 'a question of facts' than 'a question of thought'. Accordingly, he defines the 'reproach of anachronism' as follows: 'The accusation of anachronism is not the claim that something did not exist at a given date. It is the claim that something could not have existed at this date.'[82] When anachronism is about historical potentiality, it presupposes a distinct notion of what is do-able (say-able or think-able) in a certain time.[83] Thus, anachronism is tied to an understanding of 'time itself as the principle of immanence that subsumes all phenomena under a law of interiority. The truth of history is then the immanence of time as the principle of co-presence and co-belonging of phenomena.'[84] Obviously, the mechanism at work in anachronism is similar to the one implied in the 'contemporaneity of the non-contemporaneous'. In both cases, phenomena (people, processes) are 'out of time' – and both presuppose a universalising viewpoint from which to establish temporal order and to diagnose its distortion. Curiously, though – and here the politics of time set in – the topos of the 'contemporaneity of the non-contemporaneous' has evolved into a self-evident shorthand of a diversity-conscious history whereas anachronisms still count among the mortal sins in the field.[85]

Next to the notion of 'shared time', the figure of 'being out of time' has also received increasing attention lately.[86] In the wake of Fabian and others, we are used to associating non-coevalness (or non-contemporaneity) with imperial politics and colonialism. However, is the assertion of non-coevalness always an

---

[81] Osborne, 'Fiction of the Contemporary', 23 and 25–6.

[82] Jacques Rancière, 'The Concept of Anachronism and the Historian's Truth (English translation)', *InPrint* 3, 1 (2015), 21–48.

[83] Quentin Skinner, presumably anachronism's most prominent enemy, relies on a similar concept: Quentin Skinner, 'Meaning and Understanding in the History of Ideas', *History and Theory* 8, 1 (1969), 3–53, here 8–9 and passim.

[84] Rancière, 'Concept of Anachronism', 26.

[85] Cf. also Achim Landwehr and Tobias Winnerling, 'Chronisms: On the Past and Future of the Relation of Times', *Rethinking History* 23, 4 (2019), 435–55.

[86] This is what Birth, 'Creation of Coevalness', calls 'the danger of homochronism'.

imperial gesture? Or can it also be part of resistance and subversion? Berber Bevernage, a Belgian historian and theorist of history, has made a powerful case for the multiple usages and meanings of non-coevalness.[87] Building on examples from his research in transitional justice, he argues that being non-coeval can equally operate as a subaltern, critical strategy, especially tied to experience of violence and trauma. Moreover, he draws attention to the fact that the benevolent assertion of coevalness can also distort our view on inequalities even within the global North – so living as a refugee is also and decisively characterised by the absence of a future, as humans usually inhabit it as a space of expected actions. Recognising the lack of coevalness inherent in such an experience is, Bevernage argues, no imperial gesture but rather a starting point for critical action.

The problem of non-coevalness is tied to different configurations of past, present and future – and, indeed, to struggles about the very division between them. Within the context of global history, it is the ongoing debate about the legacies of colonialism and imperialism that draws attention to the diverging approaches. When issues of reparation and restitution are at stake, for instance, the relation between past and present shapes the very scope of legal and political action: Even if responsibility for past actions can be clearly attributed, it is often less clear who is to be held accountable today – and whether one can indeed claim responsibility for the past.[88] In the case of reparations for slavery and the slave trade, for instance, determining who is to pay and who is to be paid raises complex questions about identity and continuity.[89] Are reparations about individuals or about institutions and social groups? Can past wrongs be compensated by financial means? Is there even such a thing as 'restorative justice' or a 'reparatory history'?[90] A disciplined historian may easily disavow his profession's competence for such questions and dismiss the issues at stake as anachronistic. Yet, this would be too easy a way out. Even if answers remain

---

[87] Bevernage, 'Tales of Pastness'.

[88] Cf. Berber Bevernage, 'The Past Is Evil/Evil Is Past. On Retrospective Politics, Philosophy of History, and Temporal Manichaeism', *History and Theory* 54, 3 (2015), 333–52.

[89] For the long history of such demands since the eighteenth century, see Ana Lucia Araujo, *Reparations for Slavery and the Slave Trade: A Transnational and Comparative History* (London: Bloomsbury Academic, 2017); cf. also Adam Crawford, 'Temporality in Restorative Justice: On Time, Timing and Time-Consciousness', *Theoretical Criminology* 19, 4 (2015), 470–90, here 474–5, on slavery 484.

[90] Cf. for different positions: Matthew Evans and David Wilkins, 'Transformative Justice, Reparations and Transatlantic Slavery', *Social & Legal Studies* 28, 1 (2019), 137–57; Catherine Hall, 'Doing Reparatory History: Bringing "Race" and Slavery Home', *Race & Class* 60, 1 (2018), 3–21; Thomas Creamer, 'International Reparations for Slavery and the Slave Trade', *Journal of Black Studies* 49, 7 (2018), 694–713; Rhoda Howard-Hassmann, 'Reparations for the Slave Trade: Rhetoric, Law, History and Political Realities', *Revue Canadienne des Études Africaines* 41, 3 (2007), 427–54.

controversial (and they certainly will), the questions themselves remind us of the presence of the past and the way it shapes potential futures today.[91]

Conclusion

Among global historians, time and temporality are a source both of concern and hope. In the struggle against traditional periodisation and the 'denial of coevalness', temporalising practices such as synchronisation and the reference to chronology have been employed as a remedy. At the same time, pluritemporality and chronopolitics remain critical issues. To conclude, I highlight four points to further rethink temporality in global history and beyond.

1. *Global History and Its Time.* Global historians take pride in actively embracing multiple voices and plural perspectives and in critically rethinking standards and procedures of historiography in general. Calling out the 'fetish of time' by assessing pluritemporalities thus appears to be their very mission. Yet, proceeding along these lines, we can also turn back to the temporality of global history itself: if global history is the history for our time, what happens when the times are a-changing? Or when the global present does not work as an 'operative fiction' anymore? How does this change global history, its narratives and its role? Is global history an episode in a broader movement towards a decentering of history and historical scholarship?[92] Does its success lie, then, in turning global perspectives into the 'new normal'?

2. *After Modernisation.* Globalisation discourse entertains an ambiguous relation with modernity and modernisation theory.[93] The same goes for global history. Global historians, though, also grapple with modernity in a specific form – that is, the temporal regime of historicity. As the chronopolitics involved in this emerge nowhere more clearly than in the legacies of colonialism around the world, global historians can contribute to historicising historicity.[94] Studying periods before the onset of globalisation discourse, in particular, may help to make visible – even if inadvertently – silent assumptions about the 'global' and the 'modern'.

3. *At the Same Time.* Time has been described as the 'unity of difference'. While any attempt at ontological definition is beyond a historian's grasp, we have certainly observed that time is intimately connected to the making of differences: from outright denial of coevalness to the more subtle figures of anachronism and 'contemporaneity of the non-contemporary'. At the same

---

[91] Rolph-Michel Trouillot, *Silencing the Past. Power and the Production of History* (Boston: Beacon Press 2015); cf. also Jan Jansen's chapter on Teleology in this volume.

[92] See Natalie Zemon Davis, 'Decentering History: Local Stories and Cultural Crossings in a Global World', *History and Theory* 50, 2 (2011), 188–202, esp. 190–2.

[93] See Knöbl, 'After Modernization'; Cooper, 'Globalization'.

[94] Cf. Satia, *Time's Monster.*

time, a synchronising approach emerges as global history's most prominent tool to envisage more inclusive histories. 'To be at the same time' seems to carry a promise of potential equality that oscillates between ethics, representation and historical truth. Or, as Chakrabarty phrased it: 'We have "equal" histories of the past because we would like histories to be equal! Histories – actual events on the ground – do not necessarily become equal even if historiography makes them look so.'[95] If we take history seriously, we cannot do without accounting for inequalities.

4. *Doing History.* 'From wastes, papers, vegetables, indeed from glaciers and "eternal snows"', Michel de Certeau observed, 'historians *make something different*: they make history'.[96] For historians, critical reflection on temporalities is no detached academic exercise. On the contrary, it concerns the very core of their profession and their work. Rethinking time and temporality thus should lead us to consider on how we *do* history and under what circumstances: how we draw a line between the past and the present, how we routinely rely on established temporal markers to convey significance and inhabit institutions shaped by past politics of periodisation. At the same time, being historians, we also need to think about our capacity for doing things differently.

---

[95] Chakrabarty, 'Muddle of Modernity', 672.
[96] Michel de Certeau, *The Writing of History* (New York: Columbia University Press, 1988), 71, italics in the original.

4   Quantification
Measuring Connections and Comparative Development in Global History

Pim de Zwart

Global history has flourished in recent decades,[1] but has also increasingly attracted critiques by various scholars, who suggest that (some) global histories have overestimated the importance of global connections for (local) events[2] or exaggerated the impact of a particular historical figure on the course of global history.[3] Quantification may provide a preventative bulwark against such critique. In this chapter, I will address the issue of quantification in global history. To what extent have claims in global history been backed up by quantitative data, and what are the potential benefits and pitfalls of quantification for the field?

To start with, it is important to establish what global history is. At the risk of oversimplifying, it seems that two types of global histories can be discerned: one that is focused on the analysis of global connections, or what is also termed 'global connectivity' or 'globalisation', and another that is concerned with making global comparisons.[4] The former may concern the circulation of knowledge and ideologies, ecological exchange, commodity trade and migration, but also political cooperation and conflict, and tends to relate global to local developments and vice versa. A second type of global history is concerned with comparisons between developments in different parts of the world. In particular, contributions to the debate over the 'Great Divergence', or the rising gap in economic performance between the West and the Rest, fall under this heading.

---

[1] Richard Drayton and David Motadel, 'Discussion: The Futures of Global History', *Journal of Global History* 13, 1 (2018), 1–21; Jürgen Osterhammel, 'Global History', in Marek Tamm and Peter Burke (eds.), *Debating New Approaches to History* (London: Bloomsbury Academic, 2019), 21–47.

[2] David Bell, 'This Is What Happens When Historians Overuse the Idea of the Network', *New Republic*, 26 October 2013.

[3] Cornell Fleischer et al., 'How to Write a Fake Global History', *Cromohs: Cyber Review of Modern Historiography*, September 2020. https://doi.org/10.13128/cromohs-12032.

[4] James Belich et al., 'Introduction', in Belich et al. (eds.) *The Prospect of Global History* (Oxford: Oxford University Press, 2016), 1–24. They suggest global history consists of three elements: comparison, connectedness and globalisation, but the latter two seem to be largely overlapping. I do not distinguish between global connectivity/connectedness and globalisation in this chapter but consider them the same.

Both the assessment of global connections and systematic global comparisons may benefit from formal reasoning backed by quantitative evidence. In order to argue that the era of 'global connectivity' started in the eleventh, sixteenth or twentieth century, one needs to have some measure of 'global connectivity' to assess when there was *more* of it. Valerie Hansen suggests that only the *potential*, not the *actual*, presence of objects from Asia in a Viking settlement in the Americas around the year 1000 is enough to be considered the start of globalisation.[5] But there was no trade between the short-lived Viking outpost in Newfoundland and Europe, let alone Asia. Few historians will therefore agree that this was the defining moment when global connections crucially impacted the course of history.[6] But what *level* or *extent* of global connections is sufficient to be considered as globalisation? Even if we do not wish to define a particular threshold in numerical terms, we need some measure and criteria to assess the *increase/rise* or *decrease/decline* of global connectivity over time.

Analyses of the consequences of global connections for developments in some particular place imply the evaluation of causal claims, as well as the weight these claims may carry (*how much* did development X contribute to event Y). Causal claims additionally require a strategy to convince people that it was actually global factor X that had a positive relationship with local factor Y, and not factors A, B or C that were also taking place at that time – that is, that causation rather than mere correlation is involved here. Quantification helps with this, because by controlling for factors A, B and C, one can (try to) approach ceteris paribus conditions. Similarly, in global comparative history, measurement is crucial considering the language of comparisons: *equal to*, *more/less*, *higher/lower*.

Despite this need for formalisation and quantification, many historians, including global historians, do not use quantitative data and are sceptical, or even hostile, towards the systematic use of quantitative data. This is especially the case when such data are used to uncover general patterns in history, or when history is used to test social science models, as some quantitative historians do. Some historians refute the idea that human history could be properly understood by trying to uncover general patterns, as they emphasise the 'unique and particularistic nature of history'.[7] Humans, their motives and their actions are too complex to be captured by any general law.[8] As a result of such objections,

[5] Valerie Hansen, *The Year 1000: When Explorers Connected the World – and Globalization Began* (New York: Scribner, 2020).

[6] Fleischer et al., 'Fake Global History'.

[7] Robert William Fogel and G. R. Elton, *Which Road to the Past: Two Views of History* (New Haven: Yale University Press, 1983), 9.

[8] Fogel and Elton, *Which Road to the Past*, 9–10; Jared Diamond and James A. Robinson, *Natural Experiments of History* (Cambridge, MA: Belknap Press, 2013), 5.

many historians have been driven away from testing their hypotheses based on quantitative data, and, more generally, explanation and the establishing of causal relations.

From the 1960s, some historians started the study of *cliometrics* (or quantitative economic history), which sought general explanations based on research that formulated hypotheses and rigorously tested these using empirical, often quantitative, data. In the following decades, cliometrics became influential among other historians. Even Lawrence Stone, who was highly critical of cliometric work, acknowledged the benefits of quantification in *Past and Present* in 1979:

> Historians can no longer get away with saying 'more', 'less', 'growing', 'declining', all of which logically imply numerical comparisons, without ever stating explicitly the statistical basis for their assertions. It [quantification] has also made argument exclusively by example seem somewhat disreputable. Critics now demand supporting statistical evidence to show that the examples are typical, and not exceptions to the rule.[9]

Yet he criticised the cliometricians for providing tables and graphs without giving sufficient, and easily accessible, description of the methodologies used to obtain those figures. This remains a problem to this day, and the increasing complexity of quantitative techniques leaves many historians without training in statistics unable to verify the findings of more sophisticated quantitative research. Especially in the United States, the barriers between historians in humanities departments and those historians influenced by the social sciences seem greater than ever.

Certainly, quantitative, like qualitative, evidence has many problems. When data are lacking, quantitative historians may provide estimates rather than actually observed datapoints. The assumptions underlying such estimates can and should be criticised. As new data and research comes to light, assumptions may need to be adjusted, and when the bias in a particular data source turns out to be more severe than expected, necessitating further modifications this necessitates further corrections. Yet a whole body of quantitative data should not be discarded too quickly. As in the case of qualitative evidence, it is important to see what story these sources may contain. Historical data are often inaccurate, but if the inaccuracies are random (such as typos made by local administrators), the quantitative evidence can still be used to obtain reliable estimates, as the average value obtained from such data (e.g. mean income in a country) will not be significantly affected (as, given enough observations, mistakes pushing the estimate upward are equally as likely as those pushing it downward). Furthermore, even if data are affected by bias (e.g. a source exploited to estimate average incomes in a country includes far more

---

[9] Lawrence Stone, 'The Revival of Narrative Reflections on a New Old History', *Past and Present* 85 (1979), 3–24, here 10–11.

incomes at the bottom end of the income distribution than at the top), there are ways to account for such bias using additional information.

Additional problems arise when historical quantitative research relies on categories created by administrators in the past, such as colonial officials. In the Viceroyalty of Peru, colonial administrators created ethnic classifications (primarily for taxation purposes) that have very much persisted in statistical publications over time, but which ignore the complexities and changing nature of the social differentiations acknowledged by Peruvians themselves.[10] Any quantitative analysis of historical demographic databases that employ these colonial classifications will need to take this into account. It is imperative that scholars grasp the political context in which the registration of people (and their characteristics) takes place before such registry's data are employed in analysis.[11] Many historical developments are hard to capture in numbers and a focus on purely quantitative evidence would lead to availability bias (or the so-called 'streetlight effect'). For example, when examining clearly measurable indicators, like GDP, wages and life expectancy, a clear view of human progress over the last centuries emerges, while if one included variables that historically have not been extensively quantified, such as biodiversity and pollution, such a view may be reversed. Moreover, quantitative methods are better at establishing *whether* there *is* a relationship between certain variables, but are less suited to explaining *why* this relationship is there.[12]

It is easy to be overwhelmed by the issues related to historical quantitative materials, and some have concluded that because inaccurate statistics will (always) lead to inaccurate conclusions, especially when they are put in a global comparative framework, any attempt to write quantitative global history is better abandoned.[13] Many others disagree, as is evidenced, for example, by the contributions cited in the remainder of this chapter. Over recent decades, many new quantitative sources have been discovered and employed, methods have been developed and refined, and, consequently, views on global history have been *improved*: we know *more* about global history now, as a result of quantitative studies, than we did a few decades ago. Yet the historian has an obligation to be transparent about the problems with, and the reliability of, the data as a precondition for rectifying those

---

[10] David Cahill, 'Colour by Numbers: Racial and Ethnic Categories in the Viceroyalty of Peru, 1532–1824', *Journal of Latin American Studies* 26, 2 (1994), 325–46.

[11] Simon Szreter and Keith Breckenridge, 'Editor's Introduction: Recognition and Registration', in Simon Szreter and Keith Breckenridge (eds.), *Registration and Recognition: Documenting the Person in World History* (Oxford: Oxford University Press, 2012), 1–36.

[12] Angus Deaton, 'Instruments, Randomization and Learning about Development', *Journal of Economic Literature* 48, 2 (2010), 424–55.

[13] D. C. M. Platt, *Mickey Mouse Numbers in Global History: The Short View* (London: Macmillan, 1989).

problems and moving – slowly but steadily – to a more accurate picture of world history.

In the remainder of this chapter, I will discuss how and to what extent quantitative evidence has been used in two main discussions in global history: (1) the debate over the origins of globalisation and (2) discussions surrounding the 'Great Divergence' in economic fortunes between the West and the Rest. Because of my own expertise, the focus of this chapter is on discussions in global economic history, but with implications for the field at large, as it is clear that quantification and its problems are not limited to economic history.

The Origins of Globalisation

A key question in global history is *when* and *how* the world became connected to such an extent that the history of the world, and its various components in terms of regions or countries, cannot be properly understood without taking those connections into account; in other words: when the process of *globalisation* started. For several decades, scholars have put forth suggestions regarding the point at which they believed the world had become a connected space. Eminent contributors to the debate, such as Fernand Braudel, Immanuel Wallerstein and Andre Gunder Frank, emphasised the creation of a global economic system from the sixteenth century on and its role in creating global economic inequalities.[14] Quantitative economic historians, such as Patrick O'Brien, Kevin O'Rourke and Jeffrey Williamson, objected to these views.[15] They suggested that the volumes and values of the commodities traded globally before the nineteenth century were insufficient to have had transformative effects. In particular, before the 1800s there were too many obstacles to intercontinental trade, in the form of monopolies, pirates and slow oceangoing ships, to allow the global integration of markets. The 'narrow focus' on quantification and integration was criticised by Dennis Flynn and Arturo Giráldez (among others), who suggested instead that global connections before the 1800s fundamentally impacted all parts of the world, in particular from the founding of Manila in 1571.[16]

---

[14] Fernand Braudel, *Civilization and Capitalism, 15th–18th Centuries*, 3 vols. (Berkeley: University of California Press, 1992), vol. 2: *The Wheels of Commerce*; Andre Gunder Frank, *Capitalism and Underdevelopment in Latin America: Historical Studies of Chile and Brazil* (New York: Monthly Review Press, 1969); Immanuel Wallerstein, *The Modern-World System*, 4 vols. (New York/Berkeley: Academic Press/University of California Press, 1974–2011).

[15] Patrick O'Brien, 'European Economic Development: The Contribution of the Periphery', *Economic History Review* 35, 1 (1982), 1–18; Kevin H. O'Rourke and Jeffrey G. Williamson, 'When Did Globalisation Begin?', *European Review of Economic History* 6, 1 (2002), 23–50.

[16] Dennis Flynn and Arturo Giráldez, 'Path Dependence, Time Lags and the Birth of Globalization: A Critique of O'Rourke and Williamson', *European Review of Economic History* 8, 1 (2004), 81–108.

These different answers are the result of different *conceptualisations* of 'transformative connections' and 'globalisation', as well as differences in the *measurement* and the *empirical evidence* used to test the presence of those concepts in history and assess possible causality between global connections and transformative processes. It is therefore important to establish some definitions. For O'Rourke and Williamson, globalisation is equivalent to the *integration* of markets,[17] while for Flynn and Giráldez, globalisation concerns the *sustained interaction* among all of the world's heavily populated land masses on a scale that generated *deep and lasting impacts*.[18] Jürgen Osterhammel distinguishes between 'global history', which is the history of 'transformative connections', and the 'history of globalisation', which contains the added element of 'integration'.[19] Following Osterhammel, it seems that Flynn and Giráldez are concerned with the former (although they would themselves disagree), while O'Rourke and Williamson are dealing with the latter.

The concept of 'transformative connections' is relatively broad and not clearly defined. I will take a stab at it here. It contains two elements: 'connections' and 'transformation'. Flynn and Giráldez emphasise that the connections need to be 'sustained'.[20] We find this also in other works which emphasise the 'regularity' or 'stability' of connections.[21] Following the influential work of David Held et al.,[22] one may want to investigate in the 'intensity' of the connections, which concerns the volume and value of global trade, the numbers of migrants or the amount of international financial transactions. Looking at the political and cultural domains, one may be interested in the numbers of international treaties or the amounts of international movies in local theatres. Additionally, we may need to assess how geographically extensive the connections need to be in order to be considered 'global'. Abu-Lughod is content with contact between various integrated regions across Eurasia to talk of 'world-systems'.[23] For Flynn and Giráldez,[24] what they consider the three thirds of the world – with the Pacific Ocean spanning a third of the Earth's surface, the Americas and the Atlantic another third and Afro-Eurasia the final third – need to be in regular contact in order to count as global. Connections across Afro-Eurasia alone, in their view, certainly cannot count as globalisation.

---

[17] O'Rourke and Williamson, 'When Did Globalisation Begin?'
[18] Flynn and Giráldez, 'Path Dependence'.   [19] Osterhammel, 'Global History', 28.
[20] Flynn and Giráldez, 'Path Dependence'.
[21] Belich et al., 'Introduction'; Jürgen Osterhammel and Niels P. Petersson, *Globalization: A Short History* (Princeton: Princeton University Press, 2005).
[22] David Held et al., *Global Transformations. Politics, Economics and Culture* (Stanford: Stanford University Press, 1999).
[23] Janet L. Abu-Lughod, *Before European Hegemony. The World System AD 1250–1350* (Oxford: Oxford University Press, 1989).
[24] Flynn and Giráldez, 'Path Dependence'.

What about the transformative effects, or what in the work of Held et al. and Flynn and Giráldez is termed 'impact'?[25] A crucial question is what do we consider 'transformative' or 'deep' and 'lasting' impacts?[26] For Wallerstein, the creation of a global division of labour is crucial,[27] and he notes that labour in the capitalist core of the world economy is free and remunerated with wages, while labour in the periphery is coerced. For Andre Gunder Frank and Eric Williams, the accumulation of capital is essential: because exchange in the world economy was unequal, this led to a flow of capital, or profits, from the 'periphery' to the 'core'.[28] These profits were consequently invested in the capital-intensive technologies of the Industrial Revolution in Britain. For the other parts of the world, global connections meant the deepening of poverty: the more a region in the 'periphery' was engaged with the world economy, the more 'underdeveloped' it became. For Flynn and Giráldez, the impact is not only economic but contains ecological, demographic and cultural elements as well.[29] They emphasise, for example, the importance of the American potato for the growth of the Chinese population. It is clear from these works that 'transformative' change may imply something different for different parts of the globe. For Europe it may mean an economic shift from agriculture to industry; for Asia it may mean the reverse (deindustrialisation). But global connections could also have led to a further entrenchment of pre-existing patterns and hinder development that could have taken place in their absence. The latter example may count as a deep and lasting impact, but 'transformative change' would be a misnomer. In the next section, we will look at the quantitative data that sheds light on this.

Measuring Connections

To assess the regularity and intensity of interaction in the early modern era, economic historians have relied on two sources: observations of prices of goods and volumes of trade flows from the accounts of internationally operating trading companies, as well as customs records.

First, prices of goods (and services) are at the centre of much economic history. They provide basic information about trends in supply and demand in (market) economies. In general, we know that when a product (or service) becomes more expensive compared to other goods or services, this is a sign of scarcity, while if a good becomes relatively cheaper this suggests an abundance

---

[25] Held et al., *Global Transformations*; Flynn and Giráldez, 'Path Dependence'.

[26] Flynn and Giráldez, 'Path Dependence'.

[27] Wallerstein, *Modern World-System*, vol 1, 126–129.

[28] Frank, *Capitalism and Underdevelopment*; Eric Williams, *Capitalism and Slavery* (Chapel Hill: University of North Carolina Press, 1944).

[29] Flynn and Giráldez, 'Path Dependence'.

of supply. As O'Rourke notes: 'most economic data, like the quantities of output of various types of products in a country, require someone that counted these quantities, which, when we are counting the output across an entire city, province or country, implies a certain level of bureaucracy, which was generally lacking before the nineteenth century.'[30] Yet throughout history, from antiquity to the present, people and institutions have been buying and selling stuff. While most of these transactions went undocumented, many institutions, especially those that have been in existence for extended periods – such as churches, orphanages or chartered trading companies (such as the *Vereenigde Oost-Indische Compagnie*, VOC) – kept records of their incomes and expenses, and these have often have been preserved.[31] Additional price quotations can be compiled from price currents that were published weekly in some of the major urban commodity markets like Amsterdam and London.[32] By comparing such price currents with prices observed in, for example, the VOC's own accounts of the sales of their commodities at auction, it becomes clear that these are very closely correlated, giving credence to these figures.[33] Problems may arise if large institutions purchased in bulk and/or via long-term contracts with wholesalers, which implies that the prices paid by the institutions may be different from those in the local market place. By taking observations from a variety of such institutions in different cities, however, it is possible to compute price series that, at least in respect of the longer-term trends, seem robust. Economic historians have been compiling these price data since the late nineteenth century, and most of these figures are now relatively accessible. Drawing on the huge body of work on prices in economic history,[34] local series have been scrutinised for their reliability – for example, by checking whether price hikes can be related to local harvest failures or whether price declines are related to increased output and supply – and from this it emerges that price data are quite reliable overall.

Second, we have comparatively abundant information on early modern seaborne trade for two reasons: (1) it was conducted by large trading companies that kept extensive records of their activities; and (2) many states and cities from the late Middle Ages meticulously recorded seaborne trade for customs

---

[30] Kevin H. O'Rourke, 'The Economist and Global History', in Belich et al., *The Prospect of Global History*, 44–63, here 46.

[31] E.g.: N.W. Posthumus, *Nederlandsche Prijsgeschiedenis*, 2 vols. (Leiden: Brill, 1943–1964).

[32] J.M. Price, 'Note on some London Price-Currents, 1667–1715', *Economic History Review* 7 (1954), 240–250.

[33] Pim de Zwart, *Globalization and the Colonial Origins of the Great Divergence* (Leiden: Brill, 2016); Pim de Zwart, 'Globalization in the Early Modern Era: New Evidence from the Dutch-Asiatic Trade, 1600–1800', *Journal of Economic History* 76 (2016), 520–58.

[34] The literature is far too voluminous to cite here, but Robert C. Allen's seminal paper is a good start: 'The Great Divergence in European Wages and Prices from the Middle Ages to the First World War', *Explorations in Economic History* 38, 4 (2001), 411–47.

reasons. These data have been gathered, assessed and published for most European countries.[35] The trade between Europe and Asia in the early modern period is exceptionally well-documented because it was monopolised by a handful of chartered trading companies (the VOC, EIC, *Compagnie des Indes*, etc.) whose records on trade flows have been largely kept (only documents from the Portuguese *Casa da India* were lost in the Lisbon earthquake of 1755). These records allow for the construction of a complete image of Euro-Asian trade in the pre-1800 period.[36] For the trade between the Americas and Europe we are on significantly less firm ground, as that trade was operated by many smaller traders and not all those records have been localised. Nonetheless, on the basis of customs records in America and Europe and figures from the Spanish colonial fleet, some estimates of those trading volumes can be made as well, although the error margins are clearly larger.[37]

What can such data tell us about the regularity and intensity of connections? In the centuries before the discovery of the passage to India via the Cape of Good Hope, intercontinental connections – those between Africa, Asia and Europe – took place partially over land and partially across the seas. The overland routes between Europe and Asia, the Silk Road, thrived at various point in time: in antiquity when it connected Han China with the Roman Empire, or during the *Pax Mongolica* in the thirteenth and fourteenth centuries. Scholars such as Abu-Lughod have emphasised the importance of global interaction and the existence of early, non-Western 'world-systems' in the thirteenth and fourteenth centuries.[38] Overland routes, however, were vulnerable to political instability: armed conflict and bandits could severely disrupt trade flows for years. Connections along the Silk Road were thus not regular or stable. Neither were they intensive: volumes traded along those routes were small and amounted to only a fraction of the volume of goods brought back by Portuguese ships in the first decades of the sixteenth century.[39]

---

[35] See sources underlying Robert C. Allen, 'Progress and Poverty in Early Modern Europe', *Economic History Review* 56, Issue 3 (2003), 403–43; Jan de Vries, 'Connecting Europe and Asia: A Quantitative Analysis of the Cape-route Trade, 1497–1795', in Arturo Giráldez and Dennis O. Flynn (eds.), *Global Connections and Monetary History, 1470–1800* (Aldershot: Ashgate, 2003), 35–106.

[36] De Vries, 'Connecting Europe'.

[37] Jan de Vries, 'The Limits of Globalization in the Early Modern World', *Economic History Review* 63, 3 (2010), 710–33. De Vries based his work on studies such as Antonio García-Baquerro González, *Cadiz y el Atlántico (1717–1778): El comercio colonial español bajo el monopolio gaditano* (Sevilla: Escuela de Estudios Hispano-Americanos, 1976) and John R. Fischer, *Commercial Relations Between Spain and Spanish America in the Era of Free Trade, 1778–1796* (Liverpool: University of Liverpool, 1985).

[38] Abu-Lughod, *Before European Hegemony*.

[39] Ronald Findlay and Kevin O'Rourke, *Power and Plenty: Trade, War and the World Economy in the Second Millennium* (Princeton: Princeton University Press 2007), 140; Om Prakash, *European Commercial Enterprise in Pre-Colonial India* (Cambridge: Cambridge University Press, 1998), 34.

It was thus only after $c.1500$ that intercontinental interactions became more regular, more intensive and more global. Trade was steady from then as each year a large number of ships left European ports for Asian destinations and even more sailed in the Atlantic triangular trade.[40] Overall trade volumes, both between Europe and Asia and between Europe and the Americas, increased substantially over the period between 1500 and 1800. Total volumes in Eurasian trade grew by an estimated 1.1 per cent per annum. Sustained over a period of 300 years, this implies a 25-fold increase of annual trading volumes: from 2,000 tonnes per annum around 1500 to 50,000 tonnes per annum by 1800.[41] Trade across the Atlantic, where distances were shorter and there was greater competition among a multitude of smaller traders, probably grew even faster.[42]

On the basis of a wide variety of studies of international trade in different countries of the globe (based on underlying customs and company records, as discussed earlier), O'Rourke and Williamson estimated that intercontinental trade grew by 1.06 per annum in the period between 1500 and 1800.[43] This implies that trade grew four times as fast as (estimates of) world population and more than twice as fast as (estimated) economic activity.[44] Over these three centuries, global connections, at least in terms of goods trade, thus became two to three times more important. Despite this impressive growth and the increasing importance of international connections, the total amount of trade as measured in quantities per person in many parts of the world remained remarkably low. The amount of Asian goods that landed in Europe was a measly 0.5 kg per capita per annum. For Asia at the end of the eighteenth century, the net inflow of silver constituted only 0.32 grams per person per annum,[45] which was less than 10 per cent of a daily unskilled wage in China.[46]

So, what were the impacts of this small but growing global trade on local developments? A clear indication that Vasco Da Gama's journeys mattered for European consumers are developments in the real price of pepper in Europe.[47] Over the course of the sixteenth century, the real price of pepper decreased fivefold, whereas before 1500 the real price had gone up. This implies that pepper was becoming more affordable for a wider range of consumers across Europe. In the seventeenth and eighteenth centuries in particular, when competition on

---

[40] De Vries, 'Connecting Europe'; De Vries, 'Limits'.   [41] De Vries, 'Limits', 720.

[42] De Vries, 'Limits', 719.

[43] Kevin H. O'Rourke and Jeffrey G. Williamson, 'Once More: When Did Globalisation Begin?', *European Review of Economic History* 8, 1 (2004), 109–17.

[44] Findlay and O'Rourke, *Power and Plenty*, 305.   [45] De Vries, 'Limits', 718.

[46] Robert Allen et al., 'Wages, Prices, and Living Standards in China, 1738–1925: in Comparison with Europe, Japan, and India', *Economic History Review* 64, s1 (2011), 8–38. The Chinese unskilled wage at the time was about 0.1 silver tael of 37 grams.

[47] Kevin H. O'Rourke and Jeffrey G. Williamson, 'Did Vasco Da Gama Matter for European Markets?', *Economic History Review* 62, 3 (2009), 655–84.

oceanic routes became fiercer with the entrance of northern Europeans and total volumes increased further, many exotic luxuries came within economic reach of large parts of the population. Various studies have documented the rise in consumption, including among the lower middle classes, of goods such as sugar, coffee and tea.[48] It is difficult to understand this crucial European development, also known as the early modern 'consumer revolution', without acknowledging the importance of international trade.

For early modern Europe, where documentation is best, quantification of the impact of global trade has developed the furthest. Formal econometric analyses have established a positive relationship between the volume of international trade and the development in GDP, real wages and urbanisation in Europe.[49] For other parts of the world, where historical documentation of trade patterns and economic indicators is less abundantly available and where trade may have represented a smaller part of total economic activity, such exercises are largely lacking. Formal quantitative assessment of the slave trades for African economic development has focused only on current economic outcomes and contains little information about immediate impacts.[50] Assessment of the role of international trade on economic development in the early modern Americas, Africa and Asia thus largely consists of argumentative reasoning on the basis of recently calculated figures on urbanisation, GDP and real wages in different parts of the world.[51]

Measuring Globalisation

Thus far, we have looked at some of the price and trade evidence that has been used to say something about 'transformative connections' in the early modern era. But what about 'globalisation' or the study of 'integration'? Measuring global market integration is relatively straightforward. O'Rourke and Williamson note that the best evidence for market integration is that of the convergence of international commodity prices.[52] The main characteristic of a single market is a unified price structure: two shops on the same street offering the same product need to charge the same prices (unless there are

[48] Anne McCants, 'Poor Consumers as Global Consumers: The Diffusion of Tea and Coffee Drinking in the Eighteenth Century', *Economic History Review* 61, s1 (2008), 172–200.

[49] Allen, 'Progress and Poverty'; Daron Acemoglu et al., 'The Rise of Europe: Atlantic Trade, Institutional Change, and Economic Growth', *American Economic Review* 95, 3 (2005), 546–79; Alexana M. de Pleijt and Jan Luiten van Zanden, 'Accounting for the Little Divergence: What Drove Economic Growth in Pre-Industrial Europe, 1300–1800?', *European Review of Economic History* 20, 4 (2016), 387–409.

[50] Nathan Nunn, 'The Long-Term Effects of Africa's Slave Trades', *Quarterly Journal of Economics* 123, 1 (2008), 139–76.

[51] Pim De Zwart and Jan Luiten Van Zanden, *The Origins of Globalisation: World Trade in the Making of the Global Economy* (Cambridge: Cambridge University Press, 2018).

[52] O'Rourke and Williamson, 'When Did Globalisation Begin?'

differences in quality) in order to both maintain customers; '[s]imilarly, in a single international market, prices for identical commodities will only differ across locations to the extent that trade costs . . . make arbitrage expensive'.[53] Evidence of commodity price convergence also automatically implies that there is an (economic) impact of this globalisation, as a change in prices resulting from international exchange will result in a reshuffling of resources in those economies that experienced price shifts.[54] To give an example: the rise of the wheat trade between the United States and Britain in the nineteenth century led to a massive decline in wheat prices in Britain. This allowed for a transfer of workers from the agricultural sector to the manufacturing sector and thus a crucial change in the economy and society: from an agricultural to an industrial society.

When did global commodity markets become integrated? Following O'Rourke and Williamson, the answer to this question until recently was: in the nineteenth century.[55] Before that era, deficient shipping technology, information asymmetries and monopolies, as well as low trading volumes compared with total population meant that domestic prices remained unaffected by global trade and events. It was only after the Napoleonic wars that technological progress involving steamships and railroads, as well as the demise of monopolies by chartered companies, caused commodity prices to converge globally.[56] This view has been highly influential among economists, and many economic historians also tend to refer to the nineteenth century as 'the first age of globalisation' without bothering to explain why.[57]

Some recent research, however, has put this view in doubt. There is evidence of market integration along all major trade routes (between America and Europe, Africa and America, America and Asia, and Europe and Asia). Flynn and Giráldez had long observed a convergence of silver prices (expressed in gold) during both the seventeenth and eighteenth centuries, which – since silver was the main medium of exchange globally – clearly indicates integration of global markets.[58] Klas Rönnback's analysis showed price convergences for sugar between Brazil and Europe, coffee between Asia and Europe and tea between China and Europe, among others.[59] Additional evidence of integrating

---

[53] O'Rourke, 'Economist and Global History', 48.
[54] O'Rourke and Williamson, 'When Did Globalisation Begin?'.
[55] O'Rourke and Williamson, 'When Did Globalisation Begin?'; O'Rourke and Williamson, 'Once More'.
[56] O'Rourke and Williamson, 'When Did Globalisation Begin?'.
[57] For example, Patrick D. Alexander and Ian Keay, 'Responding to the First Era of Globalization: Canadian Trade Policy, 1870–1913', *Journal of Economic History* 79, 3 (2019), 826–61.
[58] Dennis Flynn and Arturo Giráldez, 'Born with a "Silver Spoon": The Origin of World Trade in 1571', *Journal of World History* 6, 2 (1995), 201–21.
[59] Klas Rönnback, 'Integration of Global Commodity Markets in the Early Modern Era', *European Review of Economic History* 13, 1 (2009), 95–120.

Atlantic markets came from an analysis by Rafael Dobado-Gonzáles and others of a large database of prices in grain markets in the Americas and Europe.[60] They suggest that, at least regarding grain markets, transatlantic integration started during the eighteenth century. Extensive work on trade between Europe and Asia was recently done based on new primary materials extracted from Dutch East India Company (VOC) archives.[61] The VOC was the dominant party in the trade between Europe and Asia, responsible for 59 per cent of total Eurasian shipping in the seventeenth century and 44 per cent of the total in the eighteenth century. Most of the goods traded by the VOC exhibited price convergence between 1600 and 1800, and especially prices for those goods that became more important in the eighteenth century, such as textiles and tea, converged significantly. There is thus substantial evidence of price convergence across many goods and routes in the early modern era.

The integration of global commodity markets continued in the 1800s, after a temporary dip during the Napoleonic wars. Prices converged faster than in the preceding centuries.[62] Nonetheless, establishing a new chronology for the process of globalisation is important as it substantially alters our interpretation of the drivers of global inequality. If one considers the nineteenth century as the dawn of globalisation, this puts emphasis on the role of the Industrial Revolution in determining the gap between rich and poor, while seeing, for example, the activities of chartered trading companies and the Atlantic slave trades as being inconsequential for long-term patterns of development. On the other hand, establishing globalisation as an early modern process highlights the crucial effects of the Columbian exchange, early colonialism and the Atlantic slave trade, among others, in determining the current global income distribution.

The Great Divergence

The debate over the Great Divergence has spurred a huge amount of comparative global history research in the past two decades.[63] The main questions in this discussion concern the *when* and *why* of the rise in global economic inequality. The debate takes its name from the eponymous book by Kenneth Pomeranz, considered to be 'perhaps the most influential book in global history ever written'.[64] In a special issue of the *Journal of Global History*, Stephen Broadberry and Jack Goldstone both noted that Pomeranz put forth a decisively

---

[60] Rafael Dobado-Gonzáles et al., 'The Integration of Grain Markets in the Eighteenth Century: Early Rise of Globalization in the West', *Journal of Economic History* 72, 3 (2012), 671–707.

[61] De Zwart, *Globalization*; De Zwart, 'Globalization'.   [62] De Zwart, 'Globalization'.

[63] See also Peer Vries, *Escaping Poverty: The Origins of Modern Economic Growth* (Vienna: Vienna University Press, 2013).

[64] Osterhammel, 'Global History', 12; Drayton and Motadel, 'Discussion', 6.

quantitative thesis about the Great Divergence, containing suggestions about levels of urbanisation, consumption, trade and incomes, on the basis of very limited quantitative evidence.[65] The same can be said of the contributions of other scholars of the so-called 'California School'. R. Bin Wong suggests that both pre-industrial Europe and China experienced 'Smithian growth' and 'shared a common world of harvest insecurities and material limitations' in a book that contains only one table (on life expectancy), no graphs and hardly any quantitative observations.[66] Susan Hanley suggested that Japanese living standards and physical well-being before the Meiji Restoration were not much below that in Britain before industrialisation, while providing little quantitative evidence for Japan and almost no comparative information on material living standards in other parts of the world.[67] Prasannan Parthasarathi, who can be credited with bringing India into this discussion, based his assessment of a late Indo-European divergence on three observations of weavers' wages and three estimates of spinners' incomes in Southern India in the mid-eighteenth century, the 1790s and 1800.[68] In his book of 2011, he gives six separate observations of real wages in South India, of which only three support his argument of high wages, while he also brings three additional observations for Bengal (north-eastern India).[69] It is hard to be convinced of the core arguments given such a fragile empirical basis.

It is important to note that these works represent a response to the conventional view of an early rise of the West, which was not based on much (reliable) quantitative evidence either. These views, which suggested that Western Europe forged ahead of the rest of the world in terms of per capita GDP, urbanisation and living standards, were in terms of underlying quantitative data based largely on the work of Paul Bairoch and Angus Maddison.[70] Maddison's data of per capita GDP for non-Western countries pre-1820s were no more than conjectures.[71] It is only since the early 2000s that, in response to the work of Pomeranz and others, serious efforts have been made

[65] Stephen Broadberry and Jack A. Goldstone, 'Arenas in Global History', *Journal of Global History* 16, 2 (2021), 266–314; Kenneth Pomeranz, *The Great Divergence: China, Europe and the Making of the Modern World Economy* (Princeton: Princeton University Press, 2000).
[66] R. Bin Wong, *China Transformed. Historical Change and the Limits of European Experience* (Ithaca: Cornell University Press, 1997), 31–32.
[67] Susan B. Hanley, *Everyday Things in Premodern Japan. The Hidden Legacy of Material Culture* (Berkeley: University of California Press, 1997).
[68] Prasannan Parthasarathi, 'Rethinking Wages and Competitiveness in the Eighteenth Century: Britain and South India', *Past and Present* 158, 1 (1998), 79–109.
[69] Prasannan Parthasarathi, *Why Europe Grew Rich and Asia Did Not: Global Economic Divergence 1600–1850* (Cambridge: Cambridge University Press, 2011).
[70] For a critique of their underlying data, see also Platt, *Mickey Mouse Numbers*.
[71] See Angus Maddison, *The World Economy: A Millennial Perspective* (Paris: OECD, 2003), 250–9 for his approach to estimating GDP for countries in Latin America, Asia and Africa before the 1820s.

to improve the data, especially for non-Western countries. While studies have also compared other economic indicators, such as human stature and market performance,[72] the focus in the remainder of this chapter will be on the two indicators that have been most prominent in the discussion: real wages and GDP. Whereas Pomeranz observed that 'it seems likely that average incomes in Japan, China, and parts of Southeast Asia were comparable to (or higher than) those in Western Europe, even in the late eighteenth century',[73] most of the latest quantitative research suggests otherwise.[74] Establishing the correct chronology for the Great Divergence is, of course, an important prerequisite for understanding the reasons for that divergence.

Measuring Comparative Incomes: GDP

Per capita GDP is by far the most widely used and accepted variable to measure the development of economic performance and income in societies. GDP is an 'empirical construct that does not exist in the real world',[75] and its calculation has become exceedingly complicated due to both the rising complexities of modern economies and the increasing sophistication of statistical methods. There are three ways to estimate GDP – these being expenditure, output and income approaches – but the general idea is to get an overview of total economic activity in a country, measured at market value. For this, one needs to estimate either the total expenditure of consumers, investors and government (expenditure approach), an estimate of total goods and services produced in a society minus intermediates (output), or the total incomes obtained from land, labour and capital (income). These data are difficult to obtain and require various assumptions and choices. Dealing with technological change and the construction of a price index to correct GDP figures for inflation generates additional problems. Despite this, GDP still provides a good indication of how rapidly or slowly economies are growing.[76]

Difficulties in obtaining the necessary data increase when investigating GDP in the period before the late nineteenth century, when governmental statistical agencies started producing national statistics. Scholars need to make assumptions about the level of local consumption and production of food and clothing,

---

[72] For example, Roman Studer, 'India and the Great Divergence: Assessing the Efficiency of Grain Markets in Eighteenth- and Nineteenth-Century India', *Journal of Economic History* 68, 2 (2008), 393–437; Carol Shiue and Wolfgang Keller, 'Markets in China and Europe on the Eve of the Industrial Revolution', *American Economic Review* 97, 4 (2007), 1189–1216.

[73] Pomeranz, *The Great Divergence*, 49.

[74] As he himself had to admit: Kenneth Pomeranz, 'Ten Years After: Responses and Reconsiderations', *Historically Speaking* 12, 4 (2011), 20–5.

[75] Diane Coyle, *GDP: A Brief but Affectionate History* (Princeton: Princeton University Press, 2014), 24.

[76] Coyle, *GDP*, 136.

for example, on the basis of wage and price developments and exploit the latest research on price elasticities of demand for these products (which allows estimation of consumed quantities).[77] In addition, even when there are relatively good estimates, assumptions need to be made to capture non-market income, such as the work of spouses within the household or food grown for domestic consumption. Further problems arise with non-marketed output, such as unpaid housework and 'black market' activities,[78] which are often substantial in pre-industrial economies.

As a result, historical GDP figures are generally expected and acknowledged to contain a certain margin of error.[79] There are methods to estimate such error, using information about the variability of the series and their underlying components; indeed, some recent historical GDP studies have calculated the margin of error.[80] Such error margins should be calculated in case errors are randomly distributed. Potential biases in data can be dealt with by calculating GDP series using a variety of assumptions to see how the results change and whether this alters the general picture sketched by the GDP numbers ('robustness tests'). Calculating GDP in different ways (expenditure, output and income) can also help increase the robustness of findings. Over recent decades, various scholars have gathered figures from state tax records, customs accounts, probate inventories, farm accounts and many other sources,[81] in combination with the latest tried-and-tested assumptions, to estimate new series of GDP from the late Middle Ages for a number of countries.

This new research into GDP largely upholds Maddison's earlier conjectures. The latest evidence confirms that around the year 1000, higher incomes per capita were reached in Song China than in (what is now) Britain, but this was hardly in dispute. Yet by 1400, for which new estimates on China have recently become available, incomes in (what are now) Italy, Britain and the Netherlands were already substantially higher. England was one of the poorer parts of Europe in the Middle Ages, while Italy was one of the richer areas, so 'it is likely that Italy was already ahead by 1300, and perhaps even earlier'.[82] The gap only

[77] If the price for a product changes, so does the demand for it. In general, when prices increase, demand declines. The extent to which this takes place (i.e. the price elasticity of demand) differs per product. Basic necessities generally have lower price elasticities (as people need to consume them to survive, no matter the price change).
[78] Coyle, *GDP*, 38.
[79] Jutta Bolt and Jan Luiten van Zanden, 'The Maddison Project: Collaborative Research on Historical National Accounts', *Economic History Review* 67, 3 (2014), 627–51.
[80] Jan Luiten van Zanden and Bas van Leeuwen, 'Persistent but Not Consistent: The Growth of National Income in Holland 1347–1807', *Explorations in Economic History* 49, 2 (2012), 119–30.
[81] See Stephen Broadberry, 'Accounting for the Great Divergence', CEPR Discussion Paper 15936 (2021).
[82] Stephen Broadberry et al., 'China, Europe, and the Great Divergence: A Study in Historical National Accounting, 980–1850', *Journal of Economic History* 78, 4 (2018), 955–1000.

increased as GDP per head declined in China and would not return to 1400 levels until the twentieth century. The latest work on Japan shows lower incomes there than in China until the nineteenth century, and thus an even larger gap with the leading economies of Europe. The trend in Japan does suggest very slow improvement in incomes in the pre-industrial period. The first GDP estimates for India are available for 1600, when they are slightly higher than in China, but below those in Britain. After 1600 Indian incomes continuously decline, further increasing the gap. What is striking in the new research is that the gap between the economic leader in Europe and other parts of Europe was also very large. In the seventeenth century, average incomes in the Dutch Republic (now the Netherlands) were more than twice as high as in Britain.

On the basis of the problems outlined herein, even quantitative economic historians have been critical of historical GDP estimates. In particular, Deng and O'Brien have questioned earlier Chinese GDP estimates as they found the data to be of too low quality and not voluminous enough to produce consistent series of GDP or population. They argue that there are severe dangers in quantification on the basis of a limited and problematic body of evidence as the 'origins and accuracy of such figures are too rarely investigated or questioned'.[83] Stephen Broadberry (and colleagues) responded two years later by presenting a large body of new data that did exactly that: investigating and revising earlier estimates of Chinese GDP.[84] Furthermore, when Peter Solar pointed out problems with their government output data, they updated their figures to take his suggestions into account.[85] This shows the benefits of these quantitative approaches that are based on generally accepted comparative methodologies: as the assumptions and underlying data are discussed openly, they can readily be criticised and improved. New estimates are then easily entered into the same comparative framework.

Measuring Comparative Incomes: Real Wages

A further issue with per capita GDP is that it is an estimate of the average income in a society and may give little information about the standard of living of the majority of the population. While there is a clear correlation between GDP and various aspects of well-being, the correlation is not perfect, and GDP itself, as Diane Coyle emphasises several times, is 'not a measure of welfare'.[86]

---

[83] Kent Deng and Patrick O'Brien, 'China's GDP Per Capita from the Han Dynasty to Communist Times', *World Economics Journal* 17 (2016), 79–123.

[84] Broadberry et al., 'China'.

[85] Peter Solar, 'China's GDP: Some Corrections and the Way Forward', *Journal of Economic History* 81, 3 (2021), 943–57; Stephen Broadberry et al., 'China, Europe, and the Great Divergence: A Restatement', *Journal of Economic History* 81, 3 (2021), 958–74.

[86] Coyle, *GDP*, 40, 73–5, 91, 140.

Due to a high degree of social inequality, large parts of a population can be denied decent schooling or healthcare, despite the relatively high GDP per capita of the states in which they reside. This, and the issues sketched earlier, have led to the search for alternative measures of living standards. Real wages – the purchasing power of an (often unskilled male building) labourer – represent a good alternative for the following reasons: (1) data on wages and prices are relatively widely available for a large number of countries far back in time; (2) as wage labour has existed since antiquity it requires no anachronistic concept or statistical artefact like 'GDP'; (3) it directly measures incomes of those at the lower end of the income distribution. Real wages studies essentially ask very basic questions: how much did the average person earn for a day's work; how did this change over time; and was a worker better off in Delhi or in London in the early 1800s?

But real wage comparisons are not without problems, either: how can the real value of the wage of a worker in medieval England, who lighted his house using wax candles and warmed himself by a fireplace full of firewood, be compared with a worker in the twentieth century who used electricity and a coal stove? Or how can the income of an eighteenth-century worker in England, who ate bread and meat and drank beer, be compared with that of a Japanese labourer in the same period who mainly consumed rice, beans and fish? In order to deal with this issue, Robert Allen developed a consumption basket based on necessary nutritional intake.[87] The aim of this methodology was to compare both the purchasing power of workers in the same region over time and the purchasing power of similar workers in different regions. A basket was defined that delivered the necessary nutrients, some 1,940 kcal and 40 grams of protein per day, mainly from the cheapest available staple in a region, as well as some required clothing and fuel (for heating and lighting). By defining a basket in this way, it was possible to compare the value of the wage relative to an early modern poverty line.

Using this methodology, real wages have been widely used in the Great Divergence debate and the last two decades have seen not only new estimates for various parts of Europe and North America, but also for China, India, Japan, Sri Lanka and Indonesia. On the basis of these newly gathered data, the basic conclusion of a comparatively early Great Divergence (significantly before the Industrial Revolution) is essentially confirmed. In contrast to GDP estimates, real wages are often taken from urban areas and thus reflect the standard of living in the capital, or another major city, of a country. The first global comparative figures for 1600 suggest there was already a gap in real incomes between workers in Europe and India. In particular, wages in Amsterdam were

---

[87] Allen, 'Great Divergence'; Allen et al., 'Wages, Prices'.

substantially higher.[88] From the late seventeenth century, data for Batavia (now Jakarta, Java) become available, suggesting that these were also well below those in Western Europe.[89] Similar conclusions can be drawn on the basis of the evidence about Chinese and Japanese wages, with the latter in particular being at an extraordinarily low level.[90]

These real wage estimates have also received a fair deal of criticism. With regard to the high wages observed for London, the extent to which the observed 'wages' actually reflect the money that entered the pockets of local workers has been questioned, as opposed to the price paid to labour organisers and recruiters, who also retained a share of that money.[91] Taking this into account, London's real wages may have been about 30 per cent lower than earlier estimates suggest.

For China as well as South and Southeast Asia, critics of real wage studies have noted that as these were predominantly agricultural societies, the wages of often urban workers cannot be taken as representative for the income of the broader population.[92] Deng and O'Brien argue that wage rates cannot be compared across Eurasia because the ratio of wage-dependent workers is very different: in Qing China, wage workers represented about 3 per cent of the total workforce. By contrast, in the seventeenth-century Dutch Republic this figure may have exceeded 50 per cent,[93] and similar figures may be expected for England and other parts of Western Europe. Despite this, when labour markets function more or less freely, as they did in Qing China according to Pomeranz, one may assume a certain relationship between wages earned and the living standards of rural populations, at least in the long term. If wages represent a far lower standard of living than that earned by agriculture, simply not enough workers would show up to perform the necessary work. This labour scarcity would then increase wages to a level where it provides an attractive enough alternative to other activities. Similarly, wages cannot consistently represent a far higher standard of living than that earned by the average peasant in the countryside as that would likely cause an abundance of labour offered on

---

[88] Pim de Zwart and Jan Lucassen, 'Poverty or Prosperity in Northern India? New Evidence on Real Wages, 1590s–1870s', *Economic History Review* 73, 3 (2020), 644–67.

[89] Pim de Zwart and Jan Luiten van Zanden, 'Labor, Wages and Living Standards in Java, 1680–1914', *European Review of Economic History* 19, 3 (2015), 215–34.

[90] Allen et al., 'Wages, Prices'.

[91] Judy Stephenson, '"Real" Wages? Contractors, Workers, and Pay in London Building Trades, 1650–1800', *Economic History Review* 71, 1 (2018), 106–32.

[92] Kent Deng and Patrick O'Brien, 'Establishing Statistical Foundations of a Chronology for the Great Divergence: A Survey and Critique of the Primary Sources for the Construction of Relative Wage Levels for Ming–Qing China', *Economic History Review* 69, 4 (2016), 1057–182.

[93] Jan Lucassen, 'Proletarianization in Western Europe and India: Concepts and Methods', mimeograph, 2005.

the market, which would put downward pressure on wages.[94] Therefore, as Bin Wong and Jean-Laurent Rosenthal write, 'we know that when economies are growing rapidly, wages rise, and when economies run into trouble, wages fall'.[95] Deng and O'Brien, while primarily focused on China, extend their critical claims of real wages studies to other parts of Asia, such as India. Yet for pre-modern India, in particular around Calcutta, most sources suggest a highly competitive labour market, where wages clearly responded to supply and demand. From the 1750s to the 1770s, there is evidence that when the wages offered by the British in Calcutta were not high enough compared with private employers, this resulted in a shortage of workers. When the British needed a large number of construction workers to build a new gun carriage factory in 1804, they were well aware that they had to set the wages high enough to attract sufficient applicants.[96]

Deng and O'Brien also dispute the evidence on which the Chinese wage series is based. As was the case with some of the price series discussed earlier, the sources of wage figures are often large institutions (governments, large companies, churches, etc.) that may not have paid market rates. Data on wages in China were gathered from such sources: government records (stating the costs incurred on construction projects), international companies (which hired labourers to load their ships), in addition to domestic firms (workers in local fuel stores). For Deng and O'Brien, these sources 'seem to be neither voluminous, transparent, nor contextualised enough to serve as proxies for average daily wages or for the standards of living afforded by the private sector of the Chinese economy to a definable group of unskilled urban and agricultural workers at the bottom end of an income distribution scale'.[97] In addition, they observe that these wages are difficult to interpret because the non-monetary incomes of workers (such as board and lodging) remain unspecified, and, as these payments in kind were often substantial, they cannot form the basis for any wage comparisons. Other critics have questioned whether incomes based solely on male earnings provide an accurate image of household earnings. If in one part of the globe the contribution of women and children was much higher than in others, this could have implications for the gap in incomes.[98] The little information that we have on female incomes does suggest that women had higher incomes (relative to men) in parts of Asia, but that even

---

[94] Deng and O'Brien ('Establishing') consider such assumptions to be false, although they present no evidence that contradicts such a model. Bin Wong and Pomeranz suggest functioning 'Smithian' markets: see Wong, *China Transformed*, 18–21; Pomeranz, *Great Divergence*, 80–91: 'the evidence we have so far does not suggest that European labor markets conformed more closely to neoclassical norms than did those of Japan or China', 90.

[95] R. Bin Wong and Jean-Laurent Rosenthal, *Before and Beyond Divergence: The Politics of Economic Change in China and Europe* (Cambridge, MA: Harvard University Press, 2011), 43.

[96] De Zwart and Lucassen, 'Poverty or Prosperity', 650–51.

[97] Deng and O'Brien, 'Establishing', 1703.   [98] Pomeranz, *Great Divergence*.

including such incomes in the comparison is unlikely to close the gap.[99] Further issues have been raised regarding the seasonality of labour and the number of days per year and hours per week worked.[100]

What matters, however, is whether issues related to the data are likely to alter the conclusions that can be drawn from these studies. The latest research on real wages in the Great Divergence does not suggest that any of these issues may actually affect the levels and trends to such an extent that the current picture needs significant adjustment. One analyst of London wage series, Judy Stephenson, observed that, taking into account the money that ended up in the pockets of labour organisers, wages in London were probably still higher than those elsewhere in the early modern period, and that the overall picture sketched by the real wage work thus remains unaltered.[101] When Deng and O'Brien offer alternative observations of the number of calories obtained via unskilled wage labour in China, they suggest these data 'might also support an inference that the great divergence could well have been on stream for some time before 1700'.[102]

In order to arrive at final conclusions about the Great Divergence (as well as the origins of globalisation), one needs to look at a variety of indicators which, taken together, can show the full picture of economic development in an area. If there are large differences in the picture that emerges (e.g. between estimates of GDP and those of human stature or urbanisation), then it needs to be asked where these differences come from. Can they be explained convincingly, or do they suggest problems with (one of) the indicators? For now, it seems that most evidence, not only that on GDP and real wages, but also that on heights and urbanisation rates, points in more or less the same direction: to an early start of the Great Divergence.[103]

Conclusion

Over recent decades, economic historians have been feverishly gathering data on both global connections and comparative economic performance in differ-ent parts of the world. This recent research largely confirms many older

---

[99] Pomeranz, *Great Divergence*; De Zwart, *Globalization*; De Zwart and Lucassen, 'Poverty or Prosperity'.

[100] See, for example, John Hatcher and Judy Stephenson, *Seven Centuries of Unreal Wages: The Unreliable Data, Sources and Methods That Have Been Used for Measuring Standards of Living in the Past* (London: Palgrave Macmillan, 2018).

[101] Stephenson, '"Real" Wages?'

[102] They also suggest evidence showing the opposite, thus claiming the problems related to such figures. Deng and O'Brien, 'Establishing', 1077.

[103] For the size of cities, but also energy consumption, see Ian Morris, *The Measure of Civilization: How Social Development Decides the Fate of Nations* (Princeton: Princeton University Press, 2013), chs 3 and 4.

insights, such as those put forth in the works of Immanuel Wallerstein and Angus Maddison. Global connections increased substantially over the early modern era and integration of global markets ensued. Efforts to formally estimate the impact of these connections for Europe suggest a significant positive association between international trade and economic outcomes. For other parts of the world, data demonstrating such links are less abundant, but it is certainly likely that the benefits of trade were not shared with most parts of Africa and Asia.[104] In addition, new estimates on GDP and real wages clearly go against the arguments of Pomeranz and other revisionists who have sug- gested that the Great Divergence took place in the decades following 1800.

Discussions surrounding the various issues related to the measurement of either globalisation or the Great Divergence are unlikely to stop anytime soon. Nor should they: for the process of knowledge accumulation in global history to take place, it is crucial that historians are transparent about not only the strengths but also the weaknesses of their data. When new data comes to light that suggest that, for example, the level of export trade in a certain country was substantially higher than initially thought, or that agricultural productivity was greater, this may mean an upward correction of GDP estimates and we may have to alter our views of the timing (and probably also the causes) of the Great Divergence. This is not a weakness of quantitative global history, but rather its strength. Because numbers can more easily be compared than qualitative information, and as the researchers are explicit about what is compared, new research can easily build on what is already available, gather new data for estimates that are shaky and investigate assumptions that seem disputable.

Quantification and the use of robustness tests with different assumptions allows such a validation and therefore presents a valuable contribution to global history research. This has put some earlier observations about the rise of a global economy and the divergence in living standards on a much firmer empirical footing and led to a more accurate chronology of these developments. It does not replace but complements qualitative research, especially since many historical events, processes and developments are difficult, if not impossible, to capture in numbers, giving rise to availability bias. It is hard to imagine a purely quantitative global history of philosophy, science or politics, even if it may aid in such endeavours. Quantification allows us to strengthen or debunk some claims about global trade and income comparisons, just as it obscures elements of world history that are less easily translated into numbers, making continuous conversations between quantitative and qualitative historians indispensable for an improved understanding of global history.

---

[104] De Zwart and Van Zanden, *Origins*.

Part II

Concepts and Metaphors

5   The Global and the Earthy

Taking the Planet Seriously as a Global Historian

Sujit Sivasundaram

In the 2020s, it seems more obvious than ever that globalisation has a halting and reversible course. After a pandemic which had socially and culturally isolating effects, and as the geopolitics of superpower rivalry becomes manifest in what some see as a return to a Cold War, the mantra of connection giving rise to a world of utopian possibility and cosmopolitan oneness seems to have evaporated. If so, how should global history be characterised today?

In extant defences of the field, from one direction, everything, it is said, could have a global history. Such a claim sets its stall in opposition to the boundedness of national history and civilisational history before it.[1] This definition of global history continues to be politically important. From another direction, defenders argue that global history is as old as scholarship itself.[2] For intellectually cogent reasons, this view casts global history as a global practice rather than one which originated in early modern Europe, or even in the late-twentieth-century era of decolonisation or within the corridors of the American academe.[3] This allows a response to the view that global history is imperialist or even telescopic with respect to the conditions of the Global South. Most would agree that global history involves attention to connection and comparison, divergence and integration, and transfer and exchange. But it also involves attention to disconnection and anomaly, disintegration and theft, and differentiation and mistranslation. In the midst of critiques of the field as obsessed with frictionless mobility, this second cluster of terms and other concepts which are

---

[1] For an excellent introduction to global history, see Sebastian Conrad, *What Is Global History?* (Princeton: Princeton University Press, 2016), 6: 'one way to approach global history is to equate it with the history of everything'.

[2] For the origins of global history, see Katja Naumann, 'Long-Term and Decentred Trajectories of Doing History from a Global Perspective', *Journal of Global History* 14, 3 (2019), 335–54.

[3] For one recent exposition of the American origins of interest in globalisation and transnationalism, see Paul A. Kramer, 'How Did the World Become Global?: Transnational History, Beyond Connection', *Reviews in American History* 49, 1 (2021), 119–41. He reviews Isaac A. Kamola, *Making the World Global: US Universities and the Production of the Global Imaginary* (Durham: Duke University Press, 2019).

similar have become more salient.[4] To make matters even more confusing, alongside the resonant power of the 'global' a series of other terms are arranged, including 'world', 'transnational' and 'transcultural'.

In such a context of definitions and redefinitions, and a flourishing of so many mesmerising concepts, it would be unwise to offer one statement about what global history is. In order to interrogate the nature of this word – 'global' – I proceed by considering it as *a mode of cartography*. There are different ways of identifying the operative cartographic models. First, relationality is central to 'global' historiographical mapping: this includes, for instance, the relation between subjects and the world, the relation between objects and modes of consumption and collection, the relation between commodities and trading systems, and the relation between local traditions and universal ideologies of domination, homogenisation or differentiation. Second, a mapping impulse is evident in the scalar preoccupations of the field and in discussions about the ways to move from the small to the big, the micro to the macro, and to layer different scales in explanations of the past.[5] Words such as 'network', 'flow' or 'web' bear out the need to model and map. Third, there is both a move towards detachment, to seeing the world from above, and a keenness to fill in geographical gaps in the search for completeness, and these are both characteristic of a cartographic impulse.

Historians describe modelling, of which mapping is one example, as central to knowledge-making. As a way of tabulating phenomena into a digestible and understandable form, modelling is compatible with the quest to theorise phenomena.[6] Effective models can be non-linguistic means of summarising knowledge; models can generate disciplinary languages around them. They can play important roles in training practitioners in the field. They can support engagements with publics and funders. Models can become crucial where knowledge meets government, for instance around war or trade.

If this is the case for the widest category of models as they are used in geostrategy, physics or economics, it is also true of the way the word 'global', as a model, operates in history. Meanwhile maps are a particular class of models that represent and redefine territory. If so, global history is also linked with a cartographic impulse in attempting to reterritorialise the human past. Meanwhile, the modelled logics of global history have been driven in part by the way theoretical paradigms have weighed down on this sub-discipline of

---

[4] For instance, see Zoltán Biedermann, '(Dis)connected History and the Multiple Narratives of Global Early Modernity', *Modern Philology* 119, 1 (2021), 13–32.

[5] John-Paul A. Ghobrial, 'Introduction: Seeing the World Like a Microhistorian', *Past & Present* 242, supplement 14 (2019), 1–22.

[6] Soraya de Chadarevian and Nick Hopwood (eds.), *Models: The Third Dimension of Science* (Stanford: Stanford University Press, 2004), and Mary Morgan and Margaret Morrison, *Models as Mediators: Perspectives on Natural and Social Sciences* (Cambridge: Cambridge University Press, 1999).

history in order to make sense of the totality of history: this runs from Enlightenment science and orientalism to world-systems theory. It is a long-standing and often structuralist story.

This chapter has a set of discrete objectives. In its first section, it links the creation of the 'globe' as a model or map to the history of History. It also highlights how the elision of nature and the delimitation of subject areas were significant elements in the emergence of modern historiography. Both aspects were key to the emergence of the global historian as a modeller. The chapter then moves into a particular case study of mapping and historicism, namely the island of Taprobane. It does this with a view to reading beneath these intellectual impulses to the materiality of a particular and evolving island space. In other words, it makes room again for nature by claiming that signs of the Earth's materiality are evident in the long historical narrations of Taprobane. The third section shifts into methodological reflections on current preoccupations in historical writing around environmental history, agricultural history, oceanic history, animal history and the history of medicine, and the extent to which they engage both the global and the Earth as matter. The chapter concludes with some views on the debate around the Anthropocene. In this way, the survey of historiography runs from the origins of humanist history to debates on posthumanism.

As a provocation, this argument moves from the globe as artifice in global history, a taken-for-granted signifier, to what lies beyond that sensibility: the Earth as a fissured, crusted, summited, atmospheric and terraqueous platform. In broad terms, it takes up Dipesh Chakrabarty's invocation: 'The global is a humanocentric construction; the planet, or the Earth system, decentres the human.'[7] Critically, however, this analysis is not a call for a history determined by nature, nor should it be simplified as a call to replace the global with the Earthy. It is an exploration of a more multi-disciplinary and materially aware global history, in tune with that advocated elsewhere, which can include the Earth itself as a vital agent.[8]

Throughout, in order to illustrate points, the chapter uses literature with a focus on South Asia to moor the argument in a historiography which engages the world outside the West.

---

[7] Dipesh Chakrabarty, *The Climate of History in a Planetary Age* (Chicago: University of Chicago Press, 2021), 19
[8] One recent intervention in favour of vitalism is Amitav Ghosh, *The Nutmeg's Curse: Parables for a Planet in Crisis* (Chicago: University of Chicago Press, 2021).

The Global, the Natural, the Human and the Origins of Modern History

The planet we inhabit is not globular: it is an oblate spheroid. I recently joked in print that global history should be renamed oblate spheroidic history.[9] Such a proposal is useful at least simply to generate critical reflection on the taken-for-grantedness of this artificial concept, the 'global', in our thought and scholarship.

The production of the globe as object has a rich historiography, though often a Eurocentric one, linked to the Copernican Revolution and the use of the globe as a signifier of political and economic power in Europe.[10] One influential view is that the theorising of the planet as rotund and the emergence of the modern were interrelated; but another view would be that the casting of pre-moderns as flat Earthers was itself a modern exaggeration.[11] Rather than sketching a teleology around modernity, it may be useful to follow Jerry Brotton, who writes:

It is precisely upon the figure of the globe, as both a visual image and a material object, that many of the social and cultural hopes and anxieties of the period came to be focused. For if the development of the terrestrial globe was coterminous with the geographical expansion of the horizons of the early modern world, then the intellectual and material transactions which went into its production were also symptomatic of the expanding intellectual, political and commercial horizons of this world.[12]

The globe spread with empires and with programmes of power and diplomatic exchange and slipped from the hands of elite patrons and monarchs to publics as the forms of its representation also changed. Indeed, it is a heavily represented idea and the frequency and varied modes of its representation have been the key to its taken-for-grantedness. To see it as quintessentially European is to forget the rich strands of counter-thought around the globe in other regions of the world.

For instance, when the globe was introduced into India in the late sixteenth century, as Sumathi Ramaswamy highlights, Mughal emperors were depicted with a globe in thirty or so images in the decades that followed. She astutely

---

[9] Sujit Sivasundaram, 'Making the Globe: A Cultural History of Science in the Bay of Bengal', *Cultural History* 9, 2 (2020), 217–40.

[10] See, for instance, Lesley Cormack, 'The World at Your Fingertips: Renaissance Globes as Comographical, Mathematical and Pedagogical Instruments', *Archives Internationales d'Histoires des Sciences* 59, 163 (2009), 485–97. Meanwhile, for 'planetary consciousness' see also Mary Louise Pratt, *Imperial Eyes: Travel Writing and Transculturation* (London: Routledge, 1992).

[11] This point is made by Sumathi Ramaswamy, *Terrestrial Lessons: The Conquest of the World as Globe* (Chicago: University of Chicago Press, 2017).

[12] Jerry Brotton, *Trading Territories: Mapping the Early Modern World* (London: Reaktion Books, 1997), 21.

analyses this visual genre as indicative of an 'assertion of difference and defiance' rather than a simple mimicry of European meanings of increasing imperial reach. The globe may be cast as an icon, a replacement for sacred relics in the West. Yet in South Asia, gods and globes co-mingle to this day, suggesting that the routes through which the globe has become a common symbol are multiple rather than singular.[13] A narrative of the role of a singular Renaissance, Enlightenment, imperial programme or indeed of the rise of European science must be avoided if we are to track the origins of the globe as object.

Another way of tracing the rise of the globe as signifier is to see it as linked to the consolidation of astronomical science. Simon Schaffer has paid attention to the relations between astronomy, orientalism and empire in South Asia.[14] In this story the British East India Company's astronomers were calibrating both rational science and rational religion. Hindu Puranic astronomy in the nineteenth century, caricatured for its commitment to flat Earth, milky oceans and moon-eating dragons, was seen as the degenerated version of a previously superior knowledge of the stars and the Earth. It was the same logic that framed orientalist engagement with Hinduism, which itself was seen to have declined into priestcraft. What was needed, then, was for Newtonian men of science to resuscitate it, and for that task it was necessary to find Newtonian science in the Vedas. In other words, astronomical and religious studies were interconnected with the disciplinary foundations of history. As astronomers interrogated Indian historical texts, they would in turn sanctify and purify both true science and religion. The making of astronomical knowledge relied on being able to travel across times and places, but even as astronomy was made secure as a modern discipline its subject became clearer. The Earth and the heavens were separated from each other as intellectual subjects.

It is worth switching more directly to the history of History. In the European history of history, in place of a universal account which was tied to a Judeo-Christian narrative there arose a sense of the unity and connectedness of humankind which was natural. This unity and connectedness was first thought to be civilisational and then evolutionary.[15] This natural ordering was then debated and even disputed as senses of race and racism as well as gender, language and climate started to structure knowledge in the modern era from stadial theory to eugenics. These debates became the province of the new

[13] See Ramaswamy, *Terrestrial Lessons*, 291, and Sumathi Ramaswamy, 'Conceit of the Globe in Mughal Visual Practice', *Comparative Studies in Society and History* 49, 4 (2007), 751–82.
[14] Simon Schaffer, 'British Orientalism on Histories of Religion and Astral Sciences in Northern India', in Bernard Lightman and Sara Qidwai, (eds.), *Evolutionary Theories and Religious Traditions* (Pittsburgh: University of Pittsburgh Press, 2023), 17–40.
[15] For a valuable account of the origins of universal history and then global history which this paragraph and the next draw on, see Franz L. Fillafer, 'A World Connecting: From the Unity of History to Global History', *History and Theory* 56, 1 (2017), 3–37.

sciences. While nature had been seen as timeless and eternal prior to 1800, the rise of new scientific disciplines of empiricism, including geology or comparative anatomy, tied in turn to sprawling enterprises of data collecting that increasingly stretched to all corners of the planet, generating newer senses of the changes of nature and humans in time. Concomitantly, the modelling of the globe was an act of statistical manipulation, tied to longitude and latitude but reaching into the air as well as into the water and underground. It also depended on this data collecting and facilitated trade.

It was in this ferment that modern historiography was born. If the new disciplines of science had taken over the subject of nature, the heavens, as well as of long time, the definition of history changed in response to that. The nineteenth century's Western historicism began with Europe and was no longer generally a universal history of humankind. Indeed, non-European history was cast into a series of other new disciplines outside the strict confines of history per se. With the rise of new empires and nations, which needed historical tellings, it was also necessary to delimit the specialisations of modern historians. Of course, this story looks rather different if the perspective we take shifts from Europe to the writing of history in other regions of the world, but there too the modern saw a delimiting of subject area and a separation of the terrain of memory and so-called 'myth' or 'religion' from history. In other words, history everywhere, by the nineteenth century, was much narrower on many counts. It was also increasingly human-centred.

In the South Asian world, for instance, there was a rich set of diverse histories in the early modern era, including dynastic narrations and traditions connected to all kinds of lineages, running across gods, humans, demons and the natural world. Kumkum Chatterjee skilfully explored these histories in Bengal in the seventeenth and eighteenth centuries and into the period of the advent of British colonialism and the impact of orientalist historiography.[16] Of relevance here is the fact that they had long and often cyclical or otherwise shaped senses of time and wide geographies; they blurred the factual and the fictional and they stretched across Sanskrit as well as Persian traditions in addition to various regional vernaculars. They could take verse form. They had a sense of authority, expertise and function. This means, following Chatterjee, that British and European histories in India should not be seen as the first to be scientific and rational, despite the centrality of such latter histories to conceptions of nationalism, literacy and middle-class sensibility in India by the end of the nineteenth century. Relatedly and for Sri Lanka, I have argued that its palm-leaf manuscript

---

[16] Kumkum Chatterjee, *The Cultures of History in Early Modern India: Persianization and Mughal Culture in Bengal* (Oxford: Oxford University Press, 2009). Another vital and important contribution for another region of South Asia, is Velcheru N. Rao, David Shulman and Sanjay Subrahmanyam, *Textures of Time: Writing History in South India, 1600–1800* (New York: Other Press LLC, 2003).

histories held their popular power and resonance into the era of printed-colonial histories.[17] It is not that palm-leaf gave way to print. Rather, history came to be defined by printed and supposedly 'empirical' narrations; palm-leaf texts were cast outside the discipline.

It is useful to consider today's global history as a mode of modelling and mapping which reaches beyond this historiographical drawing of the curtains of the nineteenth and twentieth centuries. Yet in contesting the delimited foundations of modern historiography, which global historians aim to do, it is also necessary to challenge the disciplinary specialisms which generated a separation between the right subject of history and the right subject of science.

Behind Map and Model: The Changeable Earth

Working from the premise that mapping, modelling and global history are interrelated, some alternative fragments of cartography of the wider world will be followed to see what lies beneath this relation and whether it is possible to work towards nature.

A good site for me to focus attention on is the gigantically proportioned island of 'Taprobane', which is often said to come from Claudius Ptolemy's *Geographia*. The cartographic rendition of this island, said to be today's Sri Lanka, occupies approximately twelve times the extent of present-day Sri Lanka.[18] This late-fourteenth- or early-fifteenth-century version is from the British Library, and arrived there through the collections of the eighteenth-century classical and musical scholar Charles Burney (Figure 5.1).[19] The reason for the exaggerated cartographic rendition continues to confound recent historians: did Ptolemy mistake a part of India as belonging to the island of present-day Sri Lanka? One response to the problem is that Ptolemy inherited this idea of Taprobane from sailors arriving in Alexandria, who knew the coast of west India well but not the island of Sri Lanka and especially the island's eastern coast, which could only be reached after going around the island.[20] Much more recently, after the tsunami of 2004, accounts of the gigantic

[17] Sujit Sivasundaram, 'Materialities in the Making of World Histories: South Asia and the South Pacific' in Ivan Gaskell and Sarah Anne Carter (eds.), *The Oxford Handbook of History and Material Culture* (Oxford: Oxford University Press, 2020), 513–34.
[18] There has been some debate about whether Ptolemy's Taprobane refers to Sri Lanka or Sumatra. For more on this, see R. L. Brohier, *Land, Maps and Surveys: Descriptive Catalogue of Historical Maps in the Surveyor General's Office, Colombo* (Colombo: Ceylon Government Press, 1951), vol. 2, 23; and John Whitchurch Bennett, *Ceylon and Its Capabilities* (London: W. H. Allen & Co., 1843), 11. Taprobane is equated with Sri Lanka in J. Lennart Berggren and Alexander Jones, *Ptolemy's Geography: An Annotated Translation of the Theoretical Chapters* (Princeton: Princeton University Press, 2000), 6.
[19] Berggren and Jones, *Ptolemy's Geography*, 20.
[20] Ananda Abeydeera, 'The Geographical Perceptions of India and Ceylon in the *Periplus Maris Erythraei* and in Ptolemy's *Geography*', *Terrae Icongnitae* 30, 1 (2013), 1–25.

Figure 5.1 Map labelled 'Taprobana insula', with the lowest horizontal line
representing the equator. British Library, Burney 111 fl v. British Library.

Taprobane, including this map, were utilised on the island to tell stories of the
resizing of Sri Lanka by repeated tidal waves, as part of the gods' judgement for
bad government today.

In Sebastian Münster's Latin translation and amplification of Ptolemy's
Geographia, from 1540, there appears a further version of the map of
'Taprobane' (Figure 5.2). In Münster's hand, the island is marked with mountains, rivers and cities. The equator – that marker of the globe – is shown
running through the island. Alongside the map appears a ferocious tusked
elephant as ornamentation, derived from the sketches of mapmaker Giacomo
Gastaldi, who also produced his version of Ptolemy's *Geographia*. The

❧ TABVLA ASIAE XII· ᛋ

Figure 5.2 Tabula Asiae XII; hand-coloured map by Sebastian Münster, *c*.1552. From Ptolemy's *Geographia universalis*, 1540 ed., rev. & ed. by Sebastian Münster. Sri Lanka is labelled 'Taprobana' on the map, a name which was given to Sumatra on maps in later editions of the *Geographia*. MIT.

elephant's angry eyes and serpentine trunk immediately attract the reader's attention. The way in which this elephant is depicted is in keeping with earlier European mapping traditions which sometimes represent elephants as looking like wild boars with trumpet-like trunks.[21] Ludovico di Varthema, who visited Lanka, is then cited. The island, we are told, 'exports elephants that are larger and nobler than those found elsewhere'.[22] Taprobane becomes known here for its anomalous natural history; its unusual elephants make a stand on the map. The description from Varthema continues: 'Its yield of the long pepper is likewise richer, indeed wonderful in its abundance.'[23] Soon the map was edited once again, and the elephant was made less fierce (Figure 5.3). Even while tracing the reverberations of Ptolemy's 'Taprobane' like this, one important caveat is that the idea, together with the knowledge of sailors and merchants

---

[21] See Donald F. Lach, *Asia in the Making of Europe*, vol. 2: *A Century of Wonder* (Chicago: The University of Chicago Press, 1970), Book 1, 124–31.
[22] Brohier, *Lands, Maps and Surveys*, 22.
[23] Brohier, *Lands, Maps and Surveys*, 22.

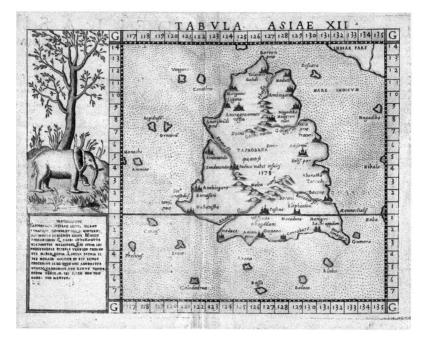

Figure 5.3 Tabula Asiae XII; hand-coloured engraved map, copied from
Sebastian Münster, in *Geografia di Claudio Tolomeo Alessandrino*, by
Giuseppe Rosaccio, 1599. Stanford University Libraries. Public Domain.

from across the Indian Ocean, fed into the work of Arab and Islamic cosmog-
raphers. Moroccan-born and Sicily-based Muhammad al-Idrisi showed Lanka
like this in the twelfth century. This image is a later reproduction. (Figure 5.4).

Rather than scrutinising this genealogy of a map of the island of Sri Lanka
for accuracy and verisimilitude, across Europe, West Asia and South Asia,
what if we track it for an alternative cartographic aesthetic? Such an aesthetic
may be connected to the physicality of the Earth. In the rendition of
'Taprobane', Sri Lanka is a fabulous island with a magnetic power at the centre
of the Indian Ocean. One could argue that this appeal is what gave rise to its
gigantic sizing and its conception as a site of human origin, even as it was later
cast as a possible location for the Garden of Eden. These maps attest to how
information about pepper and elephants travelled more easily and accurately
than information about the boundaries and limits of the island.

The history of tsunamis is another way to interrogate this map to show that
behind this cartographic impulse is an engagement with the changeable Earth.
'Taprobane' may be 'cross-contextualised' against various Indigenous palm-

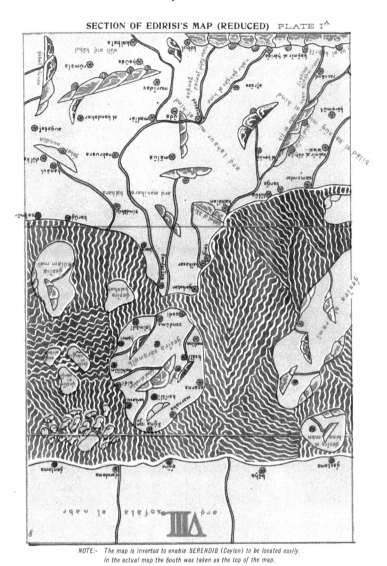

Figure 5.4 Muhammad al-Idrisi's map of Sarandib, reproduced from R. L. Brohier and J. H. O Paulusz, *Land, Maps and Surveys* (Ceylon Government Press: Colombo, 1951), Vol. 2, Plate 1A. Needham Research Institute, University of Cambridge.

leaf narrations of past tidal waves on the island, which once again point to how mappers across cultures struggled to historicise this piece of Earth. Orientalist accounts of the island's submersion borrowed heavily from what travellers were told by Indigenous peoples.

Most clearly, the elite chronicles of the *Mahavamsa*, the *Thupavamsa* and the *Rajavaliya* provide a context for appreciating often retold tales of past tidal waves and resizing of the island. The *Mahavamsa*, a Buddhist chronicle written in the sixth, thirteenth and eighteenth centuries, is today the most cherished nationalist source of Sri Lankan history.[24] The account of how the sea encroached on the kingdom based in Kelaniya, during the reign of Kalanitissa, illustrates the genre perfectly.[25] The reader is told of the foolishness of Kalanitissa's brother, Ayya-Uttika, who sleeps with the queen, and therefore rouses the wrath of his brother. Having fled Kalanitissa's kingdom, Ayya-Uttika sends a man disguised as a Buddhist priest with a secret letter to the queen. This is discovered by the king, who slays the man and throws him into the sea. The author of the *Mahavamsa* presents this as a fitful deed of anger unsuitable for a monarch. After all, the priest and his attendant were innocent; it was the king's brother who was guilty. The *Mahavamsa* continues: 'Wroth at this the sea-gods made the sea overflow the land.'[26] Another chronicle, the seventeenth century *Rajavaliya*, records: 'on account of the wickedness of Kelanitissa, 100,000 seaport towns, 970 fishers' villages, and 470 villages of pearl-fishers making altogether eleven-twelfths of Lanka, were submerged by the great sea'.[27]

This story draws on a rich pre-colonial and oral historical consciousness which itself was cartographic. For instance, Charles Pridham, a mid-nineteenth-century colonial and orientalist British historian, in writing of the flood in the reign of Kalanitissa, does not mention the *Mahavamsa*; he notes that his account of the flooding emerges from 'Singalese topographical works' such as the 'Kadaimpota and Lanka-Wistric'.[28] Pridham refers here to a set of sources that were far more accessible than the elite chronicles and which were kept safe by village elders and recited at public ceremonies. The *kadaim pot* and *vitti pot* did not attract as much

---

[24] For discussions of how to interpret Buddhist chronicles, see: Steven Kemper, *The Presence of the Past: Chronicles, Politics and Culture in Sinhala Life* (Ithaca: Cornell University Press, 1991); Gananath Obeyesekere, 'The Myth of the Human Sacrifice: History, Story and Debate in a Buddhist Chronicle', *Social Analysis* 25, 25 (1989), 78–93; Ronald Inden et al., *Querying the Medieval: Texts and the History of Practices in South Asia* (New York: Oxford University Press, 2000), 99–16.

[25] This appears in William Geiger (transl.), *The Mahāvaṃsa, or the Great Chronicle of Ceylon* (London: Frowde, 1912, reprinted London: Luzac, 1964), ch. XXII, lines 13–22.

[26] Geiger, The Mahavamsa, ch XXII, line 20.

[27] Bandusena Gunasekera (ed.), *The Rajavaliya or a Historical Narrative of Sinhalese Kings* (Ceylon: George J. A. Sheen, Government Printer, 1900; reprinted Colombo: Skeen, 1954), 23.

[28] Charles Pridham, *A Historical and Statistical Account and Statistical Account of Ceylon and Its Dependencies* (London: Boone, 1849), vol. 1, 18.

attention from the orientalist translators of the nineteenth century, who were critical in popularising texts such as the *Mahavamsa*, yet they reveal how accounts of flooding and changes to the land were transmitted in the indigenous historical memory and in geographical texts on palm-leaf.[29] The account of the fate of Kalanitissa's kingdom seems to have been something of a staple in this set of texts.[30] One of them retells the story thus:

during the days of Kalanitissa, since the king caused the death of an innocent thera by putting him into a cauldron of boiling oil, the grief-stricken gods, in their anger with their divine powers, submerged the king's territory with the waves of the ocean in order to destroy the world. At that time nine islands surrounding Lamka, twenty-nine *mudal ratas*, thirty-five thousand five hundred and four villages together with great port villages, tanks and fields and gem mines and numerous beings, without feet, two legged, four legged, many legged and structures such as cetiyas, shrine rooms, residential quarters of monks were eroded to the sea.[31]

This cross-contextualisation of sources on the geographical shape, size and casting of the island of what is now Sri Lanka and was once Taprobane is an attempt to think beyond the rise of the European map and, indeed, the globe. For the globe's artificiality and detachment as an object makes it often bypass the Earth; in symmetry, history can do so too, and the challenge for global history is to ensure it does not. These Sri Lankan sources – from all perspectives, orientalist as well as Indigenous – are trying to come to terms with how to simultaneously map and historicise a changeable island. In a place where there were tidal waves and where there has recently been a tsunami, in a site where there are elephants and pepper, how is it possible to chart the size of an island and its past?

Reconsidering global history, viewed in light of the geographical construction and stabilisation of Sri Lanka, may be about engaging with what lies beneath and behind the mapping impulse. In the case of Lanka/Taprobane/Ceylon, this is the vexed materiality of an island which is always becoming and which is set in a watery terrain beyond human control. It is about waves, animals and peoples as world-makers. These might be the building blocks of an Earthy historiography, a historical literature that accepts the instability of the ground on which history happens. Such a history will respond to the elision of nature and the delimitation of subject area which were at the heart of the origins of modern historiography, and, indeed, Enlightened sensibilities about what counts as a good source. It will also contend with the artificiality of the global.

---

[29] For more on this geographical knowledge, see Sujit Sivasundaram, 'Tales of the Land: British Geography and Kandyan Resistance in Sri Lanka, 1803–1850', *Modern Asian Studies* 41, 5 (2007), 925–65.

[30] H. A. P. Abeyawardana, *Boundary Divisions of Mediaeval Sri Lanka* (Colombo: Academy of Sri Lankan Culture, 1999), 121.

[31] Abeyawardana, *Boundary Divisions*, 208.

The Natural in Recent Historiography

In what follows, in order to assess the state of present rather than long passed historiography, I turn to *environmental history, agricultural history, the history of oceans, animal histories* and the *history of medicine*. In taking late-twentieth-century and early-twenty-first century historiography into view, it is worth emphasising that nature has not been absent, even if it has arguably never been dominant. Each of these fields has been interlinked with global history, and increasingly so. What might a further conversation between the two sides yield if we move from the global to the Earthy?

Environmental history, like global history, is traditionally said to have been born in the USA, yet it too can be said to be as old as scholarship itself.[32] Early environmental histories often proceeded on the basis of natural determinism. Theorists such as Alexander von Humboldt or Pierre Poivre played critical roles in the origins of this field in responding to the changes in nature that they witnessed in colonial territories.[33] Meanwhile, later men of science, including Charles Darwin, were curious about transformations of nature in time and history. One might follow the global environmental historian, Alfred Crosby, in tracking a demarcation of subject areas as key to why environmental history was seen, in the nineteenth century, to rightly belong with science, rather than in historiography narrowly construed: '[Historians] were trained to specialise, to devote their lives to the minute study of small patches of history; environmental historians must be genera-lists because environmental changes are rarely affairs of days, weeks or even years and are often only discernable regionally, even continentally.'[34] Environmental history's entry into historiography came via geography. By the era of decolonisation, with fears of nuclear catastrophe and pollution, and with a visual image of the Earth as an object viewed from space motivating it, environmental history went global.

Among the debates in the field is how to write 'nature-centred' rather than 'anthro-centric' histories.[35] Yet this relies on a distinction between humans and nature which itself is increasingly disputed. Additionally, the question assumes that nature has been untouched, whereas many scholars highlight the creation of what is wild – 'wilderness', for instance – through human engagement with nature over centuries. Epidemics, floods and fires have redirected historical energy towards the environment, and this in turn raises a second perennial

---

[32] Harriet Ritvo, 'History and Animal Studies', *Society and Animals* 10, 4 (2002), 403–6.

[33] Richard Grove, *Green Imperialism: Colonial Expansion, Tropical Island Edens and the Origins of Environmentalism, 1600–1860* (Cambridge: Cambridge University Press, 1996).

[34] Alfred Crosby, 'The Past and Present of Environmental History', *American Historical Review* 100, 4 (1995), 1177–89.

[35] For a start in further exploring points in this paragraph, see Joachim Radkau, *Nature and Power: A Global History of the Environment* (Cambridge: Cambridge University Press, 2008).

question about the agency of nature. But here too, a recourse to assembly and co-constitution is one of the preferred routes rather than a strict prescription of robust agency to the non-human or the separation of humans from their environments.

The environmental crisis frames environmental history, but scholars continue to push against a presumed teleology that leads into the present moment, through turning points and transitions caused by empires, modernisation, states or developmentalist projects. There is indeed a danger in seeing the pre-colonial era as one of ecological harmony, but also a danger of erasing the violent scalar environmental changes generated by European empires, their wars and their plantation systems. More broadly, key concerns in global history, such as capitalism, industrialisation, inequality, divergence and marketisation, have all generated significant environmental history literatures.[36] Yet in many standard global history text books, the environment can go missing and become an afterthought. C. A. Bayly's last book was critiqued for this reason.[37] This is despite the fact that some key practitioners – such as William H. McNeill – were pioneers in both fields. A fundamental conversation between environmental history and global history has long been in prospect.[38]

Now that the problematic dichotomy of human/nature is being overcome it may be possible for global historians too to take soil, air and water, among other elements, more seriously as part of the story and to begin with these subjects. *Agricultural history* used to be the purview of economic historians interested in demography and trade. In the context of South Asian history, it drew further strength from subaltern studies and from the foregrounding of the marginal peasant. Subaltern studies scholars illustrated how peasant politics had ramifications for wide political ideologies as well as for governance. But the turn to culture as well as to globalisation saw a move away from these interests and, indeed, the rural peasant. In this context, recent work, for instance by Neeladri Bhattacharya, has reconsidered the status of the agrarian frontier, not simply as one of social stratification or of economic inequality, but also as one generated by knowledge, culture and the law. Indeed, it is the very normalisation of the status of agriculture as rural and peasant-based which needs critiquing.[39] Just as

[36] For one key debate, divergence, as approached via the environment and South Asia, see Prasannan Parathasarathi, *Why Europe Grew Rich and Asia Did Not: Global Economic Divergence, 1600–1850* (Cambridge: Cambridge University Press, 2011).
[37] Sunil Amrith, 'The Anthropocene and the Triumph of the Imagination: An Environmental Perspective on C. A. Bayly's *Remaking the Modern World, 1900–2015*', *Journal of Asian Studies* 78, 4 (2019), 837–48.
[38] Edmund Burke III and Kenneth Pomeranz (eds.), *The Environment and World History* (Berkeley: University of California Press, 2009).
[39] Neeladri Bhattacharya, *The Great Agrarian Conquest: The Colonial Reshaping of a Rural World* (New York: SUNY Press, 2019); see also David Gilmartin, *Blood and Water: The Indus River Basin in Modern History* (Oakland: University of California Press, 2020).

much as in other areas where the historiographies of the global and the agrarian have met – for instance, around plantation complexes or the genetic manipulation of nature – it is important for this new mode of writing about the agrarian not to take categories for granted.[40] The older structuralist perspectives, often supercharged by the schema of Marxism, have given way to radical alternatives which are more critical about singular understandings of what constitutes nature as opposed to the human, and also what constitutes the local and the global.

Turning again to South Asian history, there are several examples of works which look beyond such dichotomies. Debjani Bhattacharyya has focused on tides and recast the history of Calcutta in a deltaic and moveable geography as a result.[41] Sunil Amrith has written a history of South Asia as a history of water and rivers, while Sudipta Sen has used the river Ganges to organise a long history of Indic civilisation.[42] Rohan D'Souza has argued for the role of floods as a 'biological pulse' in eastern deltaic India, since it is made up of 'soil and water admixtures rather than neatly separated into distinct domains of land and river flow'.[43]

One of the weaknesses of environmental history is that it has often-times, and certainly in its twentieth-century incarnations, been determinedly terra-centric and connected to questions, for instance, of land use, agriculture and demography. In this mode it can fold back into national history. The splurge of recent work in *oceanic history* arose partly in response and it has had an increasingly visible place in what is considered global history today. After all, oceans necessarily cross areas, regions and nations. Oceanic history also relocates long-standing maritime and naval history to an environmental landscape of shipwreck and weather events or of whales, seals and other creatures. Here, too, the lineage of the sub-discipline is a matter of debate: on the one

---

[40] For some other works in agricultural history, colonialism and globalisation, see Rebecca Woods, *The Herds That Shot around the World: Native Breeds and the British Empire, 1800–1900* (Chapel Hill: University of North California Press, 2017); Giovanni Frederico, *Feeding the World: An Economic History of World Agriculture, 1800–2000* (Princeton: Princeton University Press, 2005); and Sven Beckert, *Empire of Cotton: A New History of Global Capitalism* (London: Allen Lane, 2014).

[41] Debjani Bhattacharyya, *Empire and Ecology in the Bengal Delta: The Making of Calcutta* (Cambridge: Cambridge University Press, 2018); Debjani Bhattacharyya, 'Almanac of a Tide Country', *items*, 20 November 2010, https://items.ssrc.org/ways-of-water/almanac-of-a-tide-country. See also the set of short reflections by Surabhi Ranganathan, 'The Law of the Sea: 7 EssaysontheInterfacesofLandandSea', www.lcil.cam.ac.uk/blog/law-sea-dr-surabhi-ranganathan. These essays were first published on the Joint Center for History and Economics website at Harvard University (January 2020).

[42] Sunil Amrith, *Unruly Waters: How Mountains, Rivers and Monsoons Have Shaped South Asia's History* (London: Penguin Books, 2018); and Sudipta Sen, *Ganges: The Many Pasts of an Indian River* (New Haven: Yale University Press, 2019).

[43] Rohan D'Souza, 'Events, Processes and Pulses: Resituating Floods in Environmental Histories of South Asia', *Environment and History* 26, 1 (2020), 31–50.

hand, it is traced to the Annales school and the formative influence of Fernand Braudel, yet the argument is made that Pacific Ocean and Indian Ocean histories have much longer genealogies beyond both Mediterranean and Atlantic studies.[44] The encounter between oceanic and global history is now beginning to burst the boundaries of artificial schemas – for instance, the 'Atlantic system of slavery' or the 'Indian ocean trading world' – to yield intra-oceanic histories as well as the histories of straits, basins and bays and a rich set of diverse geographies beyond whole ocean studies. The World Ocean itself is becoming a subject of historical narration.

This augurs well for a history of the sea which is no longer constrained by human epistemologies and geographical classifications but which is, in the sense of this chapter, more Earthy and less modelled. Oceanic histories are also taking the movement of natural things more seriously, from molluscs to salmon, and the underwater itself is emerging as a site of history. Migration is being cast within, for instance, the monsoon; the hajj pilgrimage is being understood within the material conditions of travel; labour is being interrogated with respect to knowledge of nature and the tragic experience of the sea journey.[45] Both oceanic and environmental history by default centre large geographical zones and work beyond human understandings and classifications of nature. *Animal history*, the next historiographical focus point, can have the same geographic range but it intensively studies and problematises species boundaries more than geographic or political ones.

The study of animals in history arose out of work on agrarian history before taking off amid the enthusiasm for cultural history at the end of the last century. However, cultural histories of animals were often about human representations and attitudes to animals; they were regularly focused around European zoos and exhibitions.[46] In contrast, recent work in animal studies has benefitted from the methodological foundations of postcolonial history and global history and their attention to marginal agents, for at the heart of animal history is a desire to be inclusive about historical subjectivity. Recent historians have highlighted the role played by capitalism; ideas of class, race and gender; scientific knowledge and empires in organising the category of the animal. Jonathan Saha, in new work on Burma/Myanmar at the rim of British India, for instance, claims both that 'empire was always an interspecies phenomenon' and that 'species was a category that was articulated with race, class and gender'.[47] The

---

[44] For further study on the points made in this paragraph, see David Armitage et al. (eds.), *Oceanic Histories* (Cambridge: Cambridge University Press, 2017).

[45] See, for instance, Eric Tagliacozzo, *The Longest Journey: Southeast Asians and the Pilgrimage to Mecca* (Oxford: Oxford University Press, 2013).

[46] Ritvo, 'History and Animal Studies'.

[47] Jonathan Saha, *Colonizing Animals: Interspecies Empire in Myanmar* (Cambridge: Cambridge University Press, 2021).

challenge for animal historians is the same as that for environmental historians: not to lose sight of the human in focusing on animals. Rather, an agenda that demonstrates how modes of hierarchy, ideology and politics are crystallised around the policing and articulation of the boundary between the human and the non-human is more compelling.

Indeed, if an Earthy perspective is adopted, the next step is to place the human/non-human collective within a broader environmental and material context. The zoonotic disease of Covid-19 is a case in point. In addition to intensive contact between humans and animals and new styles of meat consumption in East Asia, the wildlife frontier of China is likely also to have played a role in the origins of the recent pandemic. It is now thought that Covid-19 also arose due to rapidly changing uses of land and the march of deforestation.[48] If so, one needs to bring land, life and unseen viruses together rather than working solely at the intersection of the human and the animal. The *history of medicine* seems uniquely placed to respond to such an agenda and will surely see a resurgence in the next decades.

Though it has traditionally been concerned with histories of state-making, institutionalisation, the social context of ideas of disease, the history of the body and the relations between patients and doctors, the history of medicine is showing signs of placing the triad of disease, medicine and the body into a more complex dialectic. Vernacular traditions and indigenous ideas of medicine have increasingly come into focus and have done so amidst the rise of a desire for alternative therapies and, more problematically, a nationalist authorisation of culturally particular traditions of cure. Turning once again to a historiography which begins with South Asia, Projit Mukharji's work comes to the history of Ayurveda from the technologies and material objects used to practice it and how these in turn changed views of the body and the meaning of modernity.[49] Rohan Deb Roy, in writing a history of malaria, also follows a route which is more materially aware, in being acutely conscious of the shifting significations of cinchona, quinine, fever and the body and their sprawling transnational creation.[50]

What each of these five approaches demonstrates is the already vibrant conversations afoot which include both nature and materiality within global history. An Earthy perspective would be one that builds on each of these avenues and others, such as the history of energy, waste or technology. It would contest the historiographical and historical reasons for the elision of

---

[48] See Sujit Sivasundaram, 'The Human, the Animal and the Prehistory of Covid-19', *Past and Present* 249, 1 (2021), 295–316.

[49] Projit Mukharji, *Doctoring Traditions: Ayurveda, Small Technologies and Braided Sciences* (Chicago: University of Chicago Press, 2016).

[50] Rohan Deb Roy, *Malarial Subjects: Empire, Medicine and Nonhumans in British India, 1820–1909* (Cambridge: Cambridge University Press, 2017).

nature from mainstream history and take up the promise of global history as a method which bursts various boundaries. These boundaries should of course carry on being geographical, political, agentic and cultural. But they may also now include the boundaries of human/non-human, seen/ unseen, underwater/overwater, overground/underground and other such divisions in global understanding which are not in keeping with the way the Earth works.

This is not to call for an erasure of the global, but rather to say that the makings of the global depend in turn not only on the local, but also on all those material and natural contexts which are often at the sidelines of global historiography. Such contexts can also involve a range of different scales, from oceans to airs or from insects to tigers. Such an approach would generate a more robustly multicentred set of subjects, objects and geographies for global history. In one possible path forward one might imagine that features such as waves, earthquakes or tides; garbage pits, oil spills and fire-storms; islands, oases and deltas could be used to organise histories around specific material features and planetary events without needing a naturally deterministic framework of explanation.

On the Anthropocene

There is an important debate that is worth addressing in closing these reflections about an Earthy historiography. Is the call for a global history attuned to seas and mountains, waves and rivers, and viruses and bacteria, a history of the environmental present? And, if so, is it worth casting it under the contested label, first proposed in 2000, of the 'Anthropocene'?[51]

I have consciously not engaged with the 'Anthropocene' thus far because the 'Anthropocene' itself is a universalising concept that takes the uniformity of the planet for granted. It may easily be critiqued for many of the same reasons set out here against the global. Additionally, it rests on a teleology and assumes a very narrow view of periodisation, through the assumption that environmental transformation can be precisely dated to a particular era. It is in many ways a nostalgic concept, casting everything prior to the era when humans became 'geological agents' into a sustainable prehistory. Meanwhile, it assumes a global convergence in extinction, the growth of cities and population, farming and agriculture or deforestation. It also rests on a geohistorical framework. Pratik Chakrabarti's recent work, based out of South Asia, is useful here in showing how the debate over the Anthropocene arises out of the longer disciplinary history of geology, a discipline which naturalised and lengthened

---

[51] Originating from Paul Crutzen and Eugene Stoermer.

historical time.[52] In this sense the Anthropocene still inherits the problems of disciplinary specialism highlighted earlier rather than contesting them. It can easily see a wholesale ceding, once again, of the ground of historical scholarship to science.

The concept of the Anthropocene has also been critiqued for erasing histories of racism, enslavement and dispossession, and there has been a call for a 'Billion Black Anthropocenes'.[53] The alternative terms of the 'Capitalocene' or the 'Plantationocene' are proposed to foreground capital's role in creating an abstracted nature and the exploitation of unfree labour as a racialised commodity via imperial systems in the multispecies assembly of the plantation.[54] A concomitant debate which runs through these three terms – 'Anthropocene', 'Capitalocene', 'Plantationocene' – along with others which include 'Technocene' or 'Chthulucene', is whether or not the human/non-human binary should be bridged or not in new material approaches such as those discussed in this chapter.[55] For all these reasons, the sketch of an Earthy historiography that I present here does not fit within the conception of the 'Anthropocene'. Rather, it is an invitation towards plurality and assembly and a multiplicity of scales, forces and periodisations as constitutive of historical change.

One aspect of the debate about the 'Anthropocene' that calls for attention is temporality. Making the concept of the global more Earthy is fundamentally about its terrain and materiality, but what about the temporalities of history? A less human-centred view of time would require attention to the long-term. Indeed, the drawing of the curtains of modern historiography allowed time itself to be compressed, even as the sciences were expanding time.[56] But it may be the case that we should no longer approach temporality as a linear scale: this was part and parcel of the rolling out of the humanist and Enlightened history across the world. More cyclical views of temporality may be in order in a historiography attuned to the terrain of the Earth; attention to the rise and fall of life forms, or indeed to processes of descent, kinship and evolution, could frame quite distinct modes of historical writing. Indigenous peoples

---

[52] Pratik Chakrabarti, *Inscriptions of Nature: Geology and the Naturalization of Antiquity* (Baltimore: Johns Hopkins University Press, 2020).

[53] Kathryn Yusoff, *A Billion Black Anthropocenes or None* (Minneapolis: University of Minnesota Press, 2018).

[54] For 'plantationocene' see, for instance, Michael Warren Murphy and Caitlin Schroering, 'Refiguring the Plantationocene: Racial Capitalism, World-Systems Analysis and Global Socioecological Transformation', *Journal of World-Systems Research* 26, 2 (2020), 400–15.

[55] See, for instance, Jason W. Moore, *Capitalism in the Web of Life: Ecology and the Accumulation of Capital* (London: Verso Books, 2015) and Andreas Malm, *Fossil Capital: The Rise of Steam Power and the Roots of Global Warming* (London: Verso Books, 2016) and his 'Geology of Mankind? A Critique of the Anthropocene Narrative', *Anthropocene Review* 1, 1 (2014), 62–9.

[56] For temporality, see, for instance, Reinhart Koselleck, *Futures Past: On the Semantics of Historical Time* (New York: Columbia University Press, 2004).

continue to practice modes of genealogy which orient pasts and futures in different ways to professional historians.[57] Meanwhile, deep history and attention to changes in the Earth's temperature or pollution levels could also provide interesting routes towards alternative modes of periodisation to those determined by calendrical systems. In all these ways, it may be necessary to be more 'pluri-temporal' in historical writing.

The environmental crisis that we are living through is undeniable, and it is therefore understandable that a concept such as the 'Anthropocene' is needed to do urgent scholarly work. To take one thread within this moment, we are living in an age of mass extinction. Yet even with such a claim, philosophical debates have arisen about how to define the concept of extinction and how to come to terms with programmes of de-extinction which are already afoot, as well as techniques of rewilding.[58] New technologies, encompassing frozen arks of specimens, are opening up a middle ground between the categories of 'endangered' and 'extinct'.[59] Historians of extinction are conducting work which usefully links the horrific account of violence against Indigenous peoples with that against non-human species: programmes of genocide were linked in history across the human/non-human dichotomy, especially when they occurred in the midst of settlement colonisation. To overstate the teleological march of extinction is to prevent the possibilities of resistance, persistence and return by targeted species. It takes the crisis narrative at face value, without presenting a more nuanced story with the chance of a future encompassing diverse peoples and life forms. It minimises the agentic status of nature and the dominated.

Conclusion

This chapter started out from the premise that the Earth is a material space rather than a modelled globular entity. At the same time, the production of the globe as object and history as discipline can be jointly interrogated as endeavours that have had the tendency to detach the human from the materiality of the planet and its life forms; the origins of modern historiography saw an elision of nature. Precisely for this reason, however, human attempts at mapping may be re-read and peeled back. Working with 'Taprobane' was an attempt to read the genealogy of mapping differently – to show how

---

[57] See, for instance, Warwick Anderson and Miranda Johnson (eds.), *Pacific Futures* (Honolulu: University of Hawai'i Press, 2018).

[58] This follows the ongoing work of Sadiah Qureshi. See, for instance, her presentation to the Anthropocene Histories seminar, London, www.ucl.ac.uk/anthropocene/projects-and-seminars/seminar-series/anthropocene-histories.

[59] Joanna Radin, *Life on Ice: A History of New Uses for Cold Blood* (Chicago: Chicago University Press, 2017); Cal Fyn, *Islands of Abandonment: Life in a Posthuman Environment* (London: William Collins, 2021).

Indigenous as well as colonial authors, cartographers and historians were wrestling with the question of how to size, historicise and represent a changeable island in the midst of the ocean and over the long term. Maps can be read not only for detachment and ornamentation, but also for clues to the materiality of the Earth bursting through.

And it is in this spirit that a proposal is made here for an Earthy historiography – a more materially aware global history which can move across many scales and boundaries without reducing itself to a new series of classifications or singularities. It may not be a purist post-human history, but rather one which places the human within a series of other assemblies. It would open up the possibility of a future which is more conscious of materiality yet not solely determined by a crisis narrative or by modes of reductionism. To quote Donna Haraway: 'I am a compost-ist, not a posthuman-ist: we are all compost not posthuman.'[60]

---

[60] Donna Haraway, 'Anthropocene, Capitalocene, Plantationocene, Chthulucene: Making Kin', *Environmental Humanities* 6, 1 (2015), 159–65.

6   Openness and Closure

Spheres and Other Metaphors of Boundedness in Global History

Valeska Huber

As early as 1986, the German philosopher Hans Blumenberg pointed to the impossibility of forming a general philosophical notion of the world.[1] Since then, conceptualising the globe as a whole has proved to be a challenge in many disciplines.[2] Even terms and metaphors that are less ambitious and all-encompassing and that refer to specific global processes or aspects of globality are often inadequate. This is particularly true when it comes to capturing the tension between openness and closure that characterises many, if not all, global processes: Global phenomena – from migration and mobility to labour and capitalism – can only be understood with clear reference to unevenness and inequality and to processes of exclusion as well as inclusion. Yet the language of globality still prioritises openness and fluidity at the expense of metaphors pointing to limits and boundaries.

This terminological and conceptual conundrum is not surprising at a time when unequivocally positive narratives of growing global interconnectedness have begun to fray and a fixed sense of globality has been called into question.[3] What Michael Geyer and Charles Bright referred to simply as a 'condition of globality' in the mid-1990s is now in need of further specification.[4] As a result, the vocabulary that has helped global history come of age, ranging from connection to integration and from flows to circulation, is now considered

Research for this chapter has been funded by Deutsche Forschungsgemeinschaft (DFG) – project number 289213179.

[1] Hans Blumenberg, *Die Lesbarkeit der Welt* (Frankfurt am Main: Suhrkamp, 1986).

[2] Helge Jordheim and Erling Sandmo (eds.), *Conceptualizing the World: An Exploration across Disciplines* (New York: Berghahn Books, 2018). On competing narratives of globalisation, see Olaf Bach, *Die Erfindung der Globalisierung: Entstehung und Wandel eines zeitgeschichtlichen Grundbegriffs* (Frankfurt am Main: Campus, 2013); Sabine Selchow, *Negotiations of the 'New World': The Omnipresence of Global as a Political Phenomenon* (Bielefeld: Transcript, 2017).

[3] On figures of thought, metaphors and conceptual histories of the global, see, for instance, Jo-Anne Pemberton, *Global Metaphors: Modernity and the Quest for One World* (London: Pluto Press, 2001). For the global as a 'sui generis' category, see Jens Bartelson, 'From the International to the Global?', in Andreas Gofas et al. (eds.), *The SAGE Handbook of the History, Philosophy and Sociology of International Relations* (Thousand Oaks: SAGE, 2018), 33–45.

[4] Michael Geyer and Charles Bright, 'World History in a Global Age', *American Historical Review* 100, 4 (1995), 1034–60, here 1041.

problematic by many historians, whether or not they employ an explicitly global history perspective.[5]

At the same time, few would deny that our specific moment in time – conflict-laden and crisis-ridden as it may be – is also specifically 'global'. Many of the core experiences of the present age – military conflict and the ensuing refugee movements, the Covid-19 pandemic, the climate crisis, the extinction of species and even the resurgence of populism and nationalism – are phenomena that cannot be understood within the framework of the nation-state, despite the fact that they are deeply divisive. As a result, we need figures of thought that can capture a globality that is profoundly marked by division and tension. This chapter seeks keywords and concepts that will enable us to grasp the contradictory and conflictive globality of the current moment and sharpen our analysis of equally contradictory and conflictive global pasts.

When addressing this recent unease with the vocabulary of global history, historians often resort to antonyms. They set disconnection against connection, disentanglement against entanglement, disintegration against integration or, on the most general level, deglobalisation against globalisation. This chapter searches for a figure of thought that can challenge the existing languages of the global more effectively than simply pairing each of the established terms with its opposite.

To this end, the chapter traces the history and analytic potential of a term that does not come with its opposite in tow but instead captures openness and closure in a single frame: the sphere. The Greek word *sphaira* and the Latin word *sphaera* have taken on a plethora of meanings over time, expanding from 'globular body or figure' to '(the) globe conceived as appropriate to a particular planet, hence (one's or its) province or domain'.[6] Within this semantic family, we find terms that relate to the Earth as a whole and its globular form – words like atmosphere, lithosphere, biosphere, geosphere and hydrosphere. Spheres can also refer to the 'place, position, or station in society; an aggregate of persons of a certain rank or standing'.[7] Beyond the Earth-based vocabulary, we

---

[5] See Jeremy Adelman, 'What Is Global History Now?', *Aeon*, 2 March 2017, https://aeon.co/es says/is-global-history-still-possible-or-has-it-had-its-moment; Stefanie Gänger, 'Circulation: Reflections on Circularity, Entity, and Liquidity in the Language of Global History', *Journal of Global History* 12, 3 (2017), 303–18; Sujit Sivasundaram, 'Towards a Critical History of Connection: The Port of Colombo, the Geographical "Circuit", and the Visual Politics of New Imperialism, 1880–1914', *Comparative Studies in Society and History* 59, 2 (2017), 346–84; Dániel Margócsy, 'A Long History of Breakdowns: A Historiographical Review', *Social Studies of Science* 47, 3 (2017), 307–25; Jürgen Osterhammel and Stefanie Gänger, 'Denkpause für Globalgeschichte', *Merkur* 855 (2020), 79–86.

[6] T. F. Hoad, *The Concise Oxford Dictionary of English Etymology* (Oxford: Oxford University Press, 2003), http://dx.doi.org/10.1093/acref/9780192830982.001.0001. See also Peter Sloterdijk, *Spheres*, 3 vols. (Los Angeles: Semiotext(e), 2011–16).

[7] Oxford English Dictionary, quoted in Mary Beth Norton, *Separated by Their Sex: Women in Public and Private in the Colonial Atlantic World* (Ithaca: Cornell University Press, 2011), 6.

therefore encounter expressions ranging broadly from the spheres of the brain to spheres of political influence, spheres of law and public and private spheres.

What these expressions have in common is that they highlight the bounded or closed nature of global phenomena rather than implying openness and expansion. Closure, in the way it is used in this chapter, has the advantage of connecting geographical and geopolitical considerations with ideas of social differentiation and hierarchy. Social closure as an established sociological concept dates back to Max Weber.[8] Yet, while global historians have reflected extensively on geographical entities, social boundary-making has been neglected. In its different figurations, the sphere often unites both geographical and social facets of closure.

Besides offering historians the potential to reflect more systematically on processes of closure, there is a further reason why spheres might provide a way out of the current terminological impasse in global history. As a figure of thought that draws attention to boundaries and limits, spheres can help to counter the prevailing view that globalisation leads to formlessness and fluidity, and instead show that global processes often take quite firm and exclusive forms marked by territorial, political and social boundaries and partitions. Even in regions marked by extensive communication networks, such as the 'Muslim world', for example, ideas often did not circulate freely. They reached urban populations more frequently than rural populations, men more frequently than women and speakers of majority languages sooner than speakers of minority languages.[9] Admittedly, the boundaries thus created were not impermeable, but were marked by varying degrees of porosity, allowing some people and groups to cross while excluding others.

Instead of simply postulating what ought to be done or prescribing an entirely new language for global history, this chapter explores in an experimental and deliberately open-ended fashion how thinking about global spheres can be utilised fruitfully for the current practice of history writing. A first example is the radically inclusive yet claustrophobic vision of the globe as a closed sphere from which there is no escape. Building on earlier closed-world and one-world discourses, this thinking gained prominence after the Second World War in the face of the threat of nuclear destruction and environmental degradation. A second case concerns the idea of multiple global spheres that are at the same time limited to varying degrees. Here, the chapter takes its central examples from the realm of communication and language and discusses the public sphere as an exclusionary rather than inclusionary figure of thought.

---

[8] Donald Tomaskovic-Devey and Dustin Avent-Holt, *Relational Inequalities: An Organizational Approach* (Oxford: Oxford University Press, 2019), 134–61.

[9] Cemil Aydin, *The Idea of the Muslim World: A Global Intellectual History* (Cambridge, MA: Harvard University Press, 2017); Ilham Khuri-Makdisi, *The Eastern Mediterranean and the Making of Global Radicalism* (Berkeley: University of California Press, 2013).

Openness and Closure in Global History

Many global historians have been attracted to words that allude to openness and fluidity. Three commonly employed terms evoke openness as a central characteristic of global processes: 'connection', 'circulation' and 'integration'. The most widely used of these is undoubtedly 'connection'. However vaguely defined, connections are ubiquitous, from Christopher Bayly's subtitle of *The Birth of the Modern World* ('Global Connections and Comparisons') to the ever-expanding field of connectivity studies, featuring topics ranging from human migration to the mobility of objects and ideas.[10] Given the variety of phenomena related to connection and connectivity, some authors are careful to clarify that 'connectivity is never seamless or entirely smooth and is always interrupted, often in unnoticed ways'.[11] Yet despite such efforts at differentiation, the word 'connection', or 'connectivity' for that matter, itself suggests openness rather than closure as a central driving force of global processes. The term has therefore turned into an easy target for the critics of global history.[12]

Linked to connection, the terms 'circulation' and 'flow' are part of more metaphorically expansive semantic fields and figure regularly in global history writing.[13] In her critique of the languages of fluidity, Stefanie Gänger has discussed the specific role of openness and closure in this domain. There are many examples in which this language is prevalent: for instance, in reference to the circulation of goods, people and capital, or the circulation of information. Whereas circulation typically evokes closed systems such as the body or the Earth, it also implies effortless movement within such systems, without impediment and hindrance. What is more, the rhetoric of 'everything flows' can disguise social differentiation, hierarchisation and inequality as central markers of global processes.[14]

A more analytic concept that has frequently been placed at the core of a global history perspective is integration. Sebastian Conrad has argued that

---

[10] C. A. Bayly, *The Birth of the Modern World 1780–1914: Global Connections and Comparisons* (Oxford: Blackwell, 2004); see also, for example, Emily S. Rosenberg (ed.), *A World Connecting, 1870–1945* (Cambridge, MA: Harvard University Press, 2012); Roland Wenzlhuemer, *Connecting the Nineteenth-Century World: The Telegraph and Globalization* (Cambridge: Cambridge University Press, 2012).

[11] Jan Nederveen Pieterse, *Connectivity and Global Studies* (Cambridge: Cambridge University Press, 2021), xvi; Roland Wenzlhuemer et al., 'Forum Global Dis:connections', *Journal of Modern European History* 21, 1 (2023), 2–33.

[12] David A. Bell, 'This Is What Happens When Historians Overuse the Idea of Network', *The New Republic* (26 October 2013); Paul A. Kramer, 'How Did the World Become Global? Transnational History, Beyond Connection', *Reviews in American History* 49, 1 (2021), 119–41.

[13] Gänger, 'Circulation'; Claude Markovits et al. (eds.), *Society and Circulation: Mobile People and Itinerant Cultures in South Asia, 1750–1950* (London: Anthem Press, 2006).

[14] Monika Dommann, 'Alles fließt: Soll die Geschichte nomadischer werden?', *Geschichte und Gesellschaft* 42, 3 (2016), 516–34.

global history 'ultimately rests' on the notion of integration.[15] Integration is applied to a variety of often interrelated fields, including political integration (in the case of expansive empires), economic integration (for instance into capitalist markets) and social integration (for example relating to an emerging global bourgeoisie). Integration differs qualitatively from connection in its reference to causality and explanation. It is also a concept that invites more nuanced usage than the relatively vague term 'connection'. Yet while integration can be extended to include notions of hierarchy, forced incorporation and unevenness, it still hints at the centripetal and the inclusive. Despite its more analytic focus, integration therefore also implies processes of opening rather than closure as a central characteristic of global developments, and it carries the danger of relegating those who are not 'integrated' to the margins of historical narratives.

As these brief discussions reveal, terms such as 'connection', 'circulation' and 'integration' all come with their own challenges; what they share is their tilt towards the openness end of the spectrum. Even when they are carefully qualified and differentiated, their everyday associations prevent them from adequately representing the hierarchical, conflictual and uneven nature of many, if not all, global phenomena. It is often only through their negation – in terms such as 'disconnection' and 'disintegration' – that they are able to capture processes of closure. The inevitable effect of this is that developments associated with openness are perceived as more 'global' than those associated with closure.

This shortcoming of a vocabulary of closure in global history is indicative of a deeper problem. Despite early calls for scepticism – for instance, by Roland Robertson and Arif Dirlik – much of the initial globalisation literature of the 1990s followed a similar path of prioritising openness.[16] More recently, sociologists like Hartmut Rosa and Andreas Reckwitz have accentuated the fluidity that has resulted from global developments, such as the accelerating change in media technologies, dissolving family structures and weakening social ties.[17] Yet even if unintentionally, this depiction of the global as formless and fuzzy can serve to veil the rock-hard exclusions produced by many global processes.

---

[15] Sebastian Conrad, *What Is Global History?* (Princeton: Princeton University Press, 2016), 129; see also 90–114.

[16] Early on, authors such as Roland Robertson and Arif Dirlik pointed to the co-constitutiveness of integration and fragmentation in global processes: Arif Dirlik, 'The Postcolonial Aura: Third World Criticism in the Age of Global Capitalism', in Padmini Mongia (ed.), *Contemporary Postcolonial Theory: A Reader* (London: Hodder Arnold, 1996), 294–321; Roland Robertson, 'Glocalization: Time-Space and Homogeneity-Heterogeneity', in Mike Featherstone et al. (eds.), *Global Modernities* (London: SAGE, 1995), 25–44.

[17] Andreas Reckwitz, *Society of Singularities* (Cambridge: Polity Press, 2020); Hartmut Rosa, *Social Acceleration: A New Theory of Modernity* (New York: Columbia University Press, 2015); Andreas Reckwitz and Hartmut Rosa, *Late Modernity in Crisis: Why We Need a Theory of Society* (Cambridge: Polity Press, 2023).

Regardless of long-standing debates, the dilemma of capturing globality while at the same time disclosing globality's always limited, bounded and exclusionary nature therefore remains unresolved. The first and most common response to this dilemma is to couple a word with its antonym, as noted earlier. The relationship between the two terms may either work sequentially, with phases of globalisation being followed by phases of deglobalisation, or synchronously, with processes of connection and disconnection occurring simultaneously. In both cases, however, the term and its negation are still understood as separate. However, the processes these opposites refer to are often closely intertwined, as phenomena such as global capitalism and its reliance on forced labour clearly reveal. Binaries tend to obscure the fact that openness for some leads to closure for others, and that both are equally related to globality.

Other attempts to move beyond this impasse have entailed searching for different metaphors and concepts altogether. Two metaphors of the global that have gained prominence in recent years are noteworthy in this context. In her 'ethnography of global connection', Anna Lowenhaupt Tsing uses the term 'friction' to address many of the aforementioned problems.[18] For her, the global is not marked by smoothness and interchange but by resistance and dissent, pointing to the conflictual nature of globality. Tsing's approach has resonated widely throughout the social sciences, illustrating the need for a more nuanced metaphorical language of the global which includes processes of chafing and erasure.[19]

The metaphor of friction may go some way towards considering disruptions and interferences as essential facets of the global. In Tsing's view, the global appears characterised less by seamless flows and connections than by often violent processes of eradication and conflict. Yet referring to friction and similar metaphors still tends to depict global processes as fuzzy and undefined, and thus to disguise more solidified power structures and entrenched inequalities.

World-making has become another widely employed term to capture alternative visions in globalist thought and imagination. Duncan Bell has begun to discuss how concepts of world-making in fact point to the limits of worlds rather than to an all-encompassing vision.[20] Exploring internationalism after empire, Adom Getachew has analysed how anticolonial thinkers and politicians such as W. E. B. Du Bois, Kwame Nkrumah, Julius Nyerere and George

[18] Anna Lowenhaupt Tsing, *Friction: An Ethnography of Global Connection* (Princeton: Princeton University Press, 2011).
[19] See, for example, Antoinette Burton, *Africa in the Indian Imagination: Race and the Politics of Postcolonial Citation* (Durham: Duke University Press, 2016).
[20] Duncan Bell, 'Making and Taking Worlds', in Samuel Moyn and Andrew Sartori (eds.), *Global Intellectual History* (New York: Columbia University Press, 2013), 254–80; Nelson Goodman, *Ways of Worldmaking* (Hassocks: Harvester Press, 1978).

Padmore advocated for the creation of a new postcolonial world. She shows that for them, world-making was as central a project as nation-building, which is frequently emphasised in the scholarship on postcolonial orders.[21] While the notion of world-making highlights diverse and competing understandings of globality and international orders, authors who use it as their key concept have only just begun to explore what the limits of these worlds were and how they can be understood analytically. Although they offer more satisfying conceptions of the global than the binary constructions mentioned earlier, concepts such as 'friction' and 'world-making' do not address in a sufficiently concrete manner questions of closure, boundaries and limits, or, more generally, the importance of rigid forms and structures in global processes.

Reflections on the globe as a sphere, or as composed of several distinct spheres, build on the literature around friction and world-making but probe conceptions of closure and boundary-making more explicitly. They allow historians to foreground in what manner worlds are limited, revealing how the experience of globality that Geyer and Bright took for granted is often exclusionary and based on race, class and gender inequalities and on unequal access to natural and other resources such as information or the freedom to move. When we use the figure of thought of the sphere, globality does not appear as formless and diffuse, but rather as marked by often fairly stark forms of inclusion and exclusion. This chapter goes on to show that, by using the concept of the sphere and adjacent expressions, historical actors were already thinking about globality as a phenomenon uniting openness and closure long before scholars began doing so.

Given the capaciousness of the term, it is not surprising that the German philosopher Peter Sloterdijk allowed his trilogy on spheres (consisting of three separate volumes on bubbles, globes and foams) to be sprawling and associative, ultimately filling more than 2,500 pages.[22] His 'spherology' presents a wealth of material on how globes and other round objects of various kinds figure in world history. In this way, it allows for plentiful associations and vantage points.[23] If Sloterdijk's abundance of material makes for fascinating (if time-consuming) reading, the gist of his argument is more difficult to pin down. Yet the image of the sphere – with its subfields of bubbles, globes and foams – is very fitting for a reflection on how to rethink global history, pointing to questions of global forms and their boundaries, as well as their more ephemeral or permanent features.[24]

---

[21] Adom Getachew, *Worldmaking after Empire: The Rise and Fall of Self-Determination* (Princeton: Princeton University Press, 2019).

[22] Sloterdijk, *Spheres*.

[23] See Kari van Dijk, 'The World as Sphere: Conceptualizing with Sloterdijk', in Jordheim and Sandmo, *Conceptualizing the World*, 327–338.

[24] For reflections on the ephemeral nature of bubbles, see also Simon Schaffer, 'A Science Whose Business is Bursting: Soap Bubbles as Commodities in Classical Physics', in Lorraine Daston

Unlike comparison and scale, the sphere might not immediately spring to mind as a figure of thought that historians can use to respond to the current critique of global history. This apparent challenge is at the same time an opportunity: to explore in a more experimental way whether spheres might offer an alternative to the binary solutions that have been prominent so far. Rather than providing an exercise in theorising the global, this chapter context-ualises spheres and their boundaries to highlight co-constitutive processes of opening and closing. The examples illustrate how, over the course of the twentieth century, various historical actors have perceived globality as closed and limited rather than open and expansive.

As an unusual figure of thought to denote the global, the sphere can serve to give conceptions of closure a firmer place in global history. Ranging from the shutting of geographic borders to processes of social stratification and the constraints and hierarchies of the international political system, from the restriction of opportunities to the limitation of access to resources and freedoms, closure has taken centre stage in many disciplines other than history.[25] Spheres and their boundedness can help us to move our thinking about boundary-making from the geographical terms often prevalent in global history to boundaries in the social realm.

More specifically, thinking about the global in terms of spheres leads us in two separate and distinct directions. First, the sphere can refer to the circum-scribed nature of the globe as a whole and its finite resources. In this discourse, the sphere appears as an underlying figure of imagination that amalgamates visions of globality and humanity. This notion of the sphere most often surfaces in closed-world discourses, linking the interrelatedness of humanity as a whole with the limits of humanity's habitat: the Earth. Second, the term can refer to more narrowly circumscribed domains, such as political, economic, social and communicational spheres. In this understanding, spheres are global but at the same time exclusionary, often restricted to a particular region or to a specific segment of the global population. Whereas political spheres are demarcated by geographical boundaries, public spheres are often demarcated by social boundaries.

As the following explorations show, both versions of global spheres – the more inclusive world as sphere, and the more exclusive world of many spheres – run counter to conceptions of the global that stress formlessness and fluidity. They are oriented instead toward ideas of boundary-work and

---

(ed.), *Things That Talk: Object Lessons from Art and Science* (Cambridge, MA: MIT Press, 2004), 147–94.

[25] For sociology, see Tomaskovic-Devey and Avent-Holt, *Relational Inequalities*, ch. 6, 134–61. For international relations, see Lora Anne Viola, *The Closure of the International System: How Institutions Create Political Equalities and Hierarchies* (Cambridge: Cambridge University Press, 2020).

boundary-making.[26] Spheres can grow and shrink, expand and contract, but they are usually unambiguously demarcated. In tracing spherical ideas in globalist imaginations and testing the sphere as an alternative metaphor of the global, I turn to different examples that illustrate the inclusive as well as exclusive nature of spheres and explore how spheres might contribute to solving the dilemmas of global history.

Inclusion: The World as Sphere

The most obvious use of the term 'sphere' in global history relates to the sphericity of the globe as a whole. Where and at what point in history can the emergence of this radically inclusive sphericity – or, in less abstract terms, the idea of a finite and fragile world in which humans share a single destiny – be located? The idea of a shrinking globe (or time–space compression, to use Harvey's well-worn phrase) came of age during the infrastructure and transport revolution of the late nineteenth and early twentieth centuries, continuing into the interwar period and the Second World War.[27] Closed-world discourses took centre stage in the decades after the war, when fears of environmental degradation, nuclear annihilation and rapid population growth converged in the emergence of international organisations and pro-test movements focused on the fragility of the globe.

Conceptualising the globe as a closed sphere has of course a longer history predating the twentieth century.[28] The sphere was used in geography starting in the fifth century BC and found its way into many cosmologies.[29] The 'discov-ery' of the Americas further boosted spherical thinking. Yet the idea of clearly demarcated celestial and terrestrial spheres was also present in various contexts beyond European expansionism, from the Middle Ages onwards.[30] Even if a more fully illustrated history of spheres in various cultures lies beyond the

---

[26] Thomas F. Gieryn, 'Boundary-Work and the Demarcation of Science from Non-Science: Strains and Interests in Professional Ideologies of Scientists', *American Sociological Review* 48, 6 (1983), 781–95; Andreas Wimmer, *Ethnic Boundary Making: Institutions, Power, Networks* (Oxford: Oxford University Press, 2013).

[27] David Harvey, *The Condition of Postmodernity: An Enquiry into the Origins of Cultural Change* (Cambridge, MA: Blackwell, 1990).

[28] Simon Ferdinand et al. (eds.), *Other Globes: Past and Peripheral Imaginations of Globalization* (London: Palgrave Macmillan, 2019); Sumathi Ramaswamy, *Territorial Lessons: The Conquest of the World as a Globe* (Chicago: University of Chicago Press, 2017).

[29] See the exhibition at the Bibliothèque Nationale de France: Le Monde en sphères, 16 April–21 July 2019, and the connected virtual exhibition http://expositions.bnf.fr/monde-en-spheres/; Jan Mokre and Peter E. Allmayer-Beck (eds.), *Das Globenmuseum der Österreichischen Nationalbibliothek* (Vienna: Bibliophile Edition, 2005); F. Jamil Ragep, 'Astronomy', in Kate Fleet et al. (eds.), *Encyclopedia of Islam Three* (Brill Online), http://dx.doi.org/10.1163/1573-3912_ei3_COM_22652.

[30] Pina Totaro and Luisa Valente (eds.), *Sphaera: Forma immagine e metafora tra Medioevo ed età moderna* (Florence: Olschki, 2012).

scope of this chapter, it is important to note the plurality of views and conceptions in specific contexts and cultures.

Beyond physical spheres, it was the emergence of a specifically planetary consciousness that linked geographical conceptions with the idea of humanity as a whole.[31] As a figure of thought, the sphere captured the idea that the entire globe could potentially be settled by humans and that humanity was inextricably interlinked. The image of the globe as a sphere thus intimately connected geographical and social thinking. In the closed-world discourses of the twentieth century, humanity emerged as intimately conjoined on an increasingly crowded and imperilled planet. Even if these discourses did not always employ the term 'sphere' explicitly, they related to an idea formulated by Immanuel Kant: 'the spherical surface of the earth unites all the places on its surface; for if its surface were an unbounded plane, men could be so dispersed on it that they would not come into any community with one another, and community would not then be a necessary result of their existence on the earth'.[32] In this vision, humanity – however narrowly Kant himself defined it – appeared fundamentally tied together.[33]

Moving to the twentieth century, perceptions of closure assumed a central role. The period around 1900 has often been interpreted as a time of exploration and radical openness that made new infrastructural opportunities available to many.[34] Yet even if some historical actors displayed unbridled optimism about the new communication infrastructures, the late nineteenth and early twentieth centuries should not be understood purely as a moment of expansion and growth. In this period, violent European expansionism was accompanied by perceptions of closure rather than openness. What is often depicted as an age of boundless opportunities for global entrepreneurs was also a time of growing insecurity, in which efforts were made to shield certain parts of the globe from others and to protect imperial enterprises from their growing vulnerability.

What is more, while opportunities were increasing for some, they were disappearing for others. The new sense of openness – for instance, in the 'circulation of ideas' that many global intellectual historians have been drawn to in recent years – was accompanied by processes of social closure and increasing inequality.[35] The forced sedentarisation of nomadic populations

[31] Mary Louise Pratt, *Imperial Eyes: Travel Writing and Transculturation* (London: Routledge, 1994), 15–37: 'Science, Planetary Consciousness, Interiors'.

[32] Immanuel Kant, *The Metaphysics of Morals*, transl. Lara Denis (Cambridge: Cambridge University Press, 2017), 263.

[33] For a growing literature on the concept of humanity, see Siep Stuurman, *The Invention of Humanity: Equality and Cultural Difference in World History* (Cambridge, MA: Harvard University Press, 2017).

[34] See, as part of a larger literature, Rosenberg, *A World Connecting*.

[35] Pandemics and reactions to them are an obvious case in point; see Valeska Huber, 'The Unification of the Globe by Disease? The International Sanitary Conferences on Cholera,

is emblematic of larger processes of openness and closure in this period: nomadic groups became less mobile and more tightly controlled as the world was partitioned into fields of political and economic influence. Openness and closure were thus intimately intertwined at a time when the world seemed to be growing smaller for some but was becoming less accessible for others.[36]

In the interwar period, closed-world discourses flourished.[37] Echoing the words of Immanuel Kant, Raymond Pearl, a biologist at Johns Hopkins University, clearly expressed the idea of the globe as human habitat in 1927: 'All populations of organisms live in universes with definite limits. The absolute size of the universe might be small, as in the case of the test-tube … or it may be as large as earth, most of which could conceivably be inhabited, on a pinch, by man.'[38] What Pearl called a universe might also be called a sphere. His notion connected planetary thinking with reflections on humanity as an interconnected whole sharing a common destiny.

The conception of the globe and its population as dependent on each other for their very survival gained new force and urgency in the decades after the Second World War. In the second half of the twentieth century, this gave way to a claustrophobic sense of forced inclusion. Preoccupations with the threat of nuclear destruction and concerns about environmental degradation in the Anthropocene produced a sense of close interconnectedness in an inescapably bounded and limited world. Two examples illustrate this important shift in perceptions that occurred in the period. The space age provided images that allowed human beings to see the Earth from the outside. Photographs such as those in the iconic Blue Marble series produced by the 1972 Apollo 17 mission conveyed the fragility and 'sphericity' of the globe in the truest sense of the word to a wider public.[39] Beyond the space age and its new iconography,

---

1851–1894', *Historical Journal* 49, 2 (2006), 453–76; Huber, 'Pandemics and the Politics of Difference: Rewriting the History of Internationalism through Nineteenth-Century Cholera', *Journal of Global History* 15, 2 (2020), 394–407.

[36] As an example, see Priya Satia, *Empire of Guns: The Violent Making of the Industrial Revolution* (Stanford: Stanford University Press, 2019).

[37] Alison Bashford, *Global Population: History, Geopolitics, and Life on Earth* (New York: Columbia University Press, 2014), 6: 'The closed-world idea did not belong to German imperial, Weimar, and fascist *Geopolitiker* alone, however. It was widely shared by anglophone Malthusians, economists, geographers, and the first generation of demographers.'

[38] Raymond Pearl, 'The Biology of Population Growth', in Margaret Sanger (ed.), *Population Conference Proceedings* (London: Edward Arnold, 1927), 22, quoted in Alison Bashford, 'Nation, Empire, Globe: The Spaces of Population Debate in the Interwar Years', *Comparative Studies in Society and History* 49, 1 (2007), 170–201, here 170.

[39] Denis E. Cosgrove, 'Contested Global Visions: One-World, Whole-Earth, and the Apollo Space Photographs', *Annals of the Association of American Geographers* 84, 2 (1994), 270–94; Denis E. Cosgrove, *Apollo's Cartographic Genealogy of the Earth in the Western Imagination* (Baltimore: Johns Hopkins University Press, 2001); Benjamin Lazier, 'Earthrise; or, The Globalization of the World Picture', *American Historical Review* 116, 3 (2011), 602–30; Solvejg Nitzke and Nicolas Pethes (eds.), *Imagining Earth: Concepts of Wholeness in Cultural Constructions of Our Home Planet* (Bielefeld: Transcript, 2017); Robert K. Poole,

numbers conveyed the idea of an inescapable global sphere just as urgently as images. The increase in the Earth's population from about 1.6 billion to more than 6 billion over the course of the previous century exacerbated perceptions of the globe as fragile and in need of protection.[40] A controversial 1968 bestseller by Paul Ehrlich coined the term 'population bomb', relating to a range of interventionist measures in different parts of the world.[41] The global 'tipping point' was a central metaphor of this work, with Paul Ehrlich asking in a characteristically technocratic manner: 'What is the optimum number of human beings that the earth can support?'[42]

Many authors from the 1960s expressed the distinct sense that just as the world was growing smaller with the creation of new infrastructures and modes of communication, the Earth was also becoming more fragile and threatened.[43] Diverse voices joined in this closed-world discourse of a claustrophobic and finite globe and the future of human life on it. Their works show how the globe and its inhabitants can be analysed within a single, unified framework and thereby illustrate how the sphere can be deployed as a figure of thought. Three examples from a broad sample may be sufficient here to provide an overview of the different perspectives prevalent during this time. In a 1964 publication entitled *One World or None?*, Ossip K. Flechtheim, a professor of political science in West Berlin from 1952 to 1974, reflected on the growth of global population and the fundamental threat he believed it posed to humankind. Referring to the Holocaust and the Second World War, he stressed humanity's tragic recent history and the even greater catastrophe that might lie ahead, for the first time imperilling all of humankind.[44]

In *The Oneness of Mankind*, published one year after Flechtheim's book, Indian economist Radhakamal Mukerjee also shifted easily from reflection on

---

Earthrise: How Man First Saw the Earth (New Haven: Yale University Press, 2008); Holly Henry and Amanda Taylor, 'Rethinking Apollo: Envisioning Environmentalism in Space', *Sociological Review Monograph* 57, 1 (2009), 190–203.

[40] Bashford, *Global Population*; Marc Frey, 'Neo-Malthusianism and Development: Shifting Interpretations of a Contested Paradigm', *Journal of Global History* 6, 1 (2011), 75–97; Heinrich Hartmann, '"No Technical Solution": Historische Kontexte einer Moralökonomie der Weltbevölkerung seit den 1950er Jahren', in Isabella Löhr and Andrea Rehling (eds.), *Global Commons im 20. Jahrhundert: Entwürfe für eine globale Welt* (Munich: De Gruyter Oldenbourg, 2014), 33–52; Sara Weydner, 'Reproductive Rights and Reproductive Control', *Geschichte und Gesellschaft* 44, 1 (2018), 135–61.

[41] Paul Ehrlich, *The Population Bomb* (New York: Ballantine Books, 1968); Matthew Connelly, *Fatal Misconception: The Struggle to Control World Population* (Cambridge, MA: Belknap Press, 2008).

[42] Quoted in Sabine Höhler, 'The Law of Growth: How Ecology Accounted for World Population in the 20th Century', *Distinktion: Journal of Social Theory* 8, 1 (2007), 45–64, at 56.

[43] Sabine Höhler, *Spaceship Earth in the Environmental Age 1960–1990* (London: Pickering and Chatto, 2015).

[44] Ossip K. Flechtheim, *Eine Welt oder keine? Beiträge zur Politik, Politologie und Philosophie* (Hamburg: Europäische Verlagsanstalt, 1964).

the physical world to thinking about humanity in its more metaphysical sense. Calling the twentieth century 'the age of mankind' and pointing out how science, technology and economic integration had rendered the Earth ever smaller and more closely knit, he focused on universalism, humanism, solidarity and oneness: 'both rich and poor nations belong to the brotherhood of the human race in the small, intractable planet which they by concerted enterprise have to make into a habitable home for each of them to live with decency, dignity and freedom'.[45] Mukerjee tightly coupled the future of the planet with conceptions of humanity and life on Earth.

American development economist Barbara Ward took up the same idea of a crowded and inescapable planet that occupied Mukerjee. In 1966 she coined the phrase 'Spaceship Earth'.[46] In her later work *Only One Earth* (1972), she illustrated how environmental activism was connected with thinking in terms of a united humanity: 'the careful husbandry of the Earth is the sine qua non for the survival of the human species, and for the creation of decent ways of life for all the people of the world'.[47] Even if these three visions of radical inclusion did not account clearly for who actually made up humanity in any more than the most abstract terms and also risked obfuscating social distinctions for the sake of stressing the unity of humankind, they all shared the urgent sense of a claustrophobic spherical nature of the globe from which there was no escape.

In the 1970s and 1980s, when the Club of Rome and the Brundtland Commission were more overtly discussing the limits of the world's resources and related questions of global justice, there were many further examples of how and where one-world and one-humanity thinking coalesced.[48] Postcolonial leaders such as Indira Gandhi expressed in powerful terms how nature and the use of natural resources needed to be rethought as global

---

[45] Radhakamal Mukerjee, *The Oneness of Mankind* (London: Macmillan, 1965), ix. See his participation in earlier population debates mentioned earlier: Radhakamal Mukerjee, 'The Criterion of Optimum Population', *American Journal of Sociology* 38, 5 (1933), 688–98.

[46] Barbara Ward, *Spaceship Earth* (New York: Columbia University Press, 1966), later taken up by R. Buckminster Fuller, *Operating Manual for Spaceship Earth* (New York: Simon & Schuster, 1969).

[47] Barbara Ward and Rene Dubos, *Only One Earth: The Care and Maintenance of a Small Planet* (New York: W. W. Norton, 1972).

[48] See David Kuchenbuch, '"Eine Welt": Globales Interdependenzbewusstsein und die Moralisierung des Alltags in den 1970er und 1980er Jahren', *Geschichte und Gesellschaft* 38, 1 (2012), 158–84; David Kuchenbuch, *Welt-Bildner: Arno Peters, Richard Buckminster Fuller und die Medien des Globalismus, 1940–2000* (Vienna: Böhlau, 2021); David Kuchenbuch, *Globalismen: Geschichte und Gegenwart des globalen Bewusstseins* (Hamburg: Hamburger Edition, 2023); Donella H. Meadows et al., *The Limits of Growth: A Report for The Club of Rome's Project on the Predicament of Mankind* (New York: Universe Books, 1972); Matthias Schmelzer, *The Hegemony of Growth: The OECD and the Making of the Economic Growth Paradigm* (Cambridge: Cambridge University Press, 2016); Matthias Schmelzer, *Degrowth/Postwachstum zur Einführung* (Hamburg: Junius, 2019).

commons belonging to all of humanity.[49] If the global sphere could be described as claustrophobic and as a site of fierce battles over the distribution of resources, the sense of one world also produced new perspectives on global justice and solidarity.

This short survey of spherical thinking demonstrates how in the second half of the twentieth century many actors moved from a vague sense of threat to outright fears for survival, clearly pointing to closure rather than openness as the dominant feeling associated with global processes. What is more, for authors such as Flechtheim, Mukerjee and Ward, 'the world' increasingly meant not all *places* everywhere but all *people* everywhere, evoking crowdedness and inescapability and thus amalgamating geographical and social thinking. Even if the sphere might have been a spatial metaphor to start with, the examples highlighted here show how global histories that centre on the sphericity of the Earth can shift our analytic perspectives and research designs from space and the geographic scales that have long dominated global history to humanity and human populations.[50]

Exclusion: One World, Many Spheres

Do we really inhabit one world, or just our own limited spheres of the world? And how are the boundaries of these spheres defined, guarded and – at least potentially – broken? During the Covid-19 pandemic, conceptions of hermetically sealed spaces experienced a strange and unexpected renaissance, endowing us with a new arsenal of expressions that includes 'bubbles' and 'inner circles'. New Zealand's slogan 'stay in your bubble' was taken up by other countries and used in public health campaigns worldwide, encouraging people to limit their interactions to clearly restricted spheres. At the same time, new digital communication technologies united individuals across large distances, yet again, often within clearly delineated and pre-selected spheres. Both the accelerating development of new media practices and the slogans mentioned herein echo Sloterdijk's distinction of spherical thinking into globes, bubbles and foams.

Lived experiences of closure, as in the case of the Covid-19 pandemic, are mirrored in the broader use of the word 'sphere' in the social sciences. The terminology of spheres is often used (along with synonyms such as 'universe'

---

[49] Both quoted in Elizabeth DeLoughrey and George B. Handley, 'Introduction: Toward an Aesthetics of the Earth', in Elizabeth DeLoughrey and George B. Handley (eds.), *Postcolonial Ecologies: Literatures of the Environment* (Oxford: Oxford University Press, 2011), 3–39, here 16.

[50] At the same time, the question of how to bring a critical history of the Anthroposphere and a history of humanity into closer dialogue is still largely unresolved: Bruno Latour, *Down to Earth: Politics in the New Climatic Regime* (Cambridge: Polity Press, 2018); Alison Bashford, Emily M. Kern, and Adam Bobbette (eds.), *New Earth Histories: Geo-Cosmologies and the Making of the Modern World* (Chicago: University of Chicago Press, 2023).

or simply 'world') to denote clearly demarcated geographical spheres of influence or specific social configurations – for instance, gender spheres, or public and private spheres. In many cases, these differently bounded spheres overlap. The social sciences often use the term 'spheres' in reference to exclusionary bubbles, which can stretch around the world but still leave out many. In contrast to the closed-world discourses surveyed earlier, which tend to omit social differentiation, thinking in terms of spheres in the plural highlights exclusion and boundary-making. When exploring how the language of spheres is used in global history writing, it is therefore important to consider multi-spherical approaches alongside closed-world thinking.

Most notably, the term 'spheres of influence' became prevalent in the late nineteenth century, a moment some global historians have described as one of extraordinary expansion and openness. While this sense of openness was often accompanied by a sense of planetary closure as depicted earlier, the partitioning of the world into clearly defined spheres of influence is a further factor that reveals this period as deeply divisive, but no less global for that matter. Since then, the concept of spheres of influence – sometimes separate, sometimes overlapping – has become a convenient analytic device in fields such as political science, economics and law.[51]

When thinking about spheres, geopolitical spheres of influence might still be the first point of reference. The field of international relations has also displayed a renewed interest in spheres of influence.[52] Missionary or colonial spheres of influence intentionally created separations and boundaries. Legal treaties and doctrines such as the Treaty of Tordesillas or the Monroe Doctrine clearly marked out and defined spheres of influence. Other more loosely defined concepts such as the Sinosphere, the Buddhosphere and the Islamosphere point to a central dilemma of spherical thinking: are spheres of influence distinctly delineated, or do they fray and dissolve around the edges? How can we define where one sphere of influence ends and the other begins?

Rather than dwelling on the geopolitical use of spheres of influence, the remainder of this chapter highlights another, more explicitly social, concept that includes the term 'sphere'. Located at the intersection of political theory and communication studies, public spheres represent a further common usage of spheres that has made its way into the vocabulary of the social sciences and humanities. In most cases, it is used in reference to Jürgen Habermas's

---

[51] For the 'sphere of law', see, for instance, Michael Walzer, *Spheres of Justice: A Defence of Pluralism and Equality* (Oxford: Blackwell, 1983); Lauren Benton, 'Beyond Anachronism: Histories of International Law and Global Legal Politics', *Journal of the History of International Law* 21, 1 (2019), 7–40.

[52] Susanna Hast, *Spheres of Influence in International Relations: History, Theory and Politics* (London: Routledge, 2016); Van Jackson, 'Understanding Spheres of Influence in International Politics', *European Journal of International Security* 5, 3 (2019), 1–19.

conception of the public sphere from the 1960s.[53] According to Habermas, public spheres are stages for the exchange of rational arguments marked by a certain degree of institutionalisation, distinguishing them from the more flexibly used term of 'publics'.

More recently, debates on multiple public spheres have also entered global history. Scholars have sought to answer the question of how public spheres (or less firmly institutionalised publics) could expand beyond nation-states by exploring infrastructures and media but also markets and attention economies.[54] Current debates in communication studies concerning fragmented publics, filter bubbles and echo chambers further highlight the need to look beyond the more normative conceptualisations of public spheres to focus on the boundaries and limits of communication.[55] Global communication history is an area of research that can be rethought within the framework of spheres, drawing attention to accessibility and inaccessibility as central parameters of analysis.[56] Much like the more abstract term 'integration', the concept of public spheres might imply openness at first sight. Yet access to public spheres is limited by a number of factors, making them fertile ground for probing how openness and closure can be linked more effectively.

No public sphere has ever covered the entire planet. Instead, spheres are always exclusive and exclusionary affairs, allowing access and entry to some but not to others. This is most obvious in relation to the geographies of specific public spheres. Yet, in an age of communication technologies spanning the globe, their exclusionary nature is often rooted not so much in geographical limitation as in social differentiation.[57] The investigation of public spheres and

---

[53] Although the term 'public sphere' in relation to Jürgen Habermas's work was only circulated widely after the delayed translation of the book into English in 1989, it had already appeared in an encyclopedia article of 1964: Jürgen Habermas, 'The Public Sphere: An Encyclopedia Article (1964)', transl. by Sara Lennox and Frank Lennox, *New German Critique* 3 (1974), 49–55; Martin Seeliger and Sebastian Sevignani (eds.), *Ein neuer Strukturwandel der Öffentlichkeit?* (Baden-Baden: Nomos, 2021); Jostein Gripsrud et al. (eds.), *The Public Sphere*, 4 vols. (London: SAGE, 2010).

[54] Valeska Huber and Jürgen Osterhammel (eds.), *Global Publics: Their Power and Their Limits, 1870–1990* (Oxford: Oxford University Press, 2020); Emma Hunter and Leslie James, 'Introduction: Colonial Public Spheres and the Worlds of Print', *Itinerario* 44, 2 (2020), 227–42.

[55] See, for instance, Subhayan Mukerjee, 'Rethinking Audience Fragmentation Using a Theory of News Reading Publics. Online India as a Case Study', *International Journal of Press/Politics*, 19 January 2022, https://doi.org/10.1177%2F19401612211072700; Ludovic Terren and Rosa Borge-Bravo, 'Echo Chambers on Social Media: A Systematic Review of the Literature', *Communication and Media Technologies* 9 (2021), 99–118.

[56] As an analytic category, 'access' has not yet been explored in detail. As a starting point, see Jeremy Rifkin, *The Age of Access: The New Culture of Hypercapitalism: Where All of Life Is a Paid for Experience* (New York: Putnam, 2000).

[57] For the most prominent critique of Habermas: see Nancy Fraser, 'Rethinking the Public Sphere: A Contribution to the Critique of Democracy as It Really Is', in Craig Calhoun (ed.), *Habermas and the Public Sphere* (Cambridge, MA: MIT Press, 1993), 109–42.

their geographical and social reach can therefore help uncover the making and breaking of social boundaries through communicative practices.

The most obvious parameters limiting access to public spheres are the familiar structures of race, class and gender. Recent scholarship has employed global social classes as a lens through which to view inclusion and exclusion in the development of separate spheres, with public spheres frequently mapping onto social structures.[58] This has been fuelled by new research on global classes and their networks, most notably the global bourgeoisie – a class that might have been global while at the same time sporting clear limitations of access.[59] Global gender histories might be even more interesting for exploring the limits and boundaries of public spheres. Since the dichotomy between public and private spheres is traditionally reflected in a dichotomy between male and female roles and activities, the shifting boundaries of global public spheres are especially evident in relation to gender. In many societies, gender roles have long been cemented in 'separate spheres' ideologies.[60] Over the course of the last century, however, emancipating concepts such as the 'new woman' or the 'modern girl' surfaced around the world.[61] These concepts correlated with new patterns of consumption and built on the promise that women could challenge 'traditional' gender roles and burst into public spheres that were formerly reserved for men. Yet this liberating process also led to the emergence of new female global public spheres that were reserved for a select group – for instance, upper-middle-class women. So instead of collapsing boundaries, they ended up creating new ones.

While the project of tracing the idea of the 'new woman' around the world was originally based quite heavily on research on consumption and marketing, scholars working on the role of newspapers and women's magazines in the

---

[58] Hannah Arendt, *The Human Condition* (Chicago: University of Chicago Press, 1958), part II, 22–78. Transnational civil society might be another 'sphere' worth investigating in this context. See Emma Hunter, '"Our Common Humanity": Print, Power, and the Colonial Press in Interwar Tanganyika and French Cameroun', *Journal of Global History* 7, 2 (2012), 279–301; Srilatha Batliwala and L. David Brown, 'Shaping the Global Human Project: The Nature and Impact of Transnational Civil Activism', in Srilatha Batliwala and L. David Brown (eds.), *Transnational Civil Society: An Introduction* (Bloomfield: Kumarian Press, 2006), 204–27; Peter Uwe Hohendahl and Russell A. Berman, *Öffentlichkeit – Geschichte eines kritischen Begriffs* (Stuttgart: Metzler, 2000).

[59] Christof Dejung et al. (eds.), *The Global Bourgeoisie: The Rise of the Middle Classes in the Age of Empire* (Princeton: Princeton University Press, 2019); Jürgen Osterhammel, 'Hierarchies and Connections: Aspects of a Global Social History', in Sebastian Conrad and Jürgen Osterhammel (eds.), *An Emerging Modern World 1750–1870* (Cambridge, MA: Harvard University Press, 2018), 661–888.

[60] Linda Kerber, 'Separate Spheres, Female Worlds, Woman's Place: The Rhetoric of Women's History', *Journal of American History* 75, 1 (1988), 9–39. For public and private spheres, see Joan B. Landes (ed.), *Feminism, the Public and the Private* (Oxford: Oxford University Press, 1998).

[61] Alys Eve Weinbaum et al. (eds.), *The Modern Girl Around the World: Consumption, Modernity, and Globalization* (Durham: Duke University Press, 2008).

development of female public spheres have demonstrated that new communication media played a key role in the formation of global public spheres.[62] Su Lin Lewis has shown how the use of categories such as the 'new woman' and the 'modern girl' in the Asian port cities of Singapore and Rangoon not only depended on new patterns of consumption – for instance, the adoption of new styles of fashion and cuisines and behaviour – but also on the circulation of print media and access to common languages.[63] Lewis's research on the development of global female public spheres highlights the sharply drawn boundaries between male and female forms of political engagement and social practice even within these globalised contexts. Female spheres can be global but still remain restricted and exclusive. The 'new woman' and 'modern girl' are thus prime examples of how openness and closure are intertwined.

Research on global public spheres has focused not only on how access is determined by categories of race, class and gender, but also on the role of access to technologies and media in a broader sense. Beyond those classic categories of exclusion, these include 'technologies of the intellect', such as language and literacy, but also factors such as the ability to handle new technologies or age as an excluding factor.[64] The question of 'who is in and who is out?' therefore becomes even more salient if we move beyond an analysis of consumption or of conventional media histories.

Participation in global female public spheres, for instance, depended on particular skills, most notably literacy, which has become a condition for entry to many public spheres. More generally speaking, the word 'public' itself has often been coupled with qualifying adjectives such as 'educated' public, 'informed' public and 'reading' public, pointing to the crucial boundary between a global literate public and populations that could not read or write – historically, the larger part of the global population. In the nineteenth century, mass schooling became an important objective of many modernising states, yet the majority of the global female population over fifteen years of age was still not literate and therefore remained firmly excluded from public spheres defined by print. In the twentieth century, comprehensive literacy campaigns were conducted in countries including the Soviet Union, Turkey and Cuba. International organisations, above all UNESCO, have aimed to increase literacy and provide 'education for all'. Many of these campaigns have been

---

[62] Michel Hockx et al. (eds.), *Women and the Periodical Press in China's Long Twentieth Century: A Space of Their Own?* (Cambridge: Cambridge University Press, 2018); Derek R. Peterson et al. (eds.), *African Print Cultures: Newspapers and Their Publics in the Twentieth Century* (Ann Arbor: University of Michigan Press, 2016).

[63] Su Lin Lewis, 'Asian Women and Global Publics: Interaction, Information, and the City, c. 1900-1940', in Huber and Osterhammel, *Global Publics*, 145–74.

[64] For the admittedly problematic expression 'technologies of the intellect', see Jack Goody, *The Power of the Written Tradition* (Washington DC: Smithsonian Institution, 2000), 132–51.

targeted at women. At the same time, female literacy rates still remain far below those of their male counterparts.

Global yet exclusive public spheres were also circumscribed by language barriers. Often, membership rested on knowledge of ecumenical languages such as English.[65] Yet global English also faced linguistic competitors. Chinese, Arabic and Persian language communities illustrate how global public spheres are expanding, while simultaneously remaining exclusive to those who share a common language. This point is driven home by the frequent reference to language spheres such as the Anglosphere or the Sinosphere as 'worlds' – for instance, in H. G. Wells's expression 'the English-speaking world', but also the 'Francophone world' and the 'Persianate world'.[66]

As these brief examples show, when historical actors or historians say 'world', they are often referring to a clearly demarcated global sphere. Highlighting the boundedness and social differentiation that comes with conceptions of 'world' or 'globe' might sound obvious. And it might go without saying that historical actors navigate specific and clearly circumscribed spheres rather than the planet as a whole. Yet, historians frequently reproduce the selective worldviews of their historical actors or bring their own limited frame of reference to the field rather than challenging these perspectives. At the same time, a global history perspective should ideally have the potential to spell out these limitations and boundaries and make them more visible, rather than obscuring or hiding them.

Boundaries and Limits in the Language of Global History

Instead of advocating a new language of spheres (akin to Arjun Appadurai's language of 'scapes', which has rightly been criticised as being overly schematic), the aim of this chapter is to explore how the sphere as a figure of thought permits historians to rethink openness and closure in global history.[67] Of

---

[65] Diana Lemberg, '"The Universal Language of the Future": Decolonization, Development, and the American Embrace of Global English, 1945–1965', *Modern Intellectual History* 15, 2 (2018), 561–92; Valeska Huber, 'An International Language for All: Basic English and the Limits of a Global Communication Experiment', in David Brydan and Jessica Reinisch (eds.), *Internationalists in European History: Rethinking the Twentieth Century* (London: Bloomsbury, 2021), 51–67.

[66] H. G. Wells, *World Brain* (London: Methuen, 1938); Nile Green (ed.), *The Persianate World: The Frontiers of a Eurasian Lingua Franca* (Oakland: University of California Press, 2019); Michelle Beauclair (ed.), *The Francophone World: Cultural Issues and Perspectives* (Frankfurt am Main: Peter Lang, 2007); Silke Mende, *Ordnung durch Sprache. Francophonie zwischen Nationalstaat, Imperium und internationaler Politik, 1860–1960* (Berlin: De Gruyter Oldenbourg, 2020); connecting linguistic and geopolitical spheres: Georg Glasze, *Politische Räume: Die diskursive Konstitution eines 'geokulturellen Raums' – die Frankophonie* (Bielefeld: Transcript, 2013).

[67] Arjun Appadurai, 'Disjuncture and Difference in the Global Cultural Economy', *Theory, Culture and Society* 7, 2–3 (1990), 295–310.

course, the sphere is not an overall remedy: focusing on boundaries too rigorously might in fact hide the internal structures and networks that fill the sphere. At the same time, the various ways in which historical actors referred to global spheres reviewed earlier – the globe as sphere, spheres of influence, private and public spheres – offer alternative conceptualisations of the world and its limitations. They draw attention to boundaries and boundary-making and to difference and differentiation, complementing the familiar vocabulary of connection and circulation.[68]

Rather than prescribing a new language, this chapter points to several occasions where the sphere emerges as a global concept, allowing us to show how openness and closure are intertwined in contemporary reflections on globality. Through visiting instances of radical inclusion and radical exclusion, it helps to contextualise (rather than theorise) the global. Most importantly, this chapter has hinted at an ambivalence regarding the nature of boundaries and their permeability in global history. Spheres are necessarily bounded, even if these boundaries may be more solid or more ephemeral and therefore can vary in their porosity. This holds true both for the globe as a sphere characterised by radical inclusivity and for the more exclusive multiple global spheres delimited by class, gender, media systems and skills that are described in the last part of this chapter.

In this experimental think piece, I have been particularly interested in exploring the boundaries that define these spheres. A sphere is more permanent than a bubble, which can easily burst. But is a sphere impenetrable and hermetically sealed, as in the depictions of a closed world? Or is it porous and permeable, at least for some? Can one belong to several spheres, and can one leave them at will? And how are the limits of different spheres set and guarded? When thinking about spheres, we have to pay attention to the qualities of the membranes in which they are enclosed. Such reflections on the nature of boundaries invite contemplations on stability and fragility, porosity and impermeability, rather than resorting to a language of fluidity and formlessness as central features of globality. Boundaries can dissolve and solidify as a result of global phenomena such as pandemics or wars. Consequently, thinking about global spheres calls for a more systematic exploration of boundaries and limits, borders and frontiers, as a central semantic field of global history.

Of course, there is a sprawling literature on two-dimensional borderlands in global history.[69] This literature has gone a long way towards exploring

---

[68] Jeffrey C. Alexander and Paul Colomy (eds.), *Differentiation Theory and Social Change: Comparative and Historical Perspectives* (New York: Columbia University Press, 1990).

[69] From Peter Sahlins, *Boundaries: The Making of France and Spain in the Pyrenees* (Berkeley: University of California Press, 1989) to Sören Urbansky, *Beyond the Steppe Frontier: A History of the Sino-Russian Border* (Princeton: Princeton University Press, 2020). Other work has stressed the sorting processes taking place in border situations, such as my own work on the

processes of openness and closure in the literal sense. Yet a large part of this literature refers to geographical boundaries such as the borders of nation-states, continents and seascapes. These works are therefore, not surprisingly, mainly concerned with spatial conceptions of the global.

In contrast to such two-dimensional conceptions, spheres are more frequently bounded by divisions that have nothing to do with geography. Such divisions can take the forms of glass ceilings, cell membranes and elastic skins. In this sense, spheres are related as much to the sociological literature on social closure as they are to geographical conceptions of spatial expansion and retraction. Connecting the spatial and the social in global history more closely and drawing attention to the social depth of global processes therefore adds an important third dimension. Spheres can lead us to reflect more openly on the question of the universe or cosmos inhabited by a historical actor and the limits thereof – geographically, but above all socially and communicatively. Closure emerges as a flexible category: processes of closure can be territorial, but they can also relate to phenomena of social differentiation. The three-dimensional nature of spheres and their boundaries therefore points towards new and more inclusive ways of thinking about global borders and limits.

There are many examples of non-geographical boundary-work that will come to mind beyond those emphasised in this chapter. Recently, historians have been drawn to the porosities between the spheres of humans and the worlds of animals.[70] Others have conceptualised borders as semi-permeable membranes, for instance in relation to mobility and migration, where creating opportunities for some means limiting them for others. A typology of boundaries beyond the geographical allows historians to reach out to neighbouring disciplines but also to more distant fields of research, such as the biosciences, information technology and linguistics.[71]

Thinking about spheres and related metaphors broadens our view beyond binaries such as connection and disconnection or integration and disintegration and calls for a more explicit examination of how ideas of the global in themselves can lead to exclusive and exclusionary notions. This chapter moves beyond equating the global with openness, connection and integration and instead addresses the role of closure, boundaries and limits in global history

Suez Canal as connection and boundary: Valeska Huber, *Channelling Mobilities: Migration and Globalization in the Suez Canal Region and Beyond 1869–1914* (Cambridge: Cambridge University Press, 2013); and Steffen Mau, *Sortiermaschinen: Die Neuerfindung der Grenze im 21. Jahrhundert* (Munich: C. H. Beck, 2021). For an overview, see Suzanne Conklin Akbari et al., 'AHR Conversations: Walls, Borders, and Boundaries in World History', *American Historical Review* 122, 5 (2017), 1501–53.
[70] Among others Sujit Sivasundaram, 'The Human, the Animal and the Prehistory of COVID-19', *Past and Present* 249, 1 (2020), 295–316.
[71] See for instance Samantha Frost, *Biocultural Creatures: Toward a New Theory of the Human* (Durham: Duke University Press, 2016) on the boundaries of cells and their permeability.

in a wider sense, placing inequality and differentiation at the centre. In this manner, it returns from a softer and more metaphorical language to a harder language emphasising structures and constraints, ideally without losing the interlopers and trespassers that have long fascinated global historians. In this way, the slightly unwieldy concept of spheres allows for two shifts which can prove central to global history in the long run. First, it challenges practitioners of global history to reveal how openness and closure are amalgamated in specific global processes, moving beyond the metaphorical, symbolic and somewhat indeterminate language that has characterised attempts to rethink global processes beyond connection and integration. And, second, it emphatic-ally calls for a move from geographical units (and their deconstruction) to the analysis of social units in order to reveal global inequalities and hierarchies more clearly than is often the case.

7   Scales
From Shipworms to the Globe and Back

Dániel Margócsy

> Flesh and blood animals also go about their business all around us, at all times and scales, without interaction or thought about our world of ideas.[1]

Let me start with one of the less widely cited masterpieces of global history: Julian Barnes's *A History of the World in 10 1/2 Chapters* from 1989. Written by a highly erudite writer at the moment when microhistory was asserting its challenge to global histories well beyond its original Italian context, *A History of the World* offered a shrewd and penetrating critique of the dichotomy between the micro–macro distinction that preoccupied scholars during those years. While professional historians argued with each other about whether to focus on large-scale societal transformations or on the experiences of individuals and small communities, Barnes sidestepped these debates by reimagining the history of the world from the perspective of animals. In the first chapter of Barnes's book, a woodworm tells the story of Noah's Ark, the first historical event to put a brake on globalisation. And from the perspective of the woodworm, the accounts of humans, familiar to us from the Old Testament, are put into serious doubt. The narrator writes: 'Now, I realize that accounts differ. Your species has its much repeated version, which still charms even sceptics; while the animals have a compendium of sentimental myths.'[2]

According to the woodworm, God is almost absent from the story of the Flood because he operates at a scale that is barely perceptible from below and, more generally, because things rarely go according to divine plans foisted upon the Earth from above. Human agency is also dislodged when viewed from below. The woodworm presents Noah as an incompetent leader who barely makes it through the calamities, losing much of the crew on the way. In contrast, the woodworm becomes a real agent of its own fate. It was not meant to be on the Ark (or, to be more precise, in the Ark): "I was a stowaway. I too survived; I escaped." Like the microhistorians of the period,

---

[1] Iwona Blazwick and Mark Dion, 'Mise-en-scène', in Mark Dion (ed.), *Theatre of the Natural World* (London: Whitechapel Gallery, 2019), 10–22, here 17.

[2] Julian Barnes, *A History of the World in 10 1/2 Chapters* (London: Cape, 1989).

Barnes resists the danger of telling stories from above. The connection to microhistory is probably not coincidental, and not only because the worm is also featured prominently in the title of Carlo Ginzburg's seminal *The Cheese and the Worms*.[3] Echoing Ginzburg's work, a later chapter of Barnes's book uses the narrative frame of an early modern trial to recover the forgotten voices of those who were put on trial, except that the accused happen in this case to be a number of insects. Yet *A History of the World in 10 1/2 Chapters* goes further than most microhistorians. While Barnes never trivialises the importance of recounting stories of human suffering, he does insist on acknowledging animals as agents and subjects of history.

A *History of the World in 10 1/2 Chapters* did not appear in a vacuum. Barnes was inspired by the work of Italo Calvino, the prolific writer and translator who introduced the term *microstoria* into Italian.[4] Like *A History of the World*, Calvino's *Cosmicomics* offered a whirlwind history of the cosmos from the Big Bang to the late twentieth century from the perspective of a narrator who was at once a sub-atomic particle, a variety of prehistoric animals and a human being. Like Barnes's book, Calvino's work challenged historians to include in their accounts agents that cannot be classified as human.[5] The late 1980s and early 1990s, when Barnes's book appeared, also saw the heyday of a post-modernist interest in replaying and recontextualising historical processes, as well as an important wave of works in art, literature and humanistic scholarship that put animals and the environment at the centre of interest, questioning the necessary centrality of humans in stories about our globe. The epitome of this interest is Mark Dion's *Scala naturae* (and his whole oeuvre), which critically reconstitutes and puts under erasure the Enlightenment's hierarchical understandings of nature (see Figure 7.1). Available in several variants, the *Scala naturae* presents us with a staircase or ladder (the literal meaning of *scale*, datable back to the fifteenth century), which organises natural organisms on ten different levels, with a bust of the great comparative anatomist Georges Cuvier on top. In this work, Dion emphasises the visual appeal and moral dangers inherent in hierarchical, human-centred models of the universe that do not fully acknowledge the various, alternative forms of life the Earth is replete with. Like Barnes, Dion puts all sorts of lifeforms in conversation with the work of humans to ponder how our globe is full of agents that could have a story to tell, and how, at the same time, these animals 'are emblematic of the different types of human driven extinction causes – overharvesting, habitat loss, intentional extermination, over collecting of eggs or specimens and

---

[3] Carlo Ginzburg, *The Cheese and the Worms* (Baltimore: Johns Hopkins University Press, 1980).
[4] Carlo Ginzburg, 'Microhistory: Two or Three Things That I Know about It', *Critical Inquiry* 20, 1 (1993), 10–35.
[5] Italo Calvino, *Cosmicomics* (New York: Harcourt Brace, 1968).

Figure 7.1 Mark Dion. *Scala Naturae*, 1994. Painted wooden structure, artifacts, plant specimens, taxidermy specimens and bust, 297.2 x 100 x 238.1 cm. Courtesy of the artist and Tanya Bonakdar Gallery, New York/Los Angeles.

poaching', too.[6] For Dion, the history of human globalisation is the history of the deglobalisation of many animal and plant species by human agents.

I began this review of the current historiography of scale with literature and art to highlight alternatives to the human-centred approaches of history and the other social sciences. The works of Barnes and Dion reveal to us scales of existence that historians rarely engage with: for example, those of worms, microscopic viruses or nuclear particles. While the concept of scale could be

[6] Petra Lange-Berndt, 'A Natural History That Glows in the Dark', in Mark Dion (ed.), *Our Plundered Planet* (London: Hugh Lane Gallery, 2019), 10–23, here 12. See also Ruth Erickson, *Mark Dion: Misadventures of a 21st-Century Naturalist* (New Haven: Yale University Press, 2017).

used to explore how history can be written from the sub-atomic level to the level of galaxies, historians who engage with the concept of scale use this engagement primarily to stake out their claims to one, two or three levels of observation at the most. The first half of the chapter will review the human-centred debates on micro- and macrohistory that have dominated discussions in recent decades. The second half will challenge this historiography first from the perspective of geography, and then return to animal and environmental studies to plead for a historical understanding of scale that incorporates concerns about globalisation, environmental transformation and non-human agencies.

Scale in History

Scale is a word with many meanings, ranging from the step of a ladder to the ratio between the distance measured on a map and the distance measured on the ground. In this chapter, and in the larger historical literature, scale often refers to the idea that, like a nested sphere, humans, society and the world are organised in a hierarchical manner, with distinct levels of action, such as the level of the individual, the urban, the national, the supranational and the global.[7] The idea of scale sometimes simply refers to the historian's chosen focus of observation – for example, that they study the English Civil War as it played out in the county of Kent. Alternatively, historians may use the concept of scale because they believe that it is a useful explanatory tool to understand how society and the world are organised. In this chapter, I adopt this concept of scale because it is heuristically useful when it comes to describing complex hierarchies with some regular patterns of behaviour. As I later discuss in more detail, human geographers make a convincing case that scale-based conceptual frameworks are especially helpful in understanding the functioning of unequal power structures.

   For historians, at each level of the scale, interactions between actors are governed by a separate set of rules.[8] In addition, the hierarchical nature of scale often means that events at higher levels can directly influence actions on the lower rungs of the hierarchy – for example, decisions made by a national government have a role in shaping urban policies and the lives of individuals. Curiously, the scholarship that engages with the concept of scale has focused less on how bottom-up processes may be explained in such a hierarchical order: for example, how individuals or cities may influence events and actions at the national or global level. After a discussion of the emergence of the historical

---

[7] For a good discussion of defining scale, for geography but also applicable to history, see Nina Siu-Ngan Lam and Dale A. Quattrochi, 'On the Issues of Scale, Resolution, and Fractal Analysis in the Mapping Sciences', *Professional Geographer* 44, 1 (1992), 88–98.

[8] For a non-historical exploration of scale in the humanities, see Joshua DiCaglio, *Scale Theory: A Nondisciplinary Inquiry* (Minneapolis: University of Minnesota Press, 2021).

debates on scale, the bulk of this chapter will be devoted to reconceptualising scale by taking seriously the issue of bottom-up organisation and action, and to exploring how the concept of scale can help historians move beyond the dichotomy of the micro and the macro.

As Deborah Coen has argued, the modern concept of scale emerged in the nineteenth century.[9] By then, the early modern concept of the *scala naturae*, a variant of the idea of a chain of being that reached from the lowly worm to God up in heaven, had been put out of use.[10] The advent of deep time – that is, the discovery of Earth's long geological past – dispelled the belief in the divine and the eternal order of fixed species, opening the door to a variety of proto-evolutionary theories. The old hierarchical understanding of nature was replaced by a new, complex, yet equally orderly understanding of the global environment as proposed by Alexander von Humboldt, whose work partly relied on indigenous helpers, mining professionals and colonial Latin American scholars.[11] Scale turned from a concept of vertical hierarchy to a descriptor of spatial differentiation. Humboldt's global vision emphasised universal laws that ensured broad regional similarities across the globe, while not neglecting to explore how small regions could diverge from each other based on their local microclimates. As Coen posits, however, it was in the multilingual, multinational and multiregional Habsburg Empire that the concept of scale developed even further and achieved its fullest expression, as Habsburg scientists began to provide models of the complex reasons why local regions in the Karst had drastically different weather patterns from other regions nearby. Unlike Humboldt, these geographers partially dispensed with a global vision of climate and environment because climate patterns at lower levels of observation tended to depend on their own, more local sets of laws. At different scales, phenomena on Earth depended on different sets of rules.

The historians who came after the geographical revolution freely acknowledged their debt to this tradition in their understanding of the different scales of historical action, even if they reintroduced the concept of vertical hierarchy to their discussions. The Annales school's self-proclaimed break with *histoire événementielle*, and Braudel's focus on the putatively more important medium

[9] Deborah Coen, *Climate in Motion: Science, Empire, and the Problem of Scale* (Chicago: University of Chicago Press, 2018).

[10] Arthur O. Lovejoy, *The Great Chain of Being: A Study of the History of an Idea* (Cambridge: Harvard University Press, 1936); E. M. W. Tillyard, *The Elizabethan World Picture. A Study of the Idea of Order in the Age of Shakespeare, Donne and Milton* (London: Chatto and Windus, 1943).

[11] Nicolaas A. Rupke, *Alexander von Humboldt: A Metabiography* (Chicago: University of Chicago Press, 2008); Patrick Anthony, 'Mining as the Working World of Alexander von Humboldt's Plant Geography and Vertical Cartography', *Isis* 109, 1 (2018), 28–55; Jorge Cañizares-Esguerra, *Nature, Empire, and Nation: Explorations of the History of Science in the Iberian Worlds* (Stanford: Stanford University Press, 2006).

and longue durée developments of history, owed much to the lessons they had learned from the geography of the years around 1900.[12] As Braudel programmatically explained, 'I would freely declare that the *Tableau de la géographie de la France*, published in 1903, just before Ernest Lavisse's great history of France, is a major work not only of geography but also in the canon of the French school of history.'[13]

A social and economic historian who adhered fairly strongly to environmental determinism, Braudel acknowledged three different levels of historical action, each with its own specific sets of laws and regularities. At the top level, the geographic landscape provided the environmental constraints for human activity while, one level below, cyclical economic patterns and social movements paved the way for the emergence of modern society. Even further below that scale, the history of events revealed the activities of individual humans that, frankly, did not amount to much. The achievements of a single person could never be more than the foam on top of a single wave in a vast ocean. For Braudel, even the French Revolution was a blip in human history, barely worth the attention of a real scholar. Talking of his colleague Ernest Labrousse in his inaugural lecture at the Collège de France, Braudel could barely contain his shock that Labrousse focused his attention on explaining the causes of the French Revolution, a diversion from more important developments in long history.[14] This was because Braudel emphatically believed that the direction of influence primarily flowed in one direction. While geography shaped the economy and society, and all these influenced the lives of individuals, individuals could make little difference to economics and society, and society could influence the shape of the land only to a limited degree. Braudel's world was not one in which humans could easily induce climate change on a global scale.[15]

Braudel's views had important repercussions that went well beyond the borders of France. The Annales school strongly shaped the development of

---

[12] Robert J. Mayhew, 'Historical Geography, 2009–2010: Geohistoriography, the Forgotten Braudel and the Place of Nominalism', *Progress in Human Geography* 35, 3 (2010), 409–21; Samuel Kinser, 'Annaliste Paradigm? The Geohistorical Structuralism of Fernand Braudel', *American Historical Review* 86, 1 (1981), 63–105; William Rankin, 'How the Visual Is Spatial: Contemporary Spatial History, Neo-Marxism, and the Ghost of Braudel', *History and Theory* 59, 3 (2020), 311–42.

[13] Fernand Braudel, *On History*, trans. Sarah Matthews (London: Weidenfeld and Nicolson, 1980), 17.

[14] Braudel, *On History*, 30.

[15] 'Through variations in the climate a force external to man is asserting itself and claiming its part in the most everyday explanations. Today such variations are accepted.' Fernand Braudel, *The Mediterranean and the Mediterranean World in the Age of Philip II*, 2 vols. (London: William Collins, 1972), vol. 1, 272. For a nuanced reading of Braudel, which shows the French historian's willingness to consider how humans shaped their environment to some extent, see Jason W. Moore, 'Capitalism as World-Ecology: Braudel and Marx on Environmental History', *Organization and Environment* 16, 4 (2003), 431–58.

the discipline in Italy, Latin America, Eastern Europe and even in the Anglo-American world. To give one famous example, the tripartite structure of Lawrence Stone's influential *Causes of the English Revolution* owes much to the model of the Annales school, though without the emphasis on geography.[16] Stone proposed that causation could be distributed between the socio-economic preconditions of change that accumulated over a good hundred years, the precipitates of the two decades before 1640 and the triggers that made the event an actuality as opposed to a probability. Unlike Braudel, Stone eventually acknowledged that socio-economic structures were not unaffected by changes at the level of the individual, and some of his articles proposed a more multidirectional flow of influence between socio-economic, cultural and narrative approaches:

Economic and demographic determinism has not only been undermined by a recognition of ideas, culture and even individual will as independent variables. It has also been sapped by a revived recognition that political and military power, the use of brute force, has very frequently dictated the structure of the society, the distribution of wealth, the agrarian system, and even the culture of the elite.[17]

While Stone's interest in social history never waned, the late 1970s also saw the emergence of revisionist historians of the English Civil War who challenged the primacy of preconditions of change over triggers, arguing that there was little that was pre-determined about the Civil War until it finally happened.[18] And, within the broader discipline, the coming of microhistory, developed first in Italy as a reaction to the dominance of the Annales school, refocused attention back on the histories of individuals.

Never united, microhistorians took a variety of contradictory approaches to the question of scale. For many, the essence of microhistory was to uncover the voices of those who fell through the sieves of official statistics and quantitative data. Some scholars simply turned their back on history written on a large scale and used the experiences of individuals to show how the historiography of larger societal structures failed to reveal how events on the global or national scale played out on the ground. This preference for recovering lost voices did not always imply the rejection of the importance of larger societal structures,

---

[16] Stone himself acknowledged his debt in a debate: 'Koenigsberger is correct in interpreting my arrangement of the data under the tripartite headings of preconditions, precipitation, and triggers as a more complicated version of the *structure/conjoncture* dichotomy.' Lawrence Stone, 'Early Modern Revolutions: An Exchange: The Causes of the English Revolution, 1529–1642: A Reply', *Journal of Modern History* 46, 1 (1974), 106–10, here 106.

[17] Lawrence Stone, 'The Revival of Narrative: Reflections on a New Old History', *Past and Present* 85 (1979), 3–24, here 10.

[18] Mark Kishlansky, *The Rise of the New Model Army* (Cambridge: Cambridge University Press, 1979); Conrad Russell, *Parliaments and English Politics 1621–1629* (Oxford: Oxford University Press, 1979); John Morrill, *Revolt of the Provinces: Conservatives and Radicals in the English Civil War, 1630–1650* (London: Allen and Unwin, 1976).

however. Carlo Ginzburg, for instance, used his *Cheese and the Worms* not only to give voice to the Italian miller Menocchio, an exceptional individual, but also to examine how the coming of the printed book interacted with the longue durée history of Eurasian popular culture. *The Cheese and the Worms* used the figure of Menocchio to tell a large-scale story of the socio-political emergence of confessionalisation that obliterated the popular culture that our miller was coming from. For Ginzburg, the story of Menocchio could be interpreted at both levels and did not invalidate the macro-level narratives of societal change. Importantly, some other Italian microhistorians went even further, using fine-grained studies to point out how macro-level phenomena could be described as the result of individuals organising themselves into larger hierarchical groups. These microhistorians did not take larger societal structures as given in advance. Instead, they explained how these hierarchical structures emerged thanks to the self-organisation of individuals into networked groups.[19]

Inspired partly by the influential writings of Fredrik Barth, Edoardo Grendi claimed that microhistory's aim was to 'reconstruct the evolution and dynamics of social comportments', and Giovanni Levi even argued that a focus on Catholic cultural structures could explain the formation of modern Italian-style states.[20] Such proposals found resonance on the other side of the Atlantic as well. If Grendi relied on Barth, the sociologist and historian Charles Tilly suggested that the reconciliation of micro- and macrohistory must be performed by relational realism, 'which concentrates on connections that concatenate, aggregate and disaggregate readily, form organisational structures at the same time as they shape individual behaviour'.[21] To some, the solution of aggregating individuals into social groups through the study of relational networks seemed an acceptable way of bringing together micro- and macrohistorians. Yet significant differences remained as macrohistorians accused microhistorians of using outdated models of the state and other concepts, while microhistorians challenged the actual commitment of macrohistorians to understanding microstructures.

Viewed from a French perspective, the culminating theoretical statement on the encounter between micro- and macrohistory was Jacques Revel's edited

---

[19]   Edoardo Grendi, 'The Political System of a Community in Liguria: Cervo in the Late Sixteenth and Early Seventeenth Centuries', in Ed Muir and Guido Ruggiero (eds.), *Microhistory and the Lost Peoples of Europe* (Baltimore: Johns Hopkins University Press, 1991), 119–58.

[20]   Edoardo Grendi, 'Micro-analyse et histoire sociale', *Ecrire l'histoire* 3 (2009), 67–80, here 80; Giovanni Levi, 'The Origins of the Modern State and the Microhistorical Perspective', in Jürgen Schlumbohm (ed.), *Mikrogeschichte – Makrogeschichte: Komplementär oder inkommensurabel?* (Göttingen: Wallstein, 1998), 53–82; see also Giovanni Levi, *Inheriting Power: Story of an Exorcist* (Chicago: University of Chicago Press, 1988). On Barth, see Paul-André Rosental, 'Construire le macro par le micro: Fredrik Barth et la microstoria', in Jacques Revel (ed.), *Jeux d'échelles: La micro-analyse à l'expérience* (Paris: Seuil, 1996), 141–60.

[21]   Charles Tilly, 'Micro, Macro, or Megrim?', in Schlumbohm, *Mikrogeschichte – Makrogeschichte*, 33–52, here 41.

volume *Jeux d'échelles*, which brought together a number of historians and anthropologists to reconcile the Annales's approach with the attacks of the Italians.[22] For Revel, microhistory's major benefit was to defamiliarise the historical structures that the Annales school had taken for granted, but it did not do away with these structures in the end.[23] Both approaches provided an interesting perspective on history, and neither had epistemological primacy over the other. The level of the individual was by no means more empirical or more concrete than the level of societal interactions. The best historical move was to oscillate constantly and playfully between the two levels of analysis. In the process, Revel chose to ignore the more serious challenges of microhistorians who called into question the validity of standard categories of social and economic history. It also remained unclear whether the microscopic and the macroscopic perspectives provided views on the same reality, or whether they were fundamentally irreconcilable. As Revel noted, some microhistorians, such as Sabina Loriga, explicitly modelled their writing on Akira Kurosawa's *Rashomon*, the iconic film showing how the same event could be told from different, contradictory perspectives without a resolution.[24] Consequently, Revel had very little to say on how events at one level could have repercussions on events at another level. The *jeux d'échelles* shed new light on history, but they did not imply that there would necessarily be well-defined interactions between the micro and the macro.

Despite the breath of fresh air that microhistorians brought to the discipline, their programmatic statements on the issue of scale remained trapped in the terminology and framework set by the *Annales* school. Unlike the physical geographers of climate around 1900, and unlike contemporary literary authors, microhistorians kept on understanding scale as an organisational feature limited to humans alone. Ginzburg, for instance, considered worms only to the degree that people turned them into a cosmological metaphor, and never treated them as independent agents of history. As a result, microhistorians reduced scale to a simple binary dichotomy between the micro and the macro – a dichotomy that has persisted in the discipline ever since.[25] To some degree, the rise of transnational history, in its different guises from

---

[22] Revel, *Jeux d'échelles*.

[23] 'Le changement d'échelle a joué, on l'a dit, le rôle d'un estrangement, au sens des sémioticiens: d'un dépaysement par rapport aux catégories d'analyse et aux modèles interprétatifs du discours historiographique dominant.' Jacques Revel, 'Micro-analyse et construction du social' [The changing of scale played, as has been said, the role of an estrangement, in the sense of the semioticians: of a change of scenery in relation to the categories of analysis and the interpretive models of the dominant historiographical discourse], in Revel, *Jeux d'échelles*, 15–37, here 34.

[24] Revel, 'Micro-analyse et construction du social', 32; Sabina Loriga, *Soldati: L'istituzione militare nel Piemonte del Settecento* (Venice: Marsilio, 1992).

[25] Matti Peltonen, 'Clues, Margins, and Monads: The Micro-Macro Link in Historical Research', *History and Theory* 40, 3 (2001), 347–59.

connected and entangled histories to *histoires croisées* and histories of circulation and mobilities, has seemed to confirm that networks offer a way out of the
dichotomy of micro- and macrohistory.[26] Here was an attempt that aimed to
break free from the focus on partially restricted locales to cover large distances
on the globe. Some versions of transnational history were simply a sub-genre of
world history that integrated into its macroanalysis structures that were supranational or bypassed national boundaries, such as international organisations.
Yet an important segment of this literature focused on individuals or small
groups of people whose travels across the world revealed how distant places
may have an unexpectedly strong influence on each other. While some transnational microhistorians continued to focus on Italy, others devoted themselves
to giving voice to the subaltern and the dispossessed in other places on the
globe as well. They helpfully recentred the historiography by bringing to life
the experiences and connections of enslaved Africans across the Atlantic or
Indian migrants in China and beyond.[27]

When it comes to the issue of scale, the literature on global microhistory has
tended not to use network theory to analyse how structures at different scales
may interact with each other. Instead, the aim is either to see how seemingly
local events are actually influenced by complex global forces, as proposed by
proponents of glocalism, or to explain how individuals are able to bypass urban
and state-level structures and operate at multiple locales at the same times.[28]
Such studies have made it clear that the level of the individual is not seamlessly
nested in the meso- and macro-level scales of city and nation, and have
proposed alternative social systems that structure the formation of communities. Yet it often remains rather opaque how traditional macro-level concepts
could be reconciled with these new, alternative social structures. For instance,
Michael Werner and Bénédicte Zimmermann claim both that *histoire croisée*
emphasises the 'inextricable interlinking' of the micro and the macro and that
'the notion of the scale does not refer to the micro or macro but to the different

[26] Sanjay Subrahmanyam, 'Connected Histories: Notes towards a Reconfiguration of Early
Modern Eurasia', *Modern Asian Studies* 31, 3 (1997), 735–62.
[27] For some recent examples of how historians explicitly rely on microhistory to deal with issues of
race and gender across the globe, see Cao Yin, 'The Journey of Isser Singh: A Global
Microhistory of a Sikh Policeman', *International Journal of Punjab Studies* 21, 2 (2014),
325–53; Lara Putnam, 'To Study the Fragments/Whole: Microhistory and the Atlantic
World', *Journal of Social History* 39, 3 (2006), 615–30; Julia Roos, 'An Afro-German
Microhistory: Gender, Religion, and the Challenges of Diasporic Dwelling', *Central
European History* 49, 2 (2016), 240–60; and Dale Tomich and Michael Zeuske,
'Introduction, the Second Slavery: Mass Slavery, World-Economy, and Comparative
Micro-Histories', *Review (Fernand Braudel Center)* 31, 2 (2008), 91–100.
[28] Francesca Trivellato, 'Is there a Future for Italian Microhistory in the Age of Global History?',
California Italian Studies 2, 1 (2011), https://escholarship.org/uc/item/0z94n9hq; see also
Maxine Berg, Global History of the Global and the Local, a special issue of the *Journal of
Early Modern History* 27, 1–2 (2023). On globalism as the solution to scale, see
Sebastian Conrad, *What Is Global History?* (Princeton: Princeton University Press, 2016).

spaces in which the constitutive interactions of the process being analysed are inscribed', leaving it unclear whether one should discard the concepts of the micro or the macro.[29]

In less programmatic statements, the concept of the transnational has served to reveal alternatives to state- and city-based explanations that are already well-established historical categories. In *The Familiarity of Strangers*, for instance, Francesca Trivellato showed how the Sephardic diaspora of Livorno relied partly on the urban and state structures of the early modern Mediterranean, and partly on networks based on kinship and religion that connected different parts of the Mediterranean.[30] Yet even Trivellato's account of the Sephardic diaspora did not quite explain how interpersonal relationships aggregate into urban and state structures, let alone discuss how shipworms, or the seeds of plague and other infectious diseases, shaped maritime trading networks in the Mediterranean. *The Familiarity of Strangers* instead often offered top-down explanations of how the Livorno authorities posed constraints on the lives of Sephardic Jews within their walls, implying a simple model in which macro-structures shape but do not determine actions at the individual level. As Bernhard Struck, Kate Ferris and Jacques Revel wrote in 2011, the same issues that prompted the editing of *Jeux d'échelles* twenty years earlier are also present in debates about transnational histories. These authors argued that one could not simply discard the nation-state, and that the transnational is simply a spatially extended variant of the microhistorians' idea of the local individual. Transnational history did not help decide whether it was possible to reconcile the perspectives presented by different scales and if there were ways to explore how they interacted.[31]

From today's vantage point, there is widespread agreement that, for a fruitful global history, it would be crucial to finally understand how the interplay of different scales of analysis unfolds in practice, or at least in theory. In a recent special issue of *Past and Present*, John-Paul Ghobrial writes that the literature 'could do more to explain exactly how one should play the *jeux d'échelles*', but he does not actually offer an answer, and Jan de Vries's contribution to the special issue confirms that, at least from the perspective of some social and economic historians, the dichotomy may be

[29] Michael Werner and Bénédicte Zimmermann, 'Histoire Croisée: Between the Empirical and Reflexivity', *Annales* 58, 1 (2003), 7–36, here 28.
[30] Francesca Trivellato, *The Familiarity of Strangers: The Sephardic Diaspora, Livorno, and Cross-Cultural Trade in the Early Modern Period* (New Haven: Yale University Press, 2009). For a recent discussion of microhistory and the acknowledgement of the global turn, see Thomas Robisheaux et al., *Microhistory and the Historical Imagination: New Frontiers, a special issue of The Journal of Medieval and Early Modern Studies* (2017), 47, 1.
[31] Bernhard Struck et al., 'Introduction: Space and Scale in Transnational History', *International History Review* 33, 4 (2011), 573–84. See also Etienne Anheim and Enrico Castelli Gattinara, 'Jeux d'échelles: Une histoire internationale', *Revue de Synthèse* 130, 4 (2009), 661–77.

irresolvable.[32] As de Vries damningly writes, 'microhistories do not, and are not intended to, aggregate to macro-level and global histories. There is no path, no methodology, no theoretical framework in the current repertoire of the microhistorian to make this move possible.'[33]

De Vries's argument hinges on his assumption that macrohistory is successful because of its alliance with the social sciences, and therefore the only microhistory that could aggregate to larger-level explanations is the controlled case study that reveals comparative differences. For de Vries, of course, the social sciences primarily mean economics and quantitative sociology. Yet, as we have seen, the first wave of microhistories was inspired by another social science: the anthropology of Fredrik Barth. Similarly, Tilly used 'relational realism' precisely to offer an alternative explanation for how microphenomena may aggregate to macrostructures without resorting to quantitative comparative research.[34] Curiously, microhistorians today rarely acknowledge this anthropological inspiration; even more curiously, the historical debate on global history and the problem of scale mostly ignores the parallel debates on scale that have been prevalent in the disciplines of science studies and geography.[35] If, in the middle of the twentieth century, Braudel was enthusiastic about a somewhat outdated version of geography, his enthusiasm has disappeared from the discipline completely.

Flat Ontologies and Scale Jumping

If scale means that, at different levels of analysis, agents can act according to different sets of laws, the basic question is how actions at one level could affect agents at another level. In the classic formulation of the concept of scale, with its nested hierarchies, the answer is that developments at a higher rank of hierarchy can affect events at a lower rank of the scale in a top-down manner, but not vice versa. Yet once the concept of nested hierarchies is at least partially abandoned, the solution to this issue becomes much less clear. If the actions of nation-states are governed by the rules of political economy at the macro level, for instance, can individuals affect how states develop or change?

---

[32] John-Paul A. Ghobrial, 'Introduction: Seeing the World like a Microhistorian', *Past and Present* 242, supplement 14 (2019), 1–22, here 16. For similar debates in the French historiography, and an acknowledgement that they are not new, see Romain Bertrand and Guillaume Calafat, 'La microhistoire globale: affaire(s) à suivre', *Annales* 73, 1 (2018), 1–18 and the articles in that issue.

[33] Jan de Vries, 'Playing with Scales: The Global and the Micro, the Macro and the Nano', *Past and Present* 242, supplement 14 (2019), 23–36, here 29.

[34] For a useful reminder of Barth's importance, see Giovanni Levi, 'Frail Frontiers?', *Past and Present* 242, supplement 4 (2019), 37–49.

[35] For an acknowledgement of the debate, see Christian G. De Vito, 'History without Scale: The Micro-Spatial Perspective', *Past and Present* 242, supplement 14 (2019), 348–72.

In recent years, human geographers have proposed answering this fundamental question in the affirmative by emphasising the importance of bottom-up organisation and action. Microhistorians were interested in marginalised individuals who were nonetheless able to escape the constraints of such oppressive structures as the state without necessarily challenging it outright. Geographers are instead interested in revolutionary individuals and other agents who can change macrostructures such as the national state or global economy. They propose two alternative analytical approaches to accomplish this goal. First, the argument for flat ontologies posits that all macro-level phenomena can ultimately be described using only individual agents who form networks. Second, the argument for scale jumping argues that certain shape-shifting agents are able to 'make the leap' from one level of analysis to another, and thus affect outcomes both at the micro and the macro level.

In recent decades, geography has undergone a development that is not dissimilar to the transformation of the historical discipline.[36] Human geography has become detached, to some degree, from physical geography and, ever since Henri Lefebvre's groundbreaking work, geographers carefully distinguish 'the social space [that is] a social product' from the concept of physical space.[37] As a result, human geographers also refer to scale primarily to describe the hierarchical organisation of social life, with nature and non-human agents taking the role of epiphenomena. Yet the similarities with historical discourse go deeper and show parallel developments over the past forty years. Inspired by Immanuel Wallerstein, the geographer Peter Taylor conceptualised scale as a nested hierarchy with the global level as the more powerful in 1982, but the recent literature has moved away from this angle and towards interpretations that are not unlike the radicalised versions of the Barthian solutions offered by Italian microhistorians.[38] In a series of articles, Sally Marston has argued that, once the nested hierarchies of scales are rejected, scalar explanations become inferior versions of Deleuzian rhizomatic networks and therefore the concept of scale should be abolished.[39] If all agents are able to act upon all other agents (the individual on the state, and the state on the individual) and there is no pre-established hierarchy, the illusion of scale is the result of scholars mistaking certain powerful network nodes for reified and unproblematic entities. Unlike strong versions of Deleuzian network theory, Marston nonetheless points out that not all networks need to be about endless openness, flows and fluxes. There are blockages and spatial structures that give shape to the world, just as it is

---

[36] For an overview, see Andrew Herod, *Scale* (London: Routledge, 2010).
[37] Henri Lefebvre, *The Production of Space* (Oxford: Blackwell, 1991), here 26.
[38] Peter J. Taylor, 'A Materialist Framework for Political Geography', *Transactions of the Institute of British Geographers* 7, 1 (1982), 15–34.
[39] Sallie A. Marston et al., 'Human Geography without Scale', *Transactions of the Institute of British Geographers* 30, 4 (2005), 414–32.

impossible to write a transnational history of circulation without presupposing certain nation-states or other entities between which circulation takes place. A great advantage of Marston's approach is to emphasise that a focus on scale can serve to highlight socio-economic hierarchies that overshadow alternative systems of inequalities (e.g. those based on gender).[40] A network-based analysis is better able to handle complex systems of inequalities where class, race, gender and other factors interact with each other.

Flat ontology leaves slightly unclear how unequal power structures can emerge within networks where all agents are similar at the outset.[41] For this reason, other geographers have been less enthusiastic about abandoning the concept of scale, which immediately foregrounds the structural role of inequality. These geographers have maintained the idea that partially nested hierarchies play a significant role in the organisation of society and in shaping the interaction of humans with their environments.[42] Scholars inspired by Marx, such as Neil Brenner and Neil Smith, agree that scale is a social construct, but this does not make it any less real. Scale is a useful explanatory tool because it provides a clearer understanding of unequal power structures than the somewhat vague concepts of blockages and spatial structures. While in principle somewhat malleable, scale structures can also be rigid and path-dependent, and a scale-based analysis can therefore explain why the nation-state or global economy have survived across several centuries.[43] Building on Brenner and Smith, Erik Swyngedouw has importantly argued that scales can be reconfigured at each new stage of history, with certain levels gaining particular significance in certain historical situations.[44] As Swyngedouw claims, for instance, the rise of capitalism was a key event in the emergence of the global as a separate level where power could be concentrated, with other levels (e.g. the national) losing some significance at the same time.[45] Following Neil Smith's earlier work, Swyngedouw suggests that power struggles and political upheavals play out in the construction of new scales that attempt to constrain certain actors to act at only one level of action. Much work and organisation are needed for other actors to become able to 'jump scales' and effect change.

---

[40] Sallie A. Marston, 'The Social Construction of Scale', *Progress in Human Geography* 24, 1 (2000), 219–42.

[41] For a somewhat more detailed critique of flat ontologies, see Dániel Margócsy, 'A Long History of Breakdowns: A Historiographical Review', *Social Studies of Science* 47, 3 (2017), 307–25.

[42] For a review of the debates on scale, see Andrew E. G. Jonas, 'Pro Scale: Further Reflections on the "Scale Debate" in Human Geography', *Transactions of the Institute of British Geographers* 31, 3 (2006), 399–406.

[43] Neil Brenner, *New Urban Spaces: Urban Theory and the Scale Question* (Oxford: Oxford University Press, 2019), here 107–8.

[44] Erik Swyngedouw and Mustafa Dikeç, 'Theorizing the Politicizing City', *International Journal of Urban and Regional Research* 41, 1 (2016), 1–18.

[45] For a parallel historical analysis of the emergence of the global, see Sujit Sivasundaram, 'Sciences and the Global: On Methods, Questions, and Theory', *Isis* 101, 1 (2010), 146–58.

From the late 1980s onwards, Smith was one of the major theorists of scale in geography. Just like Swyngedouw, Smith claimed that scales were powerful but unstable constructions 'produced as part of the social and cultural, economic and political landscapes of contemporary capitalism and patriarchy'. As malleable political constructs, different scales of action, though hierarchically organised, were nonetheless inherently connected, which led Smith to the realisation that 'the importance of "jumping scales" lies precisely in this active social and political connectedness of apparently different scales, their deliberate confusion and abrogation'.[46] If capital structured hierarchies in such a way that those without power were pushed to a less privileged level of action, these dispossessed agents could nonetheless use a variety of jumping strategies to regain their agency and power at a level of high importance.[47] Bottom-up organisation was difficult but not impossible. To give an example, Smith brought up the New York artist Krzysztof Wodiczko's political project of the *Homeless Vehicle*. The *Homeless Vehicle* was a mobile unit that combined a shopping cart with an upper, sheltered compartment for sleeping and also included a washbasin for daily ablutions. Through its rocketlike design, it stood out from the urban environment where it was exhibited and put into action. It made visible at the urban level those masses of homeless people that the politicians of gentrification wanted to render invisible.

Following Smith, Swyngedouw has similarly reinterpreted the history of late-twentieth-century globalisation as an issue of scale jumping. In Swyngedouw's version, the contemporary network flows that Marston has studied are therefore not simply an ahistorical given.[48] They are the result of the post-Bretton Woods era in which the welfare state is hollowed out and global markets increasingly operate at the local and individual level. It is this recent historical process that Swyngedouw calls 'glocalisation'. For Swyngedouw, glocalisation is not the microhistorical study of global forces, it is the result of global markets' late-twentieth-century reorganisation of scales. It offers an example of market forces jumping scales from the global to the local without passing through the national.

While Swyngedouw's and Smith's arguments and examples come from a determinedly Marxist interpretation of history, their claims about the construction of scale resonate with the points made by the French social theorist

---

[46] Neil Smith, 'Contours of a Spatialized Politics: Homeless Vehicles and the Production of Geographical Scale', *Social Text* 33 (1993), 54–81, here 66; see also Neil Smith, 'Spaces of Vulnerability: The Space of Flows and the Politics of Scale', *Critique of Anthropology* 16, 1 (1996), 63–77; John Paul Jones et al., 'Neil Smith's Scale', *Antipode* 49, S1 (2017), 138–52.

[47] On a recent review of the role of capitalism in history, see Andrew David Edwards et al., 'Capitalism in Global History', *Past and Present* 249, 1 (2020), e1–e32.

[48] See also Bob Jessop, 'Crisis of the National Spatio-Temporal Fix and the Tendential Ecological Dominance of Globalizing Capitalism', *International Journal of Urban and Regional Research* 24, 2 (2000), 323–61.

Bruno Latour. While Actor–Network theory has often been associated with flat ontologies, Latour was clear that his aim was to deconstruct, but not to do away with, modern hierarchical structures. Throughout Latour's work, his double aim was not only to explain how 'we have never been modern', but also how the rise of Western science brought in unequal power structures and developments between societies.[49] Actor–Network theory relies on associations in networks to explain unequal development and the establishment of hierarchies of power.[50] The difference between Marxist geographers and Latour is that Latour focuses primarily on how micro-level agents build up higher-level networks, while Smith and Swyngedouw privilege capital over micro-level agents in their explanations of the emergence of scalar hierarchies. Yet even when one acknowledges this important difference, scale jumping nonetheless finds its counterpart in Actor–Network theory and its concept of immutable mobiles. At least for the early Latour, powerful networks gained their potency from the paper tools of scalable immutable mobiles, such as maps and diagrams, that allowed modern scientists to jump scales with ease.[51] Immutable mobiles reduced the globe to the level of the individual scientist and made it possible to recreate the world in one centre of accumulation, such as the city of Paris. As Latour explained, scale models were at once scientific facts and religious fetishes (a 'factish'), as they came with the promise that their manipulation in a small laboratory could effect changes at a larger level, across the globe, leading to Western domination in modernity. More recently, John Tresch has offered a decentred, and less triumphalist, version of the factish in his studies of cosmograms across history, investigating how different societies built themselves reduced, and often hierarchical, models of the cosmos to understand and manipulate it at a reduced scale.[52] Tresch's cosmograms are at once a powerful example of how people use a variety of tools to jump scales, and they also reveal how agents other than twenty-first-century historians and geographers develop complex theories about scale and levels of action.

For historians, the geographers' perspective on scale has a number of significant advantages. First of all, it points out that scale is a political construct and, as a result, it is because of historical struggles that certain levels on the

---

[49] Bruno Latour, *We Have Never Been Modern* (Cambridge, MA: Harvard University Press, 1993); Bruno Latour, *An Inquiry into Modes of Existence: An Anthropology of the Moderns* (Cambridge, MA: Harvard University Press, 2013).

[50] For a Latourian criticism of Marston along these lines, see Chris Collinge, 'Flat Ontology and the Deconstruction of Scale: A Response to Marston, Jones and Woodward', *Transactions of the Institute of British Geographers* 31, 2 (2006), 244–51.

[51] Bruno Latour, 'Drawing Things Together', in Michael Lynch and Steve Woolgar (eds.), *Representation in Scientific Practice* (Cambridge, MA: MIT Press, 1990), 20–69.

[52] John Tresch, 'Cosmopragmatics and Petabytes', in Simon Schaffer et al. (eds.), *Aesthetics of Universal Knowledge* (London: Palgrave Macmillan, 2017), 137–68; John Tresch, 'Technological World-Pictures: Cosmic Things, Cosmograms', *Isis* 98, 1 (2007), 84–99; see also Christoph Markschies et al. (eds.), *Atlas der Weltbilder* (Berlin: Akademie-Verlag, 2011).

scale, such as the global, gain particular importance at particular moments. Consequently, there is no foundational and transhistorical level of analysis that reveals the true workings of society; moreover, neither the local nor the global are necessary, transhistorical givens. Similarly, it is also entirely possible that neither a traditional micro- or macro-level analysis is the best tool for understanding all historical events, as there may be other scales of action that are rendered invisible by capital or the archival practices of political powers.

Second, the concept of scale jumping offers historians a tool that is better equipped than Revel's *jeux d'échelles* to explain how individuals can act on the macro-level on certain occasions. Smith's ideas allow us to focus on how, once established, the different scales at which agents operate can be connected – the major issue faced by both micro- and macrohistorians both before and after the transnational turn. A categorisation of different strategies of scale jumping, from the artwork of the *Homeless Vehicle* through Latourian factishes to cosmograms, may well be the best tool to help historians of the local and historians of the global join forces. Here, for lack of space, I will only offer a few such strategies from historical writings to explain how scale jumping can be used to describe the kinds of work that need to be done for entities to occupy positions of power at a variety of levels.

While scale jumping is a relatively new concept, the phenomenon itself has long been known to writers of history and historical anthropology. These historians also acknowledged that scale jumping is not always a strategy of resistance: it can also be a tool for assuming power. Ernst Kantorowicz's classic *The King's Two Bodies* is only the most prominent example of the legal and religious work that enables an individual human to become the state.[53] As Kantorowicz explained, modern kingship emerged from the Christological literature that attempted to explain how Christ united two natures in one person and how, after Christ's ascension to heaven, Christ was present on Earth both in the host and in the church. The secularised concept of kingship discussed in similar terms how to distinguish and unite the individual person and the state-level role they play in the body of the king, only to fall apart during the English Civil War when parliamentary forces fought the king in the name of the King. It was at this moment that Thomas Hobbes appeared on the scene, offering his own analysis of how 'a multitude of persons natural are united by covenants into one person civil or body politic'.[54] Once the traditional concept of the king was truly dead, a new legal system needed to be established to make states out of people. Importantly, the double nature of kingship was not only a Western idea, as Marshall Sahlins's *Islands of History* showed for the Pacific. As Sahlins explained in terms of

[53] Ernst Kantorowicz, *The King's Two Bodies: A Study in Mediaeval Political Theory* (Princeton: Princeton University Press, 1957).
[54] Thomas Hobbes, *Human Nature and De Corpore Politico* (Oxford: Oxford University Press, 1994), here 109.

structural anthropology, in the Fijian case the levels of the individual, the state and the divine are united through their 'hierarchical encompassment in the projects of kingship'. The divine king as an individual expresses the general will and 'every day, the king recreates the world'.[55] As Sahlins himself explicitly acknowledged, his interest in kings was not a revival of the 'great-man theory of history', but lay rather in understanding how microhistorical actions map onto the canvas of macrohistory.[56] As such, it was one more example of scale jumping.

It would be rash to assert, though, that only kings have the ability to move across scales from the individual to the national level in actual history. As Kantorowicz explained, his inspiration for *The King's Two Bodies* came from the realisation that the Benedictine monastic order was an "Inc." – an incorporated business organisation in the legal landscape of the United States.[57] The formation of corporations, from medieval guilds to twenty-first-century multinational companies, is a prominent example of efforts aimed at making entities visible at ever larger scales. Arguably, an important strand of the Italian microhistorians' studies of labour organisation, often inspired by E. P. Thompson, can be similarly described as attempts to see how individual workers can come together and form a union and how they come to make a class.[58] And, in a similar manner, a major focus of contemporary geographers of scale is understanding twentieth-century labour movements and early twenty-first-century urban protests.[59] Yet, if we pay heed to Kantorowicz's point, we need to remember that the aggregation of people into agents at the macro level cannot be exclusively described by the laws of Barthian networks; we also need to pay close attention to the legal and scalar solution of incorporation that constructs a political body out of a multitude.

Back to the Worms

As the previous examples have suggested, scholars and historical actors have proposed many ingenious solutions to the problem of shifting from one level of historical action to another, and many more examples could be adduced before the list is exhausted. By way of conclusion, I would like to extend our discussion of jumping scales by considering it at levels that transcend the entrenched micro–macro dichotomy of the discipline and reach out to the less visible scales

[55] Marshall Sahlins, *Islands of History* (Chicago: University of Chicago Press, 1985), 36.
[56] Sahlins, *Islands of History*, 35; Marshall Sahlins, 'Structural Work: How Microhistories Become Macrohistories and Vice Versa', *Anthropological Theory* 5, 1 (2005), 5–30.
[57] Kantorowicz, *The King's Two Bodies*, xvii.
[58] E. P. Thompson, *The Making of the English Working Class* (London: Gollancz, 1963); Maurizio Gribaudi, *Itinéraires ouvriers: Espaces et groupes sociaux à Turin au début du XXe siècle* (Paris: Éditions de l'EHESS, 1987).
[59] Swyngedouw and Dikeç, 'Theorizing the Politicizing City'; Brenner, *New Urban Spaces*.

at which politics and nature operate. The aim is to avoid the limitations of the post-Braudelian focus of both micro- and macrohistorians on those levels of analysis that prioritise humans, answering Dipesh Chakrabarty's recent call to open up history to radically new approaches.[60] This section is an attempt to understand how the social spaces historians and geographers have explored interact with the physical space of the environment that humans share with plants, animals and lower lifeforms. The plea for extending our understanding of scale by considering levels that contain microscopic entities, insects or trees is to understand how human individuals and social action shape and are shaped by their engagement with nature.[61] Twenty years ago, Timothy Mitchell famously asked the question: 'Can the mosquito speak?' Inspired by Marxian analysis, Mitchell argued that one could not understand Egyptian history without examining how colonial technology brought in both political and natural disasters.[62] Historians have only selectively engaged with Mitchell's approach, but the 2020 pandemic has provided ample evidence that the history of globalisation cannot be written without considering the role of viruses, bacteria and other vectors of disease. And while this chapter has focused primarily on the realm of the living, the geographical concept of scale can also help incorporate in its analysis a variety of tangible and intangible material agents, from mineral resources and oceans to radio waves and nuclear or cosmic radiation.[63]

I started my chapter with Mark Dion's ladders because they are a considered exploration of how scales are political constructs even at levels that include only non-human agents at first sight. The point is not simply that the 'Great Chain of Being' is a human construct of the Renaissance world picture, but rather the environmentalist realisation that human activities, including the

[60] Dipesh Chakrabarty, 'The Climate of History: Four Theses', *Critical Inquiry* 35, 2 (2009), 197–222. For a history of globalisation that discusses its ecological consequences, see Manfred B. Steger, *Globalization: A Very Short Introduction* (Oxford: Oxford University Press, 2017); see also Tyson Retz, *Progress and the Scale of History* (Cambridge: Cambridge University Press, 2022).
[61] For Latour's fascination with these issues, see Bruno Latour, *Down to Earth: Politics in the New Climatic Regime* (Cambridge: Polity Press, 2018).
[62] Timothy Mitchell, *Rule of Experts: Egypt, Techno-Politics, Modernity* (Berkeley: University of California Press, 2002).
[63] For an example of recent work in the scale jumping politics of material culture, see Jenny Bulstrode, 'Cetacean Citations and the Covenant of Iron', *Notes and Records of the Royal Society* 73, 2 (2019) 167–85; on oceanic history, see David Armitage et al. (eds.), *Oceanic Histories* (Cambridge: Cambridge University Press, 2018); for intangible materialities, see William Rankin, 'The Geography of Radionavigation and the Politics of Intangible Artifacts', *Technology and Culture* 55, 3 (2014), 622–74; Serhii Plokhy, *Chernobyl: The History of a Nuclear Catastrophe* (New York: Basic Books, 2018); Adriana Petryna, *Life Exposed: Biological Citizenship after Chernobyl* (Princeton: Princeton University Press, 2002); Gabrielle Hecht, *Being Nuclear: Africans and the Global Uranium Trade* (Cambridge, MA: MIT Press, 2012).

development of taxonomical classification, have been actively transforming nature and the Earth for many centuries, if not millennia, and that anthropogenic global warming is only the latest act by which humanity attempts to reshape the Earth with problematic consequences.[64] That is why at its lowest rungs Dion's *Scala naturae* contains human artefacts made from natural materials, such as the wooden wheel, reminding us of the hidden presence of humans at all levels of natural organisation. While the bust of Cuvier is at the top of Dion's sculpture, the point is that humans can walk down the ladder and affect lifeforms on every step. This is the reason for Dion's fascination with debris, as manifested in his cupboards of the *Tate Thames Dig*, which used the framing device of early-twentieth-century geological cabinets to exhibit the results of his excavations of the detritus of plastic, ropes, bones and shells from the banks of the Thames in London.[65] From Dion's perspective, historians' focus on the scale of the human or the state obscures the interactions between humans, animals and plant life that is happening at other levels. While for Braudel the human could affect changes at the level of the environment only with much difficulty, for Dion (and for ecocriticism) the human is a crucial agent in the construction of the environment as we know it. Like Wodiczko's *Homeless Vehicle*, *Scala naturae* is an effort to challenge and resist the political structures, this time to prevent global environmental disaster. As Dion writes: 'My taxonomies often frustrate expectations and assumptions one may have about the nature and function of display. The point of this irritation and challenge to convention is to question the status of its objectivity and power. The authority of taxonomy is fragile, as was clearly understood by a number of Surrealists.'[66]

While Dion's *Scala naturae* focuses on the role of humans in environmental disaster, Barnes's ventriloquising history of the woodworm offers a poignant reminder about the agency of animals and other lifeforms when considering the interactions of the political and the natural, coming from the same decade that produced Latour's *Pasteurization of France*, which brought non-human actants to the fore in science studies.[67] Barnes's choice of the woodworm (or shipworm) is particularly relevant for historians of globalisation because

---

[64] Obviously, this point has also been made in the vast literature on ecocriticism and in environmental history, including Carolyn Merchant, *The Death of Nature: Women, Ecology and the Scientific Revolution* (New York: Harper and Row, 1980); Richard Grove, *Green Imperialism: Colonial Expansion, Tropical Island Edens and the Origins of Environmentalism, 1600–1860* (Cambridge: Cambridge University Press, 1995); Donna Haraway, 'Teddy Bear Patriarchy: Taxidermy in the Garden of Eden, New York City, 1908–36', *Social Text* 11 (1984), 19–64; Neil Smith, *Uneven Development: Nature, Capital, and the Production of Space* (Oxford: Blackwell, 1984).

[65] Mark Dion, *Tate Thames Dig*, wooden cabinet and other materials (London: Tate Gallery, ref: T07669).

[66] Blazwick and Dion, 'Mise-en-scène', 11–12.

[67] Bruno Latour, *The Pasteurization of France* (Cambridge, MA: Harvard University Press, 1993). For a recent exploration of non-human responses to late capitalism's ruins, see

shipworms posed the major infrastructural problem for European navies from Columbus to the coming of ironclad ships in the second half of the nineteenth century.[68] Shipworms entered the hulls of seafaring ships through barely visible holes and, once they were in the wood in sufficient numbers, they hollowed out the hull until it fell into pieces and the ship sank. While standard histories of the maritime expansion of Europe have tended to focus on naval battles and wars as the major obstacle for globalisation, a focus on scales below the level of humans reveals how lowly creatures, such as the shipworm, could multiply, jump from one plank to another, from one ship to another and from one scale to another, to shape and limit the circulation of humans and the vessels that carried them across the globe.

Like humans, shipworms travelled and propagated across the globe in the early modern period, in no small part thanks to the intensification of maritime contact across all the oceans. As these parasites migrated from one place to another, they caused epidemics of timber in a variety of novel and unexpected locations. As they quickly multiplied in these new places, they were able to jump scale, destroying the wooden infrastructures of ports to an alarming degree, thereby keeping globalisation at bay. The history of the early modern age of explorations is, at least in part, the history of the highly expensive and expansive infrastructural solutions that navies across the Earth developed to deal with the worm across the seas.

For shipworms, the 1730s were one particularly successful moment when they came to jump scale in the Netherlands. During these years, shipworms moved from the hulls of ships and decided to settle in the timber piles of the dikes of the Netherlands, causing the wood to rot and leaving the Low Lands especially prone to flooding. A worm that used to be the concern of the navy suddenly became an agent at the level of the nation and the state, together with the dikes that it attacked. News writers, natural philosophers and ministers across the country rushed to find an explanation for why shipworms were now so dangerous and how dikes could be rebuilt using new materials.[69] During the following decades, the Netherlands spent huge amounts of money and labour to repair dikes and keep the country safe. It was through these particularly significant actions that dikes became one of the symbols of Dutch nationhood.

As Abraham Zeeman's print from 1731 reveals, contemporaries already realised that the problem of shipworms was a problem of scale (see Figure 7.2). This

Anna Lowenhaupt Tsing, *The Mushroom at the End of the World: On the Possibility of Life in Capitalist Ruins* (Princeton: Princeton University Press, 2015).

[68] See Mary Brazelton and Dániel Margócsy, 'Techniques of Repair, the Circulation of Knowledge, and Environmental Transformation: Towards a New History of Transportation', *History of Science* 61, 1 (2023), 3–18.

[69] Adam Sundberg, 'An Uncommon Threat: Shipworms as a Novel Disaster', *Dutch Crossing* 40, 2 (2016), 122–38.

Figure 7.2 Abraham Zeeman. *Paalwormen die de dijkbeschoeiingen aantasten,* 1731–3. Etching. 14.5 x 17.9 cm. Amsterdam: Rijksmuseum, RP-P-OB-83.674. Public Domain.

print shows artificially magnified images of the shipworm against the background of dikes and minuscule human observers. To accurately picture the danger of shipworms, the artist needed to adjust his representational scale. Zeeman used the optical illusion of art to accurately depict the scale effects of worms upon coast-based societies. And, like Zeeman, historians can tell similar stories of scale jumping across all levels only if they expand the standard toolkits of micro- and macrohistory with the help of geography, environmental studies and science studies, as well as with the creative inspiration of artists and writers. How else could global history survive in an era marked by pandemics and climate change? And, as I put the finishing touches to this chapter in March 2024, I also need to ask: how else could global history survive in an era that is marked again by the dangers that the explosive fission of nuclei, controlled by totalitarian leaders, pose to societies across the Earth?

Part III

Configurations and Telos

8 Tacit Directionality

Processes, Teleology and Contingency in Global History[*]

Jan C. Jansen

These are hard times for teleologists. No one wants to be part of their club. Coined in the early eighteenth century by German philosopher Christian Wolff as a term for the explanation of things in view of an end, goal, aim or purpose, 'teleology' was rarely used, for most of its existence, outside of the secluded intellectual worlds of philosophers and theorists of history and the natural world. It nonetheless became the cornerstone of a powerful tradition of thought that reverberated across the world.[1] Since the 1980s, however, its use has proliferated, and in the following decade it entered the vocabulary of historians. Largely absent from research articles published in the *American Historical Review* until well into the 1980s, eight times more authors used it in the following decade, a number that then doubled again over the 2010s.[2] This increase was not due to a sudden popularity of teleological views of history, but rather to its opposite. 'Teleological' stands for an understanding of history (or of a discrete sequence in the past) that those who use the term do not embrace, and in most cases reject. 'Most historians are allergic to teleology and the idea of an end', fellow historian Holly Case quipped, 'even if it already occurred'.[3] Along with 'essentialism', 'teleology' counts among

[*] For critical reading and invaluable feedback on earlier drafts, I would like to thank the participants of the 'Rethinking Global History' workshops, and in particular the two editors, Stefanie Gänger and Jürgen Osterhammel, the participants of the research seminar of the Research Training Group 1919 'Precaution, Prevision, Prediction: Managing Contingency' at the University of Duisburg-Essen, as well as Thomas Mareite, Jannik Keindorf, Nicolás González Quintero, Ana Vergara Sierra, Yves Schmitz and Megan Maruschke. Research for this chapter has received funding from the European Research Council (ERC) under the European Union's Horizon 2020 research and innovation programme (grant agreement No 849189), including for its open access publication.

[1] Henning Trüper et al. (eds.), *Historical Teleologies in the Modern World* (London: Bloomsbury Academic, 2015); the longer philosophical tradition is retraced in Jeffrey K. McDonough, *Teleology: A History* (New York: Oxford University Press, 2020).
[2] For numbers, see the search terms 'teleology' and 'teleological' on https://books.google.com/ ngrams and https://academic.oup.com/ahr/advanced-search.
[3] 'Historiker against Future', 28 September 2019, https://science.orf.at/v2/stories/2992067. All translations in this chapter by the author.

the cardinal sins a historian (and, by extension, a social scientist[4]) can be accused of today.

It is not easy to say how and why 'teleology' came to be associated with bad historical practice. It certainly has to do with the oscillation in twentieth-century philosophical and social science theory between periods in which human agency took centre-stage and counter-reactions leading to periods that shifted away from human agency.[5] In the historical profession, the 'cultural turn' of the 1980s–1990s revaluated ideas of contingency, fragmentation and discontinuity.[6] From quite different backgrounds and traditions, proponents of microhistory (especially in the tradition of Italian *microstoria* and German *Alltagsgeschichte*) and post-modernist and postcolonial scholars agreed in their distaste of comprehensive *métarécits*. There is a correlation between the rise of the anti-teleological credo and the demise of two powerful progressivist 'grand narratives': Soviet-style historical materialism and modernisation theory – 'the most teleological of the teleologies' of the mid-twentieth century.[7] Theorists and philosophers of history have argued that the breakdown of these totalising visions of the course of history also spelled the end for the entire Western modern concept of history as a coherent and meaningful process, although they disagree about what kind of regime of temporality and 'chronopolitics' would supplant it.[8]

Global history as a sub-discipline does not fit easily into the anti-teleology/teleology divide. On the one hand, global historians have been quick to embrace an anti-teleological stance and position their approach at the vanguard of anti-teleology. They have credited global history with the mission (and potential) to overcome teleologies of the nation-state, of macro-concepts such as modernisation or globalisation and of ethnocentrism.[9] In an

---

[4]   See, for example, Alexander Wendt, 'Why a World State Is Inevitable: Teleology and the Logic of Anarchy', *European Journal of International Relations* 9, 4 (2003), 491-542, here 492.

[5]   Wolfgang Knöbl, 'Das Problem der Kontingenz in den Sozialwissenschaften und die Versuche seiner Bannung', in Frank Becker et al. (eds.), *Die Ungewissheit des Zukünftigen: Kontingenz in der Geschichte* (Frankfurt am Main: Campus, 2016), 119–37.

[6]   Ute Daniel, *Kompendium Kulturgeschichte: Theorien, Praxis, Schlüsselwörter* (Frankfurt am Main: Suhrkamp, 2001), 419–29.

[7]   Frederick Cooper, *Colonialism in Question: Theory, Knowledge, History* (Berkeley: University of California Press, 2005), 118. Cooper also points to the new teleologies emerging out of the critical literature on 'modernity' (ibid., 121–35). See also Jerry H. Bentley, 'World History and Grand Narrative', in Benedikt Stuchtey and Eckhardt Fuchs (eds.), *Writing World History, 1800–2000* (Oxford: Oxford University Press, 2003), 47–66, here 49.

[8]   François Hartog, *Régimes d'historicité: Présentisme et experiences*, expanded ed. (Paris: Seuil, 2012); Hans Ulrich Gumbrecht, *Our Broad Present: Time and Contemporary Culture* (New York: Columbia University Press, 2014); Zoltán Boldizsár Simon, *History in Times of Unprecedented Change: A Theory for the 21st Century* (London: Bloomsbury Academic, 2020).

[9]   Duncan S.A. Bell, 'History and Globalization: Reflections on Temporality', *International Affairs* 79, 4 (2003), 801–14, here 804, 813–14; Jürgen Osterhammel, 'Globalgeschichte', in Hans-Jürgen Goertz (ed.), *Geschichte: Ein Grundkurs*, 3rd ed. (Reinbek: Rowohlt, 2007), 592–610, here 597; Sebastian Conrad, *What Is Global History?* (Princeton: Princeton University Press, 2016), 66, 75, 166, 212–13.

influential statement marking the launch of the *Journal of Global History*, veteran global historian Patrick O'Brien defined the field as the antidote to 'teleological chronicles designed to reinforce people's very own set of values enshrined in canonical Christian, Muslim, Hindu, Confucian and other sacred texts'.[10] At the same time, global historians have shown much less reluctance to engage in macro-historical reflections. It was precisely the reinstatement of the 'totalizing project', the launching of 'enquiries into global issues and long-run material developments' and the return to 'generalization on a global scale' that some early proponents found most liberating.[11] O'Brien combined his rejection of ethnocentric teleologies with a call for 'cosmopolitan meta-narratives'.[12]

It is difficult to decide what to make of these statements about teleology in global history. This is largely due to the way the charge of 'teleology' is commonly employed. Its meaning remains elusive, and it has been used to critique a host of methodological sins ranging from determinism and anachronism to one-dimensional analysis and presentism. Charges of 'teleology' also usually have a polemical bent. They are often employed to discredit a particular version of the past, a particular 'teleology'. British historian Herbert Butterfield famously dissected the progressivist *Whig Interpretation of History* (1931), but would himself not shy away from offering a unilinear (i.e. whiggish?) account of the history of modern science.[13] Interestingly, historians usually remain mute about what would be the opposite of a teleological position.

Still, 'teleology' does not come down to a mere game of words, some form of sophisticated bad-mouthing or susurration of the *zeitgeist*. For 'teleology' raises crucial questions that every historian has to address in their work. These questions have been built into the modern Western concept of history as a coherent and directional process and carried into history as a modern academic discipline.[14] Even if not necessarily under the umbrella-term 'teleology', historians have thus, for generations, theorised questions related to the directionality of history. In some contexts, their debates have crystallised around concepts such as 'progress', 'Whig history', 'prehistories', 'presentism', 'process' or the

---

[10] Patrick K. O'Brien, 'Global History', https://archives.history.ac.uk/makinghistory/resources/a rticles/global_history.html; see also Patrick K. O'Brien, 'Historiographical Traditions and Modern Imperatives for the Restauration of Global History', *Journal of Global History* 1, 1 (2006), 3–39.

[11] A. G. Hopkins, 'The Historiography of Globalization and the Globalization of Regionalism', *Journal of the Economic and Social History of the Orient* 53, 1–2 (2010), 19–36, here 31.

[12] O'Brien, 'Historiographical Traditions', 32.

[13] Herbert Butterfield, *The Whig Interpretation of History* (London: Bell, 1931); Herbert Butterfield, *The Origins of Modern Science* (London: Bell, 1949).

[14] Reinhart Koselleck et al., Article 'Geschichte, Historie', in Otto Brunner et al. (eds.), *Geschichtliche Grundbegriffe: Historisches Lexikon zur politisch-sozialen Sprache in Deutschland*, vol. 2 (Stuttgart: Klett-Cotta, 1975), 593–717, esp. 647–78.

'openness of history'.[15] There is, to my knowledge, no systematic discussion of teleology or directionality as a problem of history-writing, whether from a philosopher, a theorist of historical methodology or a practising historian, comparable to the sophisticated discussions of the role of concepts, narration, the relationship between structure and historical actor, temporality and so on, of recent decades.[16] Nor have critics of teleology called for a new 'turn' or distinct methodology paralleling discussions of the micro- and macro-dimensions or materiality. I propose to map the sprawling debate on teleology in a slightly more systematic way. At the centre is the question of the directionality of history – that is, the question if (and when) a particular tendency, trend or process can be considered dominant for historical development and becomes part of the explanatory toolkit. A throng of thorny issues branches off from the question of directionality: How *inevitable* is the historical process (necessity)? How *linear* is it? How *reversible* is it? Such questions are inherently connected with debates about the form, position and role of history: of its narrative form or 'emplotment';[17] of historical responsibility for past wrongdoing;[18] of its involvement in present-day politics or ideologies;[19] and of its societal relevance, its ability to provide orientation to present generations or to allow prediction of future developments or events.[20] And, above all, the fundamental question of human freedom and agency looms large over the teleology-in-history debate.[21]

---

[15] Butterfield, *Whig Interpretation*; Adrian Wilson and T. G. Ashplant, 'Whig History and Present-Centered History', *The Historical Journal* 31, 1 (1988), 1–16; 'AHR Forum: Investigating the History in Prehistories', *American Historical Review* 113, 3 (2013), 708–801; Stiftung Historisches Kolleg (ed.), *Über die Offenheit der Geschichte* (Munich: Oldenbourg, 1996).

[16] The best overview, although steeped in analytical perspectives, is Yemima Ben-Menahem, 'Historical Necessity and Contingency', in Aviezer Tucker (ed.), *A Companion to the Philosophy of History and Historiography* (Malden: Wiley-Blackwell, 2009), 120–30; see further Anthony K. Jensen, 'Teleology', in Chiel van den Akker (ed.), *The Routledge Companion to Historical Theory* (London: Routledge, 2022), 498–514; Rob Inkpen and Derek Turner, 'The Topography of Historical Contingency', *Journal of the Philosophy of History* 6, 1 (2012), 1–19.

[17] Hayden White, *Metahistory: The Historical Imagination in Nineteenth-Century Europe* (Baltimore: Johns Hopkins University Press, 1973); Reinhart Koselleck et al. (eds.), *Formen der Geschichtsschreibung* (Munich: Deutscher Taschenbuch-Verlag, 1982).

[18] Isaiah Berlin, 'Historical Inevitability', in *Liberty*, ed. Henry Hardy (Oxford: Oxford University Press, 2002), 94–165.

[19] Richard Rorty, *Contingency, Irony, and Solidarity* (Cambridge: Cambridge University Press, 1989). A recent example is the debate about 'teleology'/'presentism' and 'identity politics'; see James H. Sweet, 'Is History History? Identity Politics and Teleologies of the Present', *Perspectives on History*, September 2022, www.historians.org/research-and-publications/per spectives-on-history/september-2022/is-history-history-identity-politics-and-teleologies-of-the-present; Malcolm Foley and Priya Satia, 'Responses to "Is History History?"', *Perspectives on History*, October 2022, www.historians.org/research-and-publications/perspectives-on-history/october-2022/responses-to-is-history-history.

[20] David Armitage and Jo Guldi, *The History Manifesto* (Cambridge: Cambridge University Press, 2014).

[21] Peter Wagner, 'Autonomy in History: Teleology in Nineteenth-Century European Social and Political Thought', in Trüper et al., *Historical Teleologies*, 323–38.

Historians are more used to taking on such fundamental questions in practice, in the study of particular objects, rather than in abstract concepts. They nevertheless have engaged with them in theoretical terms – well before 'teleology' became a buzzword. Early generations of the nineteenth-century historical profession were anxious to drive contingency and chance out of their historical narratives.[22] Still, they strove to salvage the openness of history and human agency against Georg Wilhelm Friedrich Hegel's holistic – and teleological – system of history.[23] Despite being entangled in a view of history shaped by modernisation theory, Eurocentrism and nation, historians of the 1960s, 1970s and 1980s did not shy away from debating how they construed historical processes and how they squared this with the autonomy or, as it was later called, the 'self-will' (*Eigen-Sinn*) of historical actors.[24]

Remarkably, theorists of global history today seem to be even less inclined to think about issues of directionality and teleology than have previous generations and practitioners of other historical subfields. This is certainly not for lack of need. For global history stands out, at least in its prevalent theoretical form, by its intimate relationship to the processuality of history. Most definitions of global history as a subfield centre on the idea of long-distance interconnections and their 'continuous, though not steady densification and consolidation' in time.[25] In one of the most sophisticated theoretical surveys to date, Sebastian Conrad emphasises that global history as a distinct field 'does ... rest on the notion of global integration as a defining feature'.[26] Other historical subdisciplines may also have entertained a strong interest in particular processes – the emergence of capitalism in economic history, modernisation in social history, the polarisation of public and private spheres in gender history, to name but a few – but none of them has made statements about historical directionality as the foundation of how they defined their area of study.

---

[22] Alfred Heuß, 'Kontingenz in der Geschichte', *Neue Hefte für Philosophie* 24–5 (1985), 14–43; Reinhart Koselleck, 'Der Zufall als Motivationsrest in der Geschichtsschreibung', in *Vergangene Zukunft: Zur Semantik geschichtlicher Zeiten* (Frankfurt am Main: Suhrkamp, 1989), 158–75.

[23] Daniel Little, 'Philosophy of History', *The Stanford Encyclopedia of Philosophy* (Winter 2020 Edition), https://plato.stanford.edu/archives/win2020/entries/history. They drew on concepts such as 'development' or 'historical continuity'. See, for example, Johann Gustav Droysen, *Historik: Vorlesungen über Enzyklopädie und Methodologie der Geschichte*, ed. Rudolf Hübner, 7th ed. (Munich: Oldenbourg, 1937), 12, 270, 346. See also Peter Vogt, *Kontingenz und Zufall: Eine Ideen- und Begriffsgeschichte* (Berlin: Akademie-Verlag, 2011), 347–447.

[24] Karl-Georg Faber and Christian Meier (eds.), *Historische Prozesse* (Munich: Deutscher Taschenbuch-Verlag, 1978); Alf Lüdtke, *Eigen-Sinn: Fabrikalltag, Arbeitererfahrungen und Politik vom Kaiserreich bis in den Faschismus* (Hamburg: Ergebnisse, 1993). For a theoretical critique of these attempts, see Wolfgang Knöbl, *Die Soziologie vor der Geschichte: Zur Kritik der Sozialtheorie* (Berlin: Suhrkamp, 2022), 198–205.

[25] Osterhammel, 'Globalgeschichte', 596.

[26] Conrad, *What Is Global History?*, 110.

In addition, global history is not just a statement about one particular historical process, but also about its relevance. Global history ascribes at least partial explanatory power to structures and forms of global integration, understood as regular and stable patterns of exchange and interaction. The term 'integration', however, remains conspicuously ambiguous. It designates both a particular historical *process* of growing interconnectedness reminiscent of what only a few years ago was called 'globalisation' and a *condition* or context of historical events (that may be applied to any period or event).[27] The most astute theoreticians and practitioners of global history take pains to make sure that it is not understood as a 'teleological' vision of history and gesture at the plurality of timelines and moments of disintegration.[28] But from their assumptions, global historians do privilege, or at least imply, one direction of history: the cross-border and long-distance interconnection and integration of societies across the world. Critics have hammered home this point and have asked if, limited to 'a highly abstract designator of interconnection', global integration would not 'obscure considerably more than it reveals'.[29] Some of them have depicted the history of global integration as the heir of modernisation theory and its teleological pitfalls.[30] Global history, from this perspective, is no more than the master narrative of the globalised present-day world – or, rather, of how cosmopolitan elites conceive it.[31] Some critics contend that, at its least reflective, global history is the heir to imperial worldviews or neoliberal 'connectivity talk'.[32]

Despite the embrace of integration as a defining feature by both its main theorists and critics, global history's historiographic roots diverge on these questions. For global history as a subfield grew out of several, conflicting lines of inquiry, each with its own vision of how to deal with historical directionality. Postcolonial scholars, for example – one important reference in global history – usually exhibit a strong suspicion against any kind of

---

[27] For the distinction between process and condition, see Niels P. Petersson, 'Globalisierung', in Jost Dülffer and Winfried Loth (eds.), *Dimensionen internationaler Geschichte* (Munich: Oldenbourg, 2012), 271–91, here 276.

[28] Conrad, *What Is Global History?*, 110–12.

[29] Michael Lang, 'Histories of Globalization(s)', in Prasenjit Duara et al. (eds.), *A Companion to Global Historical Thought* (Malden: Wiley, 2014), 402.

[30] Cooper, *Colonialism in Question*, 96–7, 118.

[31] Craig Calhoun, 'The Class Consciousness of Frequent Travelers: Toward a Critique of Actually Existing Cosmopolitanism', *South Atlantic Quarterly* 101, 4 (2002), 869–97; Jeremy Adelman, 'What Is Global History Now?', *Aeon*, 2 March 2017, https://aeon.co/essays/is-global-history-still-possible-or-has-it-had-its-moment.

[32] Richard Drayton, 'Where Does the World Historian Write From? Objectivity, Moral Conscience and the Past and Present of Imperialism', *Journal of Contemporary History* 46, 3 (2011), 671–85; Vanessa Ogle, *The Global Transformation of Time: 1870–1950* (Cambridge, MA: Harvard University Press, 2015), 204; Sujit Sivasundaram, 'Towards a Critical History of Connection: The Port of Colombo, the Geographical "Circuit" and the Visual Politics of New Imperialism, ca. 1880–1914', *Comparative Studies in Society and History* 59, 2 (2017), 346–84.

generalist or macro-perspectives (despite, in some cases, following their own teleology of colonial 'modernity').[33] Their stance contrasts with global history's other roots in the philosophy of history and historical sociology, a legacy that lowers the barriers to thinking about large-scale connections and contexts, at the risk of carrying along these traditions' Eurocentric and teleological baggage.[34] Global history also took shape against the backdrop of a revival of neo- and post-Hegelian philosophies of history after the Cold War.[35] In short, the fundamental tension between the universalism and unity of the past, on the one hand, and particularity and rupture, on the other, has come to a head in the intellectual milieu of global history.[36]

So why do directionality and teleology not appear higher on global historians' theoretical agenda? I think the reason why global historians have been less likely to engage in reflections about historical directionality has to do with their epistemological preferences. Since the emergence of their profession, historians have entertained a close theoretical relationship with the category of time. Global history has shifted focus to the category of space, which for a long time was thought of largely as a neutral container of history. Global historians have devoted much energy to rethinking spatial relations and movements and to exploring synchronicity and spatial alternatives to the territorially bound nation-state (networks, oceans, etc.).[37] While they have produced, for example,

<hr/>

[33] But see now Dipesh Chakrabarty, *The Climate of History in a Planetary Age* (Chicago: University of Chicago Press, 2021).
[34] Alessandro Stanziani, *Les entrelacements du monde: Histoire globale, pensée globale* (Paris: CNRS Éditions, 2018); Hervé Inglebert, *Le Monde, l'Histoire: Essai sur les histoires universelles* (Paris: Presses Universitaires de France, 2014); Dominic Sachsenmaier, *Global Perspectives on Global History: Theories and Approaches in a Connected World* (Cambridge: Cambridge University Press, 2011); Jürgen Osterhammel, 'Global History and Historical Sociology', in James Belich et al. (eds.), *The Prospect of Global History* (Oxford: Oxford University Press, 2016), 23–43. For the broader historiographic context, see George G. Iggers et al., *A Global History of Modern Historiography*, 2nd ed. (London: Routledge, 2016), 364–97; Daniel Woolf, *A Concise History of History: Global Historiography from Antiquity to the Present* (Cambridge: Cambridge University Press, 2019), 262–79; and the excellent survey of debates in Marek Tamm and Peter Burke (eds.), *Debating New Approaches to History* (London: Bloomsbury Academic, 2019).
[35] Francis Fukuyama, *The End of History and the Last Man* (London: Penguin, 1992); Krishan Kumar, 'Philosophy of History at the End of the Cold War', in Tucker, *Companion to the Philosophy of History*, 550–60.
[36] Michael Lang, 'Evolution, Rupture, and Periodization', in David Christian (ed.), *The Cambridge World History*, vol. 1: *Introducing World History, to 10,000 BCE* (Cambridge: Cambridge University Press, 2015), 84–109.
[37] Matthias Middell and Katja Naumann, 'Global History and the Spatial Turn: From the Impact of Area Studies to the Study of Critical Junctures of Globalization', *Journal of Global History* 5, 1 (2010), 149–70; Conrad, *What Is Global History?*, 115–40; Stefanie Gänger, 'Circulation: Reflections on Circularity, Entity, and Liquidity in the Language of Global History', *Journal of Global History* 12, 3 (2017), 303–18. A similar case has been made for contemporary sociology; see Göran Therborn, 'Introduction: From the Universal to the Global', *International Sociology* 15, 2 (2000), 149–50.

fascinating insights into historical 'moments' and their global ramifications in space and into the global short-term contexts of the French Revolution, global historians have been less invested, if not outright disinterested, in thinking about change over time and the temporality of global integration.[38] This neglect has produced a lopsided reflection on teleology and directionality in global history centred on spatiality. I argue that there is a lot to gain from stronger reflection on the particular challenges of time and temporality in how global historians construe historical change.

This line of argument may also help move a rather unfocused and polemical debate in a more productive direction. The question of whether global history as a historical subfield is uncritically directional or even inherently 'teleological' is too general to move the debate forward. Any conceivable response would not do justice to the diversity of the field and the different, sometimes contradictory methodological orientations and complex operations of its practitioners. That question raises a host of further questions that quickly move discussion away from global history per se, such as: Is claiming a trend or dominant direction in history necessarily teleological? When does a linear narrative turn into teleology? And why would this be a bad thing after all? For want of a – much-needed – contribution from the philosophy of history addressing these questions, this chapter seeks to ask more pragmatic questions and search for answers related to the practice of (global) historians. Seen from this point of view, global history shares a lot of the theoretical challenges and choices non-global historians face, and global historians can learn from the responses of historians active in other – including much older – subfields. The chapter will thus delve into the theory of historical processes to develop more precise questions about directionality and teleology in global history. It will then move to the responses global histories offer or may offer to the teleological pitfalls of global integration. While the directionality/teleology problem poses some particular challenges for global historians, it also offers chances to explore new research avenues. Most importantly, it can help think about not the one-and-only master narrative, but the multiple 'guiding scripts'[39] or 'framing devices'[40] global historians may use, refine and variegate in practice.

This reflection on 'guiding scripts' has its own positionality. It is based on issues of teleology and directionality as seen from the concept of history as a coherent process that has shaped history as an academic profession, while

---

[38] See, for example, Erez Manela, *The Wilsonian Moment: Self-Determination and the International Origins of Anticolonial Nationalism* (Oxford: Oxford University Press, 2009); Suzanne Desan et al. (eds.), *The French Revolution in Global Perspective* (Ithaca: Cornell University Press, 2013).

[39] Pierre-Yves Saunier, 'Comment', in Tamm and Burke, *Debating New Approaches to History*, 38.

[40] Bentley, 'World History and Grand Narrative', 49.

also mobilising critical voices from within this (Western) tradition, such as critical theory. These issues may appear entirely differently when approached from the vantage point of other cosmologies, past or present.[41]

Processes and Teleologies: Theoretical Insights

What do we mean when we speak of a series of historical facts as a 'process'? A process is not a thing, a substance to be found and explored, but an intellectual concept, a 'framing device' to integrate a number of events (or impulses) into a somewhat coherent sequence in time.[42] One and the same historical action or fact can be considered as a discrete event or as part of a comprehensive process. 'Process' and other related concepts take the incongruity of intentions of human action and their results as their starting point. They are grounded in the experience that events and historical change defied the control or intentions of individual volitional acts, a foundational experience for Western modern concepts of both history and society.[43] The 'processualisation' of the past – that is, the conception of the past as a coherent and meaningful process – has been the basis for the emergence of modern (Western) historical scholarship.[44] Long before the post-modernist and postcolonial critique of 'teleology', philosophers of history, proponents of critical theory (such as Walter Benjamin and Hannah Arendt) and practitioners of historical research have debated the implications, techniques and limits of history-as-process(es). As is the case with all thinking about history, these debates have often been informed by everyday experience outside of academia. Thus, in the looming destruction of the planet Earth through human-made climate change, an unsettling, catastrophic experience of directionality has permeated academic inquiry and life outside of academia. Conversely, unexpected political and social upheavals (such as decolonisation, '1968', '1989' or 'the Arab Spring') have often been the source of recurring discussions about 'the event' in history and its relationship to structures and processes.[45] With their weak sense for time and temporality,

---

[41] Warwick Anderson et al. (eds.), *Pacific Futures: Past and Present* (Honolulu: University of Hawai'i Press, 2018); Giorgio Riello, 'The World in a Book: The Creation of the Global in Sixteenth-Century European Costume Books', *Past & Present* 242, supplement 14 (2019), 281–317.

[42] I am following in many respects the excellent discussion by Christian Meier, 'Fragen und Thesen zu einer Theorie historischer Prozesse', in Faber and Meier, *Historische Prozesse*, 11–66. For a broader interdisciplinary survey and critique, see Knöbl, *Soziologie vor der Geschichte*.

[43] Norbert Elias, *What Is Sociology?* (London: Hutchinson, 1978), 95.

[44] Koselleck et al., 'Geschichte, Historie', 666–8; Hannah Arendt, *Between Past and Future: Eight Exercises in Political Thought* (New York: Penguin, 2006), 63–5.

[45] See Raymond Aron, *Dimensions de la conscience historique* (Paris: Plon, 1961); Edgar Morin (ed.), 'L'Evènement', *Communications* 18 (1972); Reinhart Koselleck and Wolf-Dieter Stempel

global historians' self-reflection about their 'guiding scripts' can benefit to a great extent from these debates among 'non-global' historians and sociologists of social and political change.

While theories of historical process vary, they all rest on the idea of directionality: 'The most important and probably only common feature seems to be that an incalculably large number of impulses seems to constitute a somehow coherent, uniform process. We gain its unity from the fact that we draw an arc from some kind of end to some kind of beginnings.'[46] This direction does not need to be clear at the beginning of the process, and the process does not need to be caused by one *telos*/goal. In that way, teleology, in its classical philosophical meaning, would designate only a subset of processes.

Theories of historical process combine four further elements in addition to the core notion of directionality. First, processes divide the past into clearly defined sequences independently from the question of causation. While it may be used for periodisation purposes, a process per se is not equivalent to an epoch or period as processes may overlap. Second, a process is, to a certain degree, autonomous. It is neither completely controlled by individual intentions nor entirely contingent, but 'possess[es] a relative necessity; [processes] have an autogenerative character and reproduce within particular conditions.'[47] 'Consisting of nothing but the actions of individual people, [processes] nevertheless give rise to institutions and formations which were neither intended nor planned by any single individual in the form they actually take.'[48] Similar to social institutions, there is a crucial moment, a tipping point, after which a process is able to reproduce its conditions (which may be different from its original causes). Their autonomy, however, remains conditional to the contingent historical contexts that allow them to emerge; likewise, human actions or dynamics internal to the process may change the conditions to the detriment of the process. Conflating these two elements – the identification of uniform sequences and autonomy – may result in a strongly 'teleological' vision of the past.[49] Third, there is a mutual relationship between autonomous processes and historical action and events, the latter conceived of as being, to a certain

(eds.), *Geschichte – Ereignis und Erzählung* (Munich: Deutscher Taschenbuch-Verlag, 1973); Faber and Meier, *Historische Prozesse*; Stiftung Historisches Kolleg, *Über die Offenheit der Geschichte*; Andreas Suter and Manfred Hettling (eds.), *Struktur und Ereignis* (Göttingen: Vandenhoeck & Ruprecht, 2001); François Dosse, *Renaissance de l'événement: Un défi pour l'historien: Entre sphinx et phénix* (Paris: Presses Universitaires de France, 2010); Theo Jung and Anna Karla (eds.), 'Times of the Event: Forum', *History and Theory* 60, 1 (2021), 75–149.

46 Meier, 'Fragen und Thesen zu einer Theorie historischer Prozesse', 12.

47 Wolfgang J. Mommsen, 'Der Hochimperialismus als historischer Prozeß: Eine Fallstudie zum Sinn der Verwendung des Prozeßbegriffs in der Geschichtswissenschaft', in Faber and Meier, *Historische Prozesse*, 249.

48 Norbert Elias, *The Civilizing Process: Sociogenetic and Psychogenetic Investigations*, rev. ed., vol. 1 (Malden: Blackwell, 2000), xiii.

49 Meier, 'Fragen und Thesen zu einer Theorie historischer Prozesse', 24.

degree, unpredictable and contingent. Processes only come into being through contingent historical action and events; in turn, they also shape and generate historical action and events. An event, while conditioned by structures and processes, nevertheless constitutes an interruption of a routinised sequence and yields lasting changes in the course of a process: 'Every event produces more and at the same time less than is given in its pre-given elements [*Vorgegebenheiten*]: hence its permanently surprising novelty.'[50] Fourth, historical actors may or may not be aware of processes they are part of; they may seek to shape or change them, without determining the very existence of a process (autonomy).

A theory of processes helps generate a host of questions about how a particular historical process is construed. Theorists and practitioners of global history as a history of global integration need to address questions that include (but are not limited to) the following problems (in no particular order):

(1) *Multiplicity and uniformity*: Where does one process end and another start? To what extent are subprocesses aligned to each other (unidirectionality or even simultaneity)?

(2) *Autonomy*: Is a sequence a (conditionally) autonomous *process* or a mere *trend* that remains dependent on external and contingent conditions?[51] What is the tipping point between trend and process? Which are the contingent historical conditions for the process to emerge?

(3) *Interaction of processes*: How do different processes overlap, interfere with each other and impact on one another? To what extent is their interaction shaped by contingency?

(4) *Direction*: How does the process relate to existing historical conditions? Does it change or reproduce them? Is it part of cyclical developments or 'structures of repetition' (Koselleck) in history?

(5) *End point*: What is the end point/result/outcome of a process? When can it be considered complete or discontinued?

(6) *Relationship between processes and projects/historical action/intentions*: To what extent do historical actors (from individuals to institutions) seek to regulate, steer or control a process? Do they participate in it wittingly or unwittingly? In what way do they imagine and anticipate its outcome? What relationship can be seen between intended and unintended consequences of their action?

---

[50] Reinhart Koselleck, 'Ereignis und Struktur', in Koselleck and Stempel, *Geschichte – Ereignis und Erzählung*, 560–71, here 566; see also William H. Sewell Jr., 'Historical Events as Transformations of Structures: Inventing Revolution at the Bastille', *Theory and Society* 25, 6 (1996), 841–81. A particularly elaborate version of this idea of the event is the 'critical juncture theory' in historical sociology.

[51] Wolfgang Knöbl, 'After Modernization: Der Globalisierungsbegriff als Platzhalter und Rettungsanker der Sozialwissenschaften', *Vierteljahreshefte für Zeitgeschichte* 68, 2 (2020), 297–17, here 313.

(7) *Relationship between process and event/moment*: How does a process relate to contingent events? In what way are they conditioned by the process? In what way do they disrupt it?

(8) *Causality*: To what extent and in what way can the process as a framing device help explain historical change and historical action?

(9) *Reflexivity*: To what extent and in what way is the notion of a particular process reflective of particular mindsets, interests, ideologies or experiences?

Mapping questions that grow out of the concept of historical processes may appear as overly abstract and technical. Yet it is precisely this technicality that can help denaturalise the way in which processes – in global history and beyond – are being construed. They push global historians to consider 'global integration' for what it is – a framing device, no more, but certainly no less either. Following questions like these can also help address one (if not the) key challenge of a process-centred understanding of history as embraced by theorists of global history: teleology.

Seen from the theory of historical processes, 'teleology' appears as a particular way (or pitfall) of conceiving the past as a continuous, directional and conditionally autonomous sequence. A teleological perspective highlights to its extreme one process by streamlining the past in one direction and evening out alternative paths and contingencies. It puts emphasis on necessities and constraints rather than possibilities. Given the complexity of most historical (especially long-term) processes, a teleological perspective shows itself in degrees rather than in a clearcut opposition (more or less teleological rather than teleological or not). Teleology then denotes the potential of a processual perspective to degrade

all individual things and events, every tangible and visible thing, into exponents, which have no other significance than to indicate the existence of invisible forces, and whose purpose is to fulfil certain functions within the over-all process ... The process that degrades everything and everyone to exponents has acquired a monopoly of meaning and significance, so that the individual or the particular can be meaningful only if and when they are understood as mere functions.[52]

It is this potential that has prompted some scholars to reject concepts of process as 'dangerous', for they 'impede rather than enable the grasp of social processes, because they always pretend to know tendencies of long-term historical transformation or homogenise and disambiguate heterogeneous and contradictory changes'.[53]

---

[52] Hannah Arendt, 'Geschichte und Politik in der Neuzeit', in Hannah Arendt, *Fragwürdige Traditionsbestände im politischen Denken der Gegenwart* (Frankfurt am Main: Europäische Verlagsanstalt, 1957), 81–3. An abridged English version is Arendt, *Between Past and Future*, 63–4.

[53] Hans Joas, *Die Macht des Heiligen: Eine Alternative zur Geschichte von der Entzauberung* (Berlin: Suhrkamp, 2017), 356.

While the potential of teleological alignment is inherent to the very notion of process, one may distinguish at least two versions of it. In its philosophical tradition, teleology stands for a view of the direction and meaning of history as such. Teleology with a capital 'T', as we may term it for lack of a better alternative, conceives history in its entirety as one coherent unidirectional process. Teleology with a capital T may project its *telos* well into the future and usually posits the present as an important step in this broader process. It provides history with a higher meaning or purpose.[54] More common to the practice of historical scholarship is a slightly more modest version of teleology: a description of discrete sequences in the past (teleology with a lowercase 't'). This form of teleology usually refers to an endpoint/*telos* in the past, and explains (or rather implies) why a sequence of the past had to result in the outcome we already know. To be sure, this challenge is common to everyone making sense of the past in hindsight. For, in contrast to the participant's or witness's perspective, the retrospective view knows what happened.

While some critics argue that global history does indeed tend toward a teleological vision in the mould of the philosophy of history,[55] the idea of a unidirectional process driving history as a whole is probably as foreign to most global historians as it is to most other contemporary scholars of history. Things lie differently with teleology with a lowercase t. As a sub-discipline that attaches itself so closely to the concept of a historical process – global integration – global history is in many ways prone to teleological alignment. Due to the ambiguous meaning of global integration in global history scholarship – as a process and as a condition – the challenges are twofold: the risk of over-emphasising inevitable directionality while describing the process of global integration itself, on the one hand; the risk of streamlining the past while describing and explaining historical sequences or events from the point of view of global interconnection, on the other. Turning to the practice of historical scholarship will reveal various 'guiding scripts' global historians use or may use on both these levels. A theory of global history will considerably benefit from reflecting on these practical insights.

Processes and Teleologies: Practical Insights (i)

How strongly do historians of global integration offer a unidirectional vision of the past? Are they aware of the inbuilt pitfalls of teleology that come with the concept of process, and if so, how do they deal with it? Two of the most fruitful debates that helped global history take shape have been triggered by the critical

---

[54] A very strong example of this kind of teleology is Karl Jaspers, *Vom Ursprung und Ziel der Geschichte* (Zurich: Artemis, 1949).
[55] Inglebert, *Le Monde, l'Histoire*, 948–74.

adoption of concepts from the social sciences – two 'dangerous' processes, as some would have it: (1) the debate about the emergence of 'modernity', largely understood as a model of European origin, with a strong focus on the origins of industrial capitalism (transformed into the so-called divergence debate);[56] (2) the social science concept of 'globalisation', initially meant to underline the uniqueness of 'global' modernity of the 1990s, and then increasingly extended into earlier periods.[57] Conceived as historical master narratives, both concepts do have a strong teleological bent, and many historians operating with these concepts are well aware of their pitfalls. The strategies they use vary, and range from playing with different scales, multiplying processes and timelines, and including disruptive and disintegrating forces. Some of their responses may help us think about how to complexify directionality in global integration as a process.

(1) *Scales:* Teleology has often been cast as a problem of scale, a distortion created by a macro-view that prefers the big picture over the detail, the whole over the fragment, abstract concepts over concrete individuals. An approach that puts the question of scale on the agenda, although with a preconceived opinion, is so-called microhistory, which has been considered by some as a way around global history's methodological impasses.[58] Proponents of 'global microhistory' often cast their case in terms of bringing back the human dimension into global history, but they also touch upon teleology. Italian and German national microhistorians had already turned to the local, the quirky, the intractable with the precise aim to question and counter the grand narratives of social history, especially modernisation theory and Marxist orthodoxy. Yet we should not consider 'global microhistory' as the high road and the once-and-for-all solution to teleology. In historical fields other than global history, scholars have already turned to smaller scales precisely to find a full miniature version of macro-processes.[59] Global

---

[56] Kenneth Pomeranz, *The Great Divergence: China, Europe and the Making of the Modern World Economy* (Princeton: Princeton University Press, 2000); Jean-Laurent Rosenthal and R. Bin Wong, *Before and Beyond Divergence: The Politics of Economic Change in China and Europe* (Cambridge, MA: Harvard University Press, 2011); Peer Vries, *State, Economy and the Great Divergence: Great Britain and China 1680s–1850s* (London: Bloomsbury Academic, 2015); overview in Jonathan Daly, *Historians Debate the Rise of the West* (London: Routledge, 2014).

[57] Overviews in A. G. Hopkins (ed.), *Globalization in World History* (New York: Norton, 2002); Jürgen Osterhammel and Niels P. Petersson, *Globalization: A Short History* (Princeton: Princeton University Press, 2005).

[58] 'Global History and Microhistory', *Past & Present* 242, Supplement 14 (2019); Francesca Trivellato, 'Microstoria/Microhistoire/Microhistory', *French Politics, Culture & Society* 33, 1 (2015), 122–34; Mark Gamsa, 'Biography and (Global) Microhistory', *New Global Studies* 11, 3 (2017), 231–41; Hans Medick, 'Turning Global? Microhistory in Extension', *Historische Anthropologie* 24, 2 (2016), 241–52; Romain Bertrand and Guillaume Calafat, 'La microhistoire globale: Affaire(s) à suivre', *Annales: Histoire, Sciences Sociales* 73, 1 (2018), 1–18.

[59] Emmanuel Le Roy Ladurie, *Montaillou, village occitan de 1294 à 1324* (Paris: Gallimard, 1982); David A. Bell, 'Total History and Microhistory: The French and Italian Paradigms', in

commodity or object histories, for instance, have rarely been written to counter established narratives of the rise of capitalism and its global production chains.[60] Moreover, proponents of 'deep' or 'big history' (or of a renewed form of world history) have claimed that extending historical scales to their largest possible extent was the best way to overcome the teleology of modernity.[61] Likewise, some of the most holistic social macro-theories, notably Niklas Luhmann's theory of social systems, are emphatically anti-teleological.[62]

While there is no innate relationship between the macro-teleological and the micro-anti-teleological, consciously playing with scale (*jeux d'échelles*) is certainly a promising, and tested, way to deal with issues of historical directionality.[63] Even outside of the field of microhistory, global historians have used scale as a means to temper and complicate the notion of global integration. Global integration can thus be explored as a multi-scalar process, including how historical actors navigate and move, or even 'jump', between different scales – a particularly promising but still largely uncharted avenue of inquiry. Following their prevailing interest in space, global historians have mostly turned to reflections on *spatial* scale by showing that 'globalising' forces played out in clearly confined geographic bounds and that global integration was in fact an uneven, polycentric and partial process across the world. One example of this kind of analysis is Vanessa Ogle's history of efforts to standardise world time since the late nineteenth century.[64] Instead of presenting time standardisation as a prime example of growing global uniformity, she shows how diverging regional interests and strategies shaped the process as much as top-down efforts by Western officials or international organisations. The standardisation of the clock remained incomplete well into the 1940s, and the notion of a universal time was never fully realised (related attempts to unify calendars went nowhere). Ogle is one of a growing number of global historians

Lloyd Kramer and Sarah Maza (eds.), *A Companion to Western Historical Thought* (Malden: Blackwell, 2002), 262–76.

[60] Sidney W. Mintz, *Sweetness and Power: The Place of Sugar in Modern History* (New York: Penguin, 1985); Timothy Brook, *Vermeer's Hat: The Seventeenth Century and the Dawn of the Global World* (New York: Bloomsbury Press, 2008); Sven Beckert, *Empire of Cotton: A Global History* (New York: Knopf, 2015).

[61] Daniel Lord Smail and Andrew Shryock, 'History and the "Pre"', *American Historical Review* 118, 3 (2013), 709–37; Bentley, 'World History and Grand Narrative'.

[62] Niklas Luhmann, 'Evolution und Geschichte', *Geschichte und Gesellschaft* 2, 3 (1976), 284–309; Niklas Luhmann, 'Geschichte als Prozeß und die Theorie sozio-kultureller Evolution', in Faber and Meier, *Historische Prozesse*, 413–40; Niklas Luhmann, *Soziale Systeme: Grundriß einer allgemeinen Theorie* (Frankfurt am Main: Suhrkamp, 1984), 148–90; Niklas Luhmann, *Theory of Society*, 2 vols. (Stanford: Stanford University Press, 2012–13). Arguing for an open systems approach in world history as a way out of teleology: Patrick Manning, *Navigating World History: Historians Create a Global Past* (Basingstoke: Palgrave Macmillan, 2003), 293-4.

[63] Jacques Revel (ed.), *Jeux d'échelles: La micro-analyse à l'expérience* (Paris: Seuil, 1996).

[64] Ogle, *Global Transformation of Time*.

who cast doubt upon the directionality of global integration by questioning its uniformity in space, but few global historians have actively played with global histories' timescale. One of the few exceptions is Kenneth Pomeranz, who has reflected on the different timescales of the 'great divergence' between Europe and Asia. Pomeranz proposes a model of 'fuzzy periodisation' out of a mix of (very) long-term and short-term time scales as a way to complicate the notion of a straightforward, linear process.[65]

(2) *Multiplicities:* Pomeranz contends that construing the timescales of the 'great divergence' explicitly does not call into question the directionality of the process that unfolds within these time scales. The same applies to two strategies of gaining a closer idea of the temporality of global integration/globalisation: first, the idea of *multiple timescales* of different subprocesses (economic, political, cultural, etc.) that counters the notion of a homogeneous macro-process where all dimensions move in lockstep; and, second, concepts of historical *conjunctures* of globalisation, including aborted globalisation projects, that put capitalism-centred nineteenth- and twentieth-century globalisation into perspective and undermine its alleged uniqueness.[66] All these strategies are laudable as they inject temporal categories into the discussion of global integration, but they do not reflect on the directionality of the historical process itself.

A related strategy may precisely question the uniformity of direction. On closer inspection, historians of global integration do work on a variety of different processes that only at a cost are lumped together into one allegedly coherent macro-process of interconnection or integration. A fruitful line of inquiry consists in dissecting these multiple processes and looking at how these processes interfere. A set of more precisely defined processes like expansion, transfer/reception, densification, universalisation, convergence, polarisation, hierarchisation or standardisation (each with their own direction) may refine the vocabulary of integration.[67] It remains to be seen if the interference of, say, processes of global socio-economic polarisation (or divergence) with processes of densification of communication exchanges results in a uniform direction of integration.

[65] Kenneth Pomeranz, 'Teleology, Discontinuity, and World History: Periodization and Some Creation Myths of Modernity', *Asian Review of World Histories* 1, 2 (2013), 189–226; see also Jürgen Osterhammel, 'Vergangenheiten: Über die Zeithorizonte der Geschichte', in Jürgen Osterhammel *Die Flughöhe der Adler: Historische Essays zur globalen Gegenwart* (Munich: C. H. Beck, 2017), 183–202.
[66] A. G. Hopkins, 'Introduction: Globalization – An Agenda for Historians', in *Globalization in World History*, 1–10, here 5; C. A. Bayly, '"Archaic" and "Modern" Globalization in the Eurasian and African Arena, ca. 1750–1850', in Hopkins, *Globalization in World History*, 47–73; Osterhammel, 'Globalizations'; Darwin, *After Tamerlane*; Belich et al., *The Prospect of Global History*.
[67] Knöbl, 'After Modernization', 317; Jürgen Osterhammel, 'Globalifizierung: Denkfiguren der neuen Welt', *Zeitschrift für Ideengeschichte* 9, 1 (2015), 5–16, here 11–15.

(3) *Interruptions, Reversions, Dialectics:* The way global historians tend to deal with events – the conceptual antipode to processes – is emblematic for their neglect of temporal categories. To be sure, global 'moments' and 'events' have become a highly productive subfield of study in global history.[68] Yet they largely serve to expose synchronous effects and responses in space, and thus to illustrate global interconnection. Events' position as an interruption of continuous flows – the particular temporal structure ascribed to them by theorists of history – may transpire in the opening and closure of different paths, their multifaceted meanings and ramifications across the globe, but they tend to get lost to the gaze fascinated by spatial synchronicity.[69] Studies about the undoing of globalisation or moments of 'deglobalisation' in particular places or at particular points in time largely work without making reference to the concept of the event (or global moment).[70] Keeping up with these proliferating efforts, one may define a counter-process to each of the multiple processes one could dissect global integration into: expansion/contraction, hierarchisation/equalisation, convergence/divergence, densification/diffusion and so forth. The study of countervailing processes helps to demonstrate the fragility and reversibility of global integration; it has no implications for the directionality of globalisation or integration itself.

Things look different when we consider forces of disintegration as an integral part of global integration as a historical process. The idea that global integration and fragmentation are not mutually exclusive and pertain to discrete historical processes, but are more often mutually constitutive, has been present from the start in historical scholarship on globalisation.[71] Studies on a wide range of topics, periods and geographies provide us with a number of categories and a wealth of empirical data to rethink integration as a process in less teleological terms. They can be used as a starting point to think about what may be called the *dialectics* of global integration.[72] Over recent decades,

[68] Sebastian Conrad and Dominic Sachsenmaier (eds.), *Competing Visions of World Order: Global Moments and Movements, 1880s–1930s* (Basingstoke: Palgrave Macmillan, 2012); Manela, *Wilsonian Moment*.

[69] Good discussions of recent conceptual approaches to events: Jung and Karla, 'Times of the Event'; Frank Bösch, 'Das historische Ereignis', *Docupedia-Zeitgeschichte*, 12 May 2020, http://docupedia.de/zg/Boesch_ereignis_v1_de_2020; on the particular event of the 'turning point', see Andrew Abbott, *Time Matters: On Theory and Method* (Chicago: University of Chicago Press, 2001), 240–60; Dieter Langewiesche, *Zeitwende: Geschichtsdenken heute* (Göttingen: Vandenhoeck & Ruprecht, 2008), 41–55.

[70] Harold James, *The End of Globalization: Lessons from the Great Depression* (Cambridge, MA: Harvard University Press, 2001); Jim Tomlinson, 'The Deglobalisation of Dundee, c. 1900–2000', *Journal of Scottish Historical Studies* 29, 2 (2009), 123–40.

[71] Petersson, 'Globalisierung'; on social science globalization theory: Ian Clark, *Globalization and Fragmentation: International Relations in the Twentieth Century* (Oxford: Oxford University Press, 1997).

[72] 'Dialectics' here is borrowed from Arif Dirlik, 'Globalization as the End and the Beginning of History: The Contradictory Implications of a New Paradigm', *Rethinking Marxism* 12, 4 (2000), S. 4–22; see also Middell and Naumann, 'Global History and the Spatial Turn'.

historians have used a variety of concepts to capture this dialectical character, including:

- *Bordering*: historical border and borderland studies show how processes of territorialisation and deterritorialisation impacted everyday life in borderlands; they show that the making and unmaking of borders was not a mere reflection of a global standardisation of nationhood (as some global historians would have it), but also involved complex and disruptive processes of disentanglement and re-entanglement.[73]

- *Control*: historians of migration and mobility show that the increase of migration movements and infrastructures that facilitated them across the world went hand in hand with increasing attempts at control and forms of forced immobility; the acceleration of transportation and migration was offset by decelerating measures of quarantine, identification and regulation.[74]

- *Isolation*: historians of social discipline and punishment have pointed to the fact that the nineteenth and twentieth centuries saw globalising efforts to physically isolate people as a means of social hygiene, from the emergence of prisons and convict settlements, to therapeutic institutions and quarantine, to spaces of exile and refugee camps; in forms of convict transportation, mobility became inextricably connected with carceral immobility.[75]

- *Unmixing*: historians of forced migration and nationalism have pointed to the fact that the movement of people in many instances did not serve the emergence of an interconnected world, but the creation of homogeneity along ethnic, racial, national or political lines.[76]

---

[73] The classic example is Peter Sahlins, *Boundaries: The Making of France and Spain in the Pyrenees* (Berkeley: University of California Press, 1991); more recent: Sören Urbansky, *Beyond the Steppe Frontier: A History of the Sino-Russian Border* (Princeton: Princeton University Press, 2020).

[74] Adam M. McKeown, *Melancholy Order: Asian Migration and the Globalization of Border* (New York: Columbia University Press, 2008); Valeska Huber, *Channelling Mobilities: Migration and Globalisation in the Suez Canal Region and Beyond, 1869–1914* (Cambridge: Cambridge University Press, 2013); Renaud Morieux, *The Channel: England, France and the Construction of a Maritime Border in the Eighteenth Century* (Cambridge: Cambridge University Press, 2016); for a recent reflection in sociological theory, see Steffen Mau, *Sortiermaschinen: Die Neuerfindung der Grenze im 21. Jahrhundert* (Munich: C. H. Beck, 2021).

[75] For a survey, see Alison Bashford and Carolyn Strange (eds.), *Isolation: Places and Practices of Exclusion* (Basingstoke: Palgrave Macmillan, 2003); for penal transportation as a mix of mobility and immobility, see Clare Anderson, 'Introduction', in Anderson (ed.), *A Global History of Convicts and Penal Colonies* (London: Bloomsbury, 2018), 1–35, here 2.

[76] Rogers Brubaker, 'Aftermaths of Empire and the Unmixing of Peoples: Historical and Comparative Perspectives', *Ethnic and Racial Studies* 18, 2 (1995), 189–218; Jan C. Jansen, 'Unmixing the Mediterranean? Migration, demographische "Entmischung" und Globalgeschichte', in Boris Barth et al. (eds.), *Globalgeschichten* (Frankfurt am Main: Campus, 2014), 289–314.

Using concepts such as bordering, control, isolation and unmixing to high-light the dialectics of integration might help spur global historians to take disruptive and disconnecting forces more seriously. It may also help them avoid the trap of conceptual overcompensation that would lead them to replace teleologies of integration with teleologies of disintegration.

Processes and Teleologies: Practical Insights (ii)

The previous section focused on global integration primarily as process, and the ways in which historians may avoid getting trapped in too narrow a version of directional movement. These questions are certainly central to the self-understanding of global historians, but only marginal to the many historians working on particular topics. Most historians do not deal with macro-processes (or their local/regional ramifications); rather, they address discrete historical events or processes. How does the global historian's emphasis on interconnection affect their work in terms of teleology? What does examining and explaining an event or historical fact – for example, the 'age of revolutions' – under the condition of global integration do to the space of historical possibilities? Does the focus on synchron-ous interconnections streamline the historical process more strongly than locally or nationally framed histories? With regard to the two aforementioned examples, I see a tendency in that direction, but I will also argue that this is due to a rather one-sided use of global history's methodological toolkit. Global-integration-as-condition can also help build new arguments for a more contingency-sensitive – less teleological, if you will – understanding of history.

Given the variety of research topics, a general answer to these questions is not possible. I would like to turn to one example related to my own work: the late eighteenth-century 'age of revolutions'. The topic stands for a momentous transformation and a time of upheaval that was transnational if not global in scope, but it has been largely studied in a national framework (e.g. as the history of the American Revolution, the French Revolution . . .). Over the past two decades, however, the field has become part of the global history debate and, as a consequence, has been fundamentally reshaped. Hence, the particular revolutions in the Americas and in Europe are no longer seen in isolation, but as part of an interconnected era of upheaval that was Atlantic if not global in scope.[77] Researchers have stressed the mobilities of people and ideas between

---

[77] For surveys and syntheses of the most recent literature, see Wim Klooster (ed.), *The Cambridge History of the Age of Atlantic Revolutions*, 3 vols. (Cambridge: Cambridge University Press, 2023); David Armitage and Sanjay Subrahmanyam (eds.), *The Age of Revolutions in Global Context, c. 1760–1840* (Basingstoke: Palgrave Macmillan, 2010); Alan Forrest and Matthias Middell (eds.), *The Routledge Companion to the French Revolution in World History* (London: Routledge, 2016); Sujit Sivasundaram, *Waves Across the South: A New History of Revolution and Empire* (Chicago: University of Chicago Press, 2021). On the idea of a 'world crisis' around 1800, see C. A. Bayly, *Imperial Meridian: The British Empire and the World 1780–*

different areas of the revolutionary world around 1800. In doing so, they have placed strong emphasis on the historical actors who drove these events, as if interconnection or mobility were the sole attribute of those who may appear as the drivers of change (or even 'progress') in a highly volatile historical situation.[78]

In that sense, the global interconnection or integration argument (as it is being largely used) tends to streamline developments that local and national histories have described as highly uncertain, embattled and contingent. Each of the great revolutions around 1800 has been depicted as a violent civil war, during which the outcome of the struggles did not reflect what had been initially debated; similar to what could be seen in mid-twentieth-century decolonisation, these revolutions did not strike a straightforward path from empire to nation-state.[79] Furthermore, large exile communities of 'counter-revolutionaries' sought to carve out alternatives to the revolution and worked to undo the demise of the monarchy, the independence of a colony or the overthrow of slavery even decades after the fact.[80] Against the complexities of their local, national and imperial histories, many histories of the revolutionary era produced under the condition of global integration appear blatantly less complex and more teleological.

Is this the price one has to pay for an analytical perspective less devoted to localness and particularity? As already noted, I do not believe that teleology is purely a question of scale. It is a question of reflection on time and temporality (or the lack thereof), and it occurs to me that there are paths not properly taken by global historians. The question of how historical actors experienced and organised temporality – past, present and future – has been a common theme in social history. Their foremost theoreticians, Reinhart Koselleck above all, centred on the idea of a divergence of the historical actors' 'space of experience' and their 'horizon of expectation' due to the experience of an 'acceleration' of history; this gave way to the twin concepts of uncertainty (the unpredictability of the future)

1830 (London: Longman, 1989), 164–92; John Darwin, *After Tamerlane: The Rise and Fall of Global Empires, 1400–2000* (London: Penguin, 2008), 157–217.

[78] Janet Polasky, *Revolutions without Borders: The Call to Liberty in the Atlantic World* (New Haven: Yale University Press, 2015); applied to modern revolutions as such in David Motadel (ed.), *Revolutionary World: Global Upheaval in the Modern Age* (Cambridge: Cambridge University Press, 2021).

[79] On these complexities, see, for example, Josep M. Fradera, *The Imperial Nation: Citizens and Subjects in the British, French, Spanish and American Empires* (Princeton: Princeton University Press, 2018); Manuel Covo and Megan Maruschke, 'The French Revolution as an Imperial Revolution', *French Historical Studies* 44, 3 (2021), 371–97, here 388.

[80] For example, Jeremy Adelman, *Sovereignty and Revolution in the Iberian Atlantic* (Princeton: Princeton University Press, 2006); Eliga H. Gould, *Among the Powers of the Earth: The American Revolution and the Making of a New World Empire* (Cambridge, MA: Harvard University Press, 2012); Maya Jasanoff, *Liberty's Exiles: American Loyalists in the Revolutionary World* (New York: Knopf, 2011); Friedemann Pestel, *Kosmopoliten wider Willen: Die 'monarchiens' als Revolutionsemigranten* (Berlin: De Gruyter, 2015).

and possibility (the feasibility of history).[81] An entire research agenda has sprouted from this idea of 'futures past', uncovering imaginations and expectations, plans and projects, many of which never came into being.[82] In recent years, following a general trend towards contingency in the social sciences, historians have questioned the close connection of this agenda to European 'modernity' and turned it into a more generally applicable theory of how historical actors coped with – and sought to benefit from – historical uncertainty.[83] Even if they only rarely relate to these concepts directly, local and national historians of the revolutionary era have tapped into the same ideas and uncovered the many alternative visions and projects that were on the historical actors' minds and that made alternative futures appear to the latter no less likely than the actual paths taken.

There is no reason why history, as seen under the condition of global integration, would have to do without the historical actors' concerns about uncertainty and their ways of imagining and coping with the future, even more so as many prognoses and predictions partly motivated their historical action.[84] To capture past experiences of uncertainty and imaginations of futures past, global historians do not even have to renounce their interest in connectedness and turn into local or national historians – although they would always do well to 'muddy [their] boots in the bogs of "micro-history"'.[85] In the histories of revolution and state-building mentioned earlier, scores of connected histories of alternative futures and failed projects await them.

[81] Koselleck et al., 'Geschichte, Historie', 702–6; Reinhart Koselleck, '"Erfahrungsraum" and "Erwartungshorizont" – zwei historische Kategorien', in Koselleck, *Vergangene Zukunft*, 349–75; Koselleck, 'Über die Verfügbarkeit der Geschichte', in Koselleck, *Vergangene Zukunft*, 260–77; Koselleck, 'Die unbekannte Zukunft und die Kunst der Prognose', in Koselleck, *Vergangene Zukunft*, 203–21; Alexandre Escudier, '"Temporalisation" et modernité politique: Penser avec Reinhart Koselleck', *Revue germanique internationale* 25 (2007), 37–67. The dual character of contingency (as uncertainty and possibility) has already been emphasised by Ernst Troeltsch, 'Die Bedeutung des Begriffs der Kontingenz', *Zeitschrift für Theologie und Kirche* 20, 6 (1910), 421–30.

[82] Lucian Hölscher, *Die Entdeckung der Zukunft*, 2nd ed. (Frankfurt am Main: Fischer, 2016); Zoltán Boldizsár Simon and Maret Tamm, 'Historical Futures', *History and Theory* 60, 1 (2021), 3–22; on the praxeological dimensions of these imagined futures, see Jörn Leonhard, 'Europäisches Deutungswissen in komparativer Absicht: Zugänge, Methoden und Potentiale', *Zeitschrift für Staats- und Europawissenschaften* 4, 3 (2006), 341–63.

[83] Benjamin Scheller, 'Kontingenzkulturen – Kontingenzgeschichten: Zur Einleitung', in Becker et al., *Die Ungewissheit des Zukünftigen*, 9–30; Uwe Walter, 'Kontingenz und Geschichtswissenschaft: aktuelle und künftige Felder der Forschung', in ibid., 95–118; for the broader context, see Gerhart von Graevenitz and Odo Marquard (eds.), *Kontingenz* (Munich: Fink, 1998); Michael Makropoulos, 'Kontingenz: Aspekte einer theoretischen Semantik der Moderne', *European Journal of Sociology* 45, 3 (2004), 369–99; Vogt, *Kontingenz und Zufall*; Wolfgang Knöbl, *Die Kontingenz der Moderne: Wege in Europa, Asien und Amerika* (Frankfurt am Main: Campus, 2007).

[84] Christian Meier, 'Historiker und Prognose', in Stiftung Historisches Kolleg, *Über die Offenheit der Geschichte*, 45–81, here 52.

[85] Sanjay Subrahmanyam, 'Connected Histories: Notes towards a Reconfiguration of Early Modern Eurasia', *Modern Asian Studies* 31, 3 (1997), 735–62, here 750.

The era was shaped by numerous efforts at revolutionary state-building, stake-claiming, imperial renewal or geopolitical reordering that ultimately failed or were thwarted by others.[86] Likewise, the enemies of revolution and their ideas were no less mobile than the revolutionists. The revolutionary era saw the emergence of exile as a transnational – or, more precisely, trans-imperial – political space. In a context of high geopolitical uncertainty, revolutionary alternatives and alternatives to revolution were fiercely debated and translated into projects that in many ways resembled the ones actually undertaken.[87] Taking this connected sphere of alternative imagination and failed initiatives into account is probably less a question of historical justice. After all, they were not always part of Walter Benjamin's disruptive hidden tradition of the oppressed – the unrealised hopes and expectations of justice and salvation.[88] Many of these interconnected alternative imaginations during the revolutionary era came from enslavers, monarchists, racists or staunch imperialists. Uncovering their ideas and projects can, however, help global historians see the outcome of historical processes as much less certain than it may appear at first from a perspective of global interconnection. Whole centuries can be (re)written from the perspective of failed projects, of unexpected and unpredicted developments and of 'questions' the contemporaries sought solutions for.[89]

Does giving futures past a more prominent place in global historians' toolkit mean that teleology will be replaced by unrestrained contingency? The fact that historical actors experienced a process as open-ended and the future as uncertain does not mean that the actual outcome is unexplainable in hindsight. After all, many expectations and plans failed, and the upheavals of the late eighteenth century ended in results only a few had initially foreseen or even sought – the

---

[86] Vanessa Mongey, *Rogue Revolutionaries: The Fight for Legitimacy in the Greater Caribbean* (Philadelphia: University of Pennsylvania Press, 2020); Chelsea Stieber, *Haiti's Paper War: Post-Independence Writing, Civil War, and the Making of the Republic, 1804–1954* (New York: New York University Press, 2020); Linda Colley, *The Gun, the Ship and the Pen: Warfare, Constitutions and the Making of the Modern World* (London: Profile Books, 2021).

[87] As a case study, Jan C. Jansen, 'American Indians for Saint-Domingue? Exiles, Violence, and Imperial Geopolitics after the French and Haitian Revolutions', *French Historical Studies* 45, 1 (2022), 49–86.

[88] Walter Benjamin, 'On the Concept of History', in Walter Benjamin *Selected Writings,* vol. 4: *1938–1940,* ed. Howard. Eiland and Michael W. Jennings (Cambridge, MA: Belknap Press, 2003), 389–400, here 392.

[89] Marc Ferro, *L'aveuglement: Une autre histoire de notre monde* (Paris: Tallandier, 2015), although rather about the arrogance of elites and leaders; Simon Karstens, *Gescheiterte Kolonien – Erträumte Imperien: Eine andere Geschichte der europäischen Expansion, 1492–1615* (Cologne: Böhlau, 2021); Holly Case, *The Age of Questions* (Princeton: Princeton University Press, 2018). While not entirely congruent, the study of 'futures past' is related to counterfactual history; see, for example, Quentin Deluermoz and Pierre Singaravélou, *A Past of Possibilities: A History of What Could Have Been* (New Haven: Yale University Press, 2021).

quintessential experience of process.[90] The fact that it could have been other-wise cannot absolve historians from explaining why it eventually led to a particular result. Yet past imaginations push (global) historians to search for better explanations and to go beyond unidirectional explanations. They point to the horizons of what was imaginable and sayable at a given moment, and how global integration may have affected them. Seen from this perspective, histor-ical processes are marked by spaces of possibilities that are shaped by both opening and constraining dynamics; the outcome stems from a shrinking of this space.[91] And an important argument that global historians can make is that one such factor both of constraint and of uncertainty is to be found in global integration and interconnection.

As a consequence, historians of interconnectedness might realise that the argument of global integration may in itself hold the key to a less teleological global history: entanglement as a source of uncertainty, as the particular global history complement to the classic notion of 'acceleration' of history. Such an idea was expressed well before the advent of global 'modernity', and well before the formation of the modern historical profession: by the Greek historian Polybius, usually represented as an early thinker of historical determinism and cyclical history, but writing himself in a situation of heightened consciousness of interconnection.[92] Revolving around the rise of Rome's Mediterranean empire, his *Histories* were in fact very much a history of large-scale entangle-ment and integration. Describing it as an 'enmeshment' or 'interweaving' (*symplokē*) of spheres, Polybius considered this process of expansion and integration as a source of increasing complexity, uncertainty and unpredictabil-ity for the historical actors.[93] Borrowing from historian David Bell, one may translate this idea into the vocabulary of twenty-first-century global history with the term 'connections by disruption'.[94]

---

[90] Jane Landers, *Atlantic Creoles in the Age of Revolutions* (Cambridge, MA: Harvard University Press, 2014).

[91] Frederick Cooper, 'Possibility and Restraint: African Independence in Historical Perspective', *Jourrnal of African History* 49, 2 (2008), 167–96. See also Willibald Steinmetz, *Das Sagbare und das Machbare: Zum Wandel politischer Handlungsspielräume, England 1789–1867* (Stuttgart: Klett-Cotta, 1993). Practices of prognoses are also strongly shaped by the time regime and cosmology in a given society.

[92] Elena Isayev, 'Polybius's Global Moment and Human Mobility throughout Ancient Italy', in Martin Pitts and Miguel John Versluys (eds.), *Globalisation and the Roman World: World History, Connectivity and Material Culture* (Cambridge: Cambridge University Press, 2015), 123–40.

[93] Polybius, *The Histories*, transl. Robin Waterfield (Oxford: Oxford University Press, 2010), 1, 3–4; Frank W. Walbank, 'Symploke: Its Role in Polybius' Histories', in Donald Kagan (ed.), *Studies in the Greek Historians: In Memory of Adam Parry* (Cambridge: Cambridge University Press, 2012), 197–212; see on this point Felix K. Maier, *'Überall mit dem Unerwarteten rechnen': Die Kontingenz historischer Prozesse bei Polybius* (Munich: C. H. Beck, 2012), 162–72.

[94] David A. Bell, 'The Atlantic Revolutions', in Motadel, *Revolutionary World*, 38–65, here 43.

***

So how should global historians move on from here? Do they have to absolve themselves of their inherent teleology, or can they simply carry on as if they do not consider themselves affected by a purely polemical debate? What is certain is that they should move beyond what appear to be stale alternatives. Revealing branching and contingency in every past development is no more intellectually satisfying and convincing than the idea of a unidirectional past pervaded by anonymous necessity. While it is hailed by some as the golden path to a re-politicised academic practice, there is nothing inherently more critical in the notion that things may have been otherwise; it may even serve as the basis for complacency.[95] There is thus nothing inherently good or bad to thinking in terms of comprehensive directional processes or contingency. While a stronger attention to contingency may help break up reified ideas of historical unidirectionality, fetishised and unbounded contingency may end up in unrelated microhistories driven by local cultural determinism.[96]

This is not to say that global historians should shelve teleology as a polemical and helplessly abstract issue. Quite the contrary. They should carve out what is hidden in a seemingly ideological debate and turn it into a serious debate about their theoretical and methodological foundations. Seen from a less dramatised point of view, the teleology question raises serious issues that have been engrained in historical scholarship. The idea of the past as a directional and coherent process is an element of – and theoretical challenge to – all historical scholarship, at least in its modern Western mould. Yet it poses itself in a particularly acute way for a sub-discipline that contains a processual notion of history in its very self-understanding. While no historian can do away with issues of directionality and processuality, global historians have wedded themselves to it in a particularly strong fashion.

What about excluding integration (i.e. process) from the 'official' self-definition and closing the chapter? The actual practice of global history would defy such a parlour trick. In a variety of ways, the idea of global integration/interconnection – both as a process and as a condition – has strongly informed global history scholarship over the past two decades. In fact, it contains a wealth of ideas and approaches that a more self-reflexive global history can draw on. The result will certainly not be a new grand theory, but rather the theoretical identification and refinement of guiding scripts that inform global history scholarship. One of the greatest needs for the theory of global history is to study such guiding scripts for historians of 'globality' or

[95] See, for the case of legal history, Justin Desautels-Stein and Samuel Moyn, 'On the Domestication of Critical Legal History', *History and Theory* 60, 2 (2021), 296–310.
[96] Bentley, 'World History and Grand Narrative', 48.

'global integration' – similar to the efforts that have been devoted to national histories.[97] Such guiding scripts would reveal more clearly how global historians construe historical change. They would be intrinsically situational, and would vary depending on whether someone is writing a textbook, conceiving a research article, pitching a research proposal to funding organisations or explaining to students or a broader public why global history matters. These scripts would avoid reifying 'global integration' teleologically, by injecting temporal categories into global history's theoretical reflection. They would allow space for interceding and countervailing processes, dialectical developments, tipping points, uncertainty and, yes, the interplay of necessity and contingency. And they would devote great attention to the historical actors' experience of time and historical change – their reflections, expectations, hopes and fears and the ways in which their plans and anticipations did not capture the actual outcome. Global interconnections can thus also be revealed – in their dual character – as both unlikely outcomes and sources of uncertainty.

---

[97] For example, Stefan Berger (ed.), *Writing the Nation: A Global Perspective* (Basingstoke: Palgrave Macmillan, 2008); Christopher L. Hill, *National History and the World of Nations: Capital, State, and the Rhetoric of History in Japan, France, and the United States* (Durham: Duke University Press, 2009); Stefan Berger and Chris Lorenz (eds.), *Nationalizing the Past: Historians as Nation Builders in Modern Europe* (Basingstoke: Palgrave Macmillan 2010).

9   Distance

A Problem in Global History

Jeremy Adelman

The Problem of Distance

The problem of distance occupies a central yet obscure place among global historians. For a field that seeks to explore social connections and cross-cultural exchanges, uneven and unfair as they might be, the space that separates actors from each other (our placeholder definition of 'distance') is intrinsic to the art. Most often, it is treated as an independent variable exogenous to human action, a physical or cultural geography that has to be overcome by encounters and contacts powered by technologies and social pressures. Global historians may disagree on how far we have overcome divides. But, just as global history came of age under the umbrella of the globalisation that gave it such significance, there has been an underlying presumption – to be unpacked herein – that the demise of distance was a secular, unavoidable propensity, culminating in a sense of spatial proximity (thanks to the workings of social media) and tight economic coupling (thanks to elaborate economic supply chains). The sense of being emancipated from distance also has its darker side, thanks to the same forces, as our screens fill with images of refugees fleeing Kyiv or megaships jamming the Suez Canal.

Still, there is remarkably little reflection on how distance functions in global history, in part because it is implicitly treated as a given, an exogenous condition of human life which human curiosity, ingenuity or greed strive to surmount. The result is confusion – indeed, so much confusion that global historians often find themselves invoking two seemingly incompatible narratives at once. One narrative focuses on the arc of global history as the demise or eclipse of distance. Drawn to stories of technological change, it emphasises communications and transportation breakthroughs that shrink the time needed to travel or convey messages. According to this narrative, the space separating humans has been shrinking for centuries; distance has been in decline since 1492 (a conventional marker for global history), a process that intensified with the advent of steam-based transportation and accelerated once more after 1945 under the flag of *Pax Americana*.[1]

A second grand narrative arrives at a very different conclusion. Instead of stories about closing gaps, some global historians find themselves accenting the persistence of distance, and even its heightening. The compass, steam and satellites may have shrunk the world, but they did not dissolve the gulfs that separate humans. They did not yield the one-world idylls that have often accompanied technological euphorias, from railway manias to Silicon Valley's (now faded) magical thinking. Indeed, the same instruments could be used to dehumanise in atrocious ways. Greater proximity, in effect, is not a sufficient condition for togetherness; it can often induce brutality. What is more, distance can be made intimate. Even as spanning and connecting technologies produce more togetherness, social and cultural interactions can yield chasms.[2]

In considering the problem of distance, this chapter argues, global historians need to be more mindful of the tricks that distance can play. If global historians often proclaim their ability to produce narratives that stand above methodological nationalism and other parochialisms, to break the ramparts of bounded collective myths, at times even touting the epistemic virtues of thinking 'big', 'broadening horizons' and aligning new perspectives with global needs, this chapter urges not just more humility but more awareness of the complex and often fraught ways in which more interdependence can also produce more conflict, more chasms.[3] Distance is not just an independent variable outside human interaction but has also been its effect. To understand this, we need to treat distance as more than just a physical determinant but as a social process.

Ghost Ship

On 7 March 2020, the Bahamian-flagged cruise ship *Zaandam* set sail from Buenos Aires with 1,241 passengers and 586 crew for an extended luxurious trip 'from the end of the world'. By the time it reached Florida three weeks

---

[1] Examples include Steven G. Marks, *The Information Nexus: Global Capitalism from the Renaissance to the Present* (New York: Cambridge University Press, 2016) and Harry Blutstein, *The Ascent of Globalisation* (Manchester: Manchester University Press, 2016). Both books exemplify a style that was more prominent before the great upheavals and reactions from 2015.

[2] For a classic statement, see Gordon W. Allport, *The Nature of Prejudice* (Cambridge, MA: Perseus Books, 1954). For a recent revision, Deborah Prentice and Dale Miller (eds.), *Cultural Divides: Understanding and Overcoming Group Conflict* (New York: Russell Sage Foundation, 1999).

[3] David Armitage, 'Horizons of History: Space, Time and the Future of the Past', *History Australia* 12,1 (2015), 207–25. The call for long-term, distance-collapsing narratives can also be seen in David Armitage and Jo Guldi's deliberately provocative *The History Manifesto* (New York: Cambridge University Press, 2014).

later, 193 on board had flu-like symptoms; 4 people had already died. Port after port rebuffed the vessel as its tiny infirmary filled up. The governor of Florida, Ron DeSantis, one of President Donald Trump's avid cheerleaders, declared that the vessel would not be permitted to dock. With about 250 Americans aboard, DeSantis's decision to turn citizens into pariahs provoked outrage. Even Donald Trump had an outburst: he didn't want the *Zaandam* to become a 'ghost ship'. DeSantis relented, allowing only the 49 Florida residents to disembark. The rest, Canadians, Europeans and others – including non-Floridian Americans – were lumped into the unwanted. For twelve days, the *Zaandam* floated offshore. Four more people died; hundreds more became infected. The president of the Holland America Line, Orlando Ashford, invoked principles of a fading era: 'The international community, consistently generous and helpful in the face of human suffering, shut itself off to *Zaandam* leaving her to fend for herself.'[4] Eventually, a deal was struck: the passengers could disembark. Given face masks, they were whisked out of Florida. Hundreds melted, untested, into the airports of Miami, Ft Lauderdale and Tampa Bay to board flights to New York, Toronto and London to infect people there and beyond.[5]

The tale of the ghost ship illustrates some of the challenges of grappling with distance in global history. Vacationers had come from all parts to gaze at a shrinking planet and its disappearing icebergs, only to be swept unawares into a pandemic that had started a few weeks earlier in Wuhan. Then, they discovered that this overheating global village was riven by fault lines and lethal differences between the rhetoric of the 'international community' and the legal walls of national ones. The ghost ship revealed how globe-trotting passengers got internally differentiated by gubernatorial edict, and how movement across any border doubles as an action that collapses distances while signifying differences.

Nor was the fate of the *Zaandam* peculiar to ways in which states doubled down on differentiators to sort people into those who deserved care and those who did not – and, lately, those who get vaccines from those who cannot. Citizens were made pariahs, persecuted and expelled, in their millions in the lead up to the outbreak of Covid-19. Even before the pandemic, strangers were persecuted across the world as nativists sought to 'unmix' nations that the

---

[4] For testimonies of the horror, 'Trump Urges Florida to Welcome Cruise Ship with Deadly Coronavirus Outbreak', Reuters News, 31 March, 2020, www.reuters.com/article/health-corona virus-cruise-zaandam/cruise-ship-with-coronavirus-outbreak-sails-to-uncertain-florida-wel come-idUKL1N2BO26F.

[5] Chris Buckley et al., '25 Days That Changed the World: How Covid-19 Slipped China's Grasp', *The New York Times*, 30 December 2020, www.nytimes.com/2020/12/30/world/asia/china-cor onavirus.html?action=click&module=Top%20Stories&pgtype=Homepage; Priscilla Wald, *Contagious: Cultures, Carriers, and the Outbreak Narrative* (Durham: Duke University Press, 2008).

world had mixed up. Their paroxysms were triggered by globalisation's blurry borders, merging markets and mixing peoples, thereby provoking what Arjun Appadurai prophetically called the 'anxiety of incompleteness'. By this, he means an affective condition of a nation's sense of beleaguered majorityhood. One can add the campaign and attempted putsch in the United States to assert minority white rule in the name of a shrinking white majority or, in extremis, the purification efforts in the borderlands of Russia and Ukraine. The question of who is entitled to be a citizen, or to have a state in the first place, enmeshes millions into webs of tribunals, census-takers, border-police, fencing and camps that regulate and invigilate the human flow.[6]

Indeed, as this chapter will show, it has been in the efforts to draw lines and borders to separate, to distinguish, that we can see the most acute evidence for the complex interaction between how technologies collapse spatial distancing and how mixing and merging produces efforts to enhance social distance.

What does this mean for global history? We global historians have tended to treat flow as a process that dissolves conceptual divides between majorities and minorities; it's a trait of Marxists looking for signs of international class solidarities, of (neo)liberals who see self-interest and comparative advantage as welding markets across borders, of cosmopolitans committed to ethics of care and curiosity for strangers. Some of us, the confidence in our guidance systems humbled by recent events, oscillate between all three. Either way, there has been a tendency to think of closing spatial distance as bringing in tow intervisibility, recognition and a sense of cultural proximity.[7]

For the first few decades of efforts to transcend the limits of methodological nationalism and Eurocentrism, global historians, myself included, leaned on the vocabularies of integration, with words like 'connection', 'entanglement', 'convergence' and 'exchange' – not to mention 'globalisation'. Of late, they have been under assault, criticised for obscuring place and particularity. The call to 're-scale' our narratives back to the natural units of comradely togetherness in the form of the nation is now in full flight; by restoring place over fluidity, belonging over mobility, the urge to reclaim patriotic narratives appears to correct for everything that de-bordering dismantled. The world financial crisis of 2008 ripped the halo off what was left of globalisation; the

[6] Arjun Appadurai, *Fear of Small Numbers: An Essay on the Geography of Anger* (Durham: Duke University Press, 2006), 8–9; on human flow, see Ai Weiwei, *Human Flow: Stories from the Global Refugee Crisis* (Princeton: Princeton University Press, 2020).
[7] At its most extreme has been the argument that globalisation brings isomorphism and the dawn of 'world society'. See in particular the work of John W. Meyer. Georg Krücken and Gili S. Drori (eds.), *World Society: The Writings of John W. Meyer* (New York: Oxford University Press, 2010). Not to be dismissed, Meyer and many colleagues have shown effectively how, starting with education systems from nurseries to universities, nations have come to share the same norms, credentials, curricula and systems of scientific validation.

nationalist wave of recent years has given way to dysphoric talk of deglobalisation, splinternets and bunkering behind epistemic walls.[8]

Yet these efforts to re-order the world into parts and hierarchies are themselves responses to the effects of how societies have managed distance, how closing spatial divides can yield to new detachments and separations. This chapter is about the ties between global flows and global fencing and the multiple, contradictory meanings of distance. It argues that global integration and ethno-racial categories have gone hand in hand; the first gives new significance to the latter; the latter offer instruments to cope with the former. The chapter points to some underlying currents in global history: the affect of incompleteness in our times, the urge to separate friends from foe, neighbours from strangers, have been recurring features of integration and responses to the collapse of spatial distance.

Until recently, we have not reckoned with how integration produces distance, how erasing spatial distances sparks efforts to separate and conceptual schema to sort – and alienate. We have tended to bracket the separating and distancing reactions to global fusions as spasmodic 'backlashes' of provincial have-nots who have been drained, as one British economist has aptly put it, of a sense of 'belonging'.[9] Instead, we might explore how incompleteness and distancing can be seen as part of integration, not its accidental side-effects.[10]

Confronting the way distance-effects are endogenous to human efforts to bridge physical and social gaps has an important ethical implication for our narratives. To start, we can draw out some continuities from imperial modes of amalgamation to latter-day globalisation to reveal interlocking patterns of integration and hierarchy and to explain why, in particular, imperial modes of sorting and organising what got fused together have such lasting appeal even after empires were on the run. Imperial progeny like 'civilisation', for instance, continue to be coordinates for ranking cultures. In this fashion, the creation of colonial subjects in earlier times and the mass production of stateless people in ours appear not just as side-shows when things go wrong. Rather: interdependence produces the need to stratify and separate. We might even understand the condition of statelessness not just as the by-product of Afghanistan or Venezuela's 'failure', but as consequences of other states' refusal to welcome strangers who have lost – as Hannah Arendt put it – their right to legality. As she noted in the 1967 preface to Part Two of her *Origins of Totalitarianism*, this ultimate form of political distancing, relegating peoples to the condition of

---

[8] Jeremy Adelman, 'The Patriot Paradox', *Aeon*, 29 April 2021, https://aeon.co/essays/liberal-nationalism-is-back-it-must-start-to-think-globally.
[9] Martin Sandbu, *The Economics of Belonging: A Radical Plan to Win Back the Left Behind and Achieve Prosperity for All* (Princeton: Princeton University Press, 2020).
[10] On self-subversion, see Albert O. Hirschman, *A Propensity to Self-Subversion* (Cambridge, MA: Harvard University Press, 1998).

living without rights to have rights, began when the expansion of empires in the nineteenth century fused with new racial modes of thinking and distinguishing. Fast forward: refugees exist not just because some states turn citizens into strangers but because other states rely on social categories to legalise their exclusion and turn to the underfunded and much-maligned international community to make up the gap and bear the brunt.[11]

This chapter points to the complex and fraught ways in which global historians have understood distance in two registers at once. It is about how distance is what gets shrunk by growing interdependence between societies; it is also about how interdependence triggers efforts to sort, to rank and to place conceptual distance between interdependents. It shares some thoughts about how we might understand the interplay between distancing and solidarity and the moments that push greater differentiation and those that pull to more solidarity. Not only will this enable us to have richer, more complex accounts of globalisations past; it may help us understand the knife edge we face in the age of climate change, a migrant crisis and ghost ships.

The Demise of Distance?

Distance is intrinsic to global history. It is to the field what water is to fish – at once perspective and subject. Looking at the past beyond the conventions of Eurocentrism, beyond the substrate of methodological nationalism and beyond the endogenous explanations of social life are key features of global history. Going 'beyond' implies distance and perspective, looking at societies from the outside-in or tracing dynamics across their boundaries. We – global historians – need and observe distance simultaneously. The combination of needing and observing distance produces tricks. We reach for an illusion of epistemic virtue of being global and unmoored from bounded attachments of place or communal affinity; we are distant. At the same time, there is an urge to underscore the importance of distance as the subject that needs explaining. One solution, as Sebastian Conrad has noted, is to be more cognisant, more disclosive, of our positionality as historians writing from specific perspectives and locations even as we often slip into Olympian perches gazing down at humanity's exchanges.[12] This can be pushed one step further to note how historical subjects manage distance by comingling necessity with separation, how the distance-collapsing activity of trade or migration also produces the need for

[11] Hannah Arendt, *The Origins of Totalitarianism* (New York; Harcourt Brace, 1968), xvii–xxii; Emma Haddad, *The Refugee in International Society: Between Sovereigns* (New York: Cambridge University Press, 2008).
[12] Sebastian Conrad, *What Is Global History?* (Princeton: Princeton University Press, 2017), in particular 162–84.

social categories that distinguish between insiders and outsiders, over heres and over theres.

It helps to reckon first with the ways in which global historians thought about distance as something that markets, technologies and environmental pressures surmounted and overcame. Indeed, this was the signature of what distinguished global historians from other branches – because they looked at how societies were bridged, connected and mixed (though not always voluntarily). The theme of bridging and entangling, transcending spatial and social distance, yielded a variety of overarching narratives. The first, and until recently the most common, underscores the importance of integration across locations and reducing the distances between them. It is perhaps best exemplified in Conrad's field-marking *What Is Global History?* Written in what we can now see as the sunset years of post–Cold War globalisation, *What Is Global History?* made the multiple ways and meanings of integration the leitmotif of global history. New technologies, social actors and wider – world-spanning – imaginaries created a growing sense of connection and fusion. To be clear: Conrad was reflecting back what a lot of us were practising in the code-wording of transnational, international and what became baptised in the early 2000s as global history. There were caricatured versions that looked back upon the past as a long voyage of human merging and mixing. An extreme variation of the integration narrative, common to the technological determinism that runs like a current through global history, turns distance crossing into distance collapsing. It is perhaps best captured in Marshall McLuhan's *The Gutenberg Galaxy: The Making of Typographic Man* of 1962, which underscored the transformative power of media technologies from the rise of moveable type to what he called the electronic age and the global village. Though many subsequent readers (if they read the book at all) tended to interpret *The Gutenberg Galaxy* as a celebration and missed McLuhan's disquiet about homogenisation, repeatability and amnesia (oral cultures, unlike print in his view, were committed to active memorisation), there was no denying the image of world shrinkage. The metaphor would catch on again after 1989, especially with the end of history prophecies and the rise of *homo digitalis*.[13]

In this mode, distance was the global subject precisely because it was the feature of social life that changed as distance became a relic of pre-digital, pre-typographic, pre-steam, pre-compass times. We might quibble over when this process began – was it the Renaissance, the one-world prophecies after 1492 or the global enlightenment of the eighteenth century? – but there is little denying the importance of a cluster of technical changes from the eighteenth century that enabled humans to see distances differently, indeed to see distance as

[13] Marshall McLuhan, *The Gutenberg Galaxy: The Making of Typographic Man* (Toronto: University of Toronto Press, 1962).

something that could be mastered and trained. Microscopes, telescopes, photography, telegraphy and electrical clocks triggered human capabilities to observe and watch more carefully across a wider range of distances, from close-ups of the cell to the nebulae in the skies, making visible what the naked eye could not see either because it was too far away or too near or small. By the 1880s, astrophotographers had pushed surveying beyond continental hinterlands on Earth to map the Moon's craters to bring its surface closer. The Director of the Paris Observatory, Ernest Amédée Mouchez, launched the Carte du Ciel project in 1887 as a network of the world's main observatories to identify all the stars. Now the Earth had been shrunk to a glittering speck among specks.[14]

Distance-smashing rhetoric – which had grown across Eurasia in the wake of 1492, upsetting the authority of traditional texts and supercharging a zeal for discovery that went well beyond Europe's Renaissance – acquired new energy with eighteenth-century commercial integration.[15] But it was with industrialisation and a new international division of labour that European champions declared a final triumph over distance. Steam, wiring and government policies facilitated long-distance communications (creating post offices, reducing levies on cross-border flows, abolishing censorship) and slashed the cost and delay of movement. A horse-drawn wagon or coach, crawling at about four miles per hour, would take at least sixteen days to travel from New York City to New Orleans. The arrival of the steam locomotive cut the travel time tenfold. One British observer marvelled in 1839 that the advent of the train would collapse the vastness that separated interior continents from coasts. 'Distances were thus annihilated', he exulted, bringing about a collapse of times and spaces into a common, industrialised, accelerated and shrinking merger.[16] The celebration of the telegraphic cable gave rise to even more exultant prophecies – not least because the effects were more instant; it took much longer for steam engines to revolutionise the political economy of shipping. Once gutta-percha, a Southeast Asian gum capable of insulating cables from corrosion, was discovered, there was a rush to submerge the telegraph; by 1871, a line finally lay across the bed of the Pacific; by 1900, around 350,000 kilograms of underwater cable interlaced the world, so stock and commodity prices, news

---

[14] David Aubin, 'The Fading Star of the Paris Observatory in the Nineteenth Century: Astronomers' Urban Culture of Circulation and Observation', *Osiris*, 18, 1 (2003), 79–100; David Aubin et al. (eds.), *The Heavens on Earth: Observatories and Astronomy in Nineteenth-Century Science and Culture* (Durham: Duke University Press, 2010); Deborah Coen, *Climate in Motion: Science, Empire, and the Problem of Scale* (Chicago: University of Chicago Press, 2018), 171–81.
[15] Anthony Grafton, *New Worlds, Ancient Texts: The Power of Tradition and the Shock of Discovery* (Cambridge, MA: Harvard University Press, 1995).
[16] Wolfgang Schivelbusch, *The Railway Journey: The Industrialization of Time and Space in the Nineteenth Century* (Berkeley: University of California Press, 1986), 34.

and travel plans could circumnavigate the planet in sixteen minutes to create a single market, especially for business news. Yrjö Kaukiainen is correct that we may read cable boosters too literally; the costs of information flows were falling even before the 'telegraphic revolution'. But the telegraph did mean that, by 1870, news that once took 145 days to go from Bombay to London now took just 3 days. Two avid news readers in London at the time – John Stuart Mill and Karl Marx – would make collapsing distances at the hands of steam and cables the inescapable drivers of capitalism and European civilisation.[17]

For good reason, global historians rely on 'integration' across distances as a keyword. Indeed, global history was imagined as a style of storytelling and analysis fit for the post–Cold War era of globalisation, in which market integration was celebrated, in Margaret Thatcher's immortal words, because 'there is no alternative'. Global historians did not necessarily echo the euphoria or endorse Thatcher's flat-world certainty. But the demise of distance was nonetheless a precept for the field to spotlight the collapse of expanses that could not be explained or understood by local narratives or methodological nationalism.[18] The instant spread of Covid-19 through the sinews of overnight travel – and, indeed, the global spread of cruise-ships for the world's vacationing (and now vaccinated) middle classes to see the 'end of the world' from their gunwales – demanded a style of history that demoted the significance of distance. Among historians, the result was a tendency to see the leitmotif for global history in the enclosure of the world into a single, jet-fuelled survival unit.

Split Worlds

If integration, shrinkage and the demise of distance have been a strong narrative current among global historians, they often obscured a counterpoint – one that has placed the accent on differentiation and separation. While observational and communications technologies enabled people to see more clearly and to convey more instantly across distances, they also re-signified distance and yielded urges to separate, to detach, to mark off and to create new distances, especially in social connectivity. Just as the world's astrophotographers were

---

[17] Yrjö Kaukiainen, 'Shrinking the World: Improvements in the Speed of Information Transmission, c. 1820–1870', *European Review of Economic History*, 5, 1 (2001), 1–28, here 20; John J. McCusker, 'Demise of Distance: The Business Press and the Origins of the Information Revolution in the Early Modern Atlantic World', *American Historical Review*, 110, 2 (2005), 295–321, here 295–8; Marks, *The Information Nexus*, 127–9.

[18] Perhaps best exemplified in Lynn Hunt, *Writing History in the Global Era* (New York: W. W. Norton, 2015), which quite rightly urges a change in some methodological precepts (such as more collaboration across distance and less individualism and Eurocentrism); but the book's timing, coming out on the eve of Brexit, the backlash against migrants, Donald Trump and Jair Bolsonaro's rise, suggests that we shared some blindspots about that 'global era'.

cataloguing the Moon's surface and shrinking what we thought about Earth, governments were forging new systems of surveillance and distinction. Legal systems of segregation and categorisation grew up in order to sort what was being mixed.

It was above all at borders that the tensions between a decline in spatial distance and the drive to produce more social distancing was clearest. Visas, passports and border controls all proliferated alongside the intensification of world shipping and migration. Around the time of its first centenary of independence, the United States, the land of immigrants par excellence, was girding to erect a monument to a myth of welcoming: the Statue of Liberty, to pose in the harbour of New York to 'enlighten the world'. If one stopped the story there (as many textbooks do) one would miss a basic counterpoint. Just as the Statue of Liberty was being erected, American legislators were promulgating new systems of exclusion and selection. The most notorious was the 1882 prohibition on Chinese immigrant workers, a pattern of racially informed migration policy to keep out the unwanted which, as Erika Lee has recently explained, was all about creating and enforcing social distances between peoples, a tradition that runs through the history of American migration from colonial days and the foundations of settler capitalism all the way to Trump's infamous border wall.[19]

The United States was simply an extreme case of the more general combination of heightened mobility across distances and the sense of urgency to manage and separate the mixing that ensued, especially in imperial spaces from Canton to Cape Town. In effect: integration in the nineteenth century summoned the need for separation and segregation, perhaps most visibly in the polyglot worlds of New York, Buenos Aires and the Cape Colony. These global hubs were also the site for large-scale 'city-splitting'. In Rio de Janeiro, as Brazilian historians have shown, shantytowns in the centre of the city got pulverised to make way for Parisian boulevards, pushing cortiços northwards or up the moros, giving the poor a distant perch over which they could watch the Haussmannian beautification below and, ultimately, the southward spread of suburb beachfronts along Copacabana and Ipanema. It would fall to the forensic anthropologists of the day, such as Dr Nina Rodrigues with his skull-measuring devices, to sort out the links and lines between races and to create a legal code, inscribed in the language of scientific impartiality, that would uphold what the real estate developers were creating on the ground.[20]

[19] Erika Lee, *America for Americans: A History of Xenophobia in the United States* (New York: Basic Books, 2019).
[20] Lilia Moritz Schwarcz, *O Espectáculo das Raças: Cientistas, Instituições e Questão Racial no Brasil, 1870–1930* (São Paulo: Companhia das Letras, 1993), especially chapter 6, 189–238; Carl H. Nightingale, *Segregation: A Global History of Divided Cities* (Chicago: University of Chicago Press, 2012), 207–24 on 'city-splitting'.

The combination of the demise of distance with exclusion and city-splitting was, moreover, made visible. Indeed, the contradictions and complexity of the tricks of distance can be seen – literally – in how they were represented to viewers, as recent work on the history of nineteenth-century photography has shown. The contradiction between proximity and alienation became the staple subjects of new recording devices that intensified the sense of global merger and local segregation. Consider the effect of the camera, the instrument of accelerated global intervisibility from the 1850s onwards. The daguerreotype, for example, was not just the instrument for creating 'realistic' imagery of the Egyptian pyramids; Maxine Du Camp's portrait of the Sphinx buried up to her shoulders in sand in 1849 brought the wonder home to viewers in Paris, first in a gallery and a few years later in an album of travel photos of the world, collapsing the distance between fascinated viewers and grainy viewed – and creating a frenzy for the travel industry. Du Camp's travel companion, on the other hand, was bored to tears by the rubble and the endless sand – and resented Du Camp's immediate celebrity. For those who campaigned against slavery, the possibilities of 'shooting' imagery of enslaved suffering were immediate; they used photographs of human bondage to stir sympathies far away. Slaveowners also saw the potential: they countered with pastoral, feel-good images of plantation domesticity.[21]

The war of images that prevailed over the contested ground of distance – how far apart were free and unfree, migrant and citizen, tourist and spectator? – could also be intimate, unfolding within divided households and split cities. It was in lower Manhattan that the Danish-born reporter Jacob Riis catalogued and photographed the city's tenements structured into Italian, Irish and Jewish ethnic enclaves of squalor. Experimenting with the use of flash technologies to capture the nocturnal city (he started with flashlights and then found a German innovation of mixing magnesium with potassium chlorate an effective way of illuminating while shooting – 'carrying your light where you carry your camera'), Riis shocked the sensibilities of New York's well-heeled, who preferred to keep the urchins of their city out of sight and thus out of mind. Now, togetherness became visible, splashed across the pages of newspapers and magazines, and yielded a rising sense that perhaps the welcoming creed had gone too far – or had at least exaggerated its own triumphs. Riis's images had contradictory effects that I will discuss shortly, of attaching and detaching at the same time. They also informed a model that would be picked up worldwide by socially reforming journalists,

---

[21] Elizabeth Anne McCauley, 'The Photographic Adventures of Maxine Du Camp' in Davie Olihpant and Thomas Zigal (eds.), *Perspectives on Photography* (Austin: University of Texas Press, 1982), 19–51; Matthew Fox-Amato, *Exposing Slavery: Photography, Human Bondage, and the Birth of Modern Visual Politics in America* (New York: Oxford University Press, 2019), 70–101.

armed with their new, ultra-mobile (for the time) Kodaks, by the end of the 1890s.[22] Perhaps the most infamous was this image of three boys – barefoot – sleeping on Mulberry Street (Figure 9.1).

What disturbed the gentry was not just the indigence. It was the sensation that worlds were merging in their city but classes were diverging; it was that the differences and disparities were brought close, nearby: those hungry, needy kids from Italy or Galicia were underfoot. This was an affront to the prevailing Gilded Age narrative of welcoming at the height of nineteenth-century integration. Closing distance cast light – literally and figuratively – on widening differences that became the obsession of social reformers. The result was a recognition that, for all that steam and cables wired the world into one survival unit, it was a world of strangers. Moreover, it was seen – and hence the importance of lens-based media – as a world divided between the familiar and the strange, the civilised and the barbarian, the haves and the have-nots, sharing one, divided, planet.

Figure 9.1 Jacob Riis, *Children sleeping in Mulberry Street*, New York City, 1890. Public Domain.

[22] Jacob Riis, *How the Other Half Lives: Studies Among the Tenements of New York* (New York: Charles Scribner, 1890).

The presence of the stranger provoked a welter of responses, from whitening myths of racial harmony in Brazil to panic about 'Asians' in America or, for that matter, a backlash against Euro-American missionaries in China. The mobility of peoples and the presence of migrants created a – perhaps *the* – signature of modernity: the society of strangers, replete with its champions and critics.[23] Collapsing distances created the need for new tools and concepts to sort, arrange and separate, to govern difference in a new, scientific, key. In this fashion, closing the distance between strangers while keeping them contained and unmixed helped define modernity.

The need to make sense of this duality of integration and estrangement has been stitched into the history of the modern social sciences and is a growing field of global intellectual history. Lately, historians have shown how governing difference required making sense of social distance. This is clear in the way demographers, geographers and ethnographers served in empire-building from the 1870s, often carrying with them skills developed in field work on peasantries and native people at home; as Alexis Dudden has noted of Nitobe Inazo, they laboured to make empires of strangers knowledgeable.[24] One who thought about the implications of enclosing strangers was Georg Simmel. He was working on a general text in 1908 when he felt compelled to reckon with the sociology of space and wrote an excursus about 'the stranger' in history. For him, the stranger is the figure who comes from afar to live in a group – call it 'society'. But the stranger was no wanderer, drifting from place to place; the stranger joined society without being of society and was thus always a potential wanderer. And so, the stranger remains 'distant' – Simmel's word – from the group's 'natives'. For Simmel, what was so potentially unsettling about the stranger was 'the unity of nearness and remoteness', at once intimate and objective, near and far 'at the same time'.[25] It was a prophetic little essay, capturing the zeitgeist of an era in which the promissory Victorian rhetoric about the unstoppable power of technology and self-interest to break down walls seemed to give way to a more apprehensive sense that new walls were rising in their place. A bit like nowadays.

The unity of nearness and remoteness is thus worth considering as a compass for global history. The demise of spatial distance coincided with, and one might say motivated, the creation of social distance. The society of strangers that

---

[23] See, for instance, James Vernon, *Distant Strangers: How Britain Became Modern* (Berkeley: University of California Press, 2014), 18–19.

[24] Alexis Dudden, 'Nitobe Inazo and the Diffusion of a Knowledgeable Empire' in Jeremy Adelman (ed.), *Empire and the Social Sciences: Global Histories of Knowledge* (London: Bloomsbury, 2019), 111–22. For a fascinating study of anthropology and empire, see also Paul A. Kramer, *The Blood of Government: Race, Empire, the United States and the Philippines* (Chapel Hill: University of North Carolina Press, 2006).

[25] George Simmel, 'The Stranger' in Donald Levine (ed.), *Georg Simmel: On Individuality and Social Forms* (Chicago: University of Chicago Press, 1971), 143–50.

collapsed distances created the need for mechanisms for sorting and selecting people, drawing on categories of distinction and exclusion to manage the affect of integration, which included unease and panic around the nation threatened or rendered 'incomplete' by the presence of strangers.

A good example of how heightened migration ignited greater urgency to distinguish and to separate was and is the passport and its sibling, the visa. When physical mobility over distances was arduous and expensive, the cost and hassle of moving functioned as natural filters. But as migration soared and elites and governments became more anxious about crowding – and diseased – cities teeming with newcomers, there was heated debate over border controls and identifications. The First World War added military security and suspicion to the mix and stoked an urgency for states to monopolise the documentary control over movement and identification. In 1914, the British government passed the Nationality and Status of Aliens Act, issuing booklets to separate citizens from strangers. Passports became the norm for crossing borders across Europe and fanned out worldwide. When the war finally ended, the new League of Nations sponsored an international conference to begin the process of standardising practices of state vigilance and the creation of national and transnational bureaucracies to surveil and monitor who could leave and who could enter the nation-states. And as passports and eventually visas became documentary evidence that permitted movement across borders – so long as they did not exceed the rising number of 'quotas' that were attached to certain nationalities and races – so too did the need to come up with solutions for those who had no state at all. In effect, no sooner did the passport become a standardised instrument for monitoring the human flow than institutions such as the League of Nations had to create instruments for the new category of the stateless, like Russians expelled during the Revolution and civil war, or Armenians driven from the nationalist crusades in Turkey. One effect was the Nansen Passport, funded, in the absence of a budget for the League Secretariat, by private contributions, direct purchases and stamp sales in Norway and France (Figure 9.2).[26]

What was and remains important to consider is that international mobility and circulation were linked to and inspired national systems of social differentiation. If global integration implied the creation of an enclosed and synchronised sense of capitalist time, it also created new forms of geographical distance marked by borders, barbed wire, walls, visas and elaborate mechanisms for sorting and selecting what and who gets to cross distances. Modern global integration, in effect, did not make distance less relevant. It created a bundle of

[26] John Torpey, *The Invention of the Passport: Surveillance, Citizenship, and the State* (New York: Cambridge University Press, 1999); Bruno Cabanes, *The Great War and the Origins of Humanitarianism, 1918–1924* (New York: Cambridge University Press, 2014), 133–88.

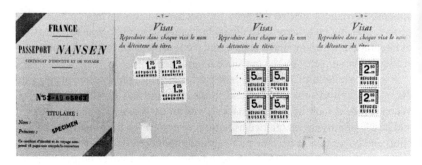

Figure 9.2 Nansen Passport with Stamps, *c.*1930 to 1940. League of Nations
Archives Original Source Citation, World Digital Library.

spatial and social sensibilities, at times converging and diverging at others, of
simultaneity and estrangement – which has been a source of difficulty for
modern social theory and global narratives alike. Integration did not so much
do away with distance as re-signify it.

Familiarity

If we can see that convergence gives new meanings to distance and does not
just make it some exogenous feature to be overcome by new technologies and
institutions, we can start to see that this complexity itself has a history that
predates the technological and modernising euphoria of pre-nineteenth-century
Victorians, their steam, their cables, their free-market credos and their print
technologies. Indeed, there is a genealogy of complex thinking about the
problem of distance that we can recover once we set aside some of the
modernisationist conventions that have governed world and global history.

The first aspect of the ambiguity of integration is the effect of making
strangers at once more familiar and more detached as part of the connecting
and integrating process. Historians of the pre-industrial world of exchange and
discovery work with a different conceptual vocabulary; instead of one-way
integration, they invoke a pluralist world of intervisible parts governed by
mores of learning and curiosity, as well as exploitation, that treat distance as
that which has to be understood rather than conquered. In a lovely book, *Quelle
heure est-il là-bas?*, Serge Gruzinski examines the ways in which exploration
and cosmography made distant cities like Istanbul and Mexico City and their
lettered elites more aware and curious about each other and created a sense of
immediacy and ubiquity, even if a lot of it was illusory or functioned through
a series of mirror games that made distant events seem imaginable. At the same
time, closing the gap had the effect of running up against inherited and

incumbent ways of doing things, of making far away people seem strange and exotic, as well as loathsome and scary, 'defamiliarising' them. When Eurasian states came into contact with each other as a result of the ways in which travel, trade and exploration were closing geographies, they created systems of translation and decipherment – inscribed in texts or paintings – to render strangers more comprehensible. When vessels began to connect Mexico City to Manila and thereafter to Istanbul, the systems of representation spanned the globe. They also ensured that the violence and conquests were also, therefore, clashes and exchanges of symbols.[27]

Gruzinski's story is part of a wider effort on the part of especially early modern historians to chart the ways in which societies, as they came into contact with each other, struggled to produce what Sanjay Subrahmanyam described as commensurable values and to create cultural repertoires to manage encounters.

This 'early modern sentiment' might be recovered for global historians and pushed into the making of the modern world to avoid some of the traps laid by proclamations that distance has been demolished, such as one finds in abundance when global history is unreflexively harnessed to the history of globalisation(s). Terms like 'mobility', 'familiarity', 'exchange', 'liminality' and, most of all, 'connection' (as opposed to 'integration') cleared ways to explore routes between and across units without dissolving the sense of – indeed, the discovery of – social distance. For instance, Subrahmanyam's *Three Ways to Be Alien* follows the travels and adventures of three men in the seventeenth century who operated between cultures. The Portuguese took an Indian prince captive. A Venetian merchant winds up in India for six decades. Subrahmanyam's purpose was to break the lock that national and regional (area studies) histories had on familiar bounded subjects and (though he exaggerated somewhat) the tyranny of comparative history, by tracking how his subjects moved across localities.[28] Natalie Zemon Davis's *Trickster Travels: A Sixteenth-Century Muslim Between Worlds* told the tale of Leo Africanus, aka Al-Hasan al-Wazzan. His was a story of 'entangled values', 'double visions' and 'multiple repertoires' that reflected the agonies and artistries of crossing pre-national, mainly devotional, borders. Raised in Fez and winding

---

[27] Serge Gruzinski, *Quelle heure est-il là-bas? Amérique et Islam à l'orée des temps modernes* (Paris: Editions du Seuil, 2008) [English translation: *What Time Is It There? America and Islam at the Dawn of Modern Times* (Cambridge: Polity, 2010)]; see also Carlo Ginzburg, *Wooden Eyes: Nine Reflections on Distance* (New York: Columbia University Press, 2001); Sanjay Subrahmanyam, *Courtly Encounters: Translating Courtliness and Violence in Earl Modern Eurasia* (Cambridge, MA: Harvard University Press, 2012). See also Serge Gruzinski, *Les quatres parties du monde: Histoire d'une mondialisation* (Paris: Éditions de la Martinière, 2006).

[28] Sanjay Subrahmanyam, *Three Ways to Be Alien: Travails and Encounters in the Early Modern World* (Boston: Brandeis University Press, 2011).

up in Rome, Al-Hasan would go on to write, translate and broker the epics of African history for European consumption.[29] These are just a few examples of how working across units and exploring connections and entanglements liberated actor-focused narratives from their places, just in time to catch or to echo the cosmopolitan sentiment, multicultural ethos and pluralistic values that (many) institutions of higher education had committed themselves to inculcate. In this way, strangers could become more familiar without being less estranged.

Distance, seen in this way, did not yield to proximity; this was not yet a shrinking world. There was no claim in Subrahmanyam's or Davis's protagonists to moving about in a Braudelian unity in travelling and trailblazing, and certainly nothing bordering on a shared ecumene. Indeed, it is fair to say that connectivity and entanglement tended to reinforce the view of ecumenes as largely locally driven, reproduced and kept apart. In a wonderful recent study of Renaissance cultural diplomacy, Natalie Rothman illuminates how 'encounters' between strangers before they became interdependent created 'trans-imperial' spaces, 'interstices' or 'borderlands'. But while Ottoman and Venetian translators, missionaries, traders and migrants widened the scope for mutual regard, understanding and tolerance, they also serviced empire-building projects of marking territories and drawing boundaries between regimes. The concern remained, resolutely, focused on subjects within domains, not on the systems that crossed them.[30]

Contrast this style of multicultural effort to create more complex world narratives about how actors wrestled with the cultural dimensions of distance with the multicultural styles that have tended to prevail of late. In recent years, globalisation euphoria and the accent on circulation and networks have tended to emphasise the familiarisation that came with contact and interdependence – as if falling short of becoming one-world denoted the incompletion of some liberal, internationalist or capitalist dream. Or for that matter, socialist. Modernists tended to presume that closing the geographic gap meant closing cultural ones, turning strangers into ever more familiar fixtures of life and, eventually, homogenising them. Or, in extremis, exterminating them. This is a signature of Marshall McLuhan's stadial account from oral to print to telegraphic modes of co-existence and merger, which remains a staple for how world-making has been plotted over the centuries. At the time, he was observing the ways in which television was creating a new mode of intervisibility and commonality through communities, networks and values that crossed and erased borders.[31] By the 1970s, 'global thinking' was becoming hot – not

[29] Natalie Zemon Davis, *Trickster Travels: A Sixteenth-Century Muslim between Worlds* (New York: Hill and Wang, 2006).
[30] Ella Natalie Rothman, *Brokering Empire: Trans-Imperial Subjects between Venice and Istanbul* (Ithaca: Cornell University Press, 2012).
[31] McLuhan, *The Gutenberg Galaxy*.

because so many senses were being aroused by hot media, but because the world was becoming more crowded, unstable, running up against its limits. With it came more and more talk about Coca-Cola-isation, multinationalisation and, after 1989, lots of flat-earth talk about liberalism and networked society (for those who thought globalisation was good) or Americanisation, neoliberalism and hegemony (for the dissenters). If early modern hubs featured mediators and translators of cultural difference, the high-water mark of late-twentieth-century globalisation was dominated by outsourcers and supply-chain builders.[32]

In the years following the end of the Cold War, there was a growing sense of attachment across nations that accompanied the lowered borders between them. Even the diffusion of the term 'global' was part of the lexicon of merging world parts and peoples into one new, scalar mode of living. An ethnography of Wall Street conducted in the late 1990s captured the bravura about a borderless, flowing world seen from its commanding, financialised heights. From such a perch, togetherness meant a simultaneous and synchronised market rhythm, a form of hypercapitalist time in which actors converged on the bankers' schedule in a common urge to be flexible, nimble, mobile, unshackled from the past, 'responsive' (as the terminology of the time liked to say) to the future. Unbound by place or location, money men sought to 'serve the needs of our clients across all geographic borders' (as one 1994 Merrill Lynch report put it). The world's places, like its factories, were becoming ever more liquid.[33]

In an early wave of global history, there was a tendency to presume that scaling-up made distance irrelevant; just-in-time global delivery systems, instantaneous messaging and network society were delivering a sense of collapsed and accelerated synchronicity. One author called for a new field of study and discipline to capture this destiny and called it 'connectography'.[34] His timing was unfortunate, for just as his futurism about 'global civilisation' rolled off the printing presses in 2016, British voters elected to secede from the European Union, Donald Trump was on his way to victory and the confidence in things global dissipated quickly. Distance, as Gruzinski would have noted, may have been bridged but this did not make it any less significant.

---

[32] The arch example is the notorious Thomas L. Friedman, *The World is Flat: A Brief History of the Twenty-First Century* (New York: Farrar, Straus and Giroux, 2007). Perhaps the best example of this is Quinn Slobodian's intellectual history of neoliberalism to fill the gap opened by the end of European empires as a mechanism for world ordering. Quinn Slobodian, *Globalists: The End of Empire and the Birth of Neoliberalism* (Cambridge, MA: Harvard University Press, 2018).

[33] Karen Ho, *Liquidated: An Ethnography of Wall Street* (Durham: Duke University Press, 2009), 242 and 302.

[34] Parag Khanna, *Connectography: Mapping the Future of Global Civil* (New York: Random House, 2016).

Estrangement

Not everyone saw the triumph of flatteners and distance-busters in the same way. For some, physical distance may have collapsed, but social distance had not. If anything, the end of the Cold War had created a semblance of unity and convergence – which overlay chasms. Eric Hobsbawm's *Age of Extremes* (1994), a survey of the 'short' twentieth century, saw the fall of the Berlin Wall as the signal eclipse of an industrial working class which had anchored socialist alternatives. But if the ideological standoff was over, Hobsbawm worried that the collapsing post-socialist and postcolonial order would trigger more violence between estranged peoples within states. Marxists were not the only ones concerned. Francis Fukuyama declared the end in less materialist terms in *The End of History and the Last Man* (1992), a book which did not have the same ebullient overtones associated with his 1989 essay, and its nuances, like McLuhan's, got lost in the clichés. Here too there was an ideological patina of unity, but Fukuyama worried that liberalism unchallenged would grow flabby and let more worrying (for him) tribal affinities prosper. Despite their differences, Fukuyama and Hobsbawm were unambiguous about the era-ending moment that dawned with globalisation. Both, however, were wise enough to disparage the rage to forecast and predict the inevitable one-world triumph, and worried that a post-ideological world might be no less violent than its precursor. Looking out at the carnage in the Balkans, Rwanda and elsewhere, they worried about a new type of violence between strangers released by the collapse of imperial and post-imperial states.[35]

Others saw deeper global cleavages revealed and took the paradox of integration one step further, arguing that it was the very forces of integration and globalisation that would produce, not erase, more estrangement and alienation between cultures; the demise of physical distance could intensify social distance. Few works captured this more trenchantly than Samuel P. Huntington's *The Clash of Civilizations and the Remaking of World Order* (1996). An epistle aimed at one-worlders whose connectography missed the ways in which interactions between peoples reinforced the sense of estrangement, it had more influence in the domain of public policy in making sense of the 'West's' relationship with Islam. Nowadays, it has been dusted off to explain the abrasion with China and the feud with Putin. Historians like to dismiss *Clash of Civilizations* for essentialising cultures into civilisations, and for good reason. But a second look reveals some important insights that overlap with global historians' interest in the production of 'commensurability' – with travellers, translators and mediators of an earlier era performing the function of making cultures intervisible. For Huntington, the modern era powered

---

[35] Eric Hobsbawm, *The Age of Extremes: The Short Twentieth Century* (New York: Vintage, 1994); Francis Fukuyama, *The End of History and the Last Man* (New York: Free Press, 1992).

integration by markets and universalising liberal ideas. It also created an ever greater difficulty in understanding social differences and bridging social distances; instead of togetherness around liberal values and market forces, Huntington saw endemic difference and potential violence. Huntington's analysis of distance was more cunning than his critics appreciated. What perpetuated distance between civilisations was precisely the dynamics unleashed by integration, first by European empires, then European cosmopolitanism and cresting with European world governance girded by human rights and private property. So it was that the demise of physical distance sired triumphalist unity rhetoric and aggressive expansion by the victors and set off a 'clash' between the interconnected cultures.[36]

For global historians, the emerging challenge in the post–Cold War era lay in resolving the tension between greater connection and estrangement, in understanding how interdependence could coincide with and even create social divides. Without necessarily taking a Huntingtonian approach, global historians did in fact turn to the paradox of integration and distance, especially in explaining why some societies grew rich and others languished or 'failed'. Market integration, especially after 1820, had spawned greater material divides between people; all the one-world talk was simply papering over the chasms in GDP. Comparative economic historians like myself plunged into the challenge of explaining why some grew rich and some did not. The most famous and debated was Kenneth Pomeranz's account of the 'great divergence': how parts of northwest Europe broke out of their Malthusian trap while parts of riverine China did not. But he was not alone; there were others studying China and Latin America who posed similar questions about how collapsing physical distances and market convergence yielded to divergence.[37] By 2008, the 'what went wrong' story-seeking was a cottage industry to explain global dividing. Needless to say, global economic historians concerned with diverging directions of society did not necessarily subscribe to the cultural fixities of 'us versus them' that marked Huntingtonian analysis. Indeed, most comparative historians tended to explain divides in terms of grubby variables like factor endowments or policy decisions. What is important to note is that the happy

[36] Samuel P. Huntington, *The Clash of Civilizations and the Remaking of World Order* (New York: Simon & Schuster, 1996).
[37] The list is long: Kenneth Pomeranz, *The Great Divergence: China, Europe, and the Making of the Modern World Economy* (Princeton: Princeton University Press, 2001); R. Bin Wong and Jean-Laurent Rosenthal, *Before and Beyond Divergence: The Politics of Economic Change in China and Europe* (Cambridge, MA: Harvard University Press, 2011); Stephen Haber (ed.), *How Latin America Fell Behind: Essays on the Economic Histories of Brazil and Mexico, 1800–1914* (Stanford: Stanford University Press, 1997); Jeremy Adelman, *Frontier Development: Land, Labour and Capital on the Wheatlands of Argentina and Canada, 1890–1914* (Oxford: Clarendon Press, 1994); Daron Acemoglu and James A. Robinson, *Why Nations Fail: The Origins of Power, Prosperity, and Poverty* (New York: Crown, 2012).

convergence narratives that accompanied globalisation did have dissenters for whom distance was not just a physical condition to be overcome with new technologies and institutions.[38]

As long as globalisation appeared to lace the world together with on-demand supply chains, cheap flights and cruises, social divides tended to pale beside the euphoria of those that prospered. Backlashing was left to protestors in Argentina, disgruntled French farmers and ethno-nationalists who seethed about the dismantling of their nations.

This ability to see social distances has, not surprisingly, come out of the shadows in recent years to replace talk of global citizenship and the dividends from liquidating everything on world markets. The fracturing of globalisation is now clearing the way for a different retrospective vision, flagged in the brutal (from the perspective of earlier human rights warriors) headline of a piece in *The Economist* commemorating the 70th anniversary of the UN Convention Against Genocide: 'Never Again, Again, and Again'. Human rights had, as Michael Ignatieff has noted, become the moral global guidance system to accompany market globalisation, lending it legitimacy and creating an infrastructure to manage those whose estrangement turned to abuse. Didier Fassin has called this 'humanitarian government'.[39]

The result has been a sceptical turn among global historians about humanitarian rhetoric and proclamations – and, indeed, all modern universalisms that masquerade as distance-busting credos to match the power of markets and technologies when in fact they often behave in the same ways as the imperial civilising missions they were designed to replace. David Rieff was among the first to call into question the conceits of humanitarianism. In its modern incarnation (there is a dispute over where to start human rights movements), it was connected to the failure of developmentalism and the demise of Third Worldism in the late 1960s. Just as the promise of closing the gap between the haves and the have-nots faded, according to Rieff, humanitarians offered new hope and championed new treaties and international laws. 'Those the gods wish to destroy', Rieff noted acidly, 'they first allow to set international norms.' Writing in the aftermath of the bloodbaths of Srebrenica (where Rieff was a reporter) and Rwanda, he reminded readers that 'no century had better norms and worse realities'.[40]

[38] Pomeranz, *The Great Divergence*; Wong and Rosenthal, *Before and Beyond Divergence*.
[39] 'Never again, again, and again', *The Economist*, 8 December 2018, www.economist.com/international/2018/12/08/can-the-world-stop-genocide; Didier Fassin, *Humanitarian Reason: A Moral History of the Present* (Berkeley: University of California Press, 2012); Michael Ignatieff, *Human Rights as Politics and Idolatry* (Princeton: Princeton University Press, 2001).
[40] David Rieff, *A Bed for the Night: Humanitarianism in Crisis* (New York: Simon & Schuster, 2002), 56 and 71.

The urge to capture the history of how global ideas and norms created the illusion of breaking down distances has transformed not just the history of humanitarianism and the governance of and for strangers, but global intellectual history tout court. Leading the way has been Samuel Moyn. In the wake of the declaration of war against Iraq in 2003, Moyn turned his sights to the history of human rights as a movement to replace the disenchantment with self-determination and decolonisation. In his view and others', a short but intense arc of events – from the war in Biafra to Prague Spring and the Helsinki Accords, to atrocities in Argentina and Cambodia – stripped nation-states of their halo as rights makers and saw them as rights takers. Movements mobilised lawyers and activists to appeal to a higher normative order, what Moyn has called the last utopia.[41] It took time for this post-national vision of a global world of networked activists working in the service of a post-national idyll to take shape. In 2003, Aryeh Neier, the founder of Human Rights Watch and later head of the Open Society Foundations, reflected back on four decades of 'struggle for rights'. He noted how the Commission on Security and Cooperation in Europe had been resisted by the Ford administration in 1975, even as it was going to subject the Soviet bloc to the scrutiny of human rights activists. It was only much later, in the 1990s, that the flowering of the treaty's significance for the new human rights regime became clear. He was shocked 'to discover years later that the CSCE [Conference on Security and Cooperation in Europe] had yielded benefits beyond our wildest imagination'.[42] To Moyn, this was the kind of self-serving retrospective that celebrated the angels of history while obscuring the effects on strangers they thought they were rescuing. Ever since, the history of world 'humanitarian government' has been seen as an effort doomed to recycle past illusions about helping strangers while separating and dividing them and creating a new global hierarchy.[43]

Strange Interdependence

Distance, as should be clear, is not just tricky; it plays tricks. Technologies and organisations that claim to close gaps often create new ones that are not always seen as the result of efforts to connect and merge. At heart, this chapter has argued, growing interdependence has produced deeply mixed responses of

---

[41] Samuel Moyn, *The Last Utopia: Human Rights in History* (Cambridge, MA: Harvard University Press, 2010).

[42] Arieh Neier, *Taking Liberties: Four Decades in the Struggle for Rights* (New York: Public Affairs, 2003), 159.

[43] Heather Curtis, *Holy Humanitarians: American Evangelicals and Global Aid* (Cambridge, MA: Harvard University Press, 2018); Michael Barnett, *Empire of Humanity: A History of Humanitarianism* (Ithaca: Cornell University Press, 2011); and for a defence of human rights as a corrective to market integration, see Kathryn Sikkink, *Evidence for Hope: Making Human Rights Work in the 21st Century* (Princeton: Princeton University Press, 2017).

integration and estrangement, new models of belonging together to some new, often abstract idea of a world community, while making the divides between peoples at home and far away not just deeper, but more visible.

Earlier in this chapter I detoured to earlier modern global historians in part because they worked with a vocabulary that was more accommodating of the greys and ambiguities of what it meant to close the distances between peoples. One reason is because early modern thinkers in Mexico City, Delhi or Paris were not yet tethered to the one-world, modernising narratives that would govern capitalist storytelling habits and the technologies they wielded from the nineteenth century onwards.

Let me conclude by recovering the idea that we need more complex approaches to the distance question that accommodate the ambiguities and contradictions produced by integration and closure. Before the triumph of world capitalism, before the pulverising effects of free trade and steam technologies (what Marx and Engels would call 'heavy artillery'), this was easier to appreciate. In *Wooden Eyes: Nine Reflections on Distance*, Carlo Ginzburg has reminded us of a moral experiment conducted by the eighteenth-century *philosophe*, Denis Diderot. Do we cease to feel compassion if a person in distress is far away; does distance 'produce the effect on us that the lack of sight produces on the blind?' Diderot asked. Presaging our current debates about drone bombings and missiles, Diderot speculated that many people would find it easier to kill a man at a distance if he 'appeared no larger than a swallow'. Distance, the appearance of things being smaller, created an illusion, a kind of trap. The eighteenth-century world had sewn its parts together through exchange and scientific curiosity and made its parts more visible to each other – more visible and yet at the same time diminished by the tricks of distance. At its extreme, it made foreigners more familiar but less human.[44]

The concern about the tricks of distance was not just ideational. Indeed, two prophets of commercial capitalism, Adam Smith and David Hume, worried about the moral consequences of closing the material gaps between strangers. It obsessed them – and set off, as Luc Boltanski has noted, an urge to 'symmetrise' the spectator and the far-away spectacle, including the spectacle of suffering strangers.[45] For Hume, commercial nations were 'both the happiest and most virtuous'. In an essay he wrote in 1752, and which deeply influenced Smith's thinking about trade, Hume explained that 'industry, knowledge, and humanity, are linked together by an indissoluble chain, and are found, from experience as well as reason, to be peculiar to the more polished, and, what are

---

[44] Ginzburg, *Wooden Eyes*, 162–70.
[45] Silvia Sebastiani, 'What Constituted Historical Evidence of the New World? Closeness and Distance in William Robertson and Francisco Javier Clavijero', *Modern Intellectual History*, 11, 3 (2014), 677–95; Luc Boltanski, *La souffrance à distance: Morale humanitaire, médias et politique* (Paris: Gallimard, 1993), 90–4.

more commonly denominated, the more luxurious ages'. It was from trade among strangers and the spread of consumption that people learned the habit of 'conversing together'. Interdependence exposes peoples of the world to different goods, tastes and desires. It 'rouses men from their indolence; and presenting the gayer and more opulent part of the nation with objects of luxury, which they never before dreamed of, raises in them a desire of a more splendid way of life than what their ancestors enjoyed'.[46] Being exposed to luxuries, goods and services beyond one's reach, especially when they came from exotic places, motivated peoples' pursuits, civilised them and made them more other-regarding. Smith was more troubled; he doubted whether sympathy might march in lockstep with self-interest. In his *Theory of Moral Sentiments* (1759) the Scottish moral philosopher wondered if a gentleman would worry more about a pain in his finger than the fate of thousands of Chinese people swallowed up by an earthquake.[47] Here were two societies connected to each other by trade and science yet separated by sentiment. Did distance diminish the capacity to identify with another's pain despite mutual interests? Even more, did the commercial contact that brought the two peoples together create the illusion of a sympathy that did not keep pace?

More than two centuries later, the same tension, the same trickery, is at work. Yes, there were voices, even at the dawn of modern globalisation, that worried that markets and cameras had created an illusion of closure. In an important work on the history of capitalist thinking, Albert O. Hirschman excavated a different story about the history of self-interest and world-making. His *Passions and the Interests: Political Arguments for Capitalism Before Its Triumph* (1977) was an effort to see markets in less triumphal ways, more open to moral considerations at their root, and to draw the reader's attention to the limits of self-interest in connecting strangers. In the same year, Susan Sontag's *On Photography* (1977) meditated on the complex tricks of the camera. She questioned the celebration of 'photographic objectivity' and the heroic photographer as the impartial witness to history that brought distant events home and closed the gap between strangers; most especially, she questioned the very notion that the image of others' suffering might make the viewer feel more attachment and empathy. In fact, a world saturated with

---

[46] 'Of Refinement in the Arts', quoted in Margaret Schabas and Carl Wennerlind, *A Philosopher's Economist: Hume and the Rise of Capitalism* (Chicago: University of Chicago Press, 2020), 114 and 127.

[47] 'If he [this imagined man of humanity] was to lose his little finger to-morrow, he would not sleep to-night; but, provided he never saw them [the suffering Chinese], he will snore with the most profound security over the ruin of a hundred millions of his brethren, and the destruction of that immense multitude seems plainly an object less interesting to him, than this paltry misfortune of his own.' Adam Smith, *The Theory of Moral Sentiments*, ed. D. D. Raphael (= The Glasgow Edition of the Works and Correspondence of Adam Smith, vol. 1) (Oxford: Clarendon Press, 1976), 233.

234   Configurations and *Telos*

images of strangers in distress was as likely to foster detachment as attachment. The lens, now mounted on our phones, the latter-day instrument most responsible for closing the distance between strangers, was equally an instrument for making those distances all the more intractable.

Sontag and Hirschman picked up where the eighteenth-century *penseurs* left off and opened trails for us to examine more ambiguous and contradictory effects of proximity, to see that closure creates new social divides. The sooner we can dispense with narratives that imply a singular logic or an inevitable shift from a world of villages to the global village – whether through the 'fix' of capital or the finesse of new media, whether in a mood of dysphoria or euphoria – the better.

10 Materiality
Global History and the Material World[*]

Stefanie Gänger

Global historians have been among the most prolific apostles of the material turn since both fields' inception in the 1990s and early 2000s.[1] Global commodity histories, accounts of the 'global lives of things'[2] and popular histories of the 'world in objects' – Benin brass portraits, Aztec double-headed serpents and Mughal miniatures that 'tell of the world for which they were made'[3] – are only the most visible tip of an iceberg comprising global environmental histories,[4] world histories of consumption[5] and global histories of human waste,[6] fashion or, indeed, epidemic disease and 'contagion'.[7] Materiality evidently is en vogue among historians adopting a global perspective – as object of study, as a prism, directing the historian's gaze, as source material or, indeed, as illustration, 'material embodiment' and evidence of world-making,

[*] I would like to gratefully acknowledge the comments on this chapter made by Jürgen Osterhammel, Liliana Feierstein, Susann Liebich, Albert Loran, Ruby Ellis and Romedio-Schmitz-Esser, the participants of the transnational and global history seminar at the École normale supérieure in Paris and the fellows of the Balzan–FRIAS group. I would also like to acknowledge the helpful and inspiring feedback of my fellow authors in this volume.

[1] Jennifer L. Roberts, 'Things: Material Turn, Transnational Turn', *American Art*, 31, 2 (2017), 64–8, here 66. For a similar observation, see Giorgio Riello, 'The "Material Turn" in World and Global History', *Journal of World History* 33, 2 (2022), 193–232, here 195–6.

[2] Anne Gerritsen and Giorgio Riello, 'Introduction: The Global Lives of Things. Material Culture in the First Global Age', in Anne Gerritsen and Giorgio Riello (eds.), *The Global Lives of Things: The Material Culture of Connections in the Early Modern World* (London: Routledge, 2016), 1–23.

[3] See Neil MacGregor, *A History of the World in 100 Objects* (London: Allen Lane, 2010), xv.

[4] See, for instance, John F. Richards, *The Unending Frontier: An Environmental History of the Early Modern World* (Berkeley: University of California Press, 2003); John R. McNeill, *Something New Under the Sun: An Environmental History of the Twentieth-Century World* (New York: Norton, 2000); Corey Ross, *Ecology and Power in the Age of Empire: Europe and the Transformation of the Tropical World* (New York: Oxford University Press, 2017).

[5] Frank Trentman, *Empire of Things. How We Became a World of Consumers, from the Fifteenth Century to the Twenty-First* (New York: HarperCollins, 2016).

[6] James L. A. Webb, *The Guts of the Matter: A Global History of Human Waste and Infectious Intestinal Disease* (Cambridge: Cambridge University Press, 2019).

[7] Mark Harrison, *Contagion: How Commerce Has Spread Disease* (New Haven: Yale University Press, 2012).

the global scale and connectivity.[8] This is in some measure paradoxical, to be sure. For matter and material cultural have long been, and remain to a degree, associated with proximity, the concrete and the 'lower order'[9] in the modern imagination: the 'micro' rather than the 'macro', the contingent rather than the universal and, indeed, the local rather than the global.

This chapter seeks to uncover a series of implicit, often unspoken assumptions that guide and inform global histories that canvass aspects of the material world. Its particular interest is in the grounds on which historians associate matter and material culture with a particular scale, context or level of observation – the global, most importantly, but also, and seemingly inconsistently, the concrete, the particular or a 'lower order'. The very words 'object', 'substance' and 'matter' suggest intransience, obduracy and self-evidence. An object is that which, literally, throws itself before and puts itself against us, with 'the self-evidence of a slap in the face';[10] a substance is that which 'stands under or grounds things' – the ontologically basic, fundamental entities of reality and 'facts of nature'.[11] And yet, matter and material culture tend to stand for something other than themselves – mud for dirt, antiquities for the past, pears for food – on account of humans making sense of them in particular ways.[12] The humanities' now nearly three-decades-long interest in the 'agency' of things, posthumanism and the 'ontological dignity' of matter has let semiotics fade into the background, but, with all due humility,[13] it is still humans – and, in this particular case, historians – who endow matter and material culture with meaning. Matter, the chapter holds, may temporarily become inextricable from the global scale – because certain forms of matter affect the entire planet, for instance, or because a global material event would have been evident as such to men and women in the past – but materiality as such has no 'natural' scale, level or context, no self-evident, obvious place in any order.

---

[8] For this typology of historians' uses of materiality, see Annette C. Cremer, 'Zum Stand der Materiellen Kulturforschung in Deutschland', in Annette C. Cremer and Martin Mulsow (eds.), *Objekte als Quellen der historischen Kulturwissenschaften. Stand und Perspektiven der Forschung* (Cologne: Böhlau, 2017), 9–22, here 17.

[9] On materiality and the 'lower order', see Fernand Braudel, *Civilization and Capitalism, 15th–18th Centuries*, 3 vols. (Berkeley: University of California Press, 1992), vol. 1, *The Structures of Everyday Life: The Limits of the Possible*, 29.

[10] Lorraine Daston, 'Introduction: The Coming into Being of Scientific Objects', in Lorraine Daston (ed.), *Biographies of Scientific Objects* (Chicago: University of Chicago Press, 2000), 1–14, here 2.

[11] Howard Robinson, 'Substance', in Edward N. Zalta (ed.), *Stanford Encyclopedia of Philosophy* (2014). https://plato.stanford.edu/archives/fall2021/entries/substance/; Theodore Schatzki, 'Nature and Technology in History, *History and Theory*, 42, 4 (2003), 82–93, here 86.

[12] Roland Barthes, 'Sémantique de l'objet', in Roland Barthes (ed.), *L'aventure sémiologique* (Paris: Éditions du Seuil, 1985), 249–60, here 251–2.

[13] Timothy LeCain, *The Matter of History: How Things Create the Past* (New York: Cambridge University Press, 2017).

In its attempt at understanding the criteria practitioners apply to connect matter and material culture with a particular scale, context or level of observation, the chapter is concerned with the entire range of matter surrounding humanity in the modern era, from plants, viruses and oxygen to chintz, plastic and pesticides. One of the most pervasive dichotomies in the Western intellectual tradition is the opposition between man-made, or artefactual, material objects on the one hand, and natural, seemingly inert material objects on the other – presumably a remnant of the Aristotelian hylomorphic model, according to which things are compounds of matter (*hyle*) and form (*morphe*).[14] Scholars have for some time now problematised that dichotomy: even the most natural-looking flower, human body or river course may be the result of human ingenuity, while even the most abstract expressions of human thought and culture – Japanese sericulture and economic growth, or Western mass democracy – could be argued to arise *also* from the 'material world'.[15] This chapter shares the conviction that differences between artefactual and natural objects of the material world are gradual rather than dichotomous, and a belief in the historicity and contingency of the dichotomy. It remains, at the same time, acutely aware of the import of the differences between various kinds of material objects. Not only does matter have properties that artefacts do not – it is divisible 'without requiring a change of name', for instance, and it can endure within other sorts of matter[16] – artefactual material objects also bear many of the cultural associations the chapter sets out to uncover precisely on account of the longevity of the hylomorphic tradition. The chapter reflects on the material world surrounding and comprising human beings in its entirety, because it is only thus that one can comprehend the sum of the historian's relation to it.

A chapter concerned with materiality, globally, could have dealt with a series of other topics, to be sure. Possibilities for emphases abound; there are various ways one might approach the relationship between global history and the material world. Some might suggest it would be better to consider the materiality of the field as such – global historians' particular dependence on airplanes, digitisation or archives in places where humidity threatens the paper records.[17] Others might think it pertinent to discuss, instead, the field's material – both organic and physical-mechanical – language: its jargon of 'circulation',

[14] Tim Ingold, 'Toward an Ecology of Materials', *Annual Review of Anthropology* 41 (2012), 427–42, here 432.
[15] LeCain, *The Matter of History*, 11, 15, 19. On carbon and democracy, see Timothy Mitchell, 'Carbon Democracy', *Economy and Society* 38, 3 (2009), 399–432.
[16] Jens Soentgen, 'Stuff: A Phenomenological Definition', in Klaus Ruthenberg and Jaap van Brakel (eds.), *Stuff: The Nature of Chemical Substances* (Würzburg: Königshausen & Neumann, 2008), 71–91, here 79.
[17] On the field's particular relationship to digitisation, see Lara Putnam, 'The Transnational and the Text-Searchable: Digitized Sources and the Shadows They Cast', *American Historical Review* 121, 2 (2016), 377–402.

238   Configurations and *Telos*

'international pressure' and 'flow'.[18] Another obvious choice might have been to study the materiality of some of global history's favourite subjects: the transport infrastructure at the basis of the global economy[19] or the submarine cables, breech-loaders and doses of quinine that made high imperialism – 'a more territorial form of [imperial] domination' – possible.[20] In centring, instead, on global historians' association of matter with a particular scale, context or level of observation, the chapter opts for a theme in line with the volume's general impetus of understanding the conceptual basis of our work as global historians; of exposing the tacit assumptions that guide our work and of holding them up for careful inspection.

Signs of the Global

Most commonly, forms of matter and material culture are seen to 'reveal a world of movement and interaction'[21] when they themselves have moved – or, more accurately, have *been* moved about the world, for matter is rarely automotive – at some point during their 'biographies'.[22] Commodities, in particular – by definition moveable and implicated in patterns of exchange[23] – have come to signify world-making, the global economy and 'connections among people ... distant and unfamiliar to each other', because, owing partly to the impact of Immanuel Wallerstein's world-systems theory, their biographies are often told through world-spanning chains of production, processing, marketing and consumption.[24] So have diplomatic gifts,[25] contagious germs[26] or medicinal imports, many of which were exchanged across boundaries in the

---

[18] See, for instance, Stefanie Gänger, 'Circulation: Reflections on Circularity, Entity and Liquidity in the Language of Global History', *Journal of Global History* 12, 3 (2017), 303–18; Stuart Alexander Rockefeller, 'Flow', *Current Anthropology* 52, 4 (2011), 557–78.
[19] Historians have long argued that the transport industry has been one of the prime forces responsible for shifting the world from an essentially national system to the global economy. See, for instance, Martin Stopford, *Maritime Economics*, 3rd ed. (London: Routledge, 2009), 2.
[20] Ross, *Ecology and Power*, 8. For one of the first iterations of the argument that technology made high imperialism possible, see Daniel R Headrick, *The Tools of Empire: Technology and European Imperialism in the Nineteenth Century* (New York: Oxford University Press, 1981), 4.
[21] Gerritsen and Riello, 'Introduction: The Global Lives of Things', 23.
[22] Igor Kopytoff, 'The Cultural Biography of Things: Commoditization as Process', in Arjun Appadurai (ed.), *The Social Life of Things: Commodities in Cultural Perspective* (Cambridge: Cambridge University Press, 1986), 64–91.
[23] Kopytoff, 'The Cultural Biography of Things', 25.
[24] Steven C. Topik and Allen Wells, 'Commodity Chains in a Global Economy', in Emily S. Rosenberg (ed.), *A World Connecting: 1870–1945* (Cambridge, MA.: Harvard University Press, 2012), 593–814, here 598.
[25] Zoltán Biedermann et al., 'Introduction: Global Gifts and the Material Culture of Diplomacy in Early Modern Eurasia', in Zoltán Biedermann (eds.), *Global Gifts* (Cambridge: Cambridge University Press, 2018), 1–33.
[26] Harrison, *Contagion*.

early or late modern era and are at present regarded as 'tangible manifestations of . . . global connections', a 'global age' and a 'global shared culture'.[27] While these things' movement and implication in worldwide connections is undeniable, one ought not to forget other features of their biographies: the circumstance that their 'globality' and movement would often have been unknown to, concealed from or – particularly from the late 1800s onwards – irrelevant for our historical subjects;[28] the fact that these materials' movement across large distances would have been short in comparison to other, less mobile stages of their biographies: plant growth, or museum display, let alone gemstone formation; and the fact that contemporaries would sometimes have condemned the things' global movement as inappropriate, erroneous or extrinsic to their nature, as in discourses about medicines, plants,[29] or, indeed, antiques. As the current, virulent debate about restitution exemplifies, to many in the present and the past, some artworks, though they may have lived decidedly 'global lives', remain firmly associated with the particular context of their origins or 'ancient seat', as Arthur Wellesley, the Duke of Wellington, put it during the Napoleonic wars, when ideas about the proper place of art first (re-)gained currency.[30] Already during the 1790s, driven by their opposition to the French revolutionaries' looting of the Italian peninsula, writers such as Antoine-Chrysostôme Quatremère de Quincy had argued that the best art, though it could not be possessed, belonged in its original setting. They condemned the displacement of artworks from 'where nature had placed them', their 'sequestration from their native country [*l'enlévement à leur pays natal*]'.[31] From that moment, at least in some strands of modern thought, many artworks were regarded as intrinsically inalienable and immovable. This is not to say that Jingdezhen porcelain, Saint-Domingue sugar or Potosí

---

[27] Anne Gerritsen and Stephen McDowall, 'Global China: Material Culture and Connections in World History', *Journal of World History* 23, 1 (2012), 3–8, here 5; Gerritsen and Riello, 'Introduction: The Global Lives of Things', 23. For a similar observation, and an extensive survey and brilliant discussion, of how scholars have taken material artefacts as a way to both explain and illustrate connectivity, see Riello, 'The "Material Turn" in World and Global History', 195–204.

[28] Alexander Engel, 'Die Globalität von Gütern und ihre Ökonomien, 1450–1900', in Christian Kleinschmidt and Jan Logemann (eds.), *Konsum im 19. und 20. Jahrhundert* (Berlin: De Gruyter Oldenbourg, 2021), 115–36, here 119; Jürgen Osterhammel, 'Warenökonomie und Mobilitätsfolklore', *Zeitschrift für Ideengeschichte* 15, 1 (2021), 5–13.

[29] See, for instance, Alix Cooper, *Inventing the Indigenous: Local Knowledge and Natural History in Early Modern Europe* (Cambridge: Cambridge University Press, 2007).

[30] The Duke of Wellington's letter to Viscount Castlereagh is dated 23 September 1815, Paris. Cited in Margaret M. Miles, *Art as Plunder: The Ancient Origins of Debate about Cultural Property* (Cambridge: Cambridge University Press, 2008), 333.

[31] A[ntoine-Chrysostôme] Q[uatremère de Quincy], 'Première Lettre', in *Lettres sur le préjudice qu'occasionneroient aux arts et à la science, le déplacement des monumens de l'art de l'Italie, le démembrement de ses Ecoles, et la spoliation de ses collections, galeries, musées* (Paris: Desenne, 1796), 5. See also Miles, *Art as Plunder*, 326.

silver may not justifiably be regarded as 'physical evidence for sustained cultural encounter on a worldwide scale'.[32] It is merely to lay bare that present-day global historians' foregrounding of such objects' globality has as much to do with the possibilities that their biographies offer as with the historians' own research interests – in global integration, connections and cosmopolitanism.[33]

The other, more important question is whether these forms of matter and material culture 'reveal a world of movement and interaction' or whether what they really reveal is 'movement and interaction' in a world of isolation, stillness or, at the very least, shorter-range (e.g. (cross-) regional) movement – whether they are 'likely to offer a distorted view' of the past, as de Vries put it in relation to the 'unusually cosmopolitan individuals' many global historians like to study.[34] Indeed, few economic historians, including those studying 'commodities that transcended national borders', would deny that 'the vast majority of economic activity in the world before 1945 was still dedicated to home and local production'.[35] Even though the integration of global commodity markets certainly began in the eighteenth century, long into the nineteenth century world trade accounted only for a small share of economic activity and material possessions, even in Western Europe or East Asia.[36] By convincing metrics, even in the late twentieth century the bulk of the world's economic activity remained national or regional.[37] Historians of migration have for some time now tempered our image of modernity as an age of unchecked mobility since only a small share of the world population migrated across oceans and continents, even in the nineteenth century – 0.36 per cent in the 1850s, 0.96 per cent in the 1880s, 1.67 per cent in the 1900s and 1.58 per cent in the 1920s.[38] The same applies to the material world: in most societies in human history the bulk of foodstuffs, tableware and medicines would have been made, or harvested, close to home. Ceramics, plants and fertilisers leading global lives were exceptions rather than the rule, unusual in their cosmopolitanism. They certainly reveal 'movement and interaction' on a global scale, but not, or at least

---

[32] Robert Finlay, *The Pilgrim Art* (Berkeley: University of California Press, 2010), 6.

[33] For the attendant critiques of global history, see Jeremy Adelman, 'What is Global History Now?', *Aeon*, 2 March 2017. https://aeon.co/essays/is-global-history-still-possible-or-has-it-had-its-moment; Paul A. Kramer, 'How Did the World Become Global? Transnational History, Beyond Connection', *Reviews in American History* 49, 1 (2021), 119–41.

[34] Jan de Vries, 'Playing with Scales: The Global and the Micro, the Macro and the Nano', *Past & Present* 242, supplement 14 (2019), 23–36, here 29.

[35] Topik and Wells, 'Commodity Chains in a Global Economy', 599.

[36] See, for instance, Jan de Vries, 'The Limits of Globalization in the Early Modern World', *Economic History Review* 63, 3 (2010), 710–33, here 718; on medicines, see Stefanie Gänger, *A Singular Remedy: Cinchona Across the Atlantic World, 1751–1820* (Cambridge: Cambridge University Press, 2020), 81.

[37] Kramer, 'How Did the World Become Global?', 133.

[38] Adam McKeown, 'Global Migration, 1846–1940', *Journal of World History* 15, 2 (2004), 155–89, here 167.

not necessarily, a 'global age' of art, trade or consumption. Critics of the wider field of global history have in recent years again and again posed the question of whether the 'global talk' of the present-day is 'a *sui generis* response to events "themselves"' in the past or a discourse that, prejudiced by the historians' global present, sculpts historic realities.[39] Practitioners in the field ought to exercise due care – weigh their evidence carefully, keep a sense of proportion and remind their readers of those proportions – in order not to fall into the latter.

This is not to say that global scholarship ought to cease to deal with the material world, only that there is no material foundation for a field based purely on what critics have come to call 'connectionism'.[40] Indeed, matter often became *temporarily* – in certain periods of history – inextricable from the global scale not because it was traded or bartered across distance, but for other reasons, such as the fact that certain forms of matter came to affect the entire planet. The pollution of air, for instance, which for half a million years – since humans first harnessed fire – had been a local issue, grew 'so comprehensive and large-scale' with high modernity that it came to upset 'the fundamentals of global atmospheric chemistry'.[41] Indeed, substances may become 'global' – as in, relate to or involve the whole world – not necessarily because humans move them about but because they happen to occur in various places at the same time. Substances such as oxygen, fresh water and clay are distinct from things precisely by virtue of their peculiarly mobile, or, rather, diffuse disposition: the propensity of stuff to exist within another, dissipate and occur at the same time in different places.[42] The same applies to less appealing sorts of matter, which have likewise come to affect and involve the entire world. While the issue of refuse is as old as humanity, the massive Cold War–era chemical manufacturing of synthetic materials entailed waste that, from the 1970s at least, was publicly recognised as hazardous, toxic and global in its implications.[43] The disposal of plastics, pesticides and synthetic fibre has become inextricable from the global scale because exports of hazardous waste to poorer, non-OECD countries became an international business in the 1970s,[44] but also because chemical waste matter, instead of fully deteriorating, dissipates and accumulates in a finite world – in landfills and open dumps and, as microplastics, heavy metal or trace chemicals, in wildlife, oceans, human

[39] Kramer, 'How Did the World Become Global?', 133.
[40] Kramer, 'How Did the World Become Global?', 120.
[41] McNeill, *Something New Under the Sun*, 4.   [42] Soentgen, 'Stuff', 78.
[43] Martin V. Melosi, *Garbage in the Cities: Refuse, Reform, and the Environment*, rev. ed. (Pittsburgh: University of Pittsburgh Press 2005]). On hazardous waste, see McNeill, *Something New Under the Sun*, 29.
[44] See, for instance, Simone M. Müller, 'Corporate Behaviour and Ecological Disaster: Dow Chemical and the Great Lakes Mercury Crisis, 1970–1972', *Business History* 60, 3 (2018), 399–422; Jennifer Clapp, 'Africa, NGOs, and the International Toxic Waste Trade', *Journal of Environment & Development* 2, 3 (1994), 17–46.

foetuses and the lithosphere alike.[45] The study of plastics, pesticides and synthetics certainly lacks the romance that comes with the study of coffee, calicos or combs, but it is, in many ways, more forcibly tied to the global scale than the latter.

To be sure, the global scale of some material events emerges only in hindsight. Studies of historic climate records for the years 1788–94/5, for instance, retrospectively reveal a global, connected climate crisis: flooding on the Peruvian coast; droughts and famines in the Caribbean, Western Europe, South Asia and southern Africa; and heavy rainfall, high temperatures and epidemic disease in North America.[46] For most contemporaries, however, these would have been unconnected, local climatic stresses, confined to their own area. The same applies to contagious disease. Historians have argued, largely based on retrospective diagnoses, that the 1790s marked the beginning of 'a great epidemiological upheaval', a 'Victorian Age of Pandemics' in which diseases such as yellow fever, plague and cholera first affected all continents simultaneously. It was only after a series of cataclysmic disease outbreaks over the late 1800s and early 1900s, however – the Russian Flu of 1889–91, the plague wave of the 1890s and the 1918 Influenza Pandemic – and owing to developments in bacteriology, medical statistics and, not least, reporting, that the connectedness of local disease outbreaks as pandemics (that is, global catastrophes) became part of contemporaries' common awareness.[47] This relates to a broader debate about the justifiability of the historian's declaring an event or moment global in hindsight, without reference to contemporary experience.[48] In the particular case of material histories, however, it also involves a discussion about the justifiable role of present-day scientific knowledge in historical scholarship: the bringing to bear of evidence from epigenetics, climatology or biochemistry on historical inquiries. To many historians, even the most 'carefully measured use of the sciences'[49] is associated with the danger of anachronism – of posing ahistorical questions, or wrenching past

[45] See, for instance, Nancy Langston, 'New Chemical Bodies: Synthetic Chemicals, Regulation, and Human Health', in Andrew C. Isenberg (ed.), *The Oxford Handbook of Environmental History* (Oxford: Oxford University Press, 2014), 259–81. Some 37 per cent of waste is currently disposed of in landfills, 33 per cent in open dumps. See Silpa Kaza et al., What a Waste 2.0: A Global Snapshot of Solid Waste Management to 2050 (Washington DC: World Bank, 2018), 5.

[46] Richard H. Grove, 'The Great El Niño of 1789–93 and Its Global Consequences: Reconstructing an Extreme Climate Event in World Environmental History', *The Medieval History Journal* 10, 1–2 (2006), 75–98.

[47] Mark Harrison, 'Pandemics', in Mark Jackson (ed.), *The Routledge History of Disease* (London: Routledge, 2016), 129–46, here: 132–33.

[48] Sebastian Conrad and Dominic Sachsenmaier, 'Introduction: Competing Visions of World Order: Global Moments and Movements, 1880s–1930s', in Sebastian Conrad and Dominic Sachsenmaier (eds.), *Competing Visions of World Order: Global Moments and Movements, 1880s-1930s* (Basingstoke: Palgrave Macmillan, 2007), 1–28.

[49] LeCain, *The Matter of History*, 195.

experiences into a present-day lexis and explanatory repertoire, in ways that would distort their understanding of the past.[50] Few would deny the potential of a closer dialogue with the sciences, however, wherever they conceive materiality, nature and the human body as changing, versatile and historicizeable.[51] The field is in urgent need of novel forms of ecologically sensitive history-writing that engage in 'the plotting of human relations with matter, nature' or animals over the long term, as Sujit Sivasundaram has argued, and that reflect on co-evolution, mutation, adaptation or, indeed, causation at the interspecies frontier, including the global history of cultured evasion and taxonomic ignorance behind zoonotic disease transfer.[52]

Other material events, processes or experiences came to be regarded as universal or global, in that they hinged upon the finitude of the globe, in the eyes of men and women in the past. As early as the late 1700s and early 1800s, for instance, the advent of 'specifics' in medicine – medications that worked 'universally', that is – entailed ideas about the modern body as physiologically alike, interchangeable and universal, regardless of temperament, gender or origin.[53] Human beings in the past may not necessarily have been connected to one another on a material level through the exchange of foodstuffs, tableware or textiles, but many would knowingly have shared a 'material existence' – as beings that endure sickness, possess a sense of smell and have a limited lifespan.[54] Much of the material world became inextricable from the global scale to contemporaries during the Cold War era. Resources came to be seen on a global scale from the mid-twentieth century onwards, for instance, because, given the post-war global imaginary of the world as a closed planet 'with finite material potential',[55] their abundance or shortage became, by definition, *global*.[56] Whereas the nineteenth century was all about expansion into an ostensibly 'endless' material world – vast tropical woodlands,[57] infinite mineral ores' yet more oilfields – along ever-advancing commodity and settlement frontiers that moved on 'once resources were depleted in any given area',[58] the

---

[50] On historians of science 'making past science wholly unfamiliar', see Lorraine Daston, 'Science Studies and the History of Science', *Critical Inquiry* 35, 4 (2009), 798–813, here 806.
[51] LeCain, *The Matter of History*, 28, 208.
[52] Sujit Sivasundaram, 'The Human, the Animal and the Prehistory of COVID-19', *Past and Present* 249, 1 (2020), 295–316.
[53] Harold J. Cook, 'Markets and Cultures: Medical Specifics and the Reconfiguration of the Body in Early Modern Europe', *Transactions of the Royal Historical Society* 21 (2011), 123–45.
[54] Braudel, *The Structures of Everyday Life*, 23–9, 31; LeCain, *The Matter of History*, 1–22.
[55] Fabien Locher, 'Cold War Pastures: Garrett Hardin and the "Tragedy of the Commons"', *Revue d'Histoire Moderne et Contemporaine* 60, 1 (2013), 7–36, here 8–9.
[56] Locher, 'Cold War Pastures', 8–9.
[57] On Brazil, see José Augusto Pádua, 'Tropical Forests in Brazilian Political Culture: From Economic Hindrance to Ecological Treasure', in Fernando Vidal and Nélia Dias (eds.), *Endangerment, Biodiversity and Culture* (New York: Routledge, 2015), 148–72; on sub-Saharan Africa and South and Southeast Asia, see Ross, *Ecology and Power*, 274, also 77.
[58] Ross, *Ecology and Power*, 199–223, here: 141.

later twentieth and twenty-first centuries were marked by many contemporaries' sense of the world's inexorable material finitude. By the 1970s the exhaustion of fossil fuels, fresh water and ores 'on the global scale' had come to be seen as, if not imminent, then within sight.[59] While into the mid-1900s the history of petroleum, for instance, was that of a moving frontier – from Upper Burmese, Sumatran and Bornean to Venezuelan, Caspian and Persian oilfields[60] – apprehensions about the 'geological limits on the world oil supply' surfaced from the 1950s and had become commonplace by the early 2000s.[61] This is not to say that changes in the biophysical environment, and awareness of it, had not well preceded the mid-twentieth century. Indeed, naturalists expressed unease about the possibility of anthropogenic resource exhaustion and species rarity as early as the late 1700s.[62] It was only from the Cold War era, however, that the view that humanity inhabited an endangered planet 'with finite material potential' became a majority discourse.[63] From that moment, resource shortages and scarcity were *by necessity* canvassed on a global scale. The way the term biodiversity – that is, species diversity – was used from the mid-1980s, as reinforcing 'the global nature of the conservation problem', is another case in point. What was at stake was no longer 'particular wild places or even individual endangered species; the threat was to the diversity of life on Earth itself.'[64] The very issue of extinction, indeed, is inextricable from its global dimension. The concept and possibility of species extinction, which was first discussed after Georges Cuvier completed his studies of living and extinct elephants between 1796 and 1806, invariably was contingent both on accurate botanical knowledge – of discrete, fixed and stable ontic unities that could appear or vanish forever – and either certainty about a species' endemism or the ability to contextualise globally. As a matter of fact, the vast swathes of poorly explored territory, where supposedly extinct species might still be found undetected, furnished – other than ideas

---

[59] McNeill, *Something New Under the Sun*, 16, 147.
[60] On the moving oil frontier, see Ross, *Ecology and Power*, 203–23. See also Timothy Mitchell, *Carbon Democracy. Political Power in the Age of Oil* (London: Verso, 2011), 45–47.
[61] Kenneth S. Deffeyes, *Hubbert's Peak: The Impending World Oil Shortage* (Princeton: Princeton University Press, 2009), x.
[62] On naturalists based on Mauritius and in the Caribbean expressing early ecological concerns, see Richard H. Grove, *Green Imperialism: Colonial Expansion, Tropical Island Edens and the Origins of Environmentalism* (Cambridge: Cambridge University Press, 1995). On the northern Andes, see Stefanie Gänger, 'Cinchona Harvest, Deforestation, and "Extinction" in the Viceroyalty of New Granada, 1752–1811', *Journal of Environmental History* 24, 4 (2019), 673–9. On tropical forests in Portuguese and Brazilian thought, see Pádua, 'Tropical Forests in Brazilian Political Culture'.
[63] Locher, 'Cold War Pastures', 8–9.
[64] Megan Raby, *American Tropics: The Caribbean Roots of Biodiversity Science* (Chapel Hill: University of North Carolina Press, 2017), 1.

about the mutability of species – a key argument against Cuvier's reasoning in the early nineteenth century.[65]

Idolatry and Fetishism

In some global material histories, objects are seen not merely to illustrate or supply evidence of world-making, the global scale and connectivity, but as the 'signal', 'material embodiment' of and agent or 'actant' in processes of global integration. The tendency is palpable in the motif of the object as storyteller, telling 'tales of other places and unknown lands', which has become almost a topos in the field. In MacGregor-style 'histories of the world in objects', which have enjoyed uncommon popularity even among a wider, non-academic public, a slave drum will 'speak for millions', Spanish pieces of eight would 'tell us about the beginning of a global currency' and an early Victorian tea-set will speak to us about the impact of empire.[66] Artefacts are regarded as 'signals from the past' that communicate messages across time and 'tell of the world for which they were made'.[67] Readings of past material culture as signals of past worlds are by no means limited to popular forms of history-writing. In the most learned, nuanced and academic of historical writings, global or not, 'the objects that move and the objects that are left behind' are imputed to have 'stories to tell', sometimes particularly about contemporaries' experience of warfare, migration and displacement.[68] This line of argument is firmly in the tradition of the early 1980s material culture studies, which was marked by the idea of representation – that artefacts reflect and reveal the 'patterns of mind' of the cultures that created them.[69]

Whereas in these studies material culture is a carrier, a projection of the more profound, immaterial beliefs lurking behind it, to the more recent scholarship in the wake of agency theory, 'the matter *is* the mind'.[70] Indeed, often where historians have adopted theories about the agency of things and the 'ontological dignity' of matter – its properties and affordances and the ways in which they act on human practices and discourses[71] – we find yet another common trope: that of

---

[65] Grove, *Green Imperialism*, 245, 350, 355; Mark Barrow Jr., *Nature's Ghosts. Confronting Extinction from the Age of Jefferson to the Age of Ecology* (Chicago: University of Chicago Press, 2009), 23–6, 40–1. On the fixity of species, see also David Sepkoski, 'Extinction, Diversity, and Endangerment', in Fernando Vidal and Nélia Dias (eds.), *Endangerment, Biodiversity and Culture* (London: Routledge, 2015), 62–86, here 63–4.

[66] MacGregor, *A History of the World in 100 Objects*, xxiii, also rear cover endorsement.

[67] MacGregor, *A History of the World in 100 Objects*, xv.

[68] Leora Auslander and Tara Zahra, 'Introduction. The Things They Carried: War, Mobility, and Material Culture', in Leora Auslander and Tara Zahra (eds.), *Objects of War: The Material Culture of Conflict and Displacement* (Ithaca: Cornell University Press, 2018), 17.

[69] The expression 'patterns of mind' is Jules Prown's phrase. For the argument outlined here, and the quote, see Roberts, 'Things', 65.

[70] Roberts, 'Things', 65.   [71] For a brief survey of these debates, see Roberts, 'Things', 65.

the commodity, diplomatic gift or artwork *connecting* people, creating global spaces and bringing about worldwide integration.[72] Global material histories make reference to forms of matter and material culture contributing to the 'creation of long-distance social and economic connections', 't[ying] together continents and fuel[ing] commerce' and as 'key agents of social cohesion and transcultural systems of value in the emergence of a global political community'.[73] Indeed, the language about pots and plants occasionally bears a striking resemblance to that commonly applied to the 'unusually cosmopolitan individuals' critiqued by Jan de Vries, who are seen to reveal the global at a human scale, 'as they overcome barriers, dissolve misunderstandings, ... and create spaces of tolerance'.[74]

Practitioners of global material history have commonly applauded the embrace of agency theory for the study of *all* societies as a way of correcting 'forms of global cultural subordination that sustain themselves on the ... derogatory function of the term "fetish"' – a close associate of the ancient idea that the 'barbarian', the 'primitive' and the 'savage' are closer to nature, and to base matter, than those who claim Christianity, civilisation or modernity for themselves.[75] As a matter of fact, the term fetish (*feitiço*) surfaced during Iberian expansion and came into its own in the eighteenth century, in enlightened ethnology and critique of religion – be it West African or Catholic – as a term designating an inanimate object irrationally reverenced for powers merely projected onto it.[76] The concept made its way into the realm of the economic in 1867 with the publication of Karl Marx's *Das Kapital*, into psychoanalysis via Sigmund Freud's 1927 writings on fetishism and thence into everyday language, invariably in close company with the charges of irrationality, inferiority and immorality.[77] Particularly given the concept's

[72] For the argument that 'artefacts, luxuries, and commodities were not the embodiment of an extraneous system of connections; they created themselves global spaces and therefore are "actants"', see also Riello, 'The "Material Turn" in World and Global History', 216.
[73] On how 'commodities tied together continents and fuelled commerce', see Topik and Wells, 'Commodity Chains in a Global Economy', 593. On artefacts contributing to the 'creation of long-distance social and economic connections', see Gerritsen and Riello, 'Introduction: The Global Lives of Things', 23. On gifts as agents, see Biedermann et al., 'Introduction: Global Gifts', 1.
[74] Vries, 'Playing with Scales', 28.
[75] Roberts, 'Things', 66. On the natives' supposed proximity to nature and matter, see Shepard Krech, *The Ecological Indian: Myth and History* (New York: W. W. Norton, 1999), 16–17; J. G. A. Pocock, *Barbarism and Religion*, vol. 4: *Barbarians, Savages and Empires* (Cambridge: Cambridge University Press, 2008), 160; Anthony Pagden, *The Fall of Natural Man: The American Indian and the Origins of Comparative Ethnology* (Cambridge: Cambridge University Press, 1982), 21.
[76] Hartmut Böhme, *Fetischismus und Kultur: Eine andere Theorie der Moderne* (Reinbek: Rowohlt, 2006), 181.
[77] Peter Pels, 'The Modern Fear of Matter: Reflections on the Protestantism of Victorian Science', in Dick Houtman and Birgit Meyer (eds.), *Things: Religion and the Question of Materiality* (New York: Fordham University Press, 2012), 37.

pejorative associations, one would certainly not wish to crudely accuse modern
material historians of fetishism, as well as its close associate, idolatry.[78] The
sense that material histories exhibit a certain affinity with fetishism in their
understanding of objects as 'material embodiment' and as possessing powers
they may exert over us is hard to refute, however. [79] A hint of it at least is
present both in the idea of 'representation' – the circumstance of the thing or
matter standing in the place of a society, with the authority to speak on its
behalf – and, more plainly, in that of 'agency', as its early proponents well
knew – the ability of the thing or matter to act on its environment.[80]

One might object that in referring to gifts as agents in the emergence of
a global community, or to a tea-set as telling us about empire, historians are
either employing a Latourian idiom that has become commonplace in the
humanities or, indeed, speaking metaphorically, employing nothing more
than a figure of speech to denote that objects convey stories. But metaphors
are not concepts; rather, they are prior to them, as historians have argued. They
conjure up a vague feeling, without specifying the exact meaning of a historical
event or process.[81] One would hardly deny that some forms of matter invite
desire in far-away places or become a necessity to distant societies more easily
than others, both on account of their imbrication with cultural attributions and
their peculiar material affordances – their functional, sensorial and technical
capacities, or their particular aesthetic, olfactory or resilient properties. [82] Nor
would anyone deny that material objects permit and encourage us to ask
different questions, occasionally even to defy established chronologies or
reframe established narratives, including that of 'connectivity'.[83] Surely, action
arises from a conglomeration of things *and* persons. The crux of the matter

[78] An important difference between the two is that the idol's truth lies not in 'its status as material
embodiment', as with the fetish, but 'in its relation of iconic resemblance to some immaterial ...
entity'. William Pietz, 'The Problem of the Fetish I', *RES: Anthropology and Aesthetics*, 9
(1985), 5–17, here 7.
[79] Liliana Ruth Feierstein has argued that in the public memorialisation of the disappeared (and
academic discourse about it) in Argentina, the objects that belonged to the dead are fetishised,
including by researchers. See Liliana Ruth Feierstein, 'Of Boxes, Draws, and Crypts or How to
Contain (the Work of) Mourning', Conference paper presented at *Visualising Violence: Art,
Memory and Dictatorship in Latin America*, CRASSH, University of Cambridge, 2012. See
also her unpublished book manuscript, Tierras de idolatría: Por una crítica del fetichismo
histórico del material turn, where the author criticizes the 'idolatrous radicalisation' of historical
analysis of materiality and objects.
[80] Already Arjun Appadurai wrote that a 'minimum level of what might be called methodological
fetishism' could not be avoided in a social analysis of things. Cited in Peter Pels, 'The Spirit of
Matter: On Fetish, Rarity, and Fancy', in Patricia Spyer (ed.), *Border Fetishisms: Material
Objects in Unstable Space* (London: Routledge, 1998), 91–121, 93.
[81] For this observation, see Hugo Fazio, 'La historia global: ¿encrucijada de la contemporaneidad?', *Revista de Estudios Sociales* 23 (2006), 59–72, here 59, 61.
[82] See, for instance, Susanne Küchler, 'Materials and Design', in Alison Clarke (ed.), *The
Anthropology of Design* (Vienna: Springer, 2010), 124–35, here 125.
[83] Riello, 'The "Material Turn" in World and Global History', 224.

is how to determine the share of material things or affordances in the making or breaking of a global community or commercial link, in relation to the many other factors that would also have gone into it: political momentum, extant economic structures or, indeed, sheer human will.

This necessary distinction is complicated further by the fact that most references to things that talk or bring about global ties are about man-made, commodified or otherwise artefactual objects: tea-sets, cotton or suitcases. Such things are already imbricated with human subjectivity in ways that further obscure the boundaries between human and non-human factors in global historical processes. However, it is precisely their close vicinity with humanity as well as their humanisation – by means of a language about tea-sets that resembles that employed to describe humans – that allows the historian to conjure up the sense that these things were our accomplices in global processes, when in fact these, and they, are at least in part *our* creation. That language implies that there was a congregation of objects that all tended toward integration and cohesion or exhibited a willingness to speak of foreign places, shared in our curiosity about them, when in reality, curiosity, *wanderlust* and free will are some of the last preserves of humanity. As philosophers of action have long argued – incidentally, a field largely unresponsive to and aloof from actor–network theory and the *new materialism*, as Andreas Malm observed – human agency is qualitatively different from that of matter in its intentionality. Fossil fuels, the morning light or a steamboat undeniably have effects, but they do not form intentions or own actions as humans do, including the causal reverberations that outrun our capacity for foresight.[84] Matter and material culture, though they certainly set constraints and offer possibilities, do not actually talk, nor do they willingly help bring about global integration. Rather, global historians may sometimes be reading their biographies, under the influence of their own time's fascination with agency, global community and cosmopolitanism,[85] to make them seem to be doing so. They really may sometimes be revering material objects for powers they themselves have projected onto them.

The Pull of the Particular

In many ways, the association between matter and the global scale is, of course, downright counterintuitive. Indeed, historically, materiality has long been, and remains to a degree, associated with immediacy, proximity and the 'lower order'.[86]

---

[84] For these observations and a critique of the new materialism in dialogue with the philosophy of action, see Andreas Malm, *The Progress of This Storm: Nature and Society in a Warming World* (London: Verso, 2018), ch. 3, 78–118.

[85] Adelman, 'What Is Global History Now?'; Kramer, 'How Did the World Become Global?'

[86] Pels, 'The Modern Fear of Matter', 33. On materiality's association with sensuousness, see Marx's reflections on fetishism. Pels, 'The Spirit of Matter', 101.

Histories of matter, and material culture, will often begin with a narrative of absence, and loss – how for more than a century after its inception as an institutionalised discipline, history was largely purblind to matter and material culture.[87] The observation is in some measure accurate, to be sure. Not only did a large part of the field, in the tradition of historicism, rely principally on written sources; its understanding of history, broadly speaking, was one in which there were no material – that is, environmental, physical, natural – constraints on human agency or thought.[88] Modern historians' oversight was expressive of a broader astigmatism of industrialised societies at large that likely had a religious substratum:[89] the theological premise – present in many of the world's principal religions, from Buddhism and Hinduism to Christianity and Judaism – that materiality, not least our 'body as the core of our sensuous existence', is that which ought to be transcended, the merely apparent 'behind which lies that which is real'.[90] Indeed, 'fear and contempt' of matter was particularly prominent in Protestant ontology – formative to historicism – which defined the value of the human in part through 'its distinctiveness from, and superiority to the material world'.[91] In the dominant Victorian use of the term, materialism – different from materiality in being prescriptive and abstract rather than descriptive – was the object of a Protestant critique of Epicureanism, lust and gluttony.[92]

It is the very association of materiality with immediacy, sensuousness and the 'lower order' that may account for some of its appeal to historians, global or not, and to a general public. For one thing, to global material historians in particular, matter and material culture carry the promise of opening up a window onto the little, least-understood details of daily life – eating, dressing, lodging – a sympathetic history that will seemingly bring us closer to our historical subjects, especially the 'indigenous', the non-European and the

---

[87] See, for instance, Alfred W. Crosby, 'Past and Present of Environmental History', *American Historical Review* 100, 4 (1995), 1177–89, here 1182. See also Ivan Gaskell and Sarah Anne Carter, 'Introduction: Why History and Material Culture?', in Gaskell and Carter (eds.), *The Oxford Handbook of History and Material Culture* (Oxford: Oxford University Press, 2020), 1–16, here 1.

[88] Jürgen Osterhammel, 'Die Wiederkehr des Raumes: Geopolitik, Geohistorie und historische Geographie', *Neue Politische Literatur* 43, 3 (1998), 347–97, here 374. On German historicism and its concept of agency, centred on the human 'spirit' (*Geist*) more broadly, see Friedrich Jäger and Jörn Rüsen, *Geschichte des Historismus. Eine Einführung* (Munich: C. H. Beck, 1992), 1.

[89] Crosby, 'Past and Present of Environmental History', 1182.

[90] Daniel Miller, 'Materiality: An Introduction', in Daniel Miller (ed.), *Materiality* (Durham: Duke University Press, 2005), 1.

[91] Pels, 'The Modern Fear of Matter', 28, 33; Webb Keane, 'Sincerity, Modernity, and the Protestants', *Cultural Anthropology* 17, 1 (2002), 65–92, here 71.

[92] Pels, 'The Modern Fear of Matter'.

'subaltern' who have not left written traces.[93] A drum formerly owned by an enslaved person or the contents of a maidservant's tie-on pocket not only 'speak for' men and women 'who were unable to write their own story',[94] moving in their very mundaneness, smallness and intimacy. To many historians, objects convey the human, individual dimensions of past lives; they 'mediate distances of time and space' in ways words and images cannot.[95] Though historians rarely work with the objects themselves – usually, they rely on inventories, accounts or testaments – material remains 'carry a special credibility' and authority for many scholars, partly because they *could* be verified through the senses.[96] Like curators and visitors of museums that offer a 'more fully embodied experience' – where people are made to smell food, feel the sun on their head or take their place in a cattle car – historical writings are a reflection of the contested, yet deep-rooted, phenomenological belief that the touching, smelling or feeling of things lends proximity, 'a more immediate sense of connection' and understanding than would a history told in words.[97]

This is treacherous, to be sure. As any sensory historian will tell you, material remains cannot be verified through the senses because the cultural and historical context overwrites physiological factors and because physiological factors change over time, partly in response to cultural and historical context.[98] What is more, the notion that contact with historical materials entails some sort of proximity or superior understanding is culturally contingent, and in some measure irrational. As Ruth Klüger, a Holocaust survivor, once put it in relation to memorial sites on former concentration camp grounds, it is 'superstition (*Aberglaube*)' to think that the ghosts cling to things or to the places where they departed from this life. Immediacy does not result from being in the same place but only from being in the same place at the same time

---

[93] Elizabeth M. Brumfiel, 'It's a Material World: History, Artifacts, and Anthropology', *Annual Review of Anthropology* 32 (2003), 205–23, here 207–8. See also Gaskell and Carter, 'Introduction: Why History and Material Culture?', 5.

[94] MacGregor, *A History of the World in 100 Objects*, xxiii. On tie-on pockets, see Barbara Burman and Ariane Fennetaux, *The Pocket: A Hidden History of Women's Lives, 1660–1900* (New Haven: Yale University Press, 2020), 15.

[95] Auslander and Zahra, 'Introduction: The Things They Carried', 17.

[96] Brumfiel, 'It's a Material World', 207–8.

[97] Auslander and Zahra, 'Introduction: The Things They Carried', 3, 17. On touch and immediacy, see Dorothee Kimmich, *Lebendige Dinge in der Moderne* (Konstanz: Konstanz University Press, 2011), 105–6.

[98] For a critique of modern science and an unreflective reliance on it, see Constance Classen, *The Deepest Sense: A Cultural History of Touch* (Urbana: University of Illinois Press, 2012). For a critique of anachronism among sensory historians, see also Mark M. Smith, 'Producing Sense, Consuming Sense, Making Sense: Perils and Prospects for Sensory History', *Journal of Social History* 40, 4 (2007), 841–58, here 841.

(*Zeitschaft*).[99] Still, the appeal of materiality on account of its association with sensuousness and the promise of immediacy is pervasive and all but inescapable; unwittingly, global historians may be affected by it.

Materiality is commonly associated not just with the tangible, the intimate and the mundane, but also, along those same lines, with particularity, 'specificity' and singularity.[100] Though by now heavily theorised, things intuitively promise stability, warmth and relief from theory, as Bill Brown put it in a 2001 article.[101] Indeed, materiality, or materialism, is widely seen as 'an aspect of a relation between the abstract and the concrete',[102] invariably falling on the side of the concrete – the 'micro' rather than the 'macro',[103] the contingent rather than the universal or, indeed, the 'local'[104] rather than the global. Untranscended materiality has often been placed in opposition to theory, 'order' and structure and, conversely, attributed an affinity with, as Peter Pels put it, ideas about 'transgression', 'fancy' and the 'fact'[105] – the 'apparently noninterpretative (numerical) description … of particulars' rather than the systematic claims derived from it.[106] Indeed, the value attributed to non-artefactual forms of matter, as a natural fact and source of certainty on which to build human knowledge, is a hallmark of Western modernity.[107] Even though, somewhat ironically, it was largely through sociohistorical processes of abstraction – the abstract space of the global market, statistical enumeration or naturalist taxonomy – that our modern 'inclination to associate the material with the concrete' came about,[108] the association is a formidable and a tenacious one. While the relationship with singularity for late-modern material culture may be more tenuous – with changes in manufacturing and the rise of industrial production affecting material culture post-1800 – that with particularity is not.[109] More recently, digitisation, especially digital surrogacy, in

---

[99] Ruth Klüger, *Weiter leben. Eine Jugend* (Göttingen: Wallstein Verlag, 1994), 76. I would like to thank Liliana Feierstein for drawing my attention to Klüger's reflections.

[100] According to Peter Pels, 'the fetish presents a *generic* singularity'. Pels, 'The Spirit of Matter', 98. On 'specificity', see Joanne Begiato, 'Moving Objects: Emotional Transformation, Tangibility, and Time Travel', in Stephanie Downes et al. (eds.), *Feeling Things: Objects and Emotions Through History* (Oxford: Oxford University Press, 2018), 229–42, here 230.

[101] Bill Brown, 'Thing Theory', *Critical Enquiry* 28, 1 (2001), 1–22, here 16.

[102] Pels, 'The Modern Fear of Matter', 31.

[103] 'Thinking with things' is commonly associated with the field of microhistory. Laurel Thatcher Ulrich et al., 'Introduction: Thinking with Things', in Laurel Thatcher Ulrich et al. (eds.), *Tangible Things. Making History through Objects* (Oxford: Oxford University Press, 2015), 1–20, here 3.

[104] On the concept of 'the local' in global history, see Stefanie Gänger, '"Lokal": Bemerkungen zur Sprache der neueren Welt- und Globalgeschichte', in Gabriele Lingelbach (ed.), *Narrative und Darstellungsweisen der Globalgeschichte* (Oldenbourg: De Gruyter, 2022), 179–88.

[105] Pels, 'The Modern Fear of Matter', 31; Pels, 'The Spirit of Matter', 110–11.

[106] Mary Poovey, *A History of the Modern Fact: Problems of Knowledge in the Sciences of Wealth and Society* (Chicago: University of Chicago Press, 1998), xiii.

[107] Pels, 'The Modern Fear of Matter', 272.   [108] Pels, 'The Modern Fear of Matter', 270.

[109] Cremer, 'Zum Stand der Materiellen Kulturforschung in Deutschland', 16.

252 Configurations and *Telos*

purporting to supersede matter and bringing it into focus, may well have further exacerbated the pull of materiality as well as its long-standing association with tactility, particularity and 'originality as authenticity', as various material historians have suggested.[110] Walter Benjamin's argument, first made in his 1936 essay 'The Work of Art in the Age of Mechanical Reproduction', that the *aura* of an object is tied to its 'unique existence', and consequently lost in reproductions, is at present widely, if controversially, applied to digital surrogates.[111]

Global historians may cherish the material world as they do because materiality's close relation to the particular, the authentic and the concrete somehow assists their cause. It certainly helps them avoid the accusation of a penchant for 'macro-perspectives', 'totality' and structuralism still sometimes levelled at them.[112] It also furthers, however, what has, for better or worse, been their most fundamental argument: the contention of a growing and more or less continuous global integration. For if even the most intimate, mundane and singular aspects of life speak to world-making and connectivity, who could deny global historians having won their case entirely? At any rate, an inquiry into the hidden premises underlying present-day global material histories – our enthusiasm for the particular, the singular and the 'auratic', and the awe of matter that permeates it – is, so the chapter holds, just as worth our while as that into Protestant historicism or enlightened ethnology. Scholars have studied for some time now how specific, local conditions affected and altered the writing of global history in various parts of the globe.[113] It may well be that modern historians' association of matter with sensuousness and immediacy, their evident enthusiasm for the particular and the 'authentic', is in some measure owing to the socioreligious (especially Protestant) and cultural texture of Northwest European and North American societies. There is no reason why historians from these parts should not, just like West African or East Asian ones, be influenced by local, contingent circumstances; it is their continued ability to set trends on a global scale, however, that may well account for some of the pull of material histories globally.

---

[110] Jasmine E. Burns, 'The Aura of Materiality: Digital Surrogacy and the Preservation of Photographic Archives', *Art Documentation: Journal of the Art Libraries Society of North America* 36, 1 (2017), 1–8, here 6.

[111] Burns, 'The Aura of Materiality', 4; Brown, 'Thing Theory', 16. For the original quote, see Walter Benjamin, 'The Work of Art in the Age of Mechanical Reproduction', in *Illuminations*, ed. Hannah Arendt (New York: Schocken Books, 1969), 1–26, here 3.

[112] For a critique of global history's supposed association with 'totality' and 'macrohistory', see Sebastian Conrad, *What Is Global History?* (Princeton: Princeton University Press, 2016), 12.

[113] Sven Beckert and Dominic Sachsenmaier, 'Introduction', in Sven Beckert and Sven Sachsenmaier (eds.), *Global History, Globally. Research and Practice around the World* (London: Bloomsbury Academic, 2018), 1–18, here 5.

Orders and Storeys

This chapter is not the place to engage in debates about the genealogy, the constructedness or, indeed, the aptness of the idea of scale, of 'upper' and 'lower levels' and of 'a layered order',[114] nor to question whether historical processes are indeed located at the level of certain storeys and whether distinct 'levels of observation can reveal different aspects',[115] or ought to be assigned fundamentally 'different heuristic potentials'.[116] It is the place to argue, however, that the association between particularity and materiality contributes to the latter's attraction: for the firmly entrenched notion that there is such a thing as 'a layered order', alongside deeply rooted dichotomies of original and copy, materiality and ideality,[117] practice and theory,[118] would have played a part in drawing historians, global or not, to the material world. The chapter is also the place to observe that materiality has no natural scale, level or context, no self-evident, obvious place in any order. It can be both intimate and intricate in atmospheric chemistry, cosmopolitan at one moment and parochial the next, both of a lower and of the highest order. Global historians have been at the forefront of critiques of scholarship that, in framing national objects of inquiry, has participated in naturalising them.[119] It is precisely in the knowledge of their own rich deconstructivist tradition and of the equally rich 'biographic' tradition in material history that global historians ought to approach the material world. Critically aware of their own times' socioreligious texture, global imaginary and discursive habits, they will be able to see the world of matter and material culture in all its changeability, elusiveness and polysemy.

---

[114] Braudel, *The Structures of Everyday Life*, 29.

[115] Christian de Vito, 'History without Scale: The Micro-Spatial Perspective', Past & Present 242, supplement 14 (2019), 348–72, here 354–5.

[116] De Vito, 'History without Scale', 353–5.   [117] Roberts, 'Things', 68.

[118] For a genealogy of the dichotomy between theory and practice, see Simon Schaffer et al., 'Introduction', in Simon Schaffer et al. (eds.), *The Mindful Hand: Inquiry and Invention from the Late Renaissance to Early Industrialisation* (Amsterdam: Koninklijke Nederlandse Akademie van Wetenschappen, 2007), 309–23.

[119] Kramer, 'How Did the World Become Global?', 126.

11 Centrisms

Questions of Privilege and Perspective in Global Historical Scholarship

Dominic Sachsenmaier

Centrisms and Centres in the Global Historian's Toolbox

In fields like political theory, the term 'centrism' has recently received quite some attention. In an age of growing social and ideological polarisation in many societies around the world, some schools understand 'centrism' as a political programme that can help the political cultures of entire countries overcome ideological divisions and extreme factionalism. It is supposed to offer a possibility of bringing a society together by first focusing on concrete problems shared by most of society and subsequently working on bipartisan approaches to solving then. Such neo-pragmatist approaches are particularly prominent in the United States, with its strong tensions between the Democratic and Republican parties.[1] To be sure, these visions of political moderation remain highly controversial in parts of the social sciences (and in the body politic), but they are certainly under discussion.

In history departments, there is no definition of centrism that would come close to the political visions mentioned here. Certainly, historians in general and global historians in particular intensely debate various kinds of centrism, but in striking contrast to some other academic fields, the term (however it might be understood) carries hardly any ecumenical meaning in the sense of standing for a vision to bridge the gap between rival worldviews. The most prominent 'centrisms' – Eurocentrism and Western-centrism – do not evoke any programmatic hopes for historians and their messages to a wider public. On the contrary, these terms carry distinctly negative connotations and express disciplinary suspicion. Other well-known centrisms – such as Afrocentrism – are meant to provide the specific experiences of suppressed

---

[1] See, for example, Charles Wheelan, *The Centrist Manifesto* (New York: Norton, 2013); Brink Lindsey et al., 'The Center Can Hold: Public Policy for an Age of Extremes', *Niskanen Center*, December 2018: www.niskanencenter.org/wp-content/uploads/old_uploads/2018/12/Niskanen-vision-paper-final-PDF.pdf.

and subalternised parts of the global population.[2] It would almost be absurd to expect that they would reach out to Eurocentric perspectives and find a common ground between them. Rather, they are based on clear visions to overcome the long tradition of hegemonic perspectives.

As I will discuss in more detail, the growing importance of global history and allied fields can hardly be fathomed without the mounting criticism of Eurocentrism and related forms of centrism. Yet before turning to this and other topics, we should pause and differentiate between the place of centres and centrisms in our current historiographical practice. While historians have made an effort to distance themselves from many forms of centrism, centring techniques have certainly not disappeared from the historian's toolbox. Academic authors usually define the focal points of their own research, whether they are writing monographs or project proposals. In other words, if historians want to meet expectations of high-quality academic work, they need to be clear about the centres of their analyses, and they also need to specify what issues and themes are relevant for their studies but are situated at the margins of their analyses. The structures of dissertations, research monographs or journal articles still resemble a drawing with a clear vanishing point; rarely do they look like an abstract painting in which perspective has been abandoned. In other words, historical research usually remains centred in terms of its overall composition and the methodologies that come with it.

To be sure, the nature and function of centres in historiography have not remained unchanged over the past few decades, let alone the past century. Likewise, it would be misleading to assume that within the current landscapes of historiography, there is a standard practice of setting centres in historical inquiry. The different subfields of global history – social history, cultural history and diplomatic history, for instance – tend to use specific centring techniques. Data-based research areas like economic history have ways of defining their objects of analysis and zooming in on them that differ significantly from global historical scholarship that investigates topics such as ideas of citizenship. In terms of centring, there are also big differences between different genres of global historical publications that range from case studies, at one end of the spectrum, to epochal syntheses, at the other end. Some influential works in the latter category have abandoned the idea of trying to view an entire epoch from a singular narrative vantage point. Instead, they focus on specific

---

[2] Examples of the (highly diverse) landscape of articulations of Afrocentrism include Molefi K. Asante, *An Afrocentric Manifesto* (Cambridge: Polity Press, 2007); Marimba Ani, *Yurugu: An African-Centered Critique of European Thought and Behavior* (Trenton: Africa World Press, 1994). Examples of the controversial debates on this topic are Clarence E. *Walker, We Can't Go Home Again: An Argument about Afrocentrism* (Oxford: Oxford University Press, 2001); Amy J. Binder, *Contentious Curricula: Afrocentrism and Creationism in American Public Schools* (Princeton: Princeton University Press, 2002).

themes in single chapters, and the concrete objects of inquiry (and their underlying timeframes) are largely conditioned by these topics and vary from chapter to chapter.[3] Such chapter-specific centring techniques in larger historical syntheses are not uncommon in similar works that are more regionally defined than global history, like European or Chinese history.[4]

To be sure, the focal point of historical research can be set on very different scales of analysis; these can vary from a single historical individual or event to a larger transformation such as the emergence of a new political ideology or the collapse of a trading system,[5] but on these different analytical scales, the criteria for successful global historical research and more locally focused historical scholarship are remarkably alike, and centring techniques are among these commonalities. To put it in a different way, when it comes to ways of defining analytical or narrative centres, the field of global history has hardly strayed beyond the boundaries of what is common in historical research. These and other congruences might be a reason why, as a designated subfield, global history has gained so much recognition in history departments (and beyond), and it was probably a precondition for its unexpected growth over the past two or three decades.[6]

Yet centring is not only a normal, commonly accepted aspect of writing global history; it is also widely acknowledged as a means of overcoming privileged perspectives. This is the case, for example, with the wide range of literature that is centred on the experiences of women in various global and local historical contexts and that has become an important voice in the mounting critique of both male-centred perspectives in academic literature and male-dominated history departments.[7] Similar things can be said about histories from below – that is, works that are centred on the under-privileged parts of society,

---

[3] Examples are Jürgen Osterhammel, *The Transformation of the World: A Global History of the Nineteenth Century* (Princeton: Princeton University Press, 2014); Timothy Brook, *Vermeer's Hat: The Seventeenth Century and the Dawn of the Global World* (London: Bloomsbury, 2009).

[4] For example: Timothy C. W. Blanning, *The Pursuit of Glory: Europe, 1648–1815* (London: Penguin, 2008); Marius B. Jansen, *The Making of Modern Japan* (Cambridge, MA: The Belknap Press of Harvard University Press, 2002).

[5] On related themes, see Valeska Huber, 'Spheres: Openness and Closure' (Chapter 6, this volume); and Dániel Margócsy, 'Scales of Nature: From Shipworms to the Globe and Back' (Chapter 7, this volume).

[6] For more details on this topic, see Dominic Sachsenmaier, 'Global History', in Mark Juergensmeyer et al. (eds.), *The Oxford Handbook of Global Studies* (New York: Oxford University Press, 2018), 113–26.

[7] For the history of gender history see, for example, Sonya O. Rose, *What Is Gender History?* (Cambridge: Polity Press, 2010), 80–121. An important earlier work reflecting on that field's historiographical context: Joan W. Scott, *Gender and the Politics of History*, revised ed. (New York: Columbia University Press, 1999). For global gender history, see Bonnie G. Smith, 'Women, Gender and the Global', in Prasenjit Duara et al. (eds.), *A Companion to Global Historical Thought* (Malden: Wiley, 2014), 437–50.

which are meant to overcome elitist biases in the cultures of historiography.[8] In all these schools, primary source-based research, case studies and, more generally, centring techniques are not at stake when it comes to outlining the parameters of a new historiographical culture.

In the 1990s, when global history was still more a postulate than an academic reality, not everyone anticipated that, in terms of its centring techniques and other methodological devices, global history would move in line with the main body of historical scholarship. At that time, some scholars envisioned global history as a project that would start thinking globally in an extreme manner, without regional emphases. For instance, in his introduction to the edited volume *Conceptualizing Global History,* published in 1993, Bruce Mazlish wrote:

> The starting point for global history lies in the following basic facts of our time (although others could be added): our thrust into space, imposing upon us an increasing sense of being one world – 'Spaceship Earth' – as seen from outside the earth's atmosphere, . . . nuclear threats in the form of either weapons or utility plants, showing how the territorial state can no longer adequately protect its citizens from either militarily or ecologically related 'invasions', environmental problems that refuse to conform to lines drawn on a map, and multinational corporations that increasingly dominate our economic lives.[9]

To be sure, during the 1990s not all the early advocates of the term 'global history' shared Mazlish's view, yet many expected this intellectual project to be centred on the present understood as a global condition. Many scholars envisioned global history operating on planetary scales; they hoped it would study facets of an allegedly new global reality that they saw as shaped by new technologies and global institutions (most of which stemmed from highly developed countries) and as facing new kinds of crises, including environmental ones. In this view, global historical research would break with mainstream historical research by operating on spatial dimensions in which archival work and local case studies would only play minor roles. In contrast to detailed historical studies, global historical methodologies were supposed to move closer to fields like macroeconomics or computational sociology – fields where the study of detailed local contexts was largely irrelevant. By implication, Eurocentrism seemed only a minor concern for this specific academic project; rather, the priority was to move beyond conventional historiographical centring techniques that usually implied a strong attention to local and regional contexts.

---

[8] An early example: Howard Zinn, *A People's History of the United States: 1492 – Present* (New York: HarperCollins, 1980).

[9] Bruce Mazlish, 'An Introduction to Global History', in Bruce Mazlish and Ralph Buultjens (eds.), *Conceptualizing Global History* (Boulder: Westview Press, 1993), 1–24, here 1–2.

In hindsight, we can say that global historical research has moved in a different direction, and that already around the turn of the millennium, the term 'global history' was related to very different academic hopes and expectations.[10] Rather than operating with planetary data, during the past two decades global historical work has been very much shaped by academic currents that emphasise local historical contingencies and are decidedly critical of Eurocentrism and many other kinds of elite-centred, privileged perspectives in history-writing.[11] Jürgen Osterhammel portrayed this trend in the following manner:

> The old hierarchy where Westerners were in charge of the general, and the Others were reduced to re-enacting their own particularity, came apart. Flattening all barriers of ethnocentrism, orientalism, and exoticism was a strong and almost utopian inspiration behind the first flowering of global history around the turn of the millennium. It involved the expectation that in a massive reversal of perspectives, non-Eurocentric takes on world history would gain equal acceptance, and that such histories would be written from a variety of novel vantage points.[12]

The main force underlying this development was the growing influence of regional studies expertise on the field of global history. No other branch of historiography has assembled such diverse regional expertise and such a broad spectrum of language competence as global history: the field has become a meeting ground for academic knowledge on very different world regions. The global history research community brings together scholars trained in Latin American history, European history, East Asian history or other regions and languages. If one checks the author list of important disciplinary forums

---

[10] To be sure, the presentist aspects and decidedly global aspects are not entirely absent today, and they are even highly visible to general audiences in different parts of the world. For instance, see Yuval Noah Harari, *Homo Deus: A Brief History of Tomorrow* (London: Vintage, 2017); Diego Olstein, *A Brief History of Now: The Past and Present of Global Power* (New York: Palgrave Macmillan, 2021).

[11] In many regards, perspectives emanating from regional studies have greatly strengthened critiques of Eurocentrism in global historical scholarship: see, for example, Rochona Majumdar, *Writing Postcolonial History* (London: Bloomsbury, 2010); Dane Kennedy, 'Postcolonialism and History', in Graham Huggan (ed.), *The Oxford Handbook of Postcolonial Studies* (Oxford: Oxford University Press, 2013), 467–88. The basic transformations of academic historiography that have led to a growing critique of Eurocentrism in the humanities in general and in history departments in particular have become increasingly an object of academic research that is looking at academic transformations in single countries or in larger, international networks. See Lutz Raphael, *Geschichtswissenschaft im Zeitalter der Extreme: Theorien, Methoden, Tendenzen von 1900 bis zur Gegenwart* (Munich: C. H. Beck, 2003); Georg G. Iggers et al., *A Global History of Modern Historiography* (Harlow: Pearson Education, 2008); Axel Schneider and Daniel Woolf (eds.), *The Oxford History of Historical Writing*, vol. 5: *Historical Writing since 1945* (Oxford: Oxford University Press, 2011); Alessandro Stanziani, *Eurocentrism and the Politics of Global History* (New York: Palgrave Macmillan, 2018), 117–44.

[12] Jürgen Osterhammel, 'Global History 2020: Fragility in Stability', *Balzan Papers* 3 (2020), 11–30, here 16.

like the *Journal of Global History*, it soon becomes evident that it includes scholars who work in very different languages and localities without necessarily operating on a global level. As there is no regionally defined entry ticket to the field, there is no shared space, no regional centre that global history is to investigate *per definitionem*.

Yet the global understood as a holistic space above and beyond all regional contexts has also not become an analytical level where the diverse groups of global historians meet. On the contrary, the levels of the local and the regional remain crucial for the main body of global historical scholarship, and the centring techniques that are most common in the field remain loyal to them. The growing involvement of regional studies expertise in the field of global history even accentuated a disciplinary culture that prioritises regional case studies and primary source work. While there are obviously great differences between transregional and global historical scholarship, on the one hand, and locally defined research, on the other, the two sides remain connected at these points.[13] Both pay attention to historical details and distrust universalising narratives or perspectives that lose sight of local specificities.

As a meeting ground of different kinds of regional expertise, the realities of global historical scholarship are quite decentred, and the fragmentation into different regional focal points fits well with some of the field's most important self-definitions. Today, the bulk of global history stands more for a set of loosely related border-crossing perspectives than any kind of holistic, technology-centred interpretation of the world. This in turn is closely tied to a wider set of intellectual and political agendas: generally speaking, global historical scholarship is decidedly critical of Eurocentrism and other hegemonic traditions.

Eurocentrism and Ways of Moving Beyond It

Needless to say, not all research that is analytically centred on aspects of European history and its global entanglements is automatically Eurocentric. What counts as Eurocentrism and Western-centrism today are hegemonic assumptions about the global significance of European history or the Western past. These are not necessarily triumphalist accounts of the worldwide significance of Western civilisation; they can also be articulated as critiques of Western modernity or Europe's roles in the world. Eurocentrism has been debated, problematised and criticised extensively, yet it is still not easy to define what exactly we mean by it. It is clear that today's problem of

---

[13] On possible definitions of global history that take this disciplinary practice into account, see Dominic Sachsenmaier, *Global Perspectives on Global History: Theories and Approaches in a Connected World* (Cambridge: Cambridge University Press, 2011), 11–58.

Eurocentric perspectives is no longer tied to the geopolitical might of Europe – Dipesh Chakrabarty famously differentiated between the 'hyperreal Europe' and the actual Europe that after the epoch of world wars and the era of decolonisation is already provincialised in the sense of no longer figuring as the main global power centre.[14]

In the past, Eurocentrism had very different faces, and many of them remain – in one form or another – as challenges and problems in historical scholarship up until the present day. Among them is the idea that only the trajectories of European history are relevant for understanding the global past, which was directly reflected not only in Hegelian thinking but also in many influential historiographical works. During the nineteenth and twentieth centuries, many world-historical overviews began their accounts with the ancient civilisations in Asia and then remained centred on European history, with the rest of the world returning to the picture only during accounts of modern colonialism and the processes it triggered in other corners of the globe. One such example is a work that is little known today but was an international bestseller: *The Story of Mankind* by the Dutch-American historian Hendrik Willem van Loon.[15] Out of sixty-four chapters, van Loon devoted nine to prehistory and ancient Western Asian and Egyptian civilisations, followed by a staggering forty-nine chapters that exclusively deal with facets of the European and then North American past, discussing topics such as the 'Medieval City' or the confrontations between Russia and Sweden. These are intersected by only two chapters on Muhammed, and Buddha and Confucius, and the final part of this work contains one chapter on colonialism and two chapters that reflect upon the new world of the present and the future to come.

Since the middle of the twentieth century, the presence of such crude Europe-centred world-historical works has greatly diminished, and a monopolisation of world history by European history à la van Loon would hardly be thinkable as a college level textbook today. Yet this does not mean that the notion of a given primacy of European or Western history has completely disappeared from the landscapes of historical scholarship as an academic research and teaching field. As I will discuss in the final section of this chapter, we can clearly see the after-effects of this worldview in the institutional designs of history departments (most notably the distribution of regional expertise in them) and the asymmetries of knowledge that come with them. We recognise them quite clearly when we start looking at historiography as a global professional field.

---

[14] Dipesh Chakrabarty, *Provincializing Europe: Postcolonial Thought and Historical Difference* (Princeton: Princeton University Press, 2000), 3–6.

[15] The work was first published in 1921, and it was originally written for children, but later was widely read by adult audiences and was translated into several languages. The latest edition dates from 2014 (New York: Liveright).

Yet Eurocentrism of course poses not only institutional challenges but also epistemological and conceptual ones. For instance, while there is a broad consensus that linear historical thinking has played an important role in Western-centric understandings of the past, it is less clear what other notions of time historians can use in today's world.[16] Another major aspect in the debates on Eurocentrism is the role played by European ideas and concepts as analytical tools in historical scholarship.[17] During the early stages of postcolonial historiography, attempts were made to abandon terms of Western provenance such as class, rights, labour, economy and nationhood as analytical categories. This intellectual move was connected to the hope that it would be possible to unearth the conceptual worlds of subalternised communities in the Indian countryside and elsewhere, and then to develop historical narratives based on these concepts. A main obstacle to these projects was the global spread of modern concepts and their influence on the semantic worlds even in allegedly remote social formations such as the South Asian or Chinese peasantry. It became quite clear that conceptual worlds virtually everywhere had been widely shaped by global connections and cross-regional entanglements, and that there was no way to ignore this. We can detect a similar pattern in the current Chinese debates on China-centred historical perspectives, as I will discuss.

This speaks to the lasting tension between the critique of certain concepts as Eurocentric historiographical tools and their wide usage in many languages around the world. In recent years, as the field of conceptual history that originally focused primarily on Western European languages and societies has experienced a global turn, historians have addressed this tension.[18] A growing number of studies explore the ways in which concepts such as 'society', the 'economy' and 'civility' started circulating globally and became

---

[16] For instance, Priya Satia points to the role of linear historical thinking in attempts to relativise the heritage of Western imperialism by embedding the latter in visions of progress and increasing connectivity. Priya Satia, *Time's Monster: How History Makes History* (Cambridge, MA: The Belknap Press of Harvard University Press, 2020). On the search for new, more complex temporalities in history-writing see Matthew S. Champion, 'The History of Temporalities: An Introduction', *Past & Present* 243, 1 (2019), 247–54.

[17] On the enduring dominance of Western categories and concepts, as well as other problems related to Eurocentrism in the field: Dipesh Chakrabarty, 'The Muddle of Modernity', *The American Historical Review* 116, 3 (2011), 663–75; Dipesh Chakrabarty, *Provincializing Europe*; Sebastian Conrad, *What Is Global History?* (Princeton: Princeton University Press, 2016), 185–205; Ge Zhaoguang, *What Is China? Territory, Ethnicity, Culture and History* (Cambridge, MA: Harvard University Press, 2018); Stanziani, *Eurocentrism and the Politics of Global History*.

[18] See, for example, Margrit Pernau and Dominic Sachsenmaier (eds.), *Global Conceptual History: A Reader* (London: Bloomsbury, 2016).

well-established in very different languages around the world.[19] There has also been an attempt to understand the local adaptations of translated concepts as well as the contradictions (conceptual, societal and political) that have accompanied such localisations. Some scholars are also interested in the ways in which global transformations impacted languages in Europe. Global conceptual history primarily seeks to understand how the complex local and translocal histories of particular globally hegemonic concepts unfolded.[20] Scholars in the field usually proceed based on case studies (that require extensive linguistic expertise and local background knowledge),[21] and research is chiefly based on concrete inquiry, not abstract theoretical debates on how to overcome Eurocentrism.[22]

Nevertheless, in the daily practice of historical research, balancing an interest in global conceptual transformations with sensitivity to local contingencies remains quite challenging. The challenge is not only conceptual, and it goes beyond the task of using the right terms (or definitions thereof) for the right types of context. As research in various fields has shown, the question of terms is often tied to normative assumptions that can often be understood as Eurocentric. For instance, labour historians have debated whether categories such as 'worker' or 'serf' are shaped by universalising assumptions that disregard locally specific sociocultural experiences and modes of societal interaction in the Global South.[23] Recognising that locally sensitive concepts alone will not solve that problem, labour historians have become increasingly cautious about positing non-Western workers as oppressed and passive victims awaiting liberation by the normative worlds of supposedly more advanced societies. Still, finding ways to convincingly combine global research agendas

---

[19] Dominic Sachsenmaier, 'Notions of Society in Early Twentieth-Century China, 1900–25', in Hagen Schulz-Forberg (ed.), *A Global Conceptual History of Asia, 1860–1940* (London: Pickering & Chatto, 2014), 61–74; Margrit Pernau et al., *Civilizing Emotions: Concepts in Nineteenth Century Asia and Europe* (Oxford: Oxford University Press, 2015).

[20] As an intellectual direction, these studies of the dynamics of conceptual hegemonies, globally and locally, are quite compatible with research trends in fields like postcolonial studies.

[21] For example: Lydia H. Liu (ed.), *Tokens of Exchange: The Problem of Translation in Global Circulations* (Durham: Duke University Press, 1999); Andrew Sartori, *Bengal in Global Concept History: Culturalism in the Age of Capital* (Chicago: University of Chicago Press, 2008).

[22] On the dangers of hegemonic suppositions in global scales of thinking: Frederick Cooper, 'What Is the Concept of Globalization Good For? An African Historian's Perspective', *African Affairs* 100 (2001), 189–213; Rebecca Karl, 'What Is World History? A Critique of Pure Ideology', in Tina M. Chen and David S. Churchill (eds.), *The Material of World History* (New York: Routledge, 2015), 18–32.

[23] See, for example, Marcel van der Linden, 'The "Globalization" of Labour and Working Class History and Its Consequences', in Jan Lucassen (ed.), *Global Labor History: A State of the Art* (Bern: Peter Lang, 2006), 13–36; Andreas Eckert and Marcel van der Linden, 'New Perspectives on Workers and the History of Work: Global Labour History', in Sven Beckert and Dominic Sachsenmaier (eds.), *Global History, Globally: Research and Practice around the World* (London: Bloomsbury, 2018), 145–62.

with sensitivity to local contingencies remains a major intellectual task. Similar things can be said about women's history, gender history and feminist history once they move to a transcultural or global level of analysis: here, too, some historians have been charged with imposing particular understandings of liberation and emancipation on different cultural contexts.[24]

In addition to problems of conceptual or normative hegemonies, in many other areas of global historical scholarship facets of Eurocentrism or Western-centrism are subject to ongoing controversy. The debates on *The Great Divergence* by Kenneth Pomeranz, an early classic of global and comparative history, are just one of many potential examples.[25] In this work, which was meant to help his field move further from Eurocentric traditions, Pomeranz famously distanced himself from earlier answers to the question of why sustained industrial growth first emerged in a European context and not China. He did so by arguing that according to some key indicators, Europe had *not* pulled away from China during the fifteenth and sixteenth centuries. He maintained that in many crucial regards, the structures and outputs of the Chinese and European economies remained remarkably similar until the eighteenth century. Pomeranz's work triggered strong reactions, with many scholars arguing that his strict focus on economic data excluded social, institutional and other factors from the picture, and, in this manner, they returned the debate on the differences between China and Europe to Weberian categories of analysis.[26] Others held that both his comparative approach and his measures of economic performance were based on Eurocentric concepts.[27] These disputes and others were part of a wider debate on whether comparative perspectives (far more common in the social sciences) are a fruitful alternative to Eurocentric vantage points or instead risk imposing similar categories of analysis on different historical contexts.[28]

As a general pattern, however, the main stream leading global history away from Eurocentric perspectives is primarily formed by individual research

---

[24] See, for example, Chandra Mohanty, 'Under Western Eyes: Feminist Scholarship and Colonial Discourses', *Feminist Review* 30, 1 (1988), 61–88; Merry Wiesner-Hanks, 'World History and the History of Women, Gender, and Sexuality', *Journal of World History* 18, 1 (2007), 53–67; Pete Sigal, 'Latin America and the Challenge of Globalizing the History of Sexuality', *American Historical Review* 114, 5 (2009), 1340–53.

[25] Kenneth Pomeranz, *The Great Divergence: China, Europe, and the Making of the Modern World Economy* (Princeton: Princeton University Press, 2000).

[26] See, for example, Peter A. Coclanis, 'Ten Years After: Reflections on Kenneth Pomeranz's The Great Divergence', *Historically Speaking* 12, 4 (2011), 10–12; Peer Vries, *State, Economy and the Great Divergence: Great Britain and China, 1680s–1850s* (London: Bloomsbury, 2015).

[27] For example, Stanziani, *Eurocentrism and the Politics of Global History*, 9–10.

[28] On this topic, see, for example, Jürgen Osterhammel, *Geschichtswissenschaft jenseits des Nationalstaats: Studien zu Beziehungsgeschichte und Zivilisationsvergleich*, 2nd ed. (Göttingen: Vandenhoeck & Ruprecht, 2003); Peter van der Veer, *The Value of Comparison* (Durham: Duke University Press, 2016).

projects rather than big, potentially politicised debates. The list of examples is very broad – almost as broad as a typology of global historical scholarship would be. There is research that problematises conceptions of history that see Europe as the centre of global flows or source of innovations without considering more complex cross-regional and global dynamics.[29] Other projects pay needed attention to the agency of groups living under colonial conditions and their capacity to build trans-continental networks and interest groups.[30] There are many studies that discuss repercussions of global entanglements for facets of the Euro-American past, and thus further erode the idea that globalisation is tantamount to Westernisation.[31] Works that focus on particular commodities (such as sugar or cotton) are quite influential and help us understand how changing patterns of production, trade and consumerism transformed regions in and out of the West, albeit in locally specific ways.[32] We could add to the picture such diverse examples as research on trading systems outside the West or attempts to view the history of world communism during the twentieth century from an East Asian vantage point.[33]

This list offers just a brief glimpse of some current global historical literature, but the point is clear: in the main landscapes of global historical scholarship, Eurocentric models of history have primarily been replaced by a decentred pattern of individual case studies. At the same time, broader alternative models of global historical thinking are not entirely absent: for example, a small but growing number of historians are trying to rethink our current planetary conditions from perspectives that are less centred on human agents and put natural forces like climate change into

---

[29] See Marwa Elshakry, 'When Science Became Western: Historiographical Reflections', *Isis* 101, 1 (2010), 98–109; David Washbrook, 'Problems in Global History', in Maxine Berg (ed.), *Writing the History of the Global: Challenges for the Twenty-First Century* (Oxford: Oxford University Press, 2013), 21–31; Stefanie Gänger, 'Circulation: Reflections on Circularity, Entity, and Liquidity in the Language of Global History', *Journal of Global History* 12, 3 (2017), 303–18.

[30] For example: Su Lin Lewis and Carolien Stolte, 'Other Bandungs: Afro-Asian Internationalisms in the Early Cold War', *Journal of World History* 30, 1 (2019), 1–19; Mona L. Siegel, *Peace on Our Terms: The Global Battle for Women's Rights after the First World War* (New York: Columbia University Press, 2020). As a related example, we can add research projects that seek to undo simplistic assumptions about Western dominance in a particular region – for instance, by economists who have revised the idea of a complete collapse of the East Asian tribute system under the weight of British-led international order. See Takeshi Hamashita, *China, East Asia and the Global Economy: Regional and Historical Perspectives* (New York: Routledge, 2008).

[31] On this topic, see Gareth Austin, 'Global History in (Northwestern) Europe: Explorations and Debates', in Beckert and Sachsenmaier, *Global History, Globally*, 21–44.

[32] For instance, Sven Beckert, *Empire of Cotton: A Global History* (New York: Knopf, 2014). On related issues, see also Stefanie Gänger, 'The Material World' (Chapter 10, this volume).

[33] For example: Janet L. Abu-Lughod, *Before European Hegemony: The World System AD 1250–1350* (New York: Oxford University Press, 1989); Wang Hui, *China's Twentieth Century: Revolution, Retreat and the Road to Equality* (London: Verso, 2016).

the foreground.[34] Nevertheless, the main body of global historical literature remains centred on smaller facets of the past.

Sinocentrism and Other Forms of Centrism

The critique of Eurocentrism is a subject of concern to scholars all over the world.[35] Yet while historians in many countries are united in their opposition to Eurocentric traditions, there is much less consensus when it comes to defining Eurocentrism and specifying its alternatives. A frequent issue of contention is the question of how to regard the modern nation-state as a container when conceptualising the past. In many states, education systems emphasise national history, which impacts the ways history is researched and taught at the university level. No matter whether in Brazil, India or South Korea, it is not untypical for state education systems to portray national history primarily as the outcome of indigenous traditions rather than as the result of modern global dynamics. It is perhaps thus hardly surprising that a strong body of historians criticises Eurocentric traditions from strictly national or even nationalist perspectives. Against these currents, other groups of scholars argue that national historiography in and of itself can be understood as an imposition of European institutions and concepts onto a previously non-national indigenous world.[36] In this context, a standard argument points out that while national history today is a global phenomenon, it has its roots in global transformations that took place under the conditions of Western hegemony. These include transfers among academic experts and educational policymakers, but also forces such as nation-building processes, the global spread of the modern research university and the emergence of national education systems.[37] On that basis, some research tries to formulate alternative visions of a pre-modern past that leave national narratives aside and search for conceptions of history that are less distorted by ideas of Western provenance.[38]

[34] For example, Dipesh Chakrabarty, *The Climate of History in a Planetary Age* (Chicago: University of Chicago Press, 2021).
[35] On this topic, see for example, Beckert and Sachsenmaier, *Global History, Globally*.
[36] For a broad account of the nationalisation of the past in modern historiography, see Stefan Berger (ed.), *Writing the Nation: A Global Perspective* (London: Palgrave Macmillan, 2007). Examples of monographs dealing with the history of historiography (including national history) from translocal and global perspectives are Christopher L. Hill, *National History and the World of Nations: Capital, State, and the Rhetoric of History in Japan, France, and the United States* (Durham: Duke University Press, 2008); Daniel Woolf, *A Global History of History* (Cambridge: Cambridge University Press, 2011).
[37] On this topic, see, for example, Iggers et al., *A Global History of Modern Historiography*; Raphael, *Geschichtswissenschaft im Zeitalter der Extreme*.
[38] For more details on this topic, see, for example, David Simo, 'Writing World History in Africa: Conditions, Stakes, and Challenges', in Beckert and Sachsenmaier, *Global History, Globally*,

Some of the scholarship that takes particular regions outside of the West as its point of departure seeks to gain new kinds of global perspectives. Based on his studies of Latin America, Walter Mignolo developed the concept of 'border gnosis', understood as a conscious negotiation between concepts of European provenance and alternative epistemes as a way of first problematising occidentalist perspectives and then moving beyond them.[39] And the Cameroonian thinker Achille Mbembe suggests seeing the entire condition of humankind through the lenses of black historical experiences. He sees a 'becoming black of the world' in an increasing age of surveillance and objectification and in the loss of all human agency in the face of impending global crises.[40] When regions like Sub-Saharan Africa or Latin America figure as enunciation centres for alternative global visions, the latter are articulated as intellectual perspectives from subalternised and marginalised voices in the world. In other words, such imaginations of a regional and global order beyond modern Western hegemony are usually not embedded in a context of concrete alternative aspirations for global power.

In the case of today's China, the situation is remarkably different. On the one hand, intellectual debates in the People's Republic are based on a historical experience with Western and Japanese imperialism that are shared with similar voices in the formerly colonised world and other regions at the receiving end of global hegemonies. On the other hand, for obvious reasons the position of today's China differs greatly from countries in Latin America, Africa and elsewhere. The PRC has become a world power that now clearly articulates global visions such as the New Silk Road or the Belt and Road Initiative. The Chinese government presents these programmes as alternatives to a Western-centric world order that could be brought about by China as an upcoming global power system. This situation is also new for China itself. About a century ago, there were many Chinese visions of an alternative order, some of which were also influential in the West.[41] Yet such critiques of the West and its global

235–49; Jie-Hyun Lim, 'World History, Nationally: How Has the National Appropriated the Transnational in East Asian Historiography?', in Beckert and Sachsenmaier, *Global History, Globally*, 251–68; Qingjia Edward Wang, 'Re-presenting Asia on the Global Stage: The Rise of Global History Study in East Asia', in Beckert and Sachsenmaier, *Global History, Globally*, 45–65.

[39] Mignolo, *Local Histories/Global Designs*.
[40] Achille Mbembe, 'Introduction: The Becoming Black of the World', in Achille Mbembe, *Critique of Black Reason* (Durham: Duke University Press, 2017), 1–9.
[41] Important thinkers in this context included Kang Youwei, the young Liang Shuming and the late Liang Qichao. An example of the comparative scholarship on corresponding voices in China and other parts of the world during the early twentieth century is Pankaj Mishra, *From the Ruins of Empire: The Intellectuals Who Remade Asia* (New York: Farrar, Straus and Giroux, 2012). More generally on the struggles with Eurocentrism in China, see, for example, Manuel Pérez García, 'From Eurocentrism to Sinocentrism: The New Challenges in Global History', *European Journal of Scientific Research* 119, 3 (2014), 337–52.

hegemonies were still formulated from a position of powerlessness and lack of international agency, which underlined their utopian character. By contrast, in today's China corresponding intellectual positions are inevitably measured against the reality of a changing world and a globally ever more influential China.

This is the case with efforts to promote the concept of 'Under Heaven' (*tianxia*) as a Chinese civilisational achievement that is of great potential relevance to our future world order. Ideas about the global implications of *tianxia* have a longer history but today's most prominent thinker on this topic is the Beijing philosopher Zhao Tingyang.[42] He envisions *tianxia* as a world system that differs from the current international order in having only internality and no externality in the sense of foreign relations. In this context, he expresses great doubts about the modern nation-state, international law and democracy as potential foundations on which a sustainable global order could be built. Rather than operating with modern theories (whose Western origins he critically emphasises), Zhao Tingyang formulates his scenario of a better future world from Confucian concepts. In line with the reversed eschatology that characterised many Confucian schools in the past, he maintains that during the early Zhou dynasty (starting about 1000 BCE), the principles of a *tianxia* system had already been realised, albeit only in one part of the world. According to him, this epoch of the early Chinese past (which various Confucian schools long treated as an ideal age) speaks to the present of both China and the world at large, offering an alternative to the current facets of international order.

Zhao Tingyang's philosophy has found its critics, within and also outside of China. Many disapproving voices not only problematise the accuracy of Zhao Tingyang's work and its power of persuasion, they also articulate concerns about its potential hegemonic qualities. For instance, the Korean scholar Baik Youngseo argues that the *tianxia* vision could be read as a philosophical programme for a revitalisation of the tribute system that had placed China at the very centre of a larger inter-state order.[43] This leads back to the specific contexts of our time, in which Zhao Tingyang formulates his idea: the vision of the *tianxia* world cannot merely be read as an anti-hegemonic programme that is formulated from the perspective of Confucianism as an ethico-political

---

[42] A key work is Zhao Tingyang, *All Under Heaven: The Tianxia System for a Possible World Order* (Berkeley: University of California Press, 2021). See also Xu Jilin, 'Tianxia zhuyi yixia zhibian jiqi zai jindai de bianyi [Tianxia-ism/Civilized-barbarian Distinctions and their Modern Transformations]', *Journal of East China Normal University (Philosophy and Social Sciences)* 6 (2012), 66–75.

[43] Bai Yongrui (Baik Youngseo), 'Zhonghua diguolun zai Dongya de yiyi: Tansuo pipingxing de Zhongguo yanjiu [The Implications of the View of 'China as an Empire' in East Asia: Exploring Critical Chinese Studies]', *Kaifang Shidai* 1 (2014), http://www.opentimes.cn/Abstract/1928.html.

tradition, and it cannot merely be heard as a voice that had been marginalised under the conditions of Western hegemony. Even though in his main work Zhao Tingyang doesn't make any direct connections with Chinese state programmes such as the Belt and Road Initiative, his ideas about a new world inevitably need to be related to Chinese public debates on similar themes. At a closer look, it turns out that Zhao's philosophy shares many elements with government positions on topics like the Belt and Road Initiative or Socialism with Chinese Characteristics. These commonalities include the notion that an allegedly purely self-interest-driven and antagonistic Western-led system could be replaced by a worldwide order based on shared interest and collaboration, and that the latter would emanate from China.

Yet also in Chinese academia, such attempts to return to indigenous traditions and make them relevant for the Chinese and global future are more controversial than is often assumed in the West. Many scholars, including the prominent Shanghai (Fudan University) historian Ge Zhaoguang, have argued that there is no evidence for the historicity of the Zhou system as it is presented by Zhao Tingyang;[44] others note that his philosophy remains very vague about the main pillars of a radically inclusive world system.[45] On a broader level, like their colleagues in other parts of the world, Chinese historians are searching for possibilities to move beyond Western dominance in both the intellectual world and the world of politics. But in contrast to Zhao Tingyang, a broad return to Confucian terminologies or epistemologies is not an option for most historians, just as it would not be possible to seek to write the history of medieval Europe with a conceptual toolbox from the age of scholasticism.[46] Consequently, the vast majority of research heading in this direction is developed with methods (including centring techniques) that are very similar to the most common methodological toolkits in Western history departments.

Many important concepts that historians use in their own research do not differ profoundly from Western historiography; field designations like 'social history' or historical methods like 'discourse analysis' have their equivalents in modern Chinese historiography. It is certainly a fact that in contrast to the situation in India, Sub-Saharan Africa and many other world regions, colonial languages such as English or French have always played a minor role in

---

[44] Ge Zhaoguang, 'Dui tianxia de xiangxiang: yige wutuobang xiangxiang beihou de zhengzhi sixiang yu xueshu [Visions of 'Tianxia' – Politics, Ideas, and Scholarship Behind a Utopian Vision]', *Sixiang* 29 (2015), 1–56.

[45] See, for example, the dialogue between Zhao Tingyang and the French philosopher Régis Debray: Régis Debray and Zhao Tingyang, *Du ciel à la terre: La Chine et l'Occident* (Paris: Arenes Edition, 2014).

[46] Zhao Tingyang's return to a philosophy based on Confucian categories lacks an equally prominent match in Chinese history departments. It would also be much more challenging to write a history of China (particularly from the mid-nineteenth century onwards) while seeking to avoid epistemologies that have become so powerful during this period.

China's intellectual and educational worlds. Nevertheless, not only did the massive conceptual imports during the late Qing and Republican periods change the Chinese language, they were closely entangled with massive social, political, intellectual and other transformations.[47] This included the emergence of modern research universities and professional history departments, so in many regards the institutional settings and disciplinary cultures of Chinese historiography are tightly interwoven in a package that is the result of global connections and entanglements.[48]

An example is the substantial body of literature that is dedicated to studying the Silk Road.[49] This research is connected with a term that was probably coined by the German geographer Ferdinand von Richthofen, and scholarship in the field hardly operates with traditional epistemologies. Nonetheless, some of the Chinese publications that deal with the history of the Silk Road try to view it from China-centred perspectives. They differ from the literature that takes the vast realms of exchange networks that are subsumed under the term 'Silk Road' as its own space of connectivity and interaction.[50] Rather, there is a strong tendency to emphasise the historical connections between China and the Silk Road, and even to treat them as extensions of traditional Chinese foreign relations. Also in this field, some of the academic literature is situated very close to the official government rhetoric.[51]

Similar things can be said about some of the other literature that seeks to rethink facets of the local and the global past from China-centred perspectives. For instance, a number of influential historians advocate new world or global histories that would be written from strictly patriotic vantage points.[52] Some of

[47] The main work on this topic is still Lydia H. Liu, *Translingual Practice: Literature, National Culture, and Translated Modernity, China 1900–1937* (Stanford: Stanford University Press, 1995).
[48] On this topic, see, for instance, Prasenjit Duara, *Rescuing History from the Nation: Questioning Narratives of Modern China* (Chicago: University of Chicago Press, 1995); Fan Xin, *World History and National Identity in China: The Twentieth Century* (Cambridge: Cambridge University Press, 2021).
[49] For more details, see Dominic Sachsenmaier, 'The Humanities and the New Silk Road', in William C. Kirby et al. (eds.), *The New Silk Road: Connecting Universities between China and Europe* (Oxford: Oxford University Press, 2020), 296–311.
[50] Examples for scholarship heading into this direction: Peter Frankopan, *The Silk Road: A New History of the World* (New York: Vintage, 2015).
[51] On this topic, see, for example, Tim Winter, *Geocultural Power: China's Questions to Revive the Silk Roads for the Twenty-First Century* (Chicago: University of Chicago Press, 2019); see also Yan Haiming, *World Heritage Craze in China: Universal Discourse, National Culture, and Local Memory* (New York: Berghahn, 2018).
[52] Some studies on this literature are available in English: Nicola Spakowski, 'National Aspirations on a Global Stage: Concepts of World/Global History in Contemporary China', *Journal of Global History* 4, 3 (2009), 475–495; Fan Xin, *World History and National Identity in China*, 153–191.

this literature is entangled with publications that emphasise China's allegedly unique character as a civilisation state– that is, as a form of political order whose boundaries are largely congruent with its cultural ones. For example, according to Zhang Weiwei, a bestselling author with close ties to the PRC political establishment, this marks a great difference between the main patterns of the Chinese past and Europe, and it will create huge advantages for China in the great power games of the twenty-first century.[53] These ideas are part of a lively debate on the impending decline of the West and the beginnings of a China-led world order that not only takes place in the Chinese media but also in academic circles.

Yet certainly not all the burgeoning literature on the matchless political, cultural and social aspects of the Chinese past is narrowly oriented on governmental policies. There is some important work that discusses the unique patterns of China's history in ways that do not fit into chauvinist understandings of nationhood, and that are far detached from disputes about geopolitics and global power competition.[54] On that basis, quite a few historians are moving in very interesting directions when it comes to rethinking the encounter zone of Chinese and global historical perspectives.[55]

Still, some of the neo-nationalistic literature in China can be categorised as Sinocentric. But there is a caveat: such publications can hardly be understood as expressions of centrism commensurate to the reach of Eurocentric ideas. In contrast to the attempts at Sinocentric worldviews mentioned earlier, Eurocentrism not only stemmed from particular historical interpretations but built on an entire global support structure that had been created by the worldwide spread of concepts and institutions of European origins. Compared with the wider hegemonic bases of Eurocentrism, there is something decidedly reactive about much of the recent literature that postulates new China-centred visions of global history from nationalistic viewpoints. In the Chinese case, many works are often formulated as a direct contrast to the alleged nature of Western civilisation and the global roles of the West. As part of this overall pattern, China has only recently begun to diversify regional expertise in history departments. Up until the present day, world history (a sizeable field in China)

---

[53] Zhang Weiwei, *The China Wave: Rise of a Civilizational State* (Hackensack: World Century, 2012).
[54] Important examples for a very diverse landscape of positions are Ge Zhaoguang, *What Is China?*; Xu Jilin, 'Xu Jilin lun xintianxia zhuyi [Xu Jilin's Arguments on Neo-Tianxia-ism]', repr. *Minzu Shehuixue Yanjiu Tongxun* 202 (2016), 13–20. (2012).
[55] For example, Wang Hui, *China from Empire to Nation-State* (Cambridge, MA: Harvard University Press, 2014), 3–29; Zhang Xupeng, 'Quanqiushi yu minzu xushi: Zhongguo tese de quanqiushi heyi keneng? [Global History and National Narrative: How Is Global History with Chinese Characteristics Possible?]', *Lishi Yanjiu* 1 (2020), 155–73.

mainly connotes the study of the Western world, Russia and Japan.[56] There are still very few historians in China with a primary expertise in South Asian, Middle Eastern, African or Latin American history; concomitantly, the main theoretical debates in fields such as global history hardly take perspectives from these world regions into the picture. They remain centred on the East Asian and the Western experiences.

Centrisms and Global Hierarchies of Knowledge

Despite the vociferous critiques of Eurocentrism, there is an attention gap between the global historical debates in China and the Western world: while Chinese historians are usually familiar with the latest Western debates in their field, the reverse tends not to be the case, even when the relevant Chinese academic literature is available in translation. When we regard the contents of history education at high schools and universities around the globe, a very unequal world emerges. For instance, while most European students still primarily study European history, history education at Chinese schools and universities is not comparably Sinocentric. Here – and in many other education systems, particularly outside the West – the geographies covered by history curricula usually follow a binary logic. They emphasise the history of one's own region (i.e. East Asia, in the Chinese case) and Western history.[57] Hardly surprisingly, the mental maps conveyed by history education have a deep impact on how large parts of society perceive historical events and thus the present.[58]

Hence, while history education in many European countries is by and large limited to Western history, the geographies covered in history education in many parts of Asia, Africa, Latin America and elsewhere are bi-cultural. The 'asymmetric ignorance'[59] resulting from this pattern of historical education has been debated, but we do not yet have a detailed enough grasp of such

---

[56] On this topic, see Xu Luo, 'Reconstructing World History in the People's Republic of China since the 1980s', *Journal of World History* 18, 3 (2007), 325–50; Sachsenmaier, *Global Perspectives on Global History*, 213–19.

[57] On the world regions that are covered in Chinese history education, see Wang Side et al., 'History Education Reform in Twenty-First Century China', in Mario Carretero et al. (eds.), *The Palgrave Handbook of Research in Historical Culture and Education* (New York: Palgrave Macmillan, 2017), 657–71. On Eurocentrism in modern Chinese world history, see Ren Dongbo, 'Ouzhou zhongxinlun yu shijieshi yanjiu–Jianlun shijieshi yanjiu de Zhongguo xuepai wenti [Generally on Eurocentrism in Modern Chinese World History – Also on the Chinese School of World History Studies]', *Shixue lilun yanjiu* 1 (2006), 41–52.

[58] An example of psychological research on this topic focusing on Turkey: Serap Özer and Gökçe Ergün, 'Social Representation of Events in World History: Crosscultural Consensus or Western Discourse? How Turkish Students View Events in World History', *International Journal of Psychology* 48, 4 (2013), 574–82.

[59] On the idea of asymmetric ignorance, see Chakrabarty, *Provincializing Europe*, 28–30. See also Peter van der Veer, 'Colonial Cosmopolitanism', in Robin Cohen and Steven Vertovec (eds.),

knowledge requirements. What we do know is that many aspects of historiography and its global professional realms remain surprisingly under-studied. For instance, we have barely begun to research the global and local sociologies of knowledge in university-based historiography. Almost no literature tries to relate the history of modern historiography to the history of daily professional life in national and international academic contexts, but it is exactly this daily academic life, with all its opportunities and pitfalls, expectations and inequities, that shapes the professional reality of most historians. Not much work has been done on exploring the transnational disciplinary cultures of historiography, including the field's global gaps in the distribution of power and influence.

While historians have not paid much attention to the quotidian realities of academic life, other fields of study have. Sociologists have conducted research on the social realities at universities and how they frame professional and private interactions.[60] There has also been some excellent work situating the history of the social sciences within the context of empires, imperialism and nation-building. In other words, most of the scholarship on the lived realities of global academic life has not been produced by historians, and it doesn't specifically investigate the realities found in history departments. Perhaps this explains why this research has had limited – or no – impact on the debates on Eurocentrism in historiography.

The lack of social and cultural understandings of modern historiography as a global field is not trivial. What is at stake is not our ability to write a detailed history of daily life in history departments, but our ability to explain how international power dynamics continue to shape our field – a theme that is key to comprehensively tackling problems related to Eurocentrism and associated historical perspectives. The shortage of scholarship on the global professional landscapes of modern academic historiography puts us in an awkward position. Critiques of Eurocentrism in history departments around the world

---

Conceiving Cosmopolitanism: Theory, Context, and Practice (Oxford: Oxford University Press, 2003), 165–80.

[60] See, for example, Pierre Bourdieu, *Homo Academicus* (Paris: Éditions de Minuit, 1984): English translation: *Homo Academicus* (Stanford: Stanford University Press, 1988); Pierre Bourdieu, 'Les conditions sociales de la circulation internationale des idées', *Actes de la recherche en sciences sociales* 145 (2002), 3–8; Raewyn Connell, *Southern Theory: The Global Dynamics of Knowledge in Social Science* (Cambridge: Polity Press, 2009); George Steinmetz (ed.), *Sociology and Empire: The Imperial Entanglements of a Discipline* (Durham: Duke University Press, 2013); Jeremy Adelman (ed.), *Empire and the Social Sciences: Global Histories of Knowledge* (London: Bloomsbury, 2019). See also Charles Kurzman, 'Scholarly Attention and the Limited Internationalization of US Social Science', *International Sociology* 32, 6 (2017), 775–95; Ken Hyland, *Disciplinary Identities: Individuality and Community in Academic Discourse* (Cambridge: Cambridge University Press, 2012); Cissy Li, 'The Study of Disciplinary Identity – Some Theoretical Underpinnings', *HKBU Papers in Applied Language Studies* 13 (2009), 80–119.

have been mounting for several decades and many scholars have come to agree that the field needs to overcome its heritage of privileged and prejudiced perspectives. Seen from this angle, it is especially surprising that professional interactions among historians have not received the same levels of attention as their ideas. Thus far, the literature challenging the heritage of Western-centrism in history departments has focused largely on historiographical thinking, on concepts, narratives and ideas. By contrast, it has paid comparatively little attention to academic historiography as a social world characterised by specific professional networks and sociologies of knowledge. The result of this lack of attention is that when it comes to professional exchanges among historians, many of the older patterns of supremacy are not on the defensive: they do not have to be, as they remain widely unchallenged. In other words, while the ways historians think may have changed, the ways they act have not changed at anything like the same rate.

From this we see that it is premature to assume that we have already entered a post-Eurocentric age of historiography. Particularly when we regard them from global perspectives, much of the disciplinary structures and cultures of historiography remains metrocentric (in a metaphorical sense) in character. At the same time, nationalism is on the rise – not only as a political force in many parts of the world but also as a historiographical agenda, and, as the Chinese example shows, it can be closely connected with global power politics. It will take a lot of effort to work on a more decentred global landscape of academic historiography while at the same time critiquing the rise of historiographical chauvinism or neo-civilisationism in many countries around the world. Given these and other challenges of the current research landscape, global history as an academic field will likely need to face many tough new questions: about the directions of its research, its underlying sociologies of knowledge and its political implications.[61] These will be hard to answer, and they may return the questions of centrism to the centre of the debate, perhaps in new and reinvigorated form.

---

[61] For a highly visible debate on related issues, see Jeremy Adelman, 'What Is Global History Now?' *Aeon*, 2 March 2017, https://aeon.co/essays/is-global-history-still-possible-or-has-it-had-its-moment; Richard Drayton and David Motadel, 'Discussion: The Futures of Global History', *Journal of Global History* 13, 1 (2018), 1–21.

Index

Abu-Lughod, Janet L., 97, 100
Acham, Karl, 32
Actor–Network theory, 176, 248
Adelman, Jeremy, 13
aesthetic, 126
agency, 131, 135, 162, 164, 165, 169, 172, 173,
    175, 176, 178, 179, 236, 245, 247, 248
  agency theory, 245, 246, 248
  animal, 162, 180
  human, 161, 186, 188
  material, 179
agricultural history, 131
Akbari, Suzanne Conklin, 84
al-Idrisi, Muhammad, 126
Allen, Robert, 109
Altschul, Nadia, 83
American Revolution, 203
Amrith, Sunil, 132
anachronism, 88, 89, 242
animal history, 133, 134, 161, 162
Annales school, 3, 50, 66, 133, 165–7, 169
Anthropocene, 9, 75, 119, 135–7
anthropology, 23, 24, 84
Appadurai, Arjun, 157, 213
area studies, 48, 64, 67, 225
Arendt, Hannah, 193, 214
Aristotle, 5, 26
Arrighi, Giovanni, 68
astronomy, 121

Baik, Youngseo, 267
Bairoch, Paul, 105
Barnes, Julian, 161–3, 180
Barth, Fredrik, 168, 172, 173, 178
Bauer, Thomas, 73
Bayly, C.A., 131, 142
Bell, David A., 36, 37, 42, 207
Bell, Duncan, 144
Belt and Road Initiative (New Silk Road), 266
Benjamin, Walter, 193, 206
Bevernage, Berber, 89
Bhattacharya, Neeladri, 131

Bhattacharyya, Debjani, 132
Binet, Laurent, 43
biodiversity, 45
Bloch, Marc, 1, 33, 62–3, 66
Blumenberg, Hans, 139
Boltanski, Luc, 232
Bonnot de Condillac, Étienne, 52
Borgolte, Michael, 80
boundaries, 139, 141, 145, 146, 153, 154, 155,
    157, 158, 159, 170
Braudel, Fernand, 96, 133, 165, 166, 172,
    180, 226
Brenner, Neil, 174
Bright, Charles, 139, 145
Britain, 57, 61, 66
Broadberry, Stephen, 104, 108
Brotton, Jerry, 120
Brundtland Commission, 151
Buddha, 260
Bunge, Mario, 29
Burney, Charles, 123
Butterfield, Herbert, 187

California School, 105
Calvino, Italo, 162
cartography, 117, 126, 128, 129
Case, Holly, 185
causation, 7, 24, 25, 39, 41, 43, 93, 167, 194
centrism, 273
  afrocentrism, 254
  anthropocentrism, 119, 122, 130, 162
  ethnocentrism, 186, 258
  eurocentrism, 4, 7, 23, 47, 50, 53, 56, 59, 66, 68,
    74, 77–9, 82, 83, 85, 120, 213, 215, 254,
    255, 257, 258, 259–65, 270, 271, 272
  sinocentrism, 261, 265, 269–71
  western-centrism, 254, 259, 261, 263,
    266, 273
Certeau, Michel de, 91
Chakrabarti, Pratik, 135
Chakrabarty, Dipesh, 48, 53, 84, 91, 119,
    179, 260

274

For EU product safety concerns, contact us at Calle de José Abascal, 56–1°, 28003 Madrid, Spain or eugpsr@cambridge.org.

www.ingramcontent.com/pod-product-compliance
Ingram Content Group UK Ltd.
Pitfield, Milton Keynes, MK11 3LW, UK
UKHW020356140625

459647UK00020B/2505